Arnhem
1944

Dedication

This book is dedicated to:

All – of both sides – who lost their lives during the Battle of Arnhem.

Those left behind to deal with the human tragedy of the Bridge Too Far.

My grandson, Theo Tutton.

Arnhem 1944

The Human Tragedy of the Bridge Too Far

Dilip Sarkar
MBE FRHistS

FRONTLINE
BOOKS

FRONTLINE
BOOKS

Arnhem 1944

First published in Great Britain in 2018 by Frontline Books,
an imprint of Pen & Sword Books Ltd, Yorkshire — Philadelphia

Copyright © Dilip Sarkar, 2018
ISBN: 978 152673 273 6

The right of Dilip Sarkar to be identified as the author of this work has been asserted by him in accordance with the Copyright, Designs and Patents Act 1988. A CIP catalogue record for this book is available from the British Library All rights reserved.

No part of this book may be reproduced or transmitted in any form or by any means, electronic or mechanical including photocopying, recording or by any information storage and retrieval system, without permission from the Publisher in writing.

Typeset in Times New Roman
and printed and bound in India by Replika Press Pvt. Ltd.

Pen & Sword Books Ltd incorporates the imprints of
Pen & Sword Archaeology, Air World Books, Atlas, Aviation, Battleground, Discovery, Family History, History, Maritime, Military, Naval, Politics, Social History, Transport, True Crime, Claymore Press, Frontline Books, Praetorian Press, Seaforth Publishing and White Owl

For a complete list of Pen & Sword titles please contact:

PEN & SWORD BOOKS LTD
47 Church Street, Barnsley, South Yorkshire, S70 2AS, UK.
E-mail: enquiries@pen-and-sword.co.uk
Website: www.pen-and-sword.co.uk
Or
PEN AND SWORD BOOKS,
1950 Lawrence Road, Havertown, PA 19083, USA
E-mail: Uspen-and-sword@casematepublishers.com
Website: www.penandswordbooks.com

Contents

Foreword by Sophie Lambrechtsen-ter Horst — vii
Introduction: The Human Tragedy of the Bridge Too Far — ix
Glossary — xiv
List of maps and drawings — xvii
Prologue — xviii

Chapter 1	Driver Robert Claude Bondy, 250 (Airborne) Light Composite Company, Royal Army Service Corps	1
Chapter 2	Major Frank Tate, 2nd Parachute Battalion	14
Chapter 3	Privates Thomas and Claude Gronert, 2nd Parachute Battalion	36
Chapter 4	Lance-Corporal William Bamsey, Privates Frederick Hopwood and Gordon Matthews, 3rd Parachute Battalion	44
Chapter 5	Lance-Corporal Ronnie Boosey, 1st Parachute Battalion	62
Chapter 6	Trooper Raymond McSkimmings, 1st Airborne Reconnaissance Squadron, Reconnaissance Corps, Royal Armoured Corps	69
Chapter 7	Private Percival William Collett, 2nd (Airborne) Battalion, The South Staffordshire Regimen	87
Chapter 8	Privates Gilbert Anderson and Harry Jenkin, 11th Parachute Battalion, and Private Gordon Best, 1st Parachute Battalion	97
Chapter 9	Private Patrick Taylor, 156th Parachute Battalion, and Private Albert Willingham, 10th Parachute Battalion	112
Chapter 10	Lieutenant Peter Brazier and Staff Sergeant Raymond Gould, Glider Pilot Regiment	140

Chapter 11	Staff Sergeant Eric 'Tom' Holloway MM, Glider Pilot Regiment, and Lieutenant Ian Meikle, 1st Airlanding Light Regiment, Royal Regiment of Artillery	166
Chapter 12	Sergeant George Thomas, 1st Airlanding Anti-Tank Battery, Royal Regiment of Artillery, and Sergeant James Sharrock, Glider Pilot Regiment	186
Chapter 13	Sergeant Thomas Watson, 1st (Airborne) Battalion, The Border Regiment	204
Chapter 14	Major Alexander Cochran and Private Samuel Cassidy, 7th (Galloway) Battalion, The King's Own Scottish Borderers	217
Chapter 15	Gunner Thomas Stanley Warwick, 1st Airlanding Anti-Tank Battery, Royal Regiment of Artillery	234
Chapter 16	Corporal 'Joe' Simpson, Lance-Corporal Daniel Neville, Sappers Norman Butterworth and Sidney Gueran – and survivor, Lance-Sergeant Harold Padfield, 1st Parachute Squadron, Royal Engineers	243
Chapter 17	Squadron Leader John Phillip Gilliard DFC, 190 Squadron, RAF	267
Chapter 18	Lance-Corporal Czeslaw Gajewnik, Signals Company, 1st Parachute Battalion, 1st Polish Independent Parachute Brigade	283
Chapter 19	*Gefallen*: German Casualties at Arnhem	301
Chapter 20	Flowers in the Wind	312
Epilogue: Walking with Ghosts		329
Acknowledgements		346
Bibliography		348
Other Books by Dilip Sarkar		355
Index		356

Foreword

by Sophie Lambrechtsen-ter Horst

Dilip Sarkar has written a uniquely special book, an intimate and loving tribute to all of those killed, including those buried at the 'Airborne Cemetery' – and whose memory remains so dear to all who have commemorated the Battle of Arnhem from a young age.

During the battle, from 17–26 September 1944, we sheltered in the cellar of our home, the former rectory next to the Old Church in Oosterbeek. I was five years old then, when above me our house was transformed into a Regimental Aid Post, where my mother, Kate ter Horst – later known as the 'Angel of Arnhem' – cared for and gave the wounded and dying courage through her kindness and words.

I remember how we, as schoolchildren, during the first Airborne Commemoration a year after the battle, were allowed to lay flowers on the bare small sand hills with metal crosses bearing names of the dead. The flowers were from our own gardens, as at the time there were no florist shops.

At the Cemetery, we all were given a personal grave to attend to and look after throughout the year. During the annual commemorations every September, we were personally able to meet the relatives of these casualties, who came over to remember their lost loved ones. So it was that many close and lasting friendships started to grow – and endure today.

With the same amount of love and care, perhaps with even more, the graves of those without a name were also looked after, their headstones inscribed with the words 'Known unto God'.

It felt as if we, through everything we had lived through together, had become one great family. A family in which these unnamed graves were automatically included, treasured and honoured.

God did not seem as far away back then as he so often does today. For example, during the surrender at Arnhem Bridge, Lieutenant-Colonel John Frost's men sent the message 'Out of ammunition: God save the King'. They had fought for God and Country.

Slowly the Cemetery became green, the metal crosses replaced by impressive rows of white headstones; plants and flowers transformed the Cemetery into the beautiful place we now know today.

It is remarkable that after over seventy years the personal histories of casualties can still be traced. In this book, Dilip gives these men back their voice, by telling and contextualising their stories. It feels like bringing these men home – an unexpected encounter, often completing the story and providing closure. It feels as though love, friendship and happiness has arisen out of all that suffering. In his Introduction, Dilip mentions the 'suffering and yet triumph of the human spirit' – making me wonder whether tragedy is actually the secret of and the meaning of life?

Thank you Dilip and friends, for your devotion, years of research and work, on behalf of all those to whom you have dedicated this book – friend and foe, relatives and, lest we forget, future generations.

Sophie Lambrechtsen-ter Horst

Dilip Sarkar and Sophie Lambrechtsen-ter Horst at the latter's famous home in May 2018. (David van Buggenum)

Introduction

The Human Tragedy of the Bridge Too Far

Hallowed ground: the immaculate Arnhem-Oosterbeek War Cemetery – universally known as the 'Airborne Cemetery'. (Karen Sarkar)

Visiting any war cemetery is a moving experience; entering the Arnhem-Oosterbeek War Cemetery, within the leafy Dutch woods of Gelderland, is to walk on hallowed ground. Walking along the rows of cold, white, headstones, anyone reflecting on the names and ages of those interred cannot, surely, fail to be moved by the tragedy of it all.

All my life, the Second World War has been an obsession, mainly because I am unable to comprehend the scale of loss and suffering involved. When I was ten years old, my father – a Quaker – took me to a small war cemetery near a Wellington bomber training base in rural Gloucestershire. It was a life-changing moment. From early adulthood onwards I began researching and publishing the stories of casualties, providing a record of these sacrifices – and years later still do. Fascinated by the Arnhem story since childhood, some years ago I began work on a book concerning casualties interred at the Arnhem-Oosterbeek War Cemetery – universally known as the 'Airborne Cemetery' – but due to a change in personal circumstances the project had to be shelved. Four years ago, however, whilst working near Utrecht, I visited the Airborne Cemetery for the first time – and from the second I walked through its gates knew that this book had to be written. Ever since that profound decision, researching the fallen of the Battle of Arnhem has been the priority, involving many miles of travel, hours of correspondence and telephone calls, and visits to Arnhem and Oosterbeek to study the ground, interview local people and liaise with immensely knowledgeable Dutch historians. Indeed, it has been quite a journey, supported every step of the way by my wife, Karen.

One of many graves known only 'unto God' at Oosterbeek. (Karen Sarkar)

The Airborne Cemetery contains 1,774 graves – 244 of them 'Known unto God'. Most of these unfortunates fell during the British and Polish airborne battle at Arnhem and Oosterbeek in September 1944 – part of the ill-fated Allied attempt to seize the Maas, Waal and Lower Rhine bridges – Operation MARKET-GARDEN – intended to open the door to Germany and end the war by Christmas 1944. As things turned out, Arnhem – the very doorstep into Germany – sixty-four miles inside enemy lines – proved to be 'a bridge too far'. Walking around the cemetery, we must remember that each grave has a story, not only that of the casualty concerned but also concerning the suffering of those left behind. Beyond doubt, these losses all too often shattered families – the impact and grief even resonating to this day, rippling through successive generations unborn in 1944. For everyone, either those personally affected or others simply moved by the Arnhem story, the immaculately maintained Airborne Cemetery is an essential place of pilgrimage. There is undoubtedly something very special about this quiet place, where past and present collide. Indeed, across the lane from the Airborne Cemetery is the Dutch civilian cemetery, which includes the graves of some who also died during the great battle. Undoubtedly, the most tragic of all is the grave of little Sibilla Hendrika Snijder, born on 8 July 1944 – and killed on 18 September 1944, when a grenade landed in her

INTRODUCTION

cot. If that, and the stories in this book, does not emphasise the human tragedy of war, I am unsure what does.

In 1974, the American Cornelius Ryan wrote his best-selling book *A Bridge Too Far*, concerning Operation MARKET-GARDEN in its entirety, drawing heavily on the first-hand accounts of survivors and thereby providing a virtually minute-by-minute, blow-by-blow account of the action. The wider effort, of course, involved two American airborne divisions, both of which achieved their allotted tasks – but, as General 'Jumpin' Jim Gavin, commander of the 82nd US Airborne Division later lamented, the world would only remember the brave but forlorn struggle of the defeated British and Polish airborne troops at Arnhem-Oosterbeek. That may be so, but the benchmark of courage carved by General Roy Urquhart's men, and the bond arising between them and the Dutch civilian population, which endures to this day, is a unique story worth both re-telling and remembering. Three years after Ryan's best-seller hit the bookshelves, Richard Attenborough and Joseph Levine translated the story to cinema screen via their global box office success of the same name – involving no less than fourteen of Hollywood's superstars. Still frequently shown on television, widely available on DVD and online, the epic movie has gone a long way towards inspiring and maintaining interest in the subject. Even in the film, though, the suffering and yet triumph of the human spirit, and the tragedy of it all, is all too evident.

This book, however, is not intended to be a definitive or even comprehensive history of the Battle of Arnhem – there are many other books to claim such mantles and that was not my objective (essential reading, of course, being *A Bridge Too Far* and Martin Middlebrook's excellent overview, *Arnhem 1944: The Airborne Battle*). However, there was a need to narrate and re-tell the story of the British and Polish battle, to contextualise the casualty stories involved. Each of these men was killed at different junctures in the fighting, often requiring virtually forensic analysis to ascertain their fates. The concept of the book is to tell that story whilst relating more information regarding who these people were, what their backgrounds were, what they had done before Arnhem – and the effect of their loss on those left behind at home. Hitherto, military history has largely been written from sources such as official documents and the memories of survivors. Today, the number of survivors decreases annually, as time marches on, and an oral historian would perhaps question the validity of recording interviews with such *combattant ancienne*. Although mentioned, the personal stories of casualties are rarely the primary focus. With survivors dwindling as a source for historians, there needs, therefore, to be a fresh approach, a new methodology for historians to apply. Instead of sticking to the norm, the unit histories and survivors' memories, tell us, please, about the casualties, bringing into sharp focus the 'hidden history' of the dead – who, unlike survivors, have no voice. This, however, is no easy task: the parents of those who gave their lives are long gone; the siblings also now beginning to pass on; subsequent generations do not sometimes have any knowledge or material connected with their ancestors' lives. So, whilst far from a traditional and accessible route, the approach is original, and, to me, not only well worth the effort but *essential*. This formula could be applied to any battle, in fact, and I hope we will see other books written through this lens as time goes on.

Another point to mention is that it is simply not possible to include a casualty from every unit of or attached to the British 1st Airborne Division or Independent Polish Parachute Brigade Group. Indeed, it proved impossible, for example, to trace any living relatives of 21st Independent Parachute Company casualties, which was a disappointment, as likewise were several dead-ends and unanswered letters concerning certain other casualties of interest. Moreover, so enormous was the RAF contribution that 474 aircrew casualties were sustained, from a plethora of squadrons and other units. Arguably, the RAF's losses, numbering 40 per cent, in fact, of those suffered by General Urquhart's division, justifies a book all of its own – but we have been able to include a chapter focussed on one particular British pilot, representative of his fellow airmen who made the ultimate sacrifice. Much more work, however, needs doing, and not least with the German side, a complicated and still sensitive scenario for reasons explained in this book.

One of the Polish airborne graves at Oosterbeek – Private Ratowski was a member of the 1st Polish Independent Parachute Brigade Group's Anti-Tank Battery, killed near the Tafelberg Hotel. (Author)

This book has taken some years to research, involving many trips to Arnhem and Oosterbeek, miles of travel around the UK, countless hours on the telephone and corresponding. Meeting the families of the casualties whose stories are told here was frequently moving and always a privilege. Indeed, over that period of time I have, it seems, got to know the dead well too. Some years ago, my French friend, Professor Bernard-Marie Dupont, became fascinated by the grave of an RAF Typhoon pilot buried in his Pas-de-Calais village. Bernard became deeply, personally, involved with this story, tracing the pilot's family and friends, and writing a modest book. In this, Bernard describes his feelings about Flight Lieutenant Richard Curtis as 'a posthumous friendship'. The research for this book has, in a way, breathed life back into these casualties, their names no longer just inscriptions on their headstones but those of real people, who lived and loved. Suffice it to say, I know exactly what Bernard means. It is a profound, unique, impossible to describe relationship – and

INTRODUCTION

a hefty responsibility being entrusted with someone's memory. Hopefully you, the reader, will feel that the work involved – made possible only through collaboration and the support of many people – has done the subject justice.

Finally, in August 2017, my wife, Karen, and I were again researching at the Airborne Cemetery when I photographed, not for the first time, the grave of Private Gordon Matthews, a twenty-year-old from my hometown of Worcester, killed serving with the 3rd Parachute Battalion on 17 September 1944. For some reason, I had previously failed to notice or grasp the significance of the epitaph on his headstone:

> *To his brave memory homage give,*
> *On history's page his deeds shall live.*

The author with the grave of Worcester's twenty-year-old Private Gordon Matthews of 3rd Parachute Battalion. (Karen Sarkar)

Glossary

The following abbreviations appear in the text:

AAC	Army Air Corps
AASF	Advanced Air Striking Force
AOER	Army Officer Emergency Reserve
BEF	British Expeditionary Force
CO	Commanding Officer
CWGC	Commonwealth War Graves Commission
DCM	Distinguished Conduct Medal
DFC	Distinguished Flying Cross
DSO	Distinguished Service Order
DZ	Drop Zone
EFTS	Elementary Flying Training School
GCU	Graves Concentration Unit
GOTU	Glider Operational Training Unit
GRU	Graves Registration Unit
GSC	General Service Corps
GTS	Glider Training School
HMS	His Majesty's Ship
HMT	His Majesty's Troopship
HQ	Headquarters
ITC	Infantry Training Centre
IWGC	Imperial War Graves Commission
LZ	Landing Zone
MBE	Member of the Most Excellent Order of the British Empire
MiD	Mentioned in Despatches
MM	Military Medal
MMG	Medium Machine Gun
MOD	Ministry of Defence
NCO	Non-Commissioned Officer
OC	Officer Commanding
OR	Other Ranks
OTC	Officer Training Corps
OTCU	Officer Cadet Training Unit
PIAT	Projector Infantry Anti-Tank
POW	Prisoner of War

GLOSSARY

RA	Royal Artillery
RAC	Royal Armoured Corps
RAF	Royal Air Force
RAMC	Royal Army Medical Corps
RAOC	Royal Army Ordnance Corps
RAP	Regimental Aid Post
RASC	Royal Army Service Corps
RE	Royal Engineers
RV	rendezvous
SOE	Special Operations Executive
STC	Survey Training Centre
TA	Territorial Army
TAF	Tactical Air Force
TB	Training Battalion
TFU	Telecommunications Flying Unit
TRE	Telecommunications Research Establishment
VC	Victoria Cross
WRNS	Women's Royal Naval Service

The following German words:

Abteilung	Unit
Afrika Korps	Africa Corps
Allgemeine-SS	The general SS
Armee	Army
Aufklärungs	Reconnaissance
Bataillon	Battalion
Blitzkrieg	Lighting War
Experte	Commonly, an ace fighter pilot
Fallschirmjäger	German airborne forces
Feldkommandanteur	Field Command HQ
Festung Europa	Fortress Europe
Flak	Anti-Aircraft Artillery
Flammpanzer	Flamethrowing tank
Flieger	Airman
Gefallen	Killed in action
Gruppe	Group
Heer	German Army
Infanterie	Infantry
Jäger	Hunter
Kampfgruppe	Battle Group

Kommandeur	Commander
Kompanie	Company
Kriegslazerett	Military hospital
Kriegsmarine	German Navy
Möbelwagen	Armoured flak vehicle
Luftwaffe	German Air Force
Oberkommando der Wehrmacht	Armed Forces High Command
Ostfront	Eastern Front
Panzer	Tank
Panzerjäger	Tank-hunter
Reichsarbeitdienst	State Labour Force
Reichsführer-SS	State-leader of SS
Ritterkreuz	Knight's Cross
Rückmarsch	The German retreat from Normandy
Schutzstaffel	Protection Squad, the 'SS'
Schwarm	Section of four fighter aircraft
Schwere Panzer Kompanie	Heavy Tank Company
Schwerpunkt	Point of main effort
Sperrline	Blocking line
Stadtkommandant	Town Commandant
Stalag	Prisoner of war camp
Sturmgeschütze	Self-propelled assault gun
Unbekanst	Unknown
Vermisst	Missing
Volksbund Deutsche Kriegsgräberfürsorge	German War Graves Commission (VDK)
Volksdeutsche	Ethnic Germans
Waffen-SS	The armed SS
Wehrmacht	German armed forces

British and *Waffen*-SS Rank Comparisons (or equivalent responsibility)

Oberstgruppenführer	General
Obergruppenführer	Lieutenant General
Gruppenführer	Major General
Brigadeführer	Brigadier
Standartenführer	Colonel
Obersturmbannführer	Lieutenant Colonel
Sturmbannführer	Major
Hauptsturmführer	Captain

GLOSSARY

Obersturmführer	Lieutenant
Untersturmführer	2nd Lieutenant
Sturmscharführer	Regimental Sergeant Major
Hauptscharführer	Battalion Sergeant Major
Oberscharführer	Company Sergeant Major
Scharführer	Platoon Sergeant Major
Unterscharführer	Sergeant
Rottenführer	Corporal
Sturmann	Lance-Corporal
Schütz	Private

* * * *

List of Maps and Drawings

1. The Operation MARKET-GARDEN plan	xxiii
2. Operation MARKET flight plan, first lift, 17 September 1944	xxv
3. Map of the Wolfheze, Oosterbeek and Arnhem areas, with the approach routes indicated	xxvi
4. Location of the landing and drop zones for Operation MARKET-GARDEN	9
5. Dispositions of 1 Parachute Brigade Group under the command of Lieutenant Colonel John Frost, CO of the 2nd Parachute Battalion, as on Monday, 18 September 1944	27
6. Map of the Oosterbeek with some of the key locations indicated	155
7. Unit dispositions in the Oosterbeek area	292

Prologue

The Road to MARKET-GARDEN

At 0200 hrs on 6 June 1944, a *coup-de-main* party of the British 6th Airborne Division was dropped near Benouville in Normandy to seize the bridges over the Caen Canal and River Orne. Four out of six gliders landed, in the dark, with perfect accuracy. Surprise was complete, the bridges captured intact and a bridgehead perimeter established. Thirty minutes later, 3rd and 5th Parachute Brigades dropped east of the Orne, quickly seizing the Merville Battery. Later, the destruction of bridges across the Dives and tributaries was successfully achieved. Confused, the Germans failed to counter-attack until 0500 hrs, when the Orne bridgehead was violently but unsuccessfully assaulted. The British airborne troops held their ground. The American 101st Airborne Division had dropped at 0130 hrs, the 82nd at 0230 hrs, and although widely dispersed owing to weather conditions, cut German communications and captured important causeways just inland of the Normandy beaches.

That night, four years after Bertram Ramsay had overseen the ignominious evacuation of the British Expeditionary Force (BEF) from the beaches of Dunkirk, the sailor was back off the French coast – now an Admiral with the greatest amphibious assault force ever assembled at his disposal. This huge armada would soon disgorge British, Canadian and American troops onto the Normandy beaches between Ouistreham and Port-en-Bessin, to establish a beachhead before pushing inland to capture the ancient Norman city of Bayeux. Achieving complete surprise, at 0515 hrs on 'D-Day', the 15in guns of HMS *Ramillies* and HMS *Warspite* opened fire on *Festung Europa*. Spitfire pilot Flight Lieutenant Bob Beardsley DFC over-flew the beaches, remembering that 'The whole target area was a mass of flames. It was both an impressive and terrifying sight. I for one was glad that I was not a German soldier.' To a Norwegian Spitfire wing leader, 'Looking down on the target area was like looking down into hell'. In the words of Wing Commander Johnnie Johnson DSO DFC, leader of the Canadian 144 Wing, 'The liberation had begun, the great adventure, the long trek into Germany'. The so-called 'Day of Days' had arrived – but the battle for Normandy would be bloody and costly for all involved.

The Germans rushed reinforcements to the battlefield, often able only to travel at night owing to complete Allied aerial supremacy. The fighting was ferocious until failure of a major German counter-attack, focussed upon Mortain, presented an opportunity to ensnare the remnants of 7th *Armee* between the Canadians, advancing towards Falaise,

PROLOGUE

and the American General Patton's XV Corps, which was turning north towards Argentan; General Bradley was to hold the Germans for two days at Mortain, enabling Patton's turn to be completed. By 8 August 1944, it was clear that the German counter-attack at Mortain was spent. On 11 August, the Allies renewed their offensive along the entire German front – which now began to crumble. On 13 August, the *Oberkommando der Wehrmacht* (OKW) issued orders for a withdrawal behind the Seine. This was much too late. A German-held pocket around Falaise, twenty-five miles wide and thirty-five miles deep, was all that separated the British 2nd Army and Canadians from the Americans. With the race on to close the 'Falaise Gap', Allied fighter-bombers dominated the sky, pulverising German columns and troops wherever they could be found. On 17 August, *Feldmarschall* von Kluge was relieved of his command by *Feldmarschall* Walther Model, who arrived from Russia to take control. During his return flight to Berlin, Von Kluge shot himself, knowing full-well that his 7th *Armee* had lost the race to safety. On that day Falaise, birthplace of William the Conqueror, fell to the Canadians. Less than fifteen miles now separated the two mighty Allied armies. The gap, however, remained open, and the battered remnants of fourteen once proud German divisions – almost 80,000 men – struggled east to reach it and escape across the river Seine.

On 18 August 1944, SS-*Obergruppenführer* 'Papa' Hausser was tasked with commanding the desperate withdrawal from the Orne salient by 5th *Panzer Armee*, 7th *Armee* and *Panzergruppe* Eberbach to a position behind the Dives. To do this, Hausser had to re-take territory north-west of Trun and hold a defensive line behind which the withdrawal could continue. The Allied 2nd Tactical Air Force (TAF), however, called in all available fighter-bombers to annihilate the retreating enemy. Countless sorties were flown to the 'Corridor of Death'. Such was the carnage, in fact, that a 65 Squadron P-51 Mustang pilot, Flying Officer Peter Taylor, recalled that 'The stench of death pervaded to a height of 1,000 feet above the battlefield'. This was the dreadful crescendo of the Battle for Normandy, the terrible proof of the crushing advantage of tactical air superiority. The daily situation report of 5th *Panzer Armee* despairingly stated that 'At the exits from the pocket, as well as inside it, constant air and fighter-bomber attacks, even hunting down individual men on foot, make any movement or assembly of units impossible. Our communication systems are largely destroyed.' Aircraft from the 2nd TAF and American 9th Air Force strafed and dive-bombed the enemy until it was too dark to see, achieving panic: the withdrawal became a rout. The end result was one of Germany's greatest defeats: some 200,000 German soldiers were killed or wounded, 12,369 tanks, guns and vehicles lost. On 19 August 1944, the British land commander, General Montgomery, considered the battle to be over, the Allied victory 'definite, complete and decisive'. Whilst the victory was certainly 'definite' and 'decisive', it was not, however, 'complete': it had taken too long to close the gap, enabling 20,000 Germans to escape across the river Dives and to safety east of the Seine. Overwhelming though the Allied victory was, a month later Montgomery would pay a high price for its demonstrable incompleteness.

Those German troops who managed to escape the hell of Falaise, now began the *Rückmarsch*, the long retreat from the killing grounds of Normandy. For Germany, 1944 was a disastrous summer. In addition to having been pushed largely back behind the Siegfried Line, the Russian advance from the east was also unstoppable. Within a week of D-Day, Soviet forces had advanced to East Prussia, cutting off Germans in the Baltic regions, and pressed on into Poland, to Warsaw. By early September, Stalin possessed the Romanian oil fields and Bulgaria had joined the Allied cause. That summer, 900,000 German soldiers were killed, wounded or missing on the *Ostfront*, and some 290,000 in the West: 23,000 killed, 67,000 wounded, 200,000 missing. Many highly-experienced German commanders were also dead or in Allied custody. The defeated German army now streaming towards safety across Belgium and into Holland, before crossing the Rhine and reaching Germany itself, was understandably demoralised and in disarray. According to Cornelius Ryan, this 'frenzied exodus' reached its peak on 5 September 1944, a day recorded in Dutch history as *Dolle Dinsdag* – 'Mad Tuesday'. Desperation was the watchword, roads choked with transport of all and various means – and broken men. Most desperate of all, perhaps, were the fleeing Belgian and Dutch Nazis, whose judgement day clearly fast approached. The undignified retreat was something that the oppressed Belgians and Dutch never thought to see, as the astonishing scene unfolded outside their windows. The Allied appreciation of the situation was that German resistance in Western Europe was on the verge of collapse.

Within a week, the British had advanced 200 miles, liberating Brussels and reaching the important deep-water port of Antwerp. September 5th 1944, may well have been *Dolle Dinsdag* to the Dutch, but it was also the day on which the Germans stopped on the Meuse-Escaut Canal and dug in – their intention being to prevent the Allies reaching Holland. Suddenly, a small provincial city on the lower river Rhine, called Arnhem, was about to become of pivotal importance as the very doorstep into Germany. The whole region of Belgium and Holland is bisected by waterways, some large, some small, many potential stop lines to a defending army. Running northwards along the German border were, of course, the prepared defences of the Siegfried Line. The Allies could not, therefore, simply turn east, but needed to continue northwards, across Belgium and into Holland. Once across the Rhine, the gateway to Germany was open – and this the Germans were determined to prevent. Although German defences were minimal, the Allies had a major issue in that it was impossible to maintain momentum owing to advancing units having over extended their supply lines. The dilemma faced by the now Field Marshal Montgomery, therefore, was how to exploit the situation before the enemy substantially recovered.

According to Montgomery, there were 'two feasible axes along which a thrust into Germany could be mounted. The first was the northern axis through Belgium to the Rhine, crossing the river north of the Ruhr industrial region; once over the Rhine, this route led into the open plains of northern Germany. The alternative axis was through

PROLOGUE

Metz and the Saar area, leading to central Germany' (the river Ijssel, east of Arnhem, also had to be crossed, however). The Supreme Commander, the American General 'Ike' Eisenhower, ultimately decided on a 'broad front' strategy, the Allied armies driving to the Rhine and effecting bridgeheads wherever possible. Until Antwerp was cleared and properly open, Eisenhower refused to thrust east and thereby exacerbate his supply problems. Montgomery knew full-well the 'tremendous difficulty of organizing troops who have carried out a long and painful march after being overwhelmed in battle; if we could give the Germans no respite, it was possible that, with their lack of immediate reserves behind, they would not be able to recover sufficiently to oppose serious resistance to our progress'. Whether the British field marshal possessed sufficient resources to 'keep the enemy on the run right back to the Rhine' was, however, 'an overriding problem'. Notwithstanding the broad front policy, Montgomery 'continued to plan the concentration of such resources as I had into a drive that would hustle the enemy straight through to that river: in order to jump it quickly before the Germans could seriously oppose us. The degree of difficulty which this project involved was directly dependent on the vital factor of speed.' Montgomery persuaded Eisenhower to support his plan to prioritise seizure of a bridgehead over the Rhine.

One advantage Montgomery had was control of two American and one British airborne division, including the Polish Independent Parachute Brigade, currently awaiting action in England. Indeed, whilst the British 6th Airborne Division had taken the glory in Normandy, the 1st had stood idly by, anxious to get into action – a deepening anxiety now, in fact, as it appeared that the Germans were collapsing. There was also a time factor governing deployment of these airborne troops: the weather would soon turn unfavourable to airborne landings. Moreover, those troops could only be used within the radius of their transport aircrafts' range. Holland, and more specifically, the city of Arnhem with its road and other bridges across the Rhine, was within that area. Various plans were hatched that summer, operations planned – but cancelled, many at the last minute, including Operation COMET, the brainchild of Field Marshal Montgomery. This plan involved 4th Parachute Brigade seizing the Maas bridge at Grave, 1st Airlanding Brigade and the Poles capturing the Waal crossings at Nijmegen, and 1st Parachute Brigade the bridges at Arnhem. With these crossings in Montgomery's hands, the 400-mile long Siegfried Line would be outflanked, the way to the North German Plain and Ruhr clear. If successful, Montgomery intended to press on, reach Berlin before the Soviets, and end the war by Christmas.

An operation to isolate northern Holland, however, became increasingly pressing after 8 September 1944, when the Germans launched the first V-2 rocket from near the Dutch coast at London. The Polish General Sosabowski, rightly, argued that the airborne force involved was too small, that another division was required. COMET was cancelled on 10 September 1944 – not because of the forthright Sosabowski's sensible objections but because the Allied race across Belgium petered out owing to supply issues – and the Germans were already stiffening their defences. Montgomery, though, was determined on an airborne operation to seize the bridges, outflanking the Siegfried Line, enabling envelopment of the Ruhr and a short drive from Arnhem to the Ijsselmeer, isolating the Germans in Holland, leading to capture of the V-2 rocket sites and bringing the major ports of Antwerp and Rotterdam into play. Eisenhower agreed, albeit making clear that Montgomery was not to be given supply priority and emphasising that his objective was not Berlin. Although still concerned, given his respect for the German soldier and disbelief that the enemy was a spent force, General Sosabowski was no doubt a little happier to know that the latest plan included two American airborne divisions. The new plan, born of COMET, was Operation MARKET-GARDEN. At last, the time had come for 1st British Airborne Division, a veteran of North Africa, Sicily and Italy, to fight in Europe.

The airborne element was MARKET; Field Marshal Montgomery: 'The essential feature of the plan was the laying of a carpet of airborne troops across these waterways (the Mass, Waal and lower Rhine) on the general access of the main road through Eindhoven to Uden, Grave, Nijmegen and Arnhem, culminating in a bridgehead force north of Arnhem. The airborne carpet and bridgehead force were to be provided by the Allied Airborne Corps consisting of two American and one British airborne divisions and the Polish Parachute Brigade.' GARDEN was the ground plan: 'Along the corridor established by the airborne carpet, XXX Corps was to advance to the Arnhem bridgehead whence it would develop operations to establish a northern flank on the Zuider Zee (Ijsselmeer) and an eastern flank on the river Ijssel with bridgeheads beyond it. As XXX Corps advanced north, VIII Corps was to relieve it of responsibility for the right flank of the corridor, and widen it to the east; on the left flank, XII Corps had a similar task with responsibility for widening the corridor to the West.' The Field Marshal continued:

> 1 Airborne Corps detailed 1 Airborne Division, with Polish Parachute Brigade under command, to capture the Arnhem bridges. 82 United States Airborne Division was to seize the bridges at Nijmegen and Grave in connection with which the capture of the high ground between Groesbeek and Nijmegen was vital. 101 United States Airborne Division was to capture the bridges and defiles on XXX Corps' axis between Grave and Eindhoven . . . Our resources in transport aircraft made it impossible to fly in the whole of the Airborne Corps in one lift, and in fact four days were required to convey the Corps to the battle area, together with provision of re-supply by air. The air lift programme therefore provided that on D-Day of the operation the American divisions were each to land three Regimental Combat Teams, while the remainder were scheduled to arrive on D+1 and D+2. 1 British Airborne Division was to land initially one parachute brigade and two thirds of the air landing brigade; the rest of the division was to land on D+1. The Polish Parachute Brigade was phased on D+2.

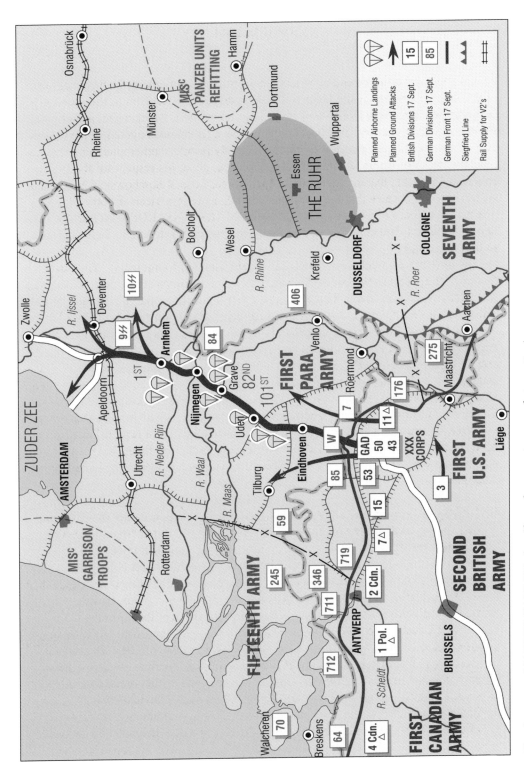

The Operation MARKET-GARDEN plan (for colour version see plate section).

Arnhem, however, was sixty-four miles behind enemy lines, much further from friendly forces than an airborne penetration had previously been dropped. Indeed, this was an airborne operation on an unprecedented scale. Tellingly, however, Montgomery also wrote that 'During the process of our re-grouping the enemy made a number of counter-attacks against bridgeheads over the Meuse-Escaut Canal, and it was becoming increasingly evident that he was succeeding in the organisation of a coordinated defensive system. For our part, the very utmost drive and energy was centred on speeding up preparations; in deciding on the target date of 17 September for the attack, time had been cut to the absolute minimum, bearing in mind the available resources at our disposal and the time taken to plan an operation of this scope involving the employment of major airborne forces.' Speed was of the essence, but the signs were already there that it was too late.

Clearly, the Germans had already begun to re-group – in no small part, of course, due to *Feldmarschall* Walter Model, a gifted defensive commander. Early in the war, when commanding 3rd *Panzer* Division, Model initiated a new system whereby his men were thrown together in *ad hoc* formations, regardless of their actual units, so that tankers trained with infantry, as infantry; engineers with reconnaissance troops, and so on. This preceded what later became standard German practice of forming composite combat groups from various units, indicating Model's forward thinking. Time and time again, in Russia Model retrieved apparently lost situations, earning for himself the sobriquet of 'Hitler's Fireman' – and the *Führer*'s personal trust and admiration. Sent to address the issues in Normandy, it was Model who convinced Hitler to permit a withdrawal over the Dives. After Von Kluge's suicide, Model temporarily assumed command of all German forces in the West, until that great German soldier *Feldmarschall* Gerd von Runstedt was recalled. Model then resumed command of Army Group 'B', setting up his headquarters at the Tafelberg Hotel in Oosterbeek, some three miles west of Arnhem. Of all the German high commanders to be in that particular area, it was a stroke of the worst possible luck that it was Model.

Another stroke of bad luck was that SS-*Oberstgruppenführer und Panzer-Generaloberst der Waffen*-SS Sepp Dietrich, commander of the new 6th SS *Panzer Armee*, decided to locate SS-*Obergruppenführer und General der Waffen*-SS Willi Bittrich's II SS *Panzer Korps* near Arnhem. Bittrich's two divisions, the 9th SS *Hohenstaufen* and 10th SS *Frundsberg* (as will be explained in more detail in due course) had been heavily engaged in Normandy and were refitting. Whilst the other SS armoured divisions were withdrawn back to Germany, Dietrich, by chance, decided to leave these two veteran formations in what was a quiet area, far from the Allied advance which was in any case slowing down. Once Dietrich's other three divisions had reached their new assembly areas on the great northern German plain, he then intended to pull out Bittrich's *Korps*. The speed of the Allied planning for MARKET-GARDEN, however, meant that the full intelligence picture was not sufficiently analysed and understood – and information from the Dutch underground regarding Bittrich's presence

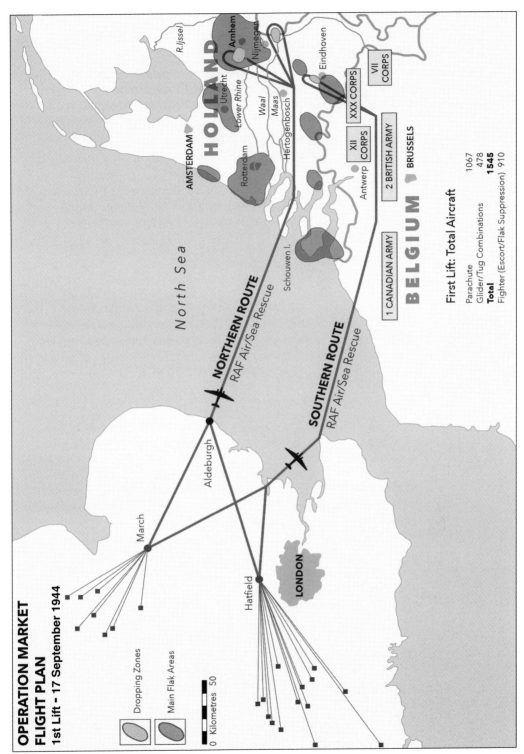

Operation MARKET flight plan, first lift, 17 September 1944 (for colour version see plate section).

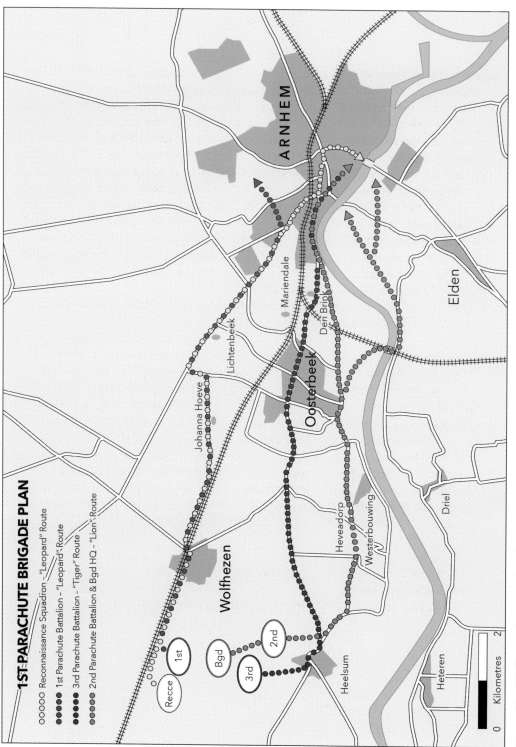

Map of the Wolfheze, Oosterbeek and Arnhem areas, with the approach routes indicated (for colour version see plate section).

PROLOGUE

was either overlooked or ignored. Major Brian Urquhart, an intelligence officer, did try, desperately, to warn General Browning, commander of the British Airborne Corps, but his insistence was dismissed as an irritant. Major Urquhart, however, was convinced that the British and Polish airborne element of MARKET was in grave danger from German armour, so ordered a reconnaissance Spitfire to take oblique photographs of the thickly wooded areas around Arnhem which might hold tanks: *Panzer* Mk IIIs and IVs were subsequently identified. Nonetheless, General Browning had no choice but to proceed as planned: this was the last great airborne opportunity, which if successful could substantially shorten the war. In any case, after Normandy these enemy armoured formations were not at full strength, and were perhaps still demoralised. It was hoped that their reaction would be slow and crumble in the face of the proposed massive airborne assault, swiftly relieved by 2nd Army. Going ahead was worth the risk – so the dissenting Major Urquhart was sent on 'gardening leave', 'desolate and miserable': Operation MARKET-GARDEN was on.

Speaking of the earlier plan, Operation COMET, Brigadier 'Shan' Hackett, commander of 4th Parachute Brigade, wrote that

> The airborne movement was very naïve. It was very good on getting airborne troops to battle, but they were innocents when it came to fighting the Germans when we arrived. They used to make a beautiful airborne plan and then add the fighting-the-Germans bit afterwards. We brigade commanders were at one of the divisional commander's conferences for COMET at Cottesmore airfield where this lovely plan was being presented. The Polish commander, Sosabowski, said in his lovely deep voice 'But the *Germans*, General, the *Germans*!' Sosabowski and I, and one or two of the others, knew that, however thin on the ground the Germans were, they could react instantly and violently when you touched something sensitive. Thank goodness COMET was cancelled; it would have been a disaster. But the same attitude persisted with the eventual Arnhem plan.

As things turned out, the bridges at Arnhem were very 'sensitive' – the German reaction fearfully instant and violent.

Thus was the scene set for the human tragedy of the 'Bridge Too Far'.

Chapter 1

Driver Robert Claude Bondy, 250 (Airborne) Light Composite Company, Royal Army Service Corps

For the inhabitants of Arnhem and Oosterbeek in the Gelderland area of the Netherlands, hard-by the river Rhine, Sunday, 17 September 1944, dawned like any other during those fearful days of Nazi occupation. Eight-year-old Wim 'Willy' van Zanten's parents, Berend and Cornelia, ran a grocery store at 20 Cornelis Koningstraat, in the upmarket leafy suburb of Oosterbeek; that morning he walked with his mother down to the Old Church at lower Oosterbeek for the morning service. It was a perfect autumnal day, the church nestling amidst an idyllic setting: to the north the houses and woods of lower

The Old Church in lower Oosterbeek, in which Wim van Zanten and congregation worshipped that fateful Sunday of 17 September 1944. This house of God would later become the scene of bitter fighting. (Author)

The polder behind the Old Church, sweeping down the river Rhine; the church's Sunday service was violently disturbed when RAF fighter-bombers attacked a German flak position here. (Author)

Oosterbeek, leading up to the Tafelberg Hotel, the Hartenstein mansion's parkland, and the main Utrechtseweg, bisecting Oosterbeek and leading eastwards to the nearby city of Arnhem. To the south, a lush, green, water meadow – polder – between the church wall and Neder Rijn. To the east, a few hundred yards away, was a railway bridge crossing the river, and to the west wooded high ground, the Westerbouwing. It was a peaceful scene, except for one thing: increased Allied air activity.

In the polder behind the church was a German flak battery – which suddenly disturbed the congregation's singing when its guns started banging away. Today, Wim remembers that 'I had to go to the toilet, which was next to the outside door, which was open due to the beautiful weather. I looked up into the blue sky at the very moment an RAF fighter dived and shot-up the German battery. Then there was silence.'

Kate ter Horst, at her lovely old former rectory home adjacent to the church, also remembered the attack:

The Ter Horst residence, the Old Rectory on Benedensdorpsweg, adjacent to the Old Church in lower Oosterbeek.

Amongst the amazed Dutch civilians rejoicing at this unprecedented aerial spectacle were Jan and Kate ter Horst. (Ter Horst Collection)

Suddenly a couple of fighters fly past. If only they would keep away with their tiresome noise, so low over our paradise . . . the baby cries out. Rikkatik-ketik! What's that? The fighters bank. Rikkatik-ketik! They're firing! Get inside! What a racket! Lower and lower they fly over the neighbourhood. Respecting nothing, they skim the very roof and we hear the sound of bullets hitting the slates . . . The planes keep flying outside and quite near us firing is continuing, while in the distance we can hear the sound of heavy explosions. Bombs? Is this an air battle? Father is on the roof with his oldest boy . . . they can see how the British fighters have hit the German Ack-Ack post behind our house. One piece is smashed and another is being dismantled; they're leaving, they're leaving!

This, though, was not some opportunist 'armed-recce' by 2nd TAF fighter-bombers – this attack was part of a large and complex air plan, paving the way for an unprecedented airborne landing. Throughout the preceding night, RAF Bomber Command had been busy, Lancasters bombed *Luftwaffe* airfields, and a combined Lancaster and Mosquito force attacked a dangerous flak concentration on the Dutch coast at Moerdijk. As Sunday dawned, 150 American 8th Army Air Force B-17 'Flying Fortress' heavy bombers pulverised batteries around Nijmegen, on the mighty river Waal. 2nd TAF Mosquitos attacked roads, river crossings and barracks situated in Arnhem, whilst American 9th Air Force medium bombers plastered the mental hospital at Wolfheze – mistakenly believed to be in use as an enemy barracks (tragically causing fifty-eight fatal casualties amongst the innocent patients), and attacked ammunition stores in the surrounding woods. A number of Dutch civilians, in fact, lost their lives during the aerial bombardment of Wolfheze. Seventy-two years later, a Dutchman told me that 'There were no German troops at the hospital or in Wolfheze. My grandfather was amongst the ninety-five civilian dead. We understand why this bombardment had to happen, mistaken though it was, but we have never had a "sorry". We would still like one.'

Hawker Typhoons of 198 and 164 Squadrons shot up German flak batteries in and around Arnhem, firing lethal 60lb RP-3 ground-attack rockets and blasting away with 20mm cannon, destroying twelve such positions – including the gun behind the Old Church at lower Oosterbeek. Wim van Zanten: 'In church the service continued and we sang "Een vaste burcht is onze God" ("A safe stronghold our God is still"), the service concluding with our national anthem. Mum and I left and crept home, running from house-to-house, as the RAF fighters were still in the air above us, shooting now and then.' What happened next was astonishing.

Early that morning, in England, men of the 1st Parachute Brigade and 1st Air Landing Brigade had prepared for what remains the biggest aerial assault of all time. Whilst the three parachute battalions were to drop at Heelsum, their objective being Arnhem Bridge some eight miles distant, 2,900 men of 1st Air Landing Brigade were to be delivered by glider to fields around Wolfheze, whilst pathfinders of the 21st Independent Parachute Company dropped by parachute, tasked with marking the drop zone ready for the main parachute landing. The gliders involved were the Airspeed Horsa and the huge General Aircraft Hamilcar. The Horsa Mk I was a high-wing cantilever monoplane with a semi-monocoque fuselage, constructed of three sections bolted together, made of wood – wingspan 88ft, length 67ft, fully-loaded weight 15,250lbs. The front section housed the dual-control cockpit, the two pilots sitting side-by-side, and main freight-loading door; benches accommodated up to fifteen soldiers in the middle section, and supply containers could be stored beneath the wings. Fitted with a tricycle undercarriage, the two main wheels could be jettisoned in flight, the glider then

A jeep being loaded into a Horsa glider. The airborne RASC performed an essential function, including collecting and distributing air-dropped supplies.

landing on its belly. Once safely down, the rear section could be removed to facilitate rapid unloading of cargo, and a hinged nose section and reinforced floor accommodated the loading, carriage and unloading of light vehicles such as the ubiquitous jeep. On the Mk I, the all-important towing cable was attached via dual points on the wing, whilst, due to the extra weight imposed by vehicles the Mk II's cable was shackled to the permanent nose-wheel oleo leg, although it remains debated whether this type was used at Arnhem. The gliders were flown by the very brave men of the Glider Pilot Regiment who piloted their unpowered craft to battle, towed by powered machines such as C-47 Dakotas and Short Stirlings. Cast off as the landing zone approached, the pilots essentially performed a controlled crash-landing. The glider pilots were considered 'Total Soldiers' who, after landing, were expected to deal with any military situation arising. These were special men indeed. Amongst those men *en route* to Wolfheze in a Horsa was Driver T/202762 Robert Claude Bondy of the Royal Army Service Corps (RASC).

Robert Bondy was born on 24 September 1908 (coincidentally I write this on 24 September 2016), and enlisted into the Territorial Army (TA) at Sutton on 6 June 1940 – two days after the Dunkirk evacuation, Operation DYNAMO, concluded and the tattered remnants of Lord Gort's once proud BEF returned to England. It was a desperate time. A volunteer, giving his address as 306 Fulham Road, Fulham, London SW10, the 31-year old, who was 5ft 9in tall with brown hair and eyes, gave his nationality as

A Horsa glider being towed off from a British airbase.

Paratroopers and gliders descending on the landing grounds near Wolfheze, 17 September 1944.

ROBERT BONDY

'English' and religion 'Church of England' and was declared 'A1' fit. He was a married man, having wed Ivy Humphrey at Brompton Parish Church on 14 January 1939, his occupation recorded as 'Chauffeur'. Robert's daughter, Pamela, born shortly before her father later flew to Arnhem:

> I know very little about my father's life before he met my mother, although I believe that he was actually half Italian and one of eight children. 'Bondy' was an Anglicised name change, but I have no knowledge of the original surname and recently discovered that the family may even have been Austrian Jews. The eight Bondy children were raised in different circumstances, two being forced emigres to Canada. My father always told my mother that he had 'nothing to tell' about his family and not to ask again. My mother was a parlour maid and cook, at Guildenhurst Manor, Billinghurst, Sussex, the home of a Mr & Mrs Rogerson, whose money was in South African diamond mining, and my father was their chauffeur.

The RASC was responsible for land, coastal and lake transport, air despatch, barracks administration, the Army Fire Service, staffing headquarters units, supplying food, water, fuel and domestic materials, and the supply of technical and military equipment. It was an essential corps, in fact, supplying a mechanised army and keeping it on the move. As a chauffeur, Robert Bondy's professional experience was directly relevant to his posting. Initially joining 31 Independent Infantry Brigade Company RASC, in December 1941, at Newbury race course, the unit then became 1st Airlanding Brigade Group Company RASC. In May 1942, the unit was re-designated 1st Airborne Division Composite Company RASC. Airborne warfare remained a comparatively new concept, and extensive training was required. Whilst the bulk of the unit existed to provide logistical support, three Parachute Platoons were tasked as their Brigade's defensive platoon, and so were trained to fight as infantry soldiers. On 23 April 1943, Driver Bondy's Army Service Record indicates another re-designation, this time to 250 (Airborne) Light Composite Company RASC, with which he embarked for North Africa on 16 May 1943. There the unit undertook more training, concentrating on supply and panier packing, and supplied the 8th Army by air. Indeed, part of 250 (Airborne) Light Composite Company undertook the first operational air supply drop during Operation SIMCOL in Italy in October 1943 – a parachute operation rescuing former British prisoners of war after the Italian Armistice the previous month. On 23 December 1943, the company disembarked from HMT *Monarch of Bermuda* at Liverpool, after a voyage not without incident: the troopship had collided with another vessel, HMT *Duchess of Bedford*, and was forced to put into Gibraltar for repair. After briefly being stationed at Boston in Lincolnshire, in February 1944, the Company went to Longhills Hall, Branston, for further air re-supply training and preparing for the next airborne operation

– which everyone knew could not be far away. It came, after sixteen cancelled proposed operations, on 17 September 1944: Operation MARKET-GARDEN.

On the side of aircraft transporting airborne soldiers to battle was chalked their individual flight numbers, known, unsurprisingly, as 'Chalk Numbers' or 'Chalks'. One Horsa conveyed the advance element of 250 (Airborne) Light Composite Company from Broadwell: Chalk 264, flown by pilots from the Glider Pilot Regiment's HQ No. 2 Wing, 'F' Squadron, 16 Flight, and 'G' Squadron's detached 10 Flight. Another glider, 265, was also detailed to lift elements of the company, but for some reason this aborted, meaning that the Company arrived at Wolfheze under-strength. Once on the ground, the RASC's men were to drive jeeps and keep 1st Airborne Division supplied with food, medical supplies and ammunition; the remainder and more substantial elements of the Company were to follow on the second lift.

On the ground at Guildenhurst Manor, that Sunday morning Mrs Bondy heard the huge aerial armada pass overhead and ran out to watch, carrying baby Pamela. Her husband had been home on leave the previous Friday, but had to be back at barracks by mid-day on Saturday. Immediately she saw the tugs and gliders droning towards the coast, she knew 'that this was it', and why Robert had been allowed leave. Known as 'Elizabeth', Mrs Bondy also knew what her husband's job was, but, he always assured her, 'There was no need to worry' because he would be 'behind the lines'. Pamela was nearly walking – Robert, she thought, had longed to see his daughter take her first steps. Elizabeth had met Robert at Guildenhurst and had been 'immediately attracted by his kindness'. After his voluntary enlistment, Elizabeth gave up their Fulham flat, returning to live and cook at the Manor. After watching the aircraft that fateful autumn afternoon in 1944, she went back inside, put Pamela in her pram – and prayed that Robert would return.

At the western end of LZ 'S' is a wooded area, part of an estate known as the Buunderkamp. The first gliders to touch down are known to have been flown by the Glider Pilot Regiment's HQ No. 2 Wing – possibly that carrying Driver Robert Bondy amongst them. Tragically, something went wrong: the Horsa in which he was flying crashed (probably being one of the four which overshot the LZ and hit the Buunderkamp's trees). Inside, the jeep he had intended to unload and drive broke free – crushing the 35-year old driver of 2 Platoon. As an anonymous soldier later explained:

> We did learn that there were areas of soft ground on some of the landing zones for the gliders, which caused serious problems on touchdown. The wheels would sink into the ground and bring the gliders to an almighty abrupt halt, causing the rear end to rise up and then crash over and begin to disintegrate. A number of glider troops were killed and injured in this way. There were also one or two collisions between some of the gliders. With the abrupt halt on touchdown the vehicles and guns broke free from their moorings as the rear lifted – rolling forward at speed, crushing troops and sometimes the pilots.

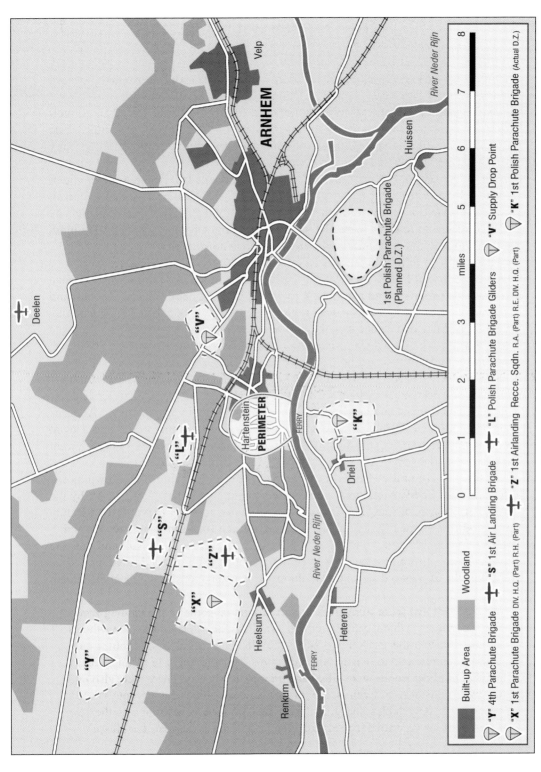

Location of the landing and drop zones for Operation MARKET-GARDEN (for colour version see plate section).

ARNHEM 1944

Today, a peaceful scene at LZ 'S', at Reijers Camp, to the north-west of Wolfheze. On 17 September 1944, four Horsas overshot and crashed into the Buunderkamp estate's woodland – including that carrying Driver Robert Bondy. (Kitty Brongers)

Elizabeth Bondy was not yet to know it, but her husband had become one of the first fatal British casualties of Operation MARKET-GARDEN. His comrades buried him adjacent to the track leading through those now-peaceful woods.

Mrs Bondy eventually learned of her husband's death on 6 October 1944, when a letter arrived – not from the War Office but from a Corporal Clay, 'who had been with him and was the sole survivor'. The Corporal enclosed a gold ring, taken from Driver Bondy's hand, which after his widow's death was passed to Pamela, who still wears it today. For Elizabeth, facing life as a single parent and War Widow, the future was 'pretty rough going at the time'. Pamela: 'My mother worked at Guildenhurst Manor for fifty-two years, we were very loyal to the family who kept her on after my father was killed. She didn't want me to grow up in someone else's house, howsoever luxurious, so worked very hard to buy a bungalow and send me to boarding school.'

In 1945, Driver Bondy's remains were exhumed from his field grave at Buunderkamp and interred at the Arnhem-Oosterbeek War Cemetery – now universally known as the 'Airborne Cemetery' (although not all graves therein are those of airborne troops). That year, on the first anniversary of the first lift, a remembrance service was held at the cemetery, during which Dutch children laid flowers on the grave. Amongst them were Wim van Zanten, witness to the Typhoon attack on the flak gun behind the Old Church, and Corry Tijssen-Rijken – who placed flowers on Driver Bondy's grave. So began many close friendships between Dutch people, the families of casualties and Arnhem veterans – which endure to this day.

ROBERT BONDY

Driver Robert Claude Bondy, one of Operation MARKET-GARDEN's first fatalities, crushed by a jeep and killed when the Horsa glider he was flying in landed heavily. (Mrs Pamela Francis-Bondy)

Driver Robert Bondy and his wife, Ivy, in happier times. (Mrs Pamela Francis-Bondy)

Driver Bondy's original grave-marker at the Airborne Cemetery. (Mrs Pamela Francis-Bondy)

The documents, photographs and airborne insignia of Driver Bondy. (Author)

In September 1976, the British *Woman's Own* magazine took three war widows, including Elizabeth Bondy, to Arnhem to visit the set of the epic Sir Richard Attenborough movie *A Bridge Too Far*. There they met General Roy Urquhart, commander of 1st British Airborne Division during the great battle; Colonel John Waddy, who had fought bravely with 156 Parachute Battalion; the film's director, and stars Sean Connery, who played the General in the film, and Anthony Hopkins, who played Lieutenant Colonel John Frost, commander of the troops who clung so desperately to the famous Arnhem bridge that now bears his name. More importantly, the widows attended the annual service at the Airborne Cemetery. It was far from the first time, however, that Mrs Bondy had been on such a pilgrimage; Pamela Francis-Bondy: 'My mother visited immediately after the war, so saw my father's original field grave. I first went with her when I was eight, staying at the bakery in Oosterbeek with Corry and her family.'

When visiting with *Woman's Own* magazine, Elizabeth Bondy went alone to see the Tijssens. 'Now Corry's children will put flowers on Robert's grave. They never forget, the Dutch, though we may have. It's the difference between having the enemy on your doorstep and having twenty-five miles of sea between you.'

That, I think, rather sets the scene for the remainder of this book.

Driver Bondy's CWGC headstone at Oosterbeek today. (8.B.7). (Kitty Brongers)

Chapter 2

Major Frank Tate, 2nd Parachute Battalion

Major Frank 'Tim' Tate jumped into action sixty miles behind the lines in enemy-occupied Holland at around 1400 hrs on Sunday 17 September 1944 – abruptly ending his wartime of largely deskbound home service. The sky all around him was full of the 1st Parachute Brigade's silken canopies, an unforgettable spectacle for anyone witness to the 2,278 British paratroopers jumping from 143 American C-47 aircraft – and which, to Dutch schoolboy Wim van Zanten 'Looked like so many snowflakes'. Even four-year-old Jan Crum, who lived in the village of Heelsum, felt that this was a significant event: 'What I remember, even after all these years, is the realisation that something of great importance was happening in the vicinity.' Flying Officer Tony Minchin, a P-51 Mustang pilot with 122 Squadron of 2nd TAF: 'We patrolled the area to keep enemy aircraft away from the gliders and paratroopers. There were aircraft of all descriptions everywhere: single and twin-engine fighters, twin-engine transport aircraft and four-engine "heavies" towing gliders.'

Previously, 320 Horsa and Hamilcar gliders had delivered the Air Landing Brigade to LZ 'S', north of the Arnhem railway line at Wolfheze, and LZ 'Z', to the south. Those sites had been successfully secured in addition to the agricultural land west of Wolfheze and north of Heelsum – DZ 'X' – which was soon covered in paratroopers. Thirty-one officers and 478 'Other Ranks' were of Lieutenant Colonel John Frost's 2nd Parachute Battalion. Some were veterans of fierce fighting in North Africa, Sicily and Italy. Others, like Major Tate, commanding Frost's HQ Company, were anxious to get into action before the war was over. Collectively, all were highly motivated and, indeed, elite troops. In their company, Major Tate was about to experience – and some! – the action he craved.

Francis Raymond Tate was born on 18 December 1904, at Fentham Road, Handsworth, Birmingham, the youngest of Joseph Bayliss Tate and Clara Elizabeth Tate's five boys. Mr Tate was a teacher, and oddly, given that it was a feminist movement, the first Honorary Secretary of the National Union of Women Teachers. Naturally, the Tates put great store in education, but were not amongst the top 5.2 per cent of Britain's socio-economic pyramid who could afford to send their children to 'public' school. These were independent fee-paying schools considered 'training grounds for leaders of the nation' in what was a society sharply divided by social class.

The Tate family pictured in happier times, at a between-the-wars family wedding; Frank 'Tim' Tate third from left, back row. (Dr John Tate)

Ninety-five per cent of children were educated through the state system, their best educational opportunity being attendance at a 'grammar' school, which imitated public schools but also charged fees. The difference was that scholarships could be won to grammar schools, thereby providing an opportunity for a small number of bright, largely middle-class, children to educate and elevate themselves. Young 'Frank', as he was known in the family, like his elder brother Bernard, won such a scholarship to King Edward VI Grammar School in New Street, Birmingham. This was a relief for the boys' father, because although not averse to the fee-paying system, as Bernard Tate, son of Bernard senior, points out: 'for a father of five, there were severe financial constraints. In fact, two of the other boys, in addition to my father and Frank, won scholarships to King Edwards.'

Like public schools, grammar schools ran Officer Training Corps (OTC) companies, grounding pupils in military training prior to being commissioned. Frank was a member of the King Edward VI OTC between 1920 and 1924, earning his 'Certificate "A"' in 1922 – confirmation of having passed the OTC examination. Armed with this piece of paper – only obtainable by those fortunate enough to attend either a public or grammar school, together with a good school report and an application counter-signed by a colonel – the bearer was entitled to a commission as of right. Such a system preserved the domain of commissions for the upper classes, certainly before the Second World War. This is clear evidence of how important to personal advancement attendance at a grammar school was for children from comparatively ordinary backgrounds. It was not into the army, clutching his Certificate 'A', that young Frank went upon leaving grammar school, though – he was Cambridge-bound.

Needless to say, the vast majority of university students in those days came from public schools. Again, however, a very small number of scholarships were available: in 1924, Frank won a state scholarship, in open competition, to read Mechanical Sciences at Caius College, Cambridge. This achievement, in fact, even made the national newspapers at the time, the same scholarship having previously been won by Frank's elder brother, Bernard. Attendance at Cambridge was a massive opportunity for someone of the Tates' socio-economic status, and arguably evidence that a degree of meritocracy existed within the framework of a society firmly gripped by the top 5.2 per cent. Clearly the Tates were bright and very capable boys deserved of such opportunities for advancement. Frank graduated with honours in 1927, becoming a patent agent, working in London. Eight years later he married Joyce, the couple's home being at 28 Teme Street, Tenbury Wells, Worcestershire, a picturesque town on the banks of the lovely river Teme, close to the Shropshire border. In 1934, Frank was elected to the Fellowship of the Chartered Institute of Patent Agents. A year earlier, however, Adolf Hitler and the Nazis had come to power in Germany – and the gathering storm clouds of war cast a menacing shadow across the Tate idyll.

A year after Hitler came to power Germany reoccupied the Rhineland, a demilitarised zone stipulated by the Versailles Peace Treaty following the First World War – a peace settlement intending to prevent further war with Germany but arguably a root cause of the global maelstrom between 1939 and 1945. Reluctantly, Britain began re-arming in 1934. Concurrently, Hitler systematically demolished the hated Versailles Treaty, massively expanding the German *Wehrmacht* even to the extent of constructing forbidden submarines and creating the *Luftwaffe*. In 1936, Hitler's new weapons and forces were tested in the Spanish Civil War, by which time many considered another war with Germany inevitable. To others, Hitler was only rectifying the injustices of what was a harsh treaty. In March 1938, however, Germany annexed Austria. September saw the so-called 'Munich Crisis', when Hitler went to the brink over re-occupying the Sudetenland, an area of Czechoslovakia populated by many ethnic Germans. Although bound to protect the Czechs, the Sudetenland was ceded to Germany in the interests of preserving an increasingly fragile peace. This, though, was a significant departure from righting the wrongs of Versailles and a clear indication of Hitler's expansionist and aggressive foreign policy. The British Prime Minister, Neville Chamberlain, returned from Munich brandishing a piece of paper bearing his signature and that of Hitler, 'guaranteeing peace in our time'. Frank Tate, like many others, was less confident and enlisted to serve his country.

FRANK TATE

On 10 October 1938, Francis Raymond Tate, Patent Agent, applied for a 'Temporary Commission in the Officers' Emergency Reserve' (OER). The OER, later called the Army Officers' Emergency Reserve (AOER), had, according to a report appearing in the *Glasgow Herald* on 31 July 1939, 'been formed in 1937 to register those possessing military experience or technical, scientific or academic qualifications prepared to give an honourable undertaking to present themselves for military service if called upon in a national emergency'. Clearly the Munich Crisis of September 1938 focussed minds, because by January 1939, the administrative process had been overwhelmed by applications, necessitating suspension of accepting further applications for six months. This initiative, however, provided a reserve of men suitable for commissions in time of war – which all but the most unrealistic 'dove' knew was coming – the only question was 'when'?

Frank's address was given as 12 Guilford Street, London WC1; religion 'Unitarian'. With eleven years' experience of chemical, mechanical and electrical engineering, and 'considerable experience in translating and reading technical German and French, relating mainly to inventions of various kinds, including chemical, electrical and mechanical inventions', the Engineers or Intelligence Corps appear obvious branches of service for this exceptional, academic, man. After registration, Frank returned to his civilian occupation and life in London, awaiting developments and the call.

Less than a year after Frank Tate registered with the OER, Hitler invaded Poland, ignoring an ultimatum to withdraw his troops; Britain and France declared war on Nazi Germany two days later, on 3 September 1939. Britain mobilised. The inevitable war, that was to consume millions of lives over the next five years, had arrived. On 5 March 1940, however, it was not into either an engineer or intelligence unit that Frank Tate was commissioned as a 2nd Lieutenant but the Royal Warwickshire Regiment – an infantry regiment. The newly-commissioned reserve officer joined the 13th Battalion, a 'Hostilities Only Battalion', upon formation in July 1940. The battalion joined 213 Independent Infantry Brigade and became part of the Norfolk County Regiment, engaged upon Home Defence. France and the Low Countries had fallen in just six weeks following Hitler's attack on the West of 10 May 1940 – and the invasion of south-east England was a very real threat. By October 1940, however, the Battle of Britain, that epic aerial conflict fought to deny Hitler the aerial supremacy required as a prelude to a seaborne invasion, had been fought and won by Fighter Command. Thereafter, the 13th Battalion remained at home, Captain Tate, as he was by then, deskbound at Regimental Headquarters in Warwick. Indeed, there he was to remain until 1 February 1943, when, perhaps surprisingly considering his age – thirty-eight – he was posted as a Major to the Parachute Regiment, Army Air Corps. How this came about is interesting.

In the autumn of 1935, a British army officer joined a Red Army exercise in the Soviet Union. Upon conclusion, he wrote that 'If I had not seen it for myself, I should not have believed such a thing possible'. What he, Archibald Wavell, had witnessed was a combined mass airborne operation, involving 1,000 paratroopers and a further 2,500 soldiers with heavy weapons landed by transport aircraft. Upon return, his advice, surprisingly, to officers of Aldershot Command was to 'forget all about it'. In Nazi Germany, though, the potential strategic advantage of this idea was fully appreciated. On 29 January 1936, Hermann Göring, Commander-in-Chief of the new *Luftwaffe*, ordered the formation of a parachute battalion. By 1 July 1938, this small force had expanded to become the 7th *Flieger* Division, comprising parachute, glider and transport units, commanded by Major-General Kurt Student. It was Student's glider troops, in fact, which landed on and took the huge Belgian Fort Eben-Emael on 10 May 1940, and parachuted in Holland. Although unfulfilled, a major role was planned for the *Fallschirmjäger* in the proposed invasion of England. In 1941, Student's men were heavily involved in the invasion of Greece and subsequently that of Crete. The British wartime Prime Minister, Winston Churchill, had already authorised the formation of a British airborne force on 22 June 1940, and so it was that the following month No. 2 Commando arrived at Ringway for conversion to paratroops. In November 1940, this was re-designated the 11th Special Air Service Battalion, comprising a headquarters, parachute and glider wing. Expansion was duly authorised and so, in September 1941, the 1st Parachute Brigade was created, made up of 1, 2 and 3 Parachute Battalions. A fourth parachute battalion was soon added, and in late 1941, the Airlanding Brigade of glider-borne troops – collectively designated the 1st Airborne Division. Brigadier Frederick 'Boy' Browning was elevated to major general and appointed 'Commander Paratroops and Airborne Troops'.

Early in 1942, the 4th Parachute Battalion was transferred to become the nucleus of 2nd Parachute Brigade, the intention being for 1st Airborne Division to comprise three brigades: 1 and 2 Parachute Brigades and the Airlanding Brigade. Paratroopers were volunteers, and only the best and fittest soldiers were presented the coveted parachutist 'wings'. The failure rate was high, and the airborne force was not altogether popular for creaming off the army's best men. Nonetheless, insufficient volunteers were qualifying as paratroopers, prompting the War Office to convert infantry battalions to the parachute role – amongst them, on 7 November 1942, the Royal Warwickshire Regiment's 13th Battalion, in which served Captain Frank Tate. So it was that Frank found himself promoted to major and posted to the new 8th (Midlands) Parachute Battalion, 3rd Parachute Brigade, Parachute Regiment, 1st Airborne Division, Army Air Corps. Major Tate, the 38-year-old former Cambridge scholar and patent agent, clearly recognising this as a unique opportunity to escape from his Warwick desk, successfully passed the demanding twelve-day parachute course to become the new parachute battalion's Adjutant. Not everyone in the 13th Battalion was enthusiastic regarding the prospect of parachute training, however, and those men remained infantry soldiers and found other units. Conversely, men from other units within the Regiment did wish to join the paratroops, so the parachute battalion essentially created from the 13th Warwickshires included men from throughout the Royal Warwickshire Regiment. Major Tate, therefore, did not have to become a paratrooper – but did so.

FRANK TATE

In May 1943, the 8th (Midlands) Parachute Battalion was transferred to the new 6th Airborne Division. Large-scale training exercises followed, the new airborne division being mobilised on 23 December 1943 and ordered to be ready for operations by 1 February 1944. Major Tate had still yet to see action, however, the 6th Airborne Division standing-by whilst the 1st Airborne Division was blooded in bitter fighting in North Africa, Sicily and Italy. These, however, were exciting times. America had entered the war after the surprise Japanese air attack on the US Navy at Pearl Harbor on 7 December 1941 – since when men and materiel had poured into Britain from across the Atlantic, ready to liberate enemy occupied Europe. That year Hitler had made the fatal error of invading the Soviet Union, a foe with enormous resources of every kind and meaning a war

Commanding 2nd Parachute Battalion's HQ Company was Major Frank 'Tim' Tate, pictured here whilst a captain serving with the Royal Warwickshire Regiment. (Dr John Tate)

Frank and Joyce Tate pictured at their Worcestershire home. (Dr John Tate)

for Germany on many fronts. Moreover, after 1942 and various Allied victories the following year, the tide had very clearly turned in the Allies' favour. By 1944, it was clear to all, including the enemy, that invasion was very much, and literally, in the air.

The 8th (Midlands) Parachute Battalion did not have an auspicious start. During training in Scotland, a 'stick' of paratroopers were accidentally dropped over the sea: only one man survived. In south-east England, an aircraft full of men flew into a hill, killing all aboard. Morale plummeted. The battalion was then taken over by Lieutenant Colonel Alastair Pearson DSO MC, a highly-respected officer, who set about overhauling his new command. Pearson personally interviewed all officers and non-commissioned officers (NCO), returning to their original units those who failed to impress. Major Tate was not amongst the failures.

The long-awaited liberation of enemy-occupied Europe began on 6 June 1944, when British, Canadian and American troops landed on the Normandy beaches. 6th Airborne Division was heavily involved on 'D-Day', securing the invasion force's left flank. Major Tate, as Adjutant, however, remained at home. The frustration of serving four years entirely in England, safe though that was for a married and comparatively elderly man, can only be imagined for a parachute officer. So, as the 6th Airborne Division tested its mettle and won battle honours in Normandy, Major Tate was left kicking his heels around the rolling Wiltshire countryside.

On 21 June 1944, Major Tate was transferred to the 2nd Parachute Battalion, of the 1st Parachute Brigade, 1st Airborne Division. Bob Peatling remembered:

> He took the place of a major who had let down our Officer Commanding (OC), Lieutenant Colonel John Frost. Major Tate became Headquarters Company Commander and was well respected. He was a lot older than everyone else and soon became known as the 'Father of the Battalion'. He showed remarkable common-sense, in fact, regarding an incident occurring during the summer of 1944, when after yet another cancelled operation we were given five days leave, to return on a Friday night at 2345 hours. This, however, did not suit the rank and file, most of which agreed to return on the Sunday night at 2345 hours. We were then put on a charge for having been Absent Without Leave, but the Battalion could not be without we defaulters due to another operation being planned for the week ahead. At the OC charge stage, and after hearing our varied and pitiful reasons for delayed return, we all ended up cleared of the charge due to a clerk's (highly suspect!) mal-administration!

As OC Headquarters Company, Major Tate was on the staff of Lieutenant Colonel Frost – a legend amongst airborne warriors. Educated at Monkton Combe, Frost was commissioned into the Cameronians in 1932. Between 1938 and 1941, he served in Iraq before returning home and becoming a paratrooper. On 27 February 1942, Major Frost's 'C' Company of 2nd Parachute Battalion undertook Operation BITING – the seizure of a German Würzburg radar from a coastal site at Bruneval. Frost's small force parachuted in, successfully achieved their objective and were safely extracted by the Royal Navy. For his part in the unique operation, Frost received the Military Cross. Churchill was delighted, and this success did great service to the fledgling airborne force's cause. Frost subsequently became OC 2nd Parachute Battalion, fighting in North Africa, Sicily and Italy. Like everyone else in the 1st Airborne Division, he enviously viewed the 6th Airborne Division's performance in Normandy and was exasperated by the succession of cancelled operations befalling 1st Airborne Division. The 1st Airborne Division represented, in fact, a significant, fresh and highly motivated reserve to unleash against the enemy – but the arrival of autumn brought with it unsettled weather unconducive to airborne operations. Time was running out – and 1st Airborne Division was spoiling for a fight.

On the Continent, the Allies had virtually destroyed the German army in Normandy, but in spite of overwhelming Allied tactical air superiority, a surprising quantity of German troops and vehicles managed to safely escape across the Seine. Reports from enemy occupied Europe confirmed that the Germans were retreating eastwards in disarray. Frost and his battalion were anxious to join the chase. The opportunity arose on Sunday 17 September 1944, with the launch of Operation MARKET-GARDEN, the largest airborne operation ever mounted, the objective of which was capturing the Rhine bridges, thus enabling 2nd Army to enter Germany, take the industrial Ruhr – and end the war by Christmas. Piece of cake – and this time, Major Frank 'Tim' Tate, to use his army nickname, was not to be left behind.

2nd Parachute Battalion emplaned in C-47 Dakotas at Saltby in Lincolnshire. The weather was perfect. It is likely, but because the Form 'B', indicating individual aircraft loadings, does not survive not certain, that Major Tate, as OC Headquarters Company, flew to Holland in the same aircraft as Colonel Frost. The latter described the scene:

> We passed the Waal, and finally the Lek, for whose bridges we were to do battle, while the red light glowed. I peered anxiously ahead at the DZ for any signs of trouble. In front and below parachutes were falling and then I was out. Once again, the thrill of falling, the great relief of feeling the harness pulling and that highly satisfactory bounce as the canopy filled with air. The rigging lines were slightly twisted, needing a vigorous pull on the lift webs to bring me round, and leave me free to enjoy the feeling of floating down. Following this came the fear of injury on hitting the ground; a last feverish pull as I touched down and then a resounding bang on the back of my helmet told me that all was well. There was no sound of enemy action, just the steady continual drone of aircraft approaching, leaving rows and clusters of parachutes in the air, followed by the fiercer note of their engines as they wheeled for home at increased speed. I felt grateful for the way they had done their task . . . The Battalion landed with practically no trouble, and there was no difficulty in finding the way to the

The 1st Parachute Brigade drops on DZ 'X', north of Renkum, 1400 hours, 17 September 1944. (Imperial War Museum)

rendezvous. *En route* some Dutch people greeted us. There was no doubting the sincerity of their welcome and they told us what they knew of the enemy.

By this time, the German airborne General Kurt Student was commanding the 1st Parachute Army, such as it was, and watched the Allied air fleet in awe from his headquarters at s'Hertogenbosch: 'It was a spectacle which impressed me deeply . . . If ever I had such resources at my disposal!', he despairingly later wrote. Stunned though they were by the shocking sight of so many aircraft, troop-carrying gliders and parachutists, the Germans were already overcoming their astonishment and reacting to the threat. Realising that the 'airborne carpet's' objective must be Arnhem's bridges, troops were mobilised and sent forth. Anyone who thought that the Germans were already a beaten and spent force was about to be violently disabused of such a misapprehension.

Although the Dutch Army had blown Arnhem Bridge in May 1940 to impede the German advance, and the city, of course, was subsequently occupied, Arnhem and its environs had largely escaped the ravages of war before 17 September 1944. Lying just east of central Holland, in Gelderland, close to the German border, the Arnhem road bridge – the reconstruction of which had only recently been completed by the Germans – was now key to Allied strategy. Hitherto, it had been very much a rear area, providing a comparatively safe haven for training units. The Arnhem garrison were not front-line troops. What the Germans were very good at, however, was re-grouping and forming *ad hoc kampfgruppen* (battle groups), composite units comprising remnants of various battered formations. Such flexibility meant that fighting capacity could be swiftly restored. Indeed, once the *Rückmarsch* from Normandy had been arrested, this is exactly what happened – and quickly. On 17 August 1944, Hitler appointed his 'Fireman' – so-called given his ability to decisively retrieve a crisis – *Generalfeldmarschall* Walter Model as Commander *Oberbefehlshaber* (OB) West. Oosterbeek, a comfortable, tree-lined suburb west of Arnhem on the main road to Utrecht, the Utrechtseweg, was chosen as Model's headquarters.

On 10 September 1944, the OKW decreed that one division of the II SS-*Panzer Korps*, which had been heavily engaged throughout the Normandy campaign and had previously seen much action on the *Ostfront*, should be replenished near the front, the other in Germany. Model decided that 10-SS *Panzer-Division Frundsberg*, which was stronger than 9-SS *Panzer-Division Hohenstaufen*, should be deployed to the Arnhem area. The latter was to hand over its armoured vehicles to *Frundsberg* and return to Germany. Two, albeit understrength, SS *Panzer-Divisions*, therefore, were in the very area 1st Airborne Division had landed in. Although after Normandy *Panzer-Divisions* really in name only, *Frundsberg* possessed a substantial amount of armour, including self-propelled guns, *Panzer* Mk IVs and the larger Panther tanks. *Hohenstaufen*, although in the process of relinquishing its vehicles to its brother division, still had a reconnaissance unit equipped with armoured cars and half-tracks, at least two self-propelled guns and several mobile flak vehicles. Commanding the II SS-*Panzer Korps* was SS-*Obergruppenführer* Wilhelm Bittrich, whose headquarters was at Doetinchem – a highly experienced general with equally motivated commanders. It is widely believed, however, that British planners had either ignored or dismissed intelligence concerning the presence of these SS divisions, but this is not actually entirely the case. The 1st Parachute Brigade Intelligence Summary, submitted by Captain W.A. Taylor on 13 September 1944, makes specific mention of 'a battle-scarred *panzer* division or two' being in the area. With limited anti-tank capacity, the lightly-armed paratroopers clearly required surprise, speed and rapid relief from Allied armour – which was indeed the plan.

Also in the Arnhem area was a training unit, SS-*Panzergrenadier-Ausbildings-und Ersatz-Bataillon* (Panzer Grenadier Depot & Reserve Battalion) 16, commanded by SS-*Sturmbannführer* Josef 'Sepp' Krafft. Whilst the majority of Krafft's young soldiers lacked combat experience, they were being trained to reinforce front-line *Waffen*-SS units by battle-hardened NCOs and officers who had fought in Russia, Normandy and elsewhere. All of these men, recruits included, were highly motivated. These were far, therefore, from the rear echelon or sub-standard troops that the 1st British Airborne Division had been briefed to expect.

So well, however, had the flight from England and drop gone, and so enthusiastically had the lead elements of the 1st Airborne Division been welcomed as liberators by the Dutch people, that the British troops gathering up their parachutes and assembling on DZ 'X' remained blissfully unaware that their intelligence picture was, to say the least, somewhat misleading. Major Digby Tatham-Warter commanded Frost's 'A' Company: 'The Battalion was dropped accurately in first class conditions. There was no opposition on dropping zone. "A" Company captured six vehicles and 12 POWs at rendezvous. Moved off at approximately 1530 hours, with "A" Company leading.'

Paratroopers rely upon surprise, speed and rapid relief. Airborne troops lack heavy weapons, although 1st Airborne Division did have a quantity of jeep-towed 6-pounder and 17-pounder anti-tank guns, and the 'Projector, Infantry, Anti-Tank' (PIAT), a hand-held, spring-loaded bomb-firing weapon. Surprise had thus far been achieved, but the 1st Parachute Brigade now had to cover, via three routes, 'Lion' (2nd Parachute Battalion), 'Tiger' (3rd Parachute Battalion) and 'Leopard' (1st Parachute Battalion), the eight miles to Arnhem Bridge – largely on foot, carrying provisions, weapons and ammunition. Given the distance and overall circumstances, John Frost and his 2nd Parachute Battalion, with supporting divisional troops, sixty miles behind enemy lines in what was shortly to become a veritable hornet's nest, set off along Lion Route, the lower of the three, towards the river Rhine.

The story of 2nd Parachute Battalion's advance to Arnhem is told elsewhere in this book, but suffice it to say here that the journey to Arnhem was not without mishap or casualties. Indeed, two miles from DZ 'X', 'A' Company, in the van, was held up by a German machine gun, and the sound of battle could be heard from the 3rd Battalion's direction, advancing along the main Utrechtseweg towards Oosterbeek. As the 2nd Battalion passed beneath a small railway viaduct near Oosterbeek-Laag Station, 'an armoured car appeared and caused some delay and casualties'. Further resistance was met beyond the viaduct. 'B' Company was sent to deal with the opposition, suffering casualties; wireless communications with both 'B' and 'C' Company's broke down. Indeed, 'nothing more was ever heard of "C" Company'. Beyond that point, German resistance was comparatively light – the rapidly-deployed and highly-effective blocking lines not yet extending all the way to the Rhine. Consequently, at 2000 hrs, Major Tatham-Warter's 'A' Company reached the Arnhem road bridge. The bridge was lightly defended but a flak gun and an armoured car swung the balance in the Germans' favour

The infamous 'Bridge Too Far'. (Author)

Appropriately, the Bridge is now 'John Frost Brug'. (Author)

– causing 'A' Company to abandon the attack it put in to capture the bridge's southern end. By this time, 2045 hrs, more of the 1st Parachute Brigade Group were arriving via the lower road, albeit excepting both the 1st and 3rd Parachute Battalions, but including Colonel Frost and his headquarters staff, which occupied buildings around Marktstraat and Eusebiusbinnensingel, close to the bridge and main Nijmegen road.

Colonel Frost:

We found a suitable house (for Battalion Headquarters and the Regimental Aid Post) on the corner overlooking the bridge and roused the owner, who spoke very good English. He was not at all happy at the prospect of billeting soldiers of any sort. The Germans, he said, had gone and he would much prefer us to chase on after them. When I convinced him that the Germans were still very much there and furthermore that we didn't merely want billets, but proposed to fortify the house in readiness for a battle, he retired to the cellar quite horrified, leaving us to our own devices.

1st Parachute Brigade Headquarters was established in the adjacent but larger Provinciehuis (County House). In 1991, (the sadly now late) Major General Frost remembered that 'Major Tate commanded Headquarters Company during the battle at Arnhem bridge. This is apt to be a rather nebulous job in battle as all the personnel are fully engaged as signallers, clerks and other administrative duties. However, at Arnhem Bridge we were all embroiled in continuous close-quarter fighting that involved everyone.' If it was action Frank wanted, he had certainly found it.

On that first day, Brigadier Gerald Lathbury, OC 1st Parachute Brigade was in company with the Divisional Commander, General Roy Urquhart, and unable to get through to Arnhem bridge – which the Brigadier and General decided they must personally do owing to the failure of wireless communications. Colonel Frost, therefore, assumed command of all units at the bridge, placing his second-in-command and friend Major David Wallis in charge of 2nd Parachute Battalion.

The initial attempt to take the northern end of Arnhem Bridge failed, however, largely owing to a machine gun located in a concrete pillbox almost adjacent to the British forward defences in houses alongside the bridge. Another attempt was made, during which a PIAT was fired at the offending pillbox, and Sapper 'Ginger' Wilkinson attempted to burn it with a flamethrower. He missed his intended target, pouring flame onto huts behind the German machine-gunner. Suddenly there was a blinding explosion as the hut – a fuel and ammunition store – erupted. The whole bridge was ablaze for the rest of the night. More Germans, however, were making sallies, and likewise paratroopers from miscellaneous units reinforced Frost, in dribs and drabs as they found a way through.

Earlier that day, before the landings began, SS-*Hauptsturmführer* Viktor Gräbner, the commander of *Hohenstaufen*'s SS-*Aufklärungs Abteilung* 9, the divisional

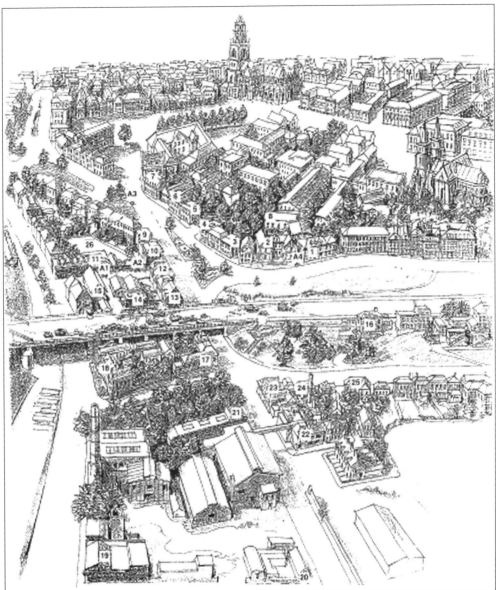

DISPOSITIONS OF 1 PARACHUTE BRIGADE GROUP UNDER THE COMMAND OF LIEUTENANT COLONEL JOHN FROST, CO OF THE 2ND PARACHUTE BATTALION, AS ON MONDAY, 18 SEPTEMBER 1944.

1. Bde Def Pl
2. HQ 1 Para Bde
3. HQ 2 Para Bn
4. Mor Pl, 2 Para Bn
5. HQ/Sp Coy, 2 Para Bn
6. HQ/Sp Coy, 2 Para Bn
7. HQ 1 Atk Bty RA
8. RASC Pl
9. B Coy, 2 Para Bn
10. B Coy, 2 Para Bn
11. Pl A Coy, 2 Para Bn
12. A Coy HQ/Pl, 2 Para Bn
13. Pl A Coy, 2 Para Bn
14. 9 Fd Coy RE (18th only)
15. Pl, A Coy/MMG 2 Para Bn
16. C Coy HQ/9 Pl, 3 Para Bn; A Tp, 1 Para Sqn RE
17. Pl, A Coy ,2 Para Bn
18. A/B Coy, 2 Para Bn
19. 8 Pl, C Coy, 3 Para Bn (overrun 18th)
20. 8 Pl, C Coy, 3 Para Bn (overrun 18th)
21. 8 Pl, C Coy, 3 Para Bn (overrun 18th)
22. Bde HQ Def Pl (overrun 18th)
23. Sigs/RASC/Ord
24. Sigs/RE
25. Sigs/RE
26. 6 pdr Atk gun/jeep park (17th)

A1. 6 pdr Atk gun (18/19th)
A2. 6 pdr Atk gun (18/19)
A3. 6 pdr Atk gun (18/19)
A4. 6 pdr Atk gun (19th)

reconnaissance unit, was awarded the coveted *Ritterkreuz* (Knight's Cross) at a ceremony in Hoenderloo for his bravery in Normandy. Although *Hohenstaufen* was transferring its vehicles and heavy weapons to *Frundsberg*, Gräbner's unit remained combat ready. Consequently SS-*Obersturmbannführer* Walter Harzer, *Hohenstaufen*'s commander, ordered Gräbner to reconnoitre and secure the bridges at Nijmegen and Arnhem. At about 1800 hrs, before the British arrived at Arnhem Bridge, Gräbner led some forty vehicles over the steel span, leaving at least one on the south side but curiously none to secure the northern end, and continued onwards with his force to Nijmegen. Also subsequently leaving vehicles on the southern side of the great Waal Bridge, he travelled to and spent the night at Elst, equidistant between the two bridges. At dawn on 18 September, Gräbner was ordered to re-cross and re-take the northern end of Arnhem Bridge. Leaving six vehicles defending Elst, Gräbner set off for Arnhem, just a few miles away, with twenty-two armoured cars and half-tracks. He was unaware of exactly where the British were, or their strength, but his plan was simple: fast armoured cars to lead the way and race across the bridge, surprising the enemy and gaining the far bank, whilst half-tracks and troop-carrying trucks followed.

From their vantage points in Arnhem, Frost's men soon reported the approaching vehicles, the recognition of black crosses dashing any hopes that this was a lead element of XXX Corps' relief column. Major Dennis Munford called in artillery from batteries supporting Frost and firing from Oosterbeek; the British fire was accurate but still the enemy advanced. Once Gräbner's vehicles were on the bridge, the artillery ceased fire, so as not to damage it. As planned, the lead armoured cars sped across the bridge unscathed, some even made it into Arnhem, but the withering fire poured down onto the SS men very violently degenerated Gräbner's once proud column into a disaster. Sergeant Cyril Robson's 6-pounder anti-tank gun destroyed more of the enemy vehicles than any other means. Halted half-tracks and lorries were set ablaze by grenades and small-arms fire, which pinned down and slaughtered the SS men. The bridge and ramp were littered with wrecked German vehicles, the most forward of which blazed away on Nijmegensweg – opposite Brigade and 2nd Parachute Battalion Headquarters. There is no question, therefore, that Major Tate saw and was a part of this successful action. Indeed, as British historian Martin Middlebrook wrote 'Nearly everyone in the British garrison was involved in the firing'.

Signalman Bill Jukes was under Major Tate's command in the 2nd Parachute Battalion Headquarters building: 'The first vehicle which drew level with the house was hit, and the second rammed into it, blocking the roadway. The rest didn't stand a chance. The crews and passengers, those still able to, began to pile out, and those of us armed with Stens joined in the general fusillade. It was impossible to say what effect my shooting had. There was such a volley coming from the windows along the street that nobody could say who shot who.' Two hours later it was all over. Some seventy Germans lay dead in and around their wrecked vehicles – including SS-*Hauptsturmführer* Viktor Gräbner. British casualties were light – and morale sky high.

Later that day Major David Wallis was killed in an incident of 'friendly fire'. Command of 2nd Parachute Battalion then went to Major Digby Tatham-Warter. By the following day, German tanks and self-propelled guns were systematically destroying the British positions around the bridge, for which there had been and would be no relief – the remainder of the 1st Parachute Brigade and 4th Parachute Brigade, the latter having arrived on the second drop, on 18 September, had been unable to get through. The situation was grim indeed, as Corporal Horace Goodrich, located in the Brigade Headquarters at the Provinciehuis, recalled: 'The enemy brought up a self-propelled gun to shell our building. I happened to be manning a Bren gun in the right place to engage it and the infantry who were standing round it. After getting off two short bursts, I observed what had all the appearance of a golden tennis ball at the mouth of the SP gun. The next moment I was lying on my back covered in dust and debris. Having got the range, they were able to fire at will until the top floor became temporarily untenable.' Just before dark, a 'Tiger tank' appeared, a round from which wounded Major Tatham-Warter, who was also 'severely affected by blast'. Command of the 2nd Parachute Battalion then passed to Major Freddie Gough of the Reconnaissance Squadron. Frequently, however, accounts refer to 'Tiger tanks' when they were not, in fact. Two Tigers of *Schwere Panzer-Kompanie* Hummel, though, had arrived in Arnhem on the evening of 19 September, so this report is probably accurate.

As night turned to another flame- and smoke-wreathed day, the pressure continued to build on the beleaguered defenders of Arnhem Bridge, critically short of all supplies. The *Luftwaffe* stepped up its operations, strafing British troops around Arnhem Bridge. *Leutnant* Hans Ransmayer of 15/JG54, however, an experienced *experte* with over thirty aerial victories to his credit, failed to see the twin spires of the St Walburgis Basillica, wreathed in smoke and situated a few hundred metres north-west of the Bridge, until it was too late. His Fw 190-A8 fighter hit the spires, killing the pilot – much to the delight of Frost's beleaguered garrison.

On that day, Colonel Frost managed to speak on the radio to General Urquhart, who had been missing for two days: there was no news of relief by XXX Corps, and no chance of reinforcements arriving from Oosterbeek. Later, 'As I was talking to Doug Crawley outside his headquarters about arranging a fighting patrol to give us more elbow-room to the north, there was a sudden savage crash beside us. I was thrown several feet and found myself lying face downwards on the ground with pain in both legs.' Wounded, Colonel Frost was taken to the Regimental Aid Post in the Battalion Headquarters building. Overall command of the pitiful remnants of the forces fighting at the bridge was passed to Major Gough, who in turn gave command of the 2nd Parachute Battalion to Major Frank Tate. By this time, the paratroopers had been 'burnt out of our positions east and immediately west of the bridge', wrote Major Tatham-Warter. News had been received that 2nd Army would reach the bridge by 5 pm that evening, '. . .This did not happen and by dark the situation had become critical. Soon after dark the few houses still standing were set on fire, and we found ourselves without

This is one of only two Schwere Panzer-Kompanie *Hummel's Tigers to reach Arnhem, photographed by* Kriegsberichter *Höppner on the eastern side of the northern ramp, and which, according to the German caption, 'eliminated the bridgehead'. (Airborne Museum Hartenstein)*

No Tigers at Arnhem Bridge today. (Author)

a position. The wounded were then surrendered, and from reports I received afterwards were well cared for, with our own doctors to look after them.' Just after dark, Brigade Headquarters in the Provinciehuis caught fire, requiring the wounded to be moved into a building behind. With no choice but very sensibly, Colonel Frost ordered 'all opposition from Brigade Headquarters to cease and the wounded to be surrendered'. The surviving 120 headquarters personnel moved north to find a new position. As the enemy appeared to deal with the wounded prisoners, those paratroopers still fighting were ordered not to fire on the Germans.

During this lull, the Germans infiltrated large numbers of troops into the Provinciehuis area. A German officer entered the garden of the house Major Tatham-Warter occupied – still a combatant and back in command of 2nd Parachute Battalion in spite of having been wounded twice – and demanded that he and his men surrender. Unable to fire owing to the ongoing evacuation of the wounded, Major Tatham-Warter ordered a move to an adjacent warehouse. Although 'A' Company took the house with little trouble, it was soon surrounded and indefensible. Late on 21 September, it was decided that the survivors should split into two groups, each of some sixty men, and try to escape back to the equally besieged British perimeter at Oosterbeek. Major Tatham-Warter was to lead one group, Major Tate the other. 2nd Lieutenant Jim Flavell was in charge of a third, smaller, separate group – many years later using such words as 'hairy', 'hell' and 'hopeless'; to describe the prevalent

The grave of Lieutenant John Grayburn VC at Oosterbeek. (13.C.11). (Author)

circumstances. According to Flavell, those involved in the break-out had no idea of enemy positions or strength, but nonetheless Major Tate led off the first group – and, silhouetted by the blazing buildings, was machine-gunned and killed almost immediately he left the sanctuary of the warehouse.

The battle for Arnhem Bridge was over. According to Major Tatham-Warter's after-action report, written whilst a prisoner, having been captured that fateful night, 'Of the 2nd Battalion, approximately 350 had reached the bridge; of this number 210 were wounded, many of whom had fought on to the end, in spite of their wounds. It is not possible to estimate the number killed, but I know of approximately 100 taken prisoner unwounded. The Battalion had fought with the utmost gallantry, in inconceivably difficult conditions, and had denied the use of the vital Bridge to the enemy for eighty hours.'

The Airborneplein Memorial near Arnhem Bridge, the twin spires of the St Walburgis Basillica beyond – into which a German fighter crashed after strafing British troops nearby. (Author)

FRANK TATE

For Colonel Frost, the virtual destruction of his battalion was heart-breaking. In the ensuing daylight, the Colonel sat with other wounded prisoners on the nearby embankment, despairingly watching the buildings previously occupied by his men burning fiercely. As if symbolic of the whole thing, he watched 'the old Battalion Headquarters collapse into a heap of smouldering rubble . . . The SS men were very polite and complimentary about the battle we had fought, but the bitterness I felt was unassuaged. No living enemy had beaten us. The Battalion was unbeaten yet, but could not have much chance with no ammunition. No. body of men could have fought more outrageously and tenaciously than the officers and men of the 1st Parachute Brigade at Arnhem Bridge.'

Major Tate's field grave was in or near the Provinciehuis – close to that of the gallant Lieutenant Jack Grayburn, awarded a posthumous Victoria Cross for his bravery fighting at the bridge. Together with 2nd Lieutenant Jim Flavell, Major Tate was recommended for a Mention in Despatches, but, as with so many recommendations arising from the Arnhem battle, this was not upheld at Division. Of sixteen 2nd Parachute Battalion officers put forward for recognition, only five, in fact, were approved.

A pre-war view of the buildings by Arnhem Bridge which were used by the used as the 1st Parachute Brigade's and 2nd Parachute Battalion's headquarters during the fighting. As CO of 2nd Para Battalion's HQ Company, Major Tate used the smaller building to the left. (Gelders Archief)

The Provinciehuis, or what was left of it after the battle, in which 1st Parachute Brigade HQ was located; 2nd Parachute Battalion's HQ was in a building to the immediate left. (Gelders Archief)

Major Francis Raymond 'Tim' Tate was posted 'Missing in Action' – a tragic status maintained for six months, when his remains were discovered and an uncertain time concluded for his widow. Joyce later re-married, living out her life at Craven Arms in Shropshire, a few miles from Tenbury Wells where she had lived with Frank; she died in 1997. After the war, Major Tate was interred at the Arnhem Oosterbeek War Cemetery (Plot 20, Row C, Grave 13). Unusually, no epitaph appears on his headstone – possibly due to his Unitarian denomination (although the family is Church of England).

Frank Tate's obituary paid tribute to him: 'an absolutely first-class soldier and a magnificent leader . . . a man of strong character, logical mind and a high sense of duty'. Certainly, he did not have to be a paratrooper but still chose to be. When the opportunity came to meet the enemy, he had not baulked at the prospect and served his country to the last. An indication of the potential mankind lost upon his death in action is provided by the achievements of his elder brother: Bernard served during the Second World War in the Royal Army Medical Corps, as a lieutenant colonel, and was made an MBE for his efforts. The family's opinion is that both Frank and Bernard were militarily inspired by two elder brothers' service during the First World War: Claude's with the Royal Navy (he also served with the Auxiliary Fire Service in Birmingham during the Second World War), and Adrian's in the Royal Warwickshire Regiment until transferring to the Royal

Flying Corps (and serving in the Home Guard in London during the Second World War). Indeed, Adrian's service in the Royal Warwickshire Regiment could explain why Frank chose to serve not in a specialist, non-combatant role more suited to his experience, but in an infantry regiment. Bernard Tate survived the Second World War to become an eminent dermatologist; he died in 1979. It is clear that, like Bernard, Frank Tate was also destined, if not for the war, to achieve greatness in his own profession and calling. Sadly, that was not to be, his story ending violently that night against the backdrop of blazing buildings near what is now, appropriately, known as 'John Frost Brug'.

The built-up area around Arnhem Bridge has totally changed, the rubble and empty shells replaced by modern buildings, making photographic comparison meaningless. This commemorative plaque can be seen today on the building now standing on the site of 2nd Parachute Battalion's HQ. (Author)

Major Tate's grave at Oosterbeek. (20.C.13). (Author)

Chapter 3

Privates Thomas and Claude Gronert, 2nd Parachute Battalion

Amongst the parachutes blossoming over DZ 'X' at Heelsum during the early afternoon of 17 September 1944, were those of the 21-year-old Gronert twins, Privates Claude and Thomas. A few hours later, both lay dead, killed in action within minutes of each other, side-by-side, as they had lived. Over the years since, the Gronert story has deeply moved many, and has rightly become a well-known tragedy of Operation MARKET-GARDEN. Indeed, should ever the day come that mankind fails to be moved by the Gronerts' story, the whole of humanity should worry.

Claude and 'Tommy' Gronert were the sons of Robert, a dustman, and Lylie Gronert of the small village of Tregajorran, on the slopes of Carn Brae, near Redruth in Cornwall. The boys were tin and copper miners at the South Crofty Mine, and as such were in a 'reserved occupation' and exempt from military service. As younger brother Bernard remembers: 'They didn't tell us what they were planning to do, and when the twins came home one day and said they'd joined up, it broke my mother's heart. I can still see her crying and asking why they'd done it, because they didn't have to go. A cousin of ours, however, was in the Army, telling us exciting stories, and I think Tom and Claude were attracted by the perceived fun of it all.'

Private Claude Gronert. (David van Buggenum)

So it was that the Gronert twins joined the Hampshire Regiment in 1941, as infantry soldiers, serving at home, before answering the call to become parachute soldiers and attending Parachute Course 63 at RAF Ringway. Upon conclusion of the twelve-day course, on 17 May 1943, the twins' instructor recorded the same remark on both brothers' reports: 'Has jumped well'. Having successfully passed the course, the Gronerts joined the Parachute Regiment, which had been formed on 1 August 1942, being sent overseas to North Africa in

Private Thomas Gronert. (David van Buggenum)

June 1943, as reinforcements for 1st Parachute Brigade. There the twins joined 2nd Parachute Battalion, and specifically 6 Platoon, commanded by Lieutenant Peter 'Cobber' Cane.

1st Parachute Brigade had been deployed to North Africa in November 1942, seeing much action there and subsequently in Sicily. Between August and September 1943, the brigade was reinforced, the new arrivals including the Gronerts and friends. Then, on 8 September 1943, 1st Airborne Division landed on Italian soil not by parachute but courtesy of the Royal Navy, at Taranto. 1st Parachute Brigade was held around the port, as Divisional reserve, moving up to Castellaneta and Altamura, before returning to England. Back home, the division trained for the liberation of enemy occupied Europe, and, as we have seen, stood by whilst 6th Airborne Division dropped and landed on D-Day, fighting throughout the Normandy campaign. After numerous cancelled operations, on 17 September 1944, Privates Claude and Tommy Gronert eventually found themselves descending over Heelsum and part of the 2nd Parachute Battalion's effort to seize Arnhem Bridge. As it turned out for so many, it was a fateful jump for both twins.

Having dropped in perfect conditions, accurately, achieving complete surprise, 1st Parachute Brigade, comprising the most experienced British parachute battalions, formed up and prepared to set off for Arnhem, eight miles away. Brigadier Lathbury's plan was for Major Freddie Gough's jeep-borne Reconnaissance Squadron to dash to Arnhem via the northernmost of three routes, codenamed 'Leopard', and seize the bridge by a *coup-de-main*. On foot, 3rd Parachute Battalion was to advance along 'Tiger' route, the main Heelsum-Arnhem road, passing through Oosterbeek, joining 2nd Parachute Battalion at Arnhem Bridge, which the latter was to approach via the lower route, 'Lion', through lower Oosterbeek and along the Rhine. 1st Parachute Battalion was to follow, along 'Leopard' route. Lathbury intended, therefore, to advance on a broad front, achieving speed and surprise, rather than one long, slow, snake-like column.

As frequently happens in war, however, the plan immediately got off to a bad start when the Reconnaissance Squadron had the grave misfortune to blunder into the northern end of the blocking line SS-*Sturmbannführer* Sepp Krafft was already putting in place. Indeed, Krafft's rapid reaction to the airborne threat over the next few hours would have a significant impact on the battle's outcome. Major Gough's casualties were heavy, and no attempt was made to proceed with his remaining two troops of jeeps. In any case, such employment was not what Gough's men were trained in, their actual intended role being to reconnoitre ahead of the main force. 3rd Parachute Battalion also ran into trouble early on, and the sound of their battle was heard by 2nd Parachute Battalion as it made a comparatively peaceful start through the woods. Colonel Frost's objective was not only the Arnhem road bridge, but also the railway bridge at lower Oosterbeek. The problem, apart from the obvious lack of a force to simultaneously attack the bridges from the far bank, was that there was some distance to walk – and as every minute ticked by, the German reaction became stronger and sharper. Infuriatingly, 2nd

Parachute Battalion's route was to take it past the operable Heavedorp ferry – of which the planners had been aware but inexplicably failed to exploit. Nonetheless, after some skirmishing with Krafft's men around Heelsum, 2nd Parachute Battalion reached Oosterbeek at or shortly before 1800 hrs – receiving a warm welcome from the ecstatic inhabitants overjoyed to be 'liberated'.

At the Old Vicarage on Benedendorpsweg in lower Oosterbeek, near the Old Church, Kate ter Horst and her young children had watched with incredulity the streams of aircraft, gliders and parachutes. The 'Moffen', as the Dutch contemptuously called their German oppressors had gone, or so it seemed; Kate ter Horst: 'We rush out of the garden and into the road. Yes, there is the impossible, incredible truth! Our unknown British liberators, like a long green serpent, are approaching, one by one, a couple of yards between each of them; the first gives us a jolly laugh from under his helmet, which is covered by a net full of green strips – an absurd sight. He spreads out his arms: "Give us a kiss!" and next moment he is gone. Behind him they come in endless files, moving rhythmically. They seem to be in no hurry, they walk so calmly. Later we realise that we cannot keep up with this camel-like walk of all those long legs. We can't keep our eyes off these soldiers who, though not marching, proceed in perfect order; we are so accustomed to the noisy marching of the Germans.' Amongst Kate's four children was five-year-old Sophie, who years later told me that 'There was huge excitement – it was like a spontaneous street party. My parents climbed the nearby church tower and draped orange flags from it. Although I was only a child, it was

The rebuilt railway bridge at lower Oosterbeek and the track across the polder taken to it by 'C' Company, 2nd Parachute Battalion, seen from Benedendorpsweg in 2017. (Author)

obvious that this was a massively significant occurrence, because of how the grown-ups were behaving, ecstatic. I will never forget it.' Amongst the paratroopers trudging past the Ter Horst house were Privates Claude and Tommy Gronert.

To the immediate south of the Ter Horst house in Benedendorpsweg, lay meadows, polder, sweeping down to the Rhine; just over a kilometre ahead was a high railway embankment, the line running south, across a river bridge, to Nijmegen. Benedendorpsweg passed through the embankment via the small Klingenbeeksweg railway viaduct. The intact Oosterbeek railway bridge was one of Colonel Frost's objectives – to which he despatched Major Victor Dover's 'C' Company. Crossing the flat, wide-open polder, Lieutenant Peter Barry's 9 Platoon gained the northern end of the bridge – then Barry decided to press on and take the southern end. Just before he reached the bridge's centre, the span exploded. No-one was hurt by the explosion, but Barry was picked out as the officer by nearby German troops and shot in the shoulder. Bitterly disappointed, 'C' Company withdrew back to Benedendorpsweg and re-joined the Battalion. This demolition completely thwarted Colonel Frost's intention to pass men across it, enabling the all-important Arnhem road bridge, which lay further on, to be seized simultaneously from both ends. Not knowing that his problem was easily solved by the nearby Heavedorp ferry, Frost pressed on – and time was increasingly of the essence. Up ahead it was also believed that a pontoon bridge existed – and Frost prayed that both, or at least one, of the two bridges, would be captured intact.

As Lieutenant Robin Vlasto led his platoon of 'A' Company through the Klingensbeeksweg viaduct, two German armoured vehicles appeared from a direction of Arnhem (these were probably from SS-*Hauptsturmführer* Viktor Gräbner's

Hohenstaufen SS-*Aufklärungs Abteilung* 9). Variously described as 'armoured cars' or unspecified 'armoured vehicles', the Germans immediately opened fire on Vlasto's men, hitting the two paratroopers either side of their leader – one being killed. 'A' Company then attempted to outflank the enemy by leaving the road, but the troublesome vehicles withdrew before a PIAT could be brought up or a 6-pounder anti-tank gun deployed. 'B' Company was then ordered to deal with the troublesome fire from Oosterbeek-Laag railway station to the north and on higher ground. Lieutenant Peter Cane's 6 Platoon was at the head of 'B' Company, ordered to taking a left turn into Spoorstraat, mounting the railway embankment with a view to outflanking the enemy's railway station position by approaching it from the north. Cane advanced with Sergeant Henry Hacker's Section, with friends and fellow Cornishmen Privates Jack Edwards and Tommy Gronert up front, scouting ahead. There was little cover, the odd shot ringing out; Cane's paratroopers took cover behind some upright wooden railway sleepers, near the station; a group of Germans was spotted and called upon to surrender – who themselves called upon the British to do likewise. A confused stand-off ensued. The Germans then held their rifles aloft, implying surrender, so Lieutenant Cane, trusting the move, got up and walked towards them, with Sergeant Hacker leading, followed by Privates Edwards and Gronert. Private Don Smith: 'The Germans didn't play straight . . . they opened fire'.

Private Jack Edwards:

> I heard Tommy shouting that there were Germans on the other side of the railway track. Again, the order came to advance; Tommy moved onto the track with the others. At that moment Claude Gronert was nearby. Our lads were in the open when the firing started, with absolutely no cover. I had just got to the end of the upright sleepers but every time I showed my head I was shot at. Then I heard Tommy shout that he had been hit. He had been shot in the mouth, the bullet passing through his neck. It all happened in a few seconds. Nobody had a ghost of a chance in that open space. There was no way we could get help to the men and the rest of us who were not in the open decided to move back to the wooden barrier, which was the only cover available. We had no way out. A German machine-gun caused the most damage and any move we made was met by fire. When we returned after the shooting had died down it was a terribly sad sight that met our eyes. Lieutenant Cane said a few words – then died. Tommy and Claude Gronert lay close to one another, both dead. Claude had received three bullets through the top of his tin hat. For me it was a shattering blow because we had been friends for a long time, were all Cornish, had joined the Parachute Regiment together from the same unit.

Having spent his last leave before Arnhem with his parents, Tommy had met up with Jack Edwards before going to the station in Truro and travelling back to Colsterworth.

The Klingenbeeksweg railway viaduct on Benedendorpsweg, on Lion Route, through which most of those British troops who reached Arnhem Bridge passed. The Gronert twins were killed up on the railway line, near Oosterbeek Laag station, a short distance to the North. (Author)

Battle damage can still be clearly seen on the viaduct. (Author)

ARNHEM 1944

Jack's wife, Barbara, went to wave them off; Tommy appeared reluctant to go, and said as much. Mrs Edwards has wondered ever since whether he had a premonition of death.

The twins were buried near the railway viaduct. Bernard Gronert: 'I remember very clearly news of the twins' deaths arriving after a long period of uncertainty. A telegram had been delivered. Mother was crying and father was comforting her. Everything changed.'

In 1945, the twins' remains were interred at the Arnhem Oosterbeek War Cemetery. Ever since, on the Sunday closest to 17 September 1944, when the 'Flower Children' place floral tributes on all 1,748 graves, Dutch twins have paid their respects to Privates Claude and Tommy Gronert.

The graves of twin Privates Claude and Thomas Gronert at Oosterbeek. (18.A.18/17). (Author)

THOMAS AND CLAUDE GRONERT

The heartbroken Mrs Gronert visited her sons' graves after the war, at the invitation of the Dutch people, and Bernard Gronert also made the pilgrimage for the 50th anniversary: 'The Dutch are lovely people and made me very welcome', he says. In fact, it is entirely appropriate to give the last word to him:

> Mother never got over it and she cried a lot for the rest of her life. The twins were talked about often in the years afterwards. We tried to think of the good times, but Christmas and birthdays were awful. After the war, when my National Service papers came, my mother was having none of it, and demanded of our local MP that given the sacrifice made by my brothers, I should not have to go. She got her way, because in any case I failed on medical grounds. I think it important for our family to continue remembering my brothers and for everyone to remember all the boys who gave their lives.

Note: The Gronert story is well-known amongst Arnhem enthusiasts, having been researched and published in detail by Dutch historian David van Buggenum in his ground-breaking *'B' Company Arrived* (2003) and *'B' Company: The Men* (see Bibliography). Both titles are highly recommended reading for anyone wishing to learn more of the twins' tragic loss.

Chapter 4

Lance-Corporal William Bamsey, Privates Frederick Hopwood and Gordon Matthews, 3rd Parachute Battalion

On 17 September 1944, thirty-six aircraft took off from Saltby and dropped the 588 men of Lieutenant Colonel John Fitch's Spalding-based 3rd Parachute Battalion over DZ 'X' at 1356 hrs. Private Henry Bennett remembered that:

> Reveille was 0430 hours, breakfast at 0500, with orders to be ready to move off at approximately 0600. After getting our kit and parachutes ready, we left Spalding by lorry roughly at 0615 for our respective aerodromes.
>
> We arrived there at 0730, and our planes, already numbered, were all lined up and ready to go. Everybody was excited and joking with each other, and as we had plenty of time, we gave our chutes their final check over. Just before we were ready to leave we met our pilot and crew, who gave us our last briefing regarding our flight. Zero Hour arrived, so orders to emplane were given, and shortly afterwards, all planes started to warm up.
>
> By this time, the sun had come out, and as there was only slight cloud, it appeared to be a nice day. Finally we started to form into our respected flights, us being Chalk 39, so we had a bit of time left to sit in our plane and watch our pals from another battalion take off. Our run in came before long, and it was dead on 0930 when we took off. It took a certain amount of time to form up, so we had the pleasure of seeing a good part of England from eight hundred to one thousand feet up.
>
> About 1030 hours, we knew we were on our way and were soon flying out over the coast of England towards the Channel. Over the water, we noticed a fair amount of vessels about (perhaps for our benefit). By this time, we had met our fighter escort, and spent our time watching them. All the way we were being told the time, and at roughly 1300 we could see the French coast, and felt that that funny feeling we get just before our descent. We noticed the flights in front of us had turned slightly to the left, and knew that we would be turning with them.
>
> At 1335 hours we passed over the coast and shore. We knew it was Holland, as everywhere was under water: farms, small villages, and you could see the

roof tops. After a while we saw the first sign of life, and for a few moments we thought we had arrived at our DZ, but that proved wrong. It was a fairly large town, and we could plainly see people in the streets waving to us. Up to now we had had no interference from the enemy, but as we were getting further inland we knew what to expect. Before long we knew we were getting close, and got what we expected. Our plane dropped and rose like a boat, but the flights on our left caught a lot more of flak than we did, but our luck must have been in, as all planes got through without mishap. Still there were no enemy fighters about, and that helped cheer us up. By now everyone was getting tense as to what to expect next, but that was soon dashed from our minds because the time arrived to prepare for the descent. It took only a short time to adjust our chutes and strap our kitbags to our legs. We were ready to go. That came next, and, as most of my pals said, it was one of our best jumps. My kitbag broke loose from about one hundred and fifty feet, and, as I watched it crash to the ground, I crossed my fingers for the boys already on the deck – as it is a fairly unpleasant thing when kitbags and containers start floating around.

It was exactly 1400 hours when I hit the deck. After regaining my kitbag, and finding my two pals, we headed for our rendezvous already marked by coloured smoke. Flights were still coming in, and on the field to our left our gliders lay everywhere, those boys having been first to land. Still we had not met any enemy resistance, however, as a few of my pals remarked. At 1500 hours, my battalion moved off towards Wolfheze. We passed quite a few Dutch people who were friendly enough and only seemed to be interested in whether they could have our chutes or not – there must have been hundreds lying about.

Brigadier Lathbury's intention, as we have seen, was for 1st Parachute Brigade to advance on a broad front, his three battalions each taking a separate route to Arnhem. Fitch was to leave DZ 'X' and proceed along 'Tiger' route, first marching south to Heelsum, then east along the Utrechtsweg, through Oosterbeek to Arnhem. There, 3rd Parachute Battalion was intended to take and hold the northern end of the bridge. After a perfect drop the battalion formed up and was soon on the move. Leading the way was Major Peter Waddy's 'B' Company, with Lieutenant Jimmy Cleminson's No. 5 Platoon scouting ahead. Amongst Cleminson's men was Private Gordon Matthews – a twenty-year-old from Worcester.

Gordon Matthews was born on 2 June 1924, the son of Frank, a former soldier and prisoner during the First World War, and Hilda Matthews of 45 The Drive, Checketts Lane, Barbourne, Worcester – just across the road from RAF Perdiswell, a busy elementary flying training school, the Tiger Moths flying from which may have inspired young Gordon's interest in aviation. A blue-eyed, brown haired, single man, 5ft 5in tall, Gordon attended St Stephen's primary school and then the Samuel Southall secondary school; a sportsman, he played football and cricket for both. Having achieved a scholarship to Worcester Technical School, when he joined up, he was an enthusiastic member of the local Home Guard unit and worked as a 'hairdresser' at Skan's – still in business today in the 'Faithful City's' Broad Street.

Gordon enlisted in the General Service Corps (GSC) at Worcester on 5 November 1942. Initially posted to Berwick-upon-Tweed for training, Private Matthews was transferred to the Royal Armoured Corps (RAC) on 16 December 1942, joining the 59th Training Regiment at Barnard Castle. It was not in a tank that Gordon would ride to battle, however: on 11 May 1943, having volunteered, he was 'Posted to Depot & School Airborne Forces, Army Air Corps', at Hardwick Hall. Like the ill-fated Gronert twins, Private Matthews was amongst replacements required by 1st Parachute Brigade to make good losses suffered during bitter fighting in North Africa – where the British paratroopers had earned the enemy's respect and the sobriquet 'Red Devils' on account of their fierce fighting abilities and distinctive maroon beret. Having passed his parachute course on his nineteenth birthday, 2 June 1943, on 17 June 1943, Private Matthews embarked on a troopship for North Africa, arriving ten days later. A month after leaving England,

The only known photograph surviving of Worcester's Private Gordon Matthews. (Author)

he joined 3rd Parachute Battalion. Four days previously, the 1st Parachute Brigade had dropped on Primosole Bridge in Sicily; a bloody two-day battle ensued until the paratroopers were relieved by the sea-landed Durham Light Infantry. The Primosole operation had cost 3rd Parachute Battalion one man in two: 250 men killed, missing or wounded. Into their shoes stepped Private Matthews, who landed with his new Battalion by sea at Taranto Harbour, Italy, on 9 September 1943. Having been used as infantry, the paratroopers embarked for 'Blighty' on 27 November 1943, arriving home on 9 December; for some, it would be their last Christmas.

As Lieutenant Cleminson's No. 5 Platoon now advanced, either side of the Utrechtseweg, they knew not what enemy strength lay ahead. Private Henry Bennett remembered Major Peter Waddy, during his pre-operation briefing, explaining that the German military presence around Arnhem was anticipated to comprise only a few thousand weak and demoralised second-rate troops and some 'beat-up armour that shouldn't cause us much trouble'. 1st Parachute Brigade, however, was about to discover how flawed this intelligence prediction was. Again as we have seen, although rebuilding after their battering in Normandy, the 9th and 10th SS Divisions were actually based in the area – and about to block the 1st and 3rd Parachute Battalion's advance was SS-*Sturmbannführer* Krafft's training unit. Krafft, a former police officer, had arrived in Oosterbeek on 9 September 1944, with his 2 and 4 *Kompanies* and heavy-weapons section. His task, as a divisional reserve, was to familiarise himself with his allotted sector along the Waal, to defend, if necessary, Arnhem's bridges and ferries, preparing them for demolition, and, significantly, 'To prepare for and attack airborne landings'. Krafft deployed his men to the woods south of the railway line between Wolfheze and Oosterbeek, around the Hotel Wolfheze, and his own headquarters at the nearby Villa Waldfriede.

On the morning of 17 September 1944, Krafft had his men exercising, in full battle order, in the woods between Wolfheze and Oosterbeek – which unwittingly put a force of armed and very dangerous *panzergrenadiers* between DZ 'X' and the 1st Parachute Brigade's objective. It is important, however, to grasp the physical significance of the wooded landscape involved. This ancient woodland is the significant feature, covering many square miles. The woods provide a degree of cover, concealing troop movement, hiding snipers, and innumerable, equally ancient, tracks bisecting them mean that armoured vehicles can easily manoeuvre. Having watched the airborne landings that afternoon, Krafft correctly guessed that the enemy's objective was Arnhem's all-important bridges; he also knew that 'the only way to draw the tooth of an airborne landing, with an inferior force, is to drive right into it'. With this very much in mind, Krafft's 2.*Kompanie* was despatched to attack the landing grounds, whilst 4 and also 9.*Kompanie*, which had now arrived on the scene, dug in along the Wolfheze road, which joined the Utrechtseweg, to the west of Oosterbeek. It was the rapid creation of this effective blocking line which would ultimately prevent the 1st and 3rd Parachute Battalions reaching their objectives – whilst 2nd Parachute Battalion was able to pass below Krafft's defences along the lower, 'Lion', route. Krafft's contribution, notwithstanding his slightly exaggerated post-action report, cannot, therefore, be over-estimated.

Sturmbannführer *Sepp Krafft – whose rapid reaction to the airborne landings did much to prevent all but 2nd Parachute Battalion and supporting divisional troops reaching Arnhem Bridge. (Gelders Archief)*

Arnhem and its environs fell within *Feldkommandanteur* 642, the *Stadtkommandant* being *Generalmajor* Friedrich Kussin, a pioneer officer who had served in the First World War. Kussin had only a small security force at his disposal to defend Arnhem, so the arrival of various SS units, including Krafft's, a few days previously was a very welcome addition to his defences. War is confusing and any commander requires accurate intelligence and as soon as possible. With this very much in mind, Kussin left his Arnhem headquarters with his aide, *Unteroffizier* Max Küster, in a camouflaged

The Bilderberg woods, surrounding the De Bilderberg Hotel – in which lurked SS-Sturmbannführer Krafft's panzergrenadiers. (Karen Sarkar)

Citroën staff car driven by *Gefreiter* Josef Willeke. Kussin was aware, of course, of the substantial British airborne landings between Heelsum and Renkum, and that SS-*Sturmbannführer* Krafft, located at the Hotel Wolfheze, was best-placed to provide an accurate situation report. It was to that location that Willeke now drove his boss.

The 3rd Parachute Battalion column, comprising walking paratroopers, twenty jeeps, including three towing 6-pounder anti-tank guns, and two Bren carriers, was over a mile along. For nearly two hours the column made good progress along the tree-lined road. Initially, there had been hardly any opposition, although 'A' Company, at the column's rear, was subjected to occasional rifle fire. Corporal Bob Allen: 'I was walking through the trees near the edge of a road; Lance-Corporal Bamsey was a few feet away to my right. We sensed enemy ahead and both paused – me behind one tree, Bamsey at the side of another. A shot rang out from the right. Bamsey collapsed like a puppet whose strings had been cut. I located the source of the shot, then dashed across and pulled Bamsey behind a tree. He had been shot through the throat, the bullet breaking his neck.' It is believed that the 21-year old Welshman from Port Talbot, Glamorgan, was the 3rd Parachute Battalion's first casualty of Operation MARKET-GARDEN.

William Bamsey was one of six children born to Griffith and Louisa, the 'close-knit and loving family' living in Marsh Street, Aberafan. 'Griff' worked at the Mansel Tin Plate Works. A passionate fan of the Welsh national game, Mr Bamsey was captain of Aberafan Harlequins 1922/23, the club today describing 'Griff' and his brother Willie as 'stalwart forwards'. It is likely that his sons also played rugby and worked at the same tin works, which also employed the three Bamsey sisters; all six Bamseys attended the National School in Aberafan, a state school close to home. Giving his civilian occupation as a 'Tinplate processor', height 5ft 6¾in, William Bamsey, a single man, enlisted into the GSC of the TA at Port Talbot on 12 February 1942. After training, on 3 July 1942, Private Bamsey joined the 10th Battalion, Somerset Light Infantry. Raised in 1940, this 'Hostilities Only' battalion served at home until being converted to 7 Parachute Battalion, 3rd Parachute Brigade, in November 1942. So it was, therefore, that Private Bamsey found himself joining the Army Air Corps and qualifying as a parachutist on 7

Private William Bamsey (centre), believed to have been the 3rd Parachute Battalion's first casualty at Arnhem, shot on the Utrechtseweg, near the junction with Wolfhezerweg, 17 September 1944. (Tracey Lodwig)

November 1942. On 10 March 1943, however, William Bamsey was promoted to Lance-Corporal and eight days later joined 3rd Parachute Battalion, along with others in this book, as replacement to make good losses sustained in North Africa. It is likely that he subsequently parachuted into Sicily with 3rd Parachute Battalion on 13 July 1943, on the Primosole Bridge operation – in which the battalion lost 250 men killed, missing or wounded (one man in two). Private Bamsey then landed by sea with the rest of 1st Parachute Brigade at Taranto, Italy, before leaving foreign shores for England on 27 November 1943.

Private Bamsey's mother (left) and sister at his graveside during a pilgrimage. (Tracey Lodwig)

Private Bamsey's grave at Oosterbeek. (19.C.1), having received a floral tribute from the 'Flower Children', September 2016. (Author)

WILLIAM BAMSEY, FREDERICK HOPWOOD, GORDON MATTHEWS

'Willie' Bamsey is remembered as 'quite feisty', one family story handed down concerning an incident occurring in the local pub when home on leave, as his niece, Tracey Lodwig, recounts:

> Another customer was harassing and shouting racist remarks to a local, so Willie politely asked him to stop. The man ignored him and continued, so Willie (I am quoting my father here) 'Knocked him out'! I also remember my grandmother telling us that Willie would go to the cinema with her whenever he was on leave; they must have gone quite often, because someone actually approached my grandfather and told him that they suspected she was having an affair with a dark haired man! What we do know is that the boys were very much loved and cherished. My grandmother had pictures of them both in her room, until she died. Her sister, Edith, would become very emotional whenever she spoke about them – I remember that. They were missed greatly.

Returning to the events of 17 September 1944, the southern end of Krafft's blocking line, along the tree-lined road running from Wolfheze to the Utrechtseweg, was occupied by SS-*Hauptsturmführer* Hans-Heinrich Köhnken's 2.*Kompanie*. Somewhat perturbed by the size of the British force now approaching his positions along the Utrechtseweg, Köhnken requested urgent assistance from his commander, based at the nearby Hotel Wolfheze. At this point, however, *Generalmajor* Kussin appeared at Krafft's headquarters, *Gefreiter* Willeke having driven west through Oosterbeek along the Utrechtseweg, then turned north-west along Wolfhezerweg – just before the lead elements of 3rd Parachute Battalion reached that junction. Having received Krafft's report, the *Stadtkommandant* now prepared to return to Arnhem via the same route – discounting Krafft's concern that the British had reached the area. Considering speed to be of the essence, and the risk worth taking, Kussin ordered Willeke to drive on.

The German staff car sped back along Wolfhezerweg towards the Utrechtseweg, through the idyllic scene of tree-lined roads and lovely houses. As the former road approaches the junction, uphill, there is no long view ahead; the road suddenly levels off, turns briefly but sharply to the right – and there is the junction, just a few metres ahead. (It is worth noting that this location is frequently but erroneously referred to as a 'crossroads', which it is not. Directly opposite, however, is the entrance to the Hoog Oorsprong estate, marked by two named brick pillars, but that is not actually a public road.) Travelling at speed, Willeke, entered the junction and, intending to turn east on the Utrechtseweg, blundered into the 3rd Parachute Battalion – the lead element of which, Lieutenant Cleminson's No. 5 Platoon, had just reached the western side of the junction. Both parties were equally surprised. Lieutenant Cleminson: 'It appeared without warning, and the front men of my leading sections, who were just behind the junction, opened fire with Stens and rifles and riddled its exposed flank. It was all over in a flash. I saw a body leaning out of the door but pressed on, leaving it to someone

The fateful Wolfhezerweg/Utrechtseweg junction. General Kussin's staff car approached from Wolfheze, blundering into the 3rd Parachute Battalion 'snake' proceeding towards Oosterbeek – with fatal consequences. (Karen Sarkar)

Generalmajor *Friedrich Kussin's grave at the German War Cemetery, Ysselsteyn, Netherlands. (Author)*

The grave of Kussin's driver at Ysselsteyn. (Author)

Kussin's interpreter's grave at Ysselsteyn. (Author)

else to sort out. I didn't know it was a general until after the war. Of course, it put all my platoon on a high.'

In fact, it had taken Cleminson's personal intervention before his men would cease fire. All three occupants of the enemy staff car were killed (although recent research argues that there were four, not three, occupants). Eight hundred yards away, SS-*Sturmbannführer* Krafft had heard the sudden outbreak of concentrated small-arms fire – and knew immediately that 'a gallant soldier' had been lost. At this early stage of the battle, the *Stadtkommandant*'s loss was a significant one to the Germans and which may explain why Lieutenant Colonel Frost and 2nd Parachute Battalion were to soon arrive at a comparatively lightly-defended Arnhem Bridge.

SS-*Hauptsturmführer* Köhnken's 2.*Kompanie* had fallen back from the junction into the grounds of the impressive De Bilderberg Hotel, set in wooded parkland adjacent to the Utrechtseweg. Krafft wasted no time in sending SS-*Obersturmführer* Günter Leiteritz's 9.*Kompanie* to assist. Leiteritz enjoyed the benefit of a flak gun, two *Pak* 36 anti-tank guns and a heavy machine-gun section – all of which were welcome reinforcements for the hard-pressed Köhnken. From the De Bilderberg's grounds, Köhnken's men poured mortar fire down on the nearby junction – at which the 1st Airborne Division's commander, General Roy Urquhart, and Brigadier Gerald Lathbury, commanding 1st Parachute Brigade, had just arrived.

Unfortunately, the 1st Airborne Division's communications had failed. There was some short-range inter-unit radio traffic, but no contact with the outside world or wider elements of the division. Like *Generalmajor* Kussin, General Urquhart had set off in a jeep to find out for himself in person what was happening. Having first liaised with the rearmost men of the 2nd Parachute Battalion's column on the lower road, the General sought out Brigadier Lathbury on 'Tiger' route. Finding the 3rd Parachute Battalion 'halted at a major junction on the Arnhem-Utrecht highway', General Urquhart 'drove to the Arnhem side of the crossing and parked the jeep in the ride between the lines of trees. I could now hear the plop and whine of mortars, and some of those bombs were falling with unsettling accuracy on the crossroads and in the woodland where many 3rd Battalion men were under cover at the south-west corner of the junction. Medical orderlies were busy, and the shouts from the wood indicated that men were being hit and wounded by tree bursts . . . The German mortar fire increased.' The accurate German mortar fire accounted for a number of fatal casualties at the junction – amongst them 26-year-old Private Frederick Hopwood.

Frederick Hopwood had been born on 16 July 1917, the youngest of James and Emily Hopwood's six children. Before enlisting, he had been a steam train foreman at the Shotton steelworks in Flintshire, at which several other family members also worked; the Hopwoods lived at Bank Farm, Shotwick, and worshipped at the village church, St Michael's. On 15 March 1940, however, Fred Hopwood enlisted at Catterick Garrison; like Gordon Matthews, he was also 5ft 5in tall. He was athletic – a boxer. Whilst serving with an anti-aircraft unit in Whitley Bay, he married a local girl, Mabel. The couple set up home in Mollington, Cheshire, their first child, also Frederick, being born on 14 May 1943. Private Hopwood had served with the 3rd Parachute Battalion in North Africa (where his best friend, Reg Madeley, was killed, and in whose memory the Hopwoods' second son would be named), Sicily and Italy. Now, the married father of two lay dead at the roadside, killed by lethal shrapnel.

Although Krafft believed that his counter-attack had been entirely successful in halting the 3rd Parachute Battalion, that was not the case. Cleminson's platoon had pressed on along the Utrechtseweg, past the De Bilderberg, towards Oosterbeek, reaching the 'major junction' referred to by General Urquhart. This was the crossroads known as 'Koude Herberg', with Utrechtseweg, on a line west to east, joined by Valkenburglaan to the north and Van Borsselenweg from the south. In this area were 9-SS *Hohenstaufen* units and vehicles, tasked with aggressively engaging the advancing British airborne men. From No. 5 Platoon's left, appeared an enemy vehicle variously described as 'a Jerry tank', 'an armoured car' and a 'self-propelled gun'. Whilst the exact type of German armoured fighting vehicle this was cannot be confirmed, the likelihood is that it was one of the vehicles deployed by *Hauptsturmführer* Gräbner and belonged to his *Hohenstaufen* reconnaissance unit. Whatever it was, the surprise appearance of German armour was a major issue for the lightly armed British paratroopers. No. 5 Platoon had but one PIAT in the leading section, which was called up but immediately spotted and destroyed by the German vehicle. Private Gordon Matthews was killed at this juncture, so it is entirely possible that this young Worcester man was behind that PIAT. This action took place adjacent to what is now the Oude Herberg Café.

Private Frederick Hopwood. (Via Neil Holmes)

Lieutenant Cleminson's other anti-tank weapon, a 6-pounder of 1st Airlanding Anti-Tank Battery, Royal Regiment of Artillery, was being towed behind a jeep and therefore facing the wrong way. Before it could be turned around, the surprisingly sluggish crew drew fire from the enemy armoured vehicle: Gunner George Robson was killed whilst his mate was wounded and captured; Lance Bombardier Lionel Dryden of the same unit was also killed in the driver's seat of his jeep (both have no known grave). Cleminson later wrote that:

> I realized that nobody had got their gammon bombs prepared to chuck at armoured vehicles, as the sticks of plastic explosive were still firmly wedged in our back pockets. I got up into a house and found myself behind the German

Shotwick War Memorial, on which Private Hopwood's death is incorrectly recorded as 18 September 1944. (Neil Holmes)

Private Hopwood's field grave, adjacent to the Hoog Ooorsprong estate on the Utrechtseweg, opposite the junction with Wolfhezerweg. The marker indicates that he was 'killed at this point' on 17 September 1944.

The field grave's location in May 2016. (Karen Sarkar)

Private Hopwood's grave at Oosterbeek. (22.B.12). (Kitty Brongers)

The Bredelaan, running north into the Bilderberg woods from the Utrechtseweg. Whether the German armoured vehicle which attacked Lieutenant Cleminson's platoon appeared from here or from Valkenburglaan, a few hundred yards east along the Utrechtseweg at the Koude Herberg crossroads, is uncertain. (Author)

View along the Utrechtseweg from the Bredelaan junction, west towards the Koude Herberg crossroads; it was somewhere along this section of road, very likely, that Private Gordon Matthews was killed and buried at the roadside with Private William Bamsey. (Author)

The area around the Koude Herberg Inn on the Utrechtseweg, located at the important crossroads with Valkenburglaan and Van Borsselenweg, was the scene of much fighting. (Author)

vehicle. I was joined by Peter Waddy [the commander of 'B' Company]. I shot a German soldier in the garden below me with my Sten and wondered what I could do to get rid of our armoured visitor. Peter suggested firing his Very light – which had singularly little effect – but, fortunately, as a result of small-arms fire and after they had collected about half a dozen prisoners, the vehicle pulled back down the road with our prisoners, their own wounded and supporting infantry.

Interestingly, before the menacing 'Jerry tank' withdrew, one of its crew leapt out, grabbed the wounded member of the 6-pounder crew and lifted him onto the front of the armoured vehicle. The Germans then withdrew, the British unable to fire further for fear of hitting their captured comrade. Some of the enemy soldiers were extremely battle-hardened, having fought on the dreadful *Ostfront* and throughout the bloody Normandy campaign; this act rather suggests that whosoever this crew were, they had plenty of combat experience and were clearly prepared to act decisively and ruthlessly.

During the mortar barrage on the crossroads, General Urquhart's jeep and signaller were hit, so both the General and Brigadier Lathbury were now stuck with Lieutenant Colonel Fitch and his 3rd Battalion – the latter in a most unenviable position, his every move scrutinised by both his Divisional and Brigade commanders. The advance along 'Tiger' had stalled. Desperate to bypass opposition and get to the bridge, still nearly five miles away, Lathbury ordered Major Peter Lewis's 'C' Company into the woods adjacent to Valkenburglaan, to find the railway line and advance along it to Arnhem. Skirmishing their way through, 'C' Company reached the bridge at 2300 hrs – a feat of arms for which 156 Parachute Battalion Arnhem veteran and historian Colonel John Waddy rightly points out '"C" Company have never been given due credit'.

ARNHEM 1944

Major Mervyn Dennison's 'A' Company, bringing up the column's rear, was ordered into the De Bilderberg grounds and woods, to clear them of the enemy and stop the mortaring. Lieutenant Ash's platoon headed due north, to locate the mortars, whilst Major Dennison joined Lieutenant Baxter's platoon, providing support. A German lookout on a water tower was dealt with and a short, sharp battle developed in the hotel's grounds and surrounding woodland. The British counter-attack was successful, however: the mortars were destroyed along with some heavy machine guns, twenty of Krafft's men were killed and eighteen more captured. 'A' Company's casualties amounted to around twenty, mostly wounded. Nonetheless, before silenced those mortars had fired 750 bombs, and had imposed a significant delay upon the 3rd Parachute Battalion.

If Lieutenant Colonel Fitch felt uncomfortable having both his Divisional and Brigade commanders urging him on, Lieutenant Cleminson of 'B' Company was in an even more unenviable position in having a general and a brigadier now tagging along with his No. 5 Platoon. As dusk gathered, Cleminson's party made slow headway along the Utrechtseweg, until reaching the parkland and tidy lawns of The Hartenstein Hotel – formerly the staff officers' mess of *Feldmarschall* Model's Army Group B, had rapidly fled the scene upon witnessing the airborne landings. With a table set with fine foods, Cleminson and his men tucked in – whilst outside the noise of battle continued. (This, however, may be a moot point, as Jan Crum explains: 'According to my information that Sunday evening 3rd Battalion had not yet taken possession of the Hartenstein. Urquhart and Lathbury spent the night in a big house along the Utrechtseweg, to the west of the Hartenstein Hotel, Utrechtseweg 269. They had not yet reached the Hartenstein Hotel due to the unexpected German reaction that first evening of the battle.') General Urquhart learned that communications remained non-existent and things were clearly not going to plan. There, in what was to be an oft-criticised decision, Brigadier Lathbury and Lieutenant Colonel Fitch decided to halt and await morning. The German reaction had been swift and sharp, and every hour the enemy became stronger whilst the British paratroopers – already weakened by their division's drop being over two days – became weaker. As Cleminson said, 3rd Parachute Battalion had 'quickly learned that advancing straight down a main road against armour with no anti-tank weapons was no way to get to the bridge'.

General Urquhart had arrived in Holland aboard a Horsa glider flown by Lieutenant Colonel Iain Murray, commanding officer of the 1st Glider Wing. Also aboard that glider being towed out of RAF Fairford in Gloucestershire, was Captain the Reverend Arnold Pare, chaplain to Murray's wing. Early on the morning of 19 September, Pare arrived at the Hartenstein, having passed over the Wolfhezerweg and Utrechtseweg junction and seeing the casualties still lying out in the open from the action two days previously. Pare was given permission to return to the scene with an armed escort, and bury the dead. The Hartenstein's tennis courts were by now in use as a prisoner of war cage, so Pare selected two young SS troopers to do the digging – little more than hungry boys, the kindly chaplain first shared out some cigarettes and chocolate before his charges began their grisly task.

Pare's party subsequently buried *Generalmajor* Kussin and his two *kameraden*, along with the 3rd Parachute Battalion dead. Private Hopwood was buried at the roadside, on the southern side of the infamous junction, at the entrance to the Hoog Oorsprong estate, together with Private Sidney Chennell, an eighteen-year-old from Chertsey, Surrey. Poignantly, two up-ended rifles planted in the ground marked the spot, along with a piece of timber bearing Hopwood's name and date of death, 17 September 1944, and a makeshift cross with Chennell's details. A Dutch civilian, Mrs Van Veelen-Van de Weerdhof and a German soldier were also buried at the same spot. According to the 'Roll of Honour', Lance-Corporal Bamsey and Private Matthews were buried 'beside Zonneheuvelweg'. The map reference provided by the Graves Registration Unit is spurious, however, and Dutch historian Chris van Roekel agrees it more likely that these field burials were along the Utrechtseweg, between the Bredelaan and Koude-Herberg crossroads.

A week later, the Matthews family received news that Gordon was 'missing', a report later appearing to that effect in the *Worcester Evening News & Times* on 13 October 1944. When the family were provided confirmation of his death in action is not known, but on that day, after weeks and possibly months of uncertainty, hope was extinguished.

Similarly, it took two months for the Hopwood family to receive confirmation of Frederick's fate, prior to which, along with the others, he was simply posted 'Missing in Action: Presumed Killed'. So confused was the administrative process in tying up all the details and loose ends, that Hopwood's date of death is incorrectly given in the official records as 18 September 1944. At the steelworks where he had previously worked, his former workmates had a whip-round for his widow and two young sons, raising £12.50 – a substantial sum in those days. Confirmation of death actually arrived in mid-October 1944, his personal effects being delivered to his widow on the same day as the Hopwoods' second son's christening. None of the families concerned knew the details of what had befallen their loved ones; both the Bamsey and Matthew families, for example, being told that their kin had parachuted behind enemy lines and been shot and killed during their descent.

On 28 August 1945, the Graves Registration Unit recovered all of the British bodies from the area of the junction. These were reinterred at the nearby Arnhem-Oosterbeek War Cemetery, where they lie at rest today. *Generalmajor* Kussin, aged forty-nine, *Gefreiter* Willeke, forty-two, and *Unteroffizier* Küster, forty, lie buried together at the German War Cemetery, Ysselsteyn – the only German war cemetery in the Netherlands, situated in the province of Limburg, close to the German border. In total, some 32,000 German soldiers killed during the Second World War are buried there – including many others who lost their lives at Arnhem in September 1944.

A sad postscript to this story concerns the eighteen-year-old younger brother of Lance-Corporal William Bamsey: Private Charles Bamsey of the 3rd Battalion, The

Private Gordon Matthews's grave at Oosterbeek. (19.B.18). (Karen Sarkar)

The village war memorial at Claines, Worcestershire, on which Private Matthews's name is commemorated. (Author)

WILLIAM BAMSEY, FREDERICK HOPWOOD, GORDON MATTHEWS

Monmouthshire Regiment. This TA infantry battalion had landed in Normandy on 14 June 1944, and was subsequently heavily involved in the fighting for 'Hill 112' and the Norman city of Caen – and, indeed, throughout the rest of the campaign. The 3rd Monmouths were a part of the 11th Armoured Division, and as infantry trained in supporting armoured warfare were the British equivalent of German *panzergrenadiers*. The battalion pursued the retreating enemy across the Seine, into Belgium and across Holland, fighting many battles along the way. When the Guards Armoured Division, of the 2nd Army's XXX Corps, started off from Bridge No.. 9 on the Bocholt-Herentals Canal, outside the town of Neerpelt, near the Belgian city of Lommel, to fight its way sixty miles to Arnhem Bridge, the 11th Armoured Division was tasked with protecting the right flank of this drive, so far as the Maas. By 25 September 1944, the 3rd Monmouths were in St Anthonis. What Private Bamsey did not then know, was that his paratrooper elder brother, fighting with the 1st British Airborne Division for possession of Arnhem Bridge, had been killed within a few hours of landing at Drop Zone 'X' on 17 September. After the drive to relieve General Urquhart's beleaguered airborne force petered out, Operation MARKET-GARDEN concluding in failure, the 3rd Monmouths remained in southern Holland. Having fought in the 'Venlo Pocket', in February 1945, the Battalion moved to the Cleve area, south of the Rhine and east of the Reichswald Forest – just a few miles south and within sight of Arnhem. There it went around the Hochwaldberg, a hilly, wooded area, sustaining casualties from artillery fire in the process, pushing on to force a bridgehead over the anti-tank defences of the so-called 'Schlieffen Line'. Heavy fighting ensued – and the teenage Bamsey lost his life in action, somewhere in the Reichswald Forest, on 27 February 1945; he has no known grave and is remembered on the Groesbeek Memorial to the missing. For Griffith and Louisa Bamsey, of Port Talbot, Glamorgan, the fighting of that last winter of war was, therefore, a double tragedy.

For the Bamsey family, there was more grief before the war's end: Private Charles Bamsey of the 3rd Monmouths, William's younger brother, was killed in action fighting near Cleve, not far from Arnhem, on 27 February 1945; he has no known grave and is remembered on the Groesbeek Memorial. (Tracey Lodwig)

Chapter 5

Lance-Corporal Ronnie Boosey, 1st Parachute Battalion

When formulating the 1st Parachute Brigade's plan to capture and hold Arnhem Bridge, Brigadier Lathbury had decided against concentrating his force on one narrow route, but to advance on a broad front via three routes. As we have seen, the 2nd Parachute Battalion took the lower route, 'Lion', whilst 3rd Parachute Battalion negotiated the middle path, 'Tiger'. To Lieutenant Colonel David Dobie's 1st Parachute Battalion fell the upper route – 'Leopard'. Dobie's task, however, was not to bludgeon his way through to the all-important bridge, but capture high ground, bisecting the Arnhem-Ede road – the Amsterdamseweg – barring the way to German reinforcements expected to use that route into the city. The plan was for 1st Parachute Battalion to hold that ground for twenty-four hours, until relieved by elements of 4th Parachute Brigade, due to arrive in the second drop on Monday 18 September 1944. Dobie was concerned, however, with the task allocated to his battalion, because the German reaction outside Arnhem was likely to be swift, and it was that northern road which the enemy were expected to use, to reinforce units defending Arnhem. Seizure of the bridge, in fact, hinged upon Major Gough's Reconnaissance Squadron's jeeps dashing ahead and executing a *coup de main* – a task for which Gough's men were not trained or properly equipped. Unfortunately, Dobie's concerns would be justified.

Lance Corporal Jack Ronald Boosey. (*Leslie Boosey*)

According to the 1st Parachute Battalion's War Diary, on Sunday 17 September 1944, Dobie's men were roused 'at an unwanted hour', and after breakfast were conveyed to Barkston Heath airfield, near Grantham in Lincolnshire. There the Battalion emplaned, along with other 1st Parachute Brigade Group units, in seventy-one C-47 Dakotas, the first wave taking off at 1130 hrs, followed by the second three minutes later. The formation crossed the English coast at Aldeburgh, heading across the North Sea towards

Holland, over which much flooding – a deliberate effort by the Germans to impede the Allied advance – was noted. There was little flak, and at 1403, the Battalion 'Dropped in the right time at the right place'. That location was DZ 'X', at Renkum Heath, from which 1st Parachute Battalion moved off at 1540. Dobie's plan was to proceed to Wolfheze station, in the Reconnaissance Squadron's wake, on foot and carrying full kit, cross the railway, travelling north, past Johannahoeve Farm, to the Amsterdamseweg, a distance of some four miles. Once at the main road, 1st Parachute Battalion was to turn east, following the road to the high ground objective. Dobie perceived this to be a risky business – and so it would prove.

Just twenty minutes after moving off, the already frustrated Lieutenant Colonel Dobie was aghast when Major Freddie Gough appeared in his jeep – by that time, Gough's squadron was supposed to have seized and been holding Arnhem Bridge, in advance of the parachute battalions travelling on foot. Gough's men, however, had met fierce resistance, suffered casualties, and had abandoned their intended *coup de main*. Ahead of 1st Parachute Battalion, however, as it turned off the road into woods, to cut the corner and shorten the distance to the Amsterdamseweg, were the northern elements of Krafft's blocking line. 'R' Company, one of Dobie's three rifle companies, was in the van, and soon engaged by *Kampfgruppe* Weber, a battle group comprising Luftwaffe personnel from nearby Deelen airfield. Weber was quickly reinforced by elements of *Kampfgruppe* Von Alloworden, which were a different proposition: SS troops and armoured vehicles from *Hohenstaufen* and *Frundsberg,* backed up by sailors pressed into the infantry role. Fierce fighting ensued, as the 1st Parachute Battalion commander's diary relates:

> 1700: 'R' Coy attacked infantry positions astride road at 673816. Enemy withdrew with casualties. 'R' Coy reached road junction 675820 after more fighting – were heavily engaged at that point by tanks and infantry. 'R' Coy took up position facing East then attacked again.
> 1800 – Remainder Bn by-passed opposition via track to South of main road to main junction. Wireless communication with 'R' Coy broke down. No. touch with Bde HQ – sent Liaison Officer off to contact (he was shot off motorcycle by enemy on main road but got back to the Bn).
> 1900 – About to advance North to main road when tanks approached from SE, along main road. Altogether five tanks and approximately fifteen-half-tracks passed X-roads 691811 (400 yards North of our position in woods). Enemy also digging in wood 694809.
> 1930 – Sent Major Bune back for 'R' Coy and decided to bypass to South again.
> 2000 – Armoured car and some infantry approached our lying up position. Engaged enemy – they withdrew, we had six casualties. Enemy in wood 695809 opened fire – returned fire and took up all-round position until 'R' Coy could come up.

2200 – Major Bune returned with 2 i/c 'R' Coy – they had 50 per cent casualties and could not get casualties away. Sent Medical Officer Field Ambulance back with 2 i/c to bring remainder Coy back to Bn. Sent patrols to main road – many enemy – spasmodic fighting and firing.

Essentially, the 1st Parachute Battalion's advance, like that of 3rd Parachute Battalion, which had halted and dug in around the Koude Herberg crossroads, just a few hundred yards east beyond the De Bilderberg Hotel, had completely stalled. Only 2nd Parachute Battalion had managed to reach and seize their objective, passing below, by chance, the southern end of Krafft's hastily-formed blocking line. Lightly-armed parachute battalions simply could not advance in the face of armour. That was the problem. Furthermore, the whole situation was compounded by the breakdown of efficient and consistent radio communication, leading to General Urquhart going off in his jeep to establish what was happening – and being unable to communicate with his commanders at a crucial moment in the battle. The situation would not improve – because every hour the defending Germans became stronger. At 0530 hrs on Monday, 18 September, David Dobie concluded that German resistance was so strong that his beleaguered battalion had no chance of reaching their high ground objective, still some three miles away. Having learned from a rare, clear, radio transmission that 2nd Battalion had reached and were desperately clinging on the bridge's northern end, the 32-year-old Lieutenant Colonel declared 'I'm not going on to the north of Arnhem; we'll try to get down to help Johnnie at the bridge'. He immediately called an 'O' Group and Major Chris Perrin-Brown's 'T' Company, in which served Lance-Corporal Jack Ronald Boosey, led off. Frequent skirmishing ensued, delaying Dobie's progress south-east, which was hard enough going as it was, given that jeep and carrier engines were switched off and the vehicles manhandled along, so as not to alert the Germans. That night, in those now peaceful woods, 1st Parachute Battalion had suffered eleven men killed, including Major Bune, and some ninety more wounded.

Thereafter, 1st Parachute Battalion made some progress, entering Oosterbeek via Stationsweg. Unaware that 3rd Parachute Battalion had abandoned 'Tiger' route, having been unable to break through German defences on the Utrechtseweg, it was east along that main road through Oosterbeek to Arnhem that Dobie now struck. As Dobie's men left the built-up area of Oosterbeek, they came under fire, and suffered more casualties, from German machine guns firing from the railway embankment. A strong defensive vantage point, Dobie sensibly decided to bypass the enemy strongpoint, by moving south, in an attempt to reach the lower road. Whereas 2nd Parachute Battalion had been able to outflank the Germans and slip through to the bridge via 'Lion' the previous day, and some of 3rd Parachute Battalion getting through earlier this day, beyond the infamous railway culvert, where the ill-fated Gronert twins had lost their lives, the enemy's defence was by now infinitely stronger. A short distance east of the culvert, the paratroopers came under very heavy fire from the German position at Den Brink – high ground to the north. With the river to his right, Dobie now had to fight his way through. 'T' Company was ordered to deal with the Den Brink Germans, supported by artillery and other heavy weapons.

Roaring the Parachute Regiment's famous battle cry, 'Waho Mohammet!', at 0900 hrs 'T' Company attacked, gaining some nearby houses – but was 'badly mauled'. The battle raged for hours; Dobie diary:

> 1400 – Second attack on factory failed [author's note: on the southern side of the road] – 20mm [fire] from River bank too strong. Met Major Dennison and made plan for co-ordinated attack – his Coy left on high ground – 'T' Coy astride road and the factory spotted by Arty (Lt. Col. Thompson and Forward Observation Officer. throughout) mortars and medium machine-guns. Anti-tank guns used against pillbox in factory area – direct hit. Caused heavy enemy casualties in this area. One enemy armoured car put out. 'S' Coy in meantime were attacked from rear and held attack which was light. T Coy reduced to 22 men. 'S' Coy 6 casualties.
> 1500 – Reached road junction 726778 – came under '88' fire, machine-gun and mortar fire from main road – gained road junction after fight. Mortars used on road junction.
> 1600 – Advanced East down main road on South side. Heavy fighting – could not advance past road junction 729779 – tanks ahead. Here mortars, artillery and medium machine-guns put out two A.A. guns on river bank – medium machine-guns shot running men. Good work.
> 1700 – Crossed road over cover of smoke and tried North side by backs of houses – came under heavy mortar fire and sniping – reached just West of hospital. Tried to get vehicles forward but quite impossible – lost one carrier.
> 1830 – In touch with bridgehead, received orders from there that must get through. Had practically no ammunition and approximately 100 men left. Decided to try right down on river bank. Heavy fire cut across main road and every side street.
> 2000 – Met OC 2nd South Staffords, who had my 'R' Coy with him (very depleted approximately 40 men) and assault pioneers, mortars and medium machine-guns – made plan to get to Bridge – Starting time 0100 hrs. Resupplied with ammunition. News came back that Bridge had been over-run. Attack put off.

This, however, was misinformation: 'Johnnie' was still desperately hanging on to Arnhem Bridge. Mention of the South Staffordshire Regiment glider-borne troops of 1st Air Landing Brigade, is significant, because this was Dobie's first confirmation, in the absence of radio communication, that the second lift, which had arrived earlier that day, had made it this far. Indeed, coming up behind, although he was unaware of it, was the 11th Parachute Battalion of 4th Parachute Brigade. The 1st and 3rd Parachute Battalions, battered and exhausted, had now drawn up together. It had been a brave and determined attempt to reach Frost, just over a mile away and equally hard-pressed at Arnhem Bridge – but the effort to reach 2nd Parachute Battalion was not yet over.

The 11th Parachute Battalion had joined the remnants of 1st and 3rd Parachute Battalions, and 2nd South Staffords, by 0100 hrs on 19 September. An order was then received to abandon the position reached at high cost, and retire on Oosterbeek; ninety minutes later, this order was cancelled and a further attack mounted at 0400 hrs, Lieutenant Colonel Fitch and his fifty 3rd Parachute Battalion survivors joining those of Dobie's 1st. The paratroopers were to advance along the river, the Onderlangs, whilst the 2nd South Staffords, following on behind, half an hour late, were to push uphill, along the Utrechtseweg past St Elizabeth Hospital. For Fitch, the only good news was that he was no longer encumbered by his brigade and divisional commanders – Brigadier Lathbury and General Urquhart having previously gone off in the wrong direction and being forced to hide in the attic of a house adjacent to the hospital. It was a sorry state of affairs: no radio communication to speak of and senior commanders incommunicado, in hiding.

At first, the advance made progress, but once daylight pervaded carnage ensued. Ranged against the airborne troops were five *Kampfgruppen* of the 9-SS *Panzer* Division *Frundsberg*. German machine guns located in houses north of the railway line, and flak guns at the brickworks on the Rhine's south bank, poured fire onto the advancing British. Nonetheless, Dobie and Fitch moved forward, but the Staffordshires and 11th Parachute Battalion, being closer to the enemy machine guns, suffered heavy casualties, slowing their advance – exposing the 1st and 3rd Parachute Battalions' left flank. Attacked by enemy armour, the two battalions on the Utrechtseweg had no option to withdraw in confusion. Those on the Onderlangs were decimated. Lieutenant Colonel Dobie was wounded and captured; Lieutenant Colonel Fitch was killed. It was a sad end to a valiant but forlorn, last attempt to 'help Johnnie at the bridge'.

At some stage in this fighting – it is not known when – Lance-Corporal 'Ronnie' Boosey of 1st Parachute Battalion's 'T' Company was very badly wounded, it is believed by a mortar shell which badly disfigured his face. Ronnie, it is fair to say, had a difficult start in life. His father, Frank, a bricklayer, had been wounded on the Somme during the Great War, and re-married between the wars. From his first marriage to May were a number of children, brought up in Walthamstow, Essex: Frank, a regular soldier and captured during the Fall of France in 1940, Ronnie, Violet, Vera, Stanley and Lesley; there were also two boys and girls from a subsequent marriage. Ronnie was brought up by his Aunt Rose, with whom his younger brother Lesley, now the last survivor, remembers he was 'happy'. Ronnie, however, enlisted on 29 May 1940, into the King's Royal Rifle Corps (embodied Territorial Army) at Whipps Cross and posted to the 7th Home Defence Battalion. He subsequently served with both the 70th and 12th Home Defence Battalions, which was clearly not to his liking given that he

The St Elisabeth Hospital on the Utrechtseweg, scene of bitter fighting as 4th Parachute Brigade attempted to reinforce Lieutenant Colonel Frost at Arnhem Bridge, a mile or so away. (Author)

No 14 Zwarteweg (middle house), adjacent to the hospital, where General Urquhart was forced to hide in the attic. (Author)

answered the call for parachute training. On 7 April 1943, he was transferred to the 1st Parachute Battalion, Army Air Corps, and after successfully completing the tough parachute course, embarked for North Africa on 15 May that year.

Ronnie Boosey, like other young men in this book, was a replacement for 1st Parachute Brigade, which had suffered 1,700 casualties in North Africa. By the time Ronnie arrived in Tunisia, the campaign was over, but then came the Allied invasion of Sicily. It is likely, therefore, that he dropped with 1st Parachute Battalion on the Primosole Bridge operation in Sicily, on 13 July 1943. Next came the 1st Parachute Brigade's seaborne landing at Taranto Harbour, Italy, on 11 September 1943. Afterwards, the brigade was used as infantry, advancing northwards to Foggia, before returning to England on 8 December 1943. The 1st Airborne Division having been held in reserve during the Normandy campaign, Lance-Corporal Boosey parachuted into Holland on Operation MARKET-GARDEN.

Having been wounded on either 19 or 20 September 1944, Lance-Corporal Boosey was captured by the Germans and taken to St Joseph's Psychiatric Hospital at Apeldoorn. Confusion, however, abounds. According to British records, Ronnie Boosey was twenty-one years old and succumbed to his dreadful wounds on 20 September 1944. Dutch records, though, record his passing as 21 September. First buried in the hospital cemetery, German records state death to have occurred on 22 September, and his age twenty-two. Such confusion illustrates why it is so difficult, and often impossible, for the historian to reach a definitive conclusion. Whether poor Ronnie Boosey died on 20, 21 or 22 September 1944, the fact remains that another young man – who had seen a great deal of action for his still-tender years – had given his life in the service of his country. In 1945, Lance-Corporal Boosey was reinterred at the Arnhem-Oosterbeek War Cemetery, where his younger brother, Lesley, made frequent annual pilgrimages to pay his respects at the graveside of his much-loved brother – 'until it all became too much'. Such is the price of war.

Lance Corporal 'Ronnie' Boosey's grave at Oosterbeek. (23.B.4). (Author)

Chapter 6

Trooper Raymond McSkimmings, 1st Airborne Reconnaissance Squadron, Reconnaissance Corps, Royal Armoured Corps

Back in England, the planners of Operation MARKET-GARDEN had anticipated only light opposition from the Germans in and around Arnhem. Acknowledging this intelligence, as we have seen, Brigadier Lathbury determined upon 1st Parachute Brigade advancing from the landing zones along a broad front, each of the three battalions taking a separate route, largely on foot, to Arnhem Bridge – eight miles away. Preceding his main force, however, the 1st Airborne Reconnaissance Squadron, 'less one troop retained as divisional reserve', and No. 3 Platoon, 9th Field Company RE, were to dash to Arnhem Bridge via the northern 'Leopard Route', along the Amserdamseweg north of the railway line. Stopping for nothing, this *coup-de-main* party in their special jeeps were to seize the all-important bridge, the Field Company men removing any demolition charges, and hold the objective until Lathbury's parachute battalions and supporting divisional troops arrived. It is fair to say that, like the Glider Pilot Regiment and 'Pathfinders' of the 21st Independent Parachute Company, the 'Recce Squadron' was an elite within an elite. Amongst their number was nineteen-year-old Trooper Ray McSkimmings.

Raymond McSkimmings was born in Carlisle on 7 February 1925, to William McSkimmings, like his father a 'fish purveyor', and his wife, Norah (née Reynolds). The McSkimmings were a well-known local family with a traditional fish and chip shop in the Caldewgate district of the city. Other children followed, but the parents separated before the war. Ray, however, was a clever lad: having passed his 11+ examination, he became a pupil at the Creighton School, a grammar school appended to Carlisle Cathedral. In 1939, Ray passed the Carlisle Council Certificate of Education, having achieved 'first class' in 'Arithmetic of Commerce' and second in both English and Geography. Living with his mother at 28 Leatham Street, the young school-leaver went to work for Harrison & Hethrington Ltd at Botchergate, Carlisle, a firm of 'Live Stock Agricultural & Estate Auctioneers, Valuers, Estate & Insurance Agents', as a 'general clerk'. Ray's ambition was to become an auctioneer, mainly of livestock, but it was not to be: as the war raged globally, on 15 April 1943, eighteen-year old Raymond McSkimmings enlisted at Carlisle into the 'Territorial Army for the duration of the

ARNHEM 1944

Toddler Ray McSkimmings (left) with sister Betty and 'Mam', Norah. (Ted McSkimmings)

Ray with sister Betty; a bright lad, Ray attended Creighton School, a grammar school appended to Carlisle Cathedral. (Ted McSkimmings)

RAYMOND MCSKIMMINGS

Emergency'. Private 14583993 McSkimmings arrived at 55 Primary Training Wing of the GSC, at Richmond, joining 'B' Company. There he would undertake six weeks of basic infantry training, including drill, rifle and pistol shooting, PT, gas training, elementary map reading and tactics. Recruits were also assessed by a Personnel Selection Board, which decided which unit the new soldiers would join after training. Clearly Ray impressed, because of 27 May 1943, he successfully passed out and was posted to the Reconnaissance Corps – a specialist unit. Next stop, therefore, was 63 Reconnaissance Training Centre at Catterick in Yorkshire.

The Reconnaissance Corps had been formed on 14 January 1941, providing infantry divisions a mobile spearhead – hence the corps' badge of a vertical spear flanked by lightning bolts. Each infantry corps thereafter had a brigade reconnaissance group of battalion strength. From 6 June 1942, the Corps, in recognition of its specialist status, adopted cavalry designations, its private soldiers becoming troopers, its companies known as squadrons and platoons likewise troops. Intelligence is everything, and it was the Reconnaissance Corps' job to be ahead of the main body, gathering and passing back accurate information regarding the enemy's disposition and deployment. As John Fairley wrote in his excellent *Remember Arnhem*, this task was 'a skilled and dangerous one'. According to historian Sir Arthur Bryant, 'Those who served had to be intelligent,

Trooper Ray McSkimmings, having been posted to the Reconnaissance Corps in May 1943. (Ted McSkimmings)

In January 1944, Ray, together with his friend Arthur Barlow, volunteered for the Airborne Reconnaissance Squadron, and are pictured here resplendent in red berets and parachutist's wings. (Ted McSkimmings)

enterprising, brave, enduring and highly skilled'. At Catterick Camp, Trooper McSkimmings met another exceptional young reconnaissance soldier, Trooper Arthur Barlow, as the latter remembered:

> When I first spoke to 'Mac', we were in the same hut. I had been called up with a chap called George Fletcher, who was the husband of my wife's sister-in-law, Valerie. Daisey, my wife, and Valerie, decided to come up to Catterick for a weekend visit. We found them some rooms in Richmond and we waited for the weekend to come around. On the Friday night before they were due to arrive, my name appeared on the notice board for Saturday night guard duty! While I was ranting and raving about what I was going to do, Mac came over to where I was stood in front of the noticeboard, a big smile on his face, as usual! 'I will do your guard duty for you', he said. Now this was a tricky business, the slightest mistake or hesitation while on parade would give the whole game away. So, we blancoed his equipment and polished his brasses, his boots shone so that we could see our own faces in them. We took his best battledress down to the laundry where it was sponged and pressed. He rehearsed and remembered my name and number, and when we got him dressed up he looked magnificent!
>
> Off went George and I to meet the girls, and after a wonderful weekend we returned to barracks on the Sunday evening after seeing them off at Richmond station. Mac's impersonation of me went perfectly, in fact he was one of the four men complimented on their smart turnout by the officer in charge of the Guard. Good job he never asked Mac his name!
>
> I offered Mac five shillings for his effort on my behalf, he refused of course but insisted we had a slap-up NAAFI supper: meat pie, chips, beans and sausage. We remained close friends for the rest of our time together.

On Saturday, 17 June 1943, Ray wrote home to his mother, Norah:

> I received your parcel today. Thanks for the new pair of socks.
>
> I suppose Betty [author's note: one of Ray's younger sisters] will be in the ATS now and wishing she was out of it. Please send her address through as soon as you get it and I will write her.
>
> We have had pretty rough weather here lately but it has turned out fine again. Today we are going swimming this afternoon if it keeps up.
>
> Well I hope you are all well at home and not worrying about me, because I'll be all right and as soon as I do go I will write and tell you.
>
> Well Mother, all my love to those at home and I'll be seeing them all again soon (I hope). So long for now, Your loving son, Ray.

RAYMOND MCSKIMMINGS

According to Trooper McSkimmings's Army Service Record, on 10 October 1943 he had passed the 'standard trade test'. On 4 December, he 'mustered as Tradesman Wireless Operator'. On 1 January 1944, the Reconnaissance Corps became absorbed by the Royal Armoured Corps. Arthur Barlow continues:

> It was about this time when the Airborne Recce Squadron came back from Italy up to Catterick for re-training and recruitment. There was a notice on the board asking for recruits who were interested in flying and parachuting! Mac looks at me, and I look at Mac. 'What do you think?', he says.
> 'It must be better than this place', I said. So off we went to Ruskington, passed the interview and stayed down there.

So it was that on 21 February 1944, Trooper McSkimmings was posted from the 80th Reconnaissance Regiment to 'No. 1 Airlanding Squadron' – which had started life in 1941, as the 31st Independent Reconnaissance Company. In November that year, the unit became glider-borne and re-designated the 1st Airlanding Reconnaissance Squadron. The unit drew recruits from other elements of the Reconnaissance Corps, and when 250 strong, in April 1943, joined the 1st Airborne Division in North Africa. Thereafter, the Squadron saw action in Sicily and Italy before returning home for Christmas 1943. Initially based at Spalding in Lincolnshire, the squadron soon moved to Ruskington, south of Lincoln. There it was decided that to relieve the logistic pressure on the provision of gliders, some members of the squadron would become parachutists. Consequently, parachute training was undertaken at Ringway – Troopers McSkimmings and Barlow volunteering accordingly; the latter recalled that:

> I remember Mac and I found a nice little pub in Manchester, it had a small stage and a microphone; customers were invited to get up and sign a song. Can you imagine Mac and me up there signing the 'Brave Paratrooper' song, accompanied by a pianist, trumpeter and a mouthorgan? The noise was incredible, but there was always a couple of free beers on the table when we sat down!

Both young troopers passed their course, although exactly which one and when is unrecorded on Ray's Army Service Record. Nonetheless, we do know from that source that as from 27 May 1944, he was 'Entitled to Parachute Pay @ 2/- per day' and 'Additional Pay Airborne Troops @ 1/- per day'. They were now very much part of a real elite – red berets and all, as Arthur Barlow remembered: 'They were good days. We did our parachute training together, got our red berets and "wings" and went into Manchester for a few beers to celebrate!'

No description of 1st Airborne Reconnaissance Squadron, as the unit became known, no matter how brief, would be complete without reference to its flamboyant and popular commander: Major Charles Frederick Howard Gough. 'Freddie' had been born into a military family on 16 September 1901, his father having served as an Indian Army officer. After leaving Cheam School, Gough briefly served as a midshipman in the Royal Navy, but not finding the sea air attractive, became a farmer and horse-breeder in India. Two years later he returned home to work for Lloyd's of London. In 1924, he was commissioned in the 5th City of London Regiment, in which he served until 1930, before transferring to the Reserve. Impending war saw him mobilised in August 1939, joining 2nd Rifles. Craving action, the 39-year-old volunteered to serve in a special ski unit formed by the Scots Guards to directly assist the Finns against the Russians. Before the detachment could be deployed, however, the Finnish war ended. Although considered too old for active service, by hook and probably crook, Gough managed to arrange an appointment as commander of No. 101 Provost Company, Corps of Military Police, at the BEF's HQ in France. After the German attack on the West in May 1940, he was amongst those troops safely brought home from the mole and beaches of Dunkirk. Afterwards, the 'Old Boys' Network' again came to the rescue, as it so often did, ignoring his age and posting him to command 31st Independent Reconnaissance Corps – which, the following month, became '1st Airlanding Company', as the squadron was first called. It is universally acknowledged that Gough was an inspirational leader, arguably in the swashbuckling, buccaneering mould of the indomitable legless air ace Douglas Bader. Gough, who played a pivotal role at Arnhem Bridge, was clearly loved by his men – and there can be no higher praise for any officer.

On an unspecified 'Monday night' whilst serving as one of 'Freddie Gough's Specials', in 'C' Troop, Trooper McSkimmings wrote home after a spell of leave:

Well I arrived back safely after being nearly 24 hours on the road. I got in about 8 o'clock Sunday morning, but everything was alright as they had not missed me.

The train from Carlisle to London was packed to the brim, but I got a seat as Jimmy Davidson booked me one when the train came in, which is just as well as the train landed in London 2 hours late and I missed my connection, but everything turned out all right excepting that I was dog-tired but I got straight into bed and did not get up until 5 o'clock at night.

The reason why I was able to go to bed is because the rest of the Troop and officers, except two of us, don't come back until tonight as they did not go on leave until Friday night.

So the two of us have just been lying in bed until dinner time and going onto the beach in the afternoon, so we've had plenty of rest.

Well, I'll just end this short note as I'm going to bed now (no, I'm not sick of it yet), so good night and God bless you.

On Saturday, 3 September 1944, Ray wrote home again:

By the time you receive this letter I shall be over there and you will know where we have gone from the news.

Don't worry, I shall be all-right and if you don't hear from me for some time, don't worry; you know what the postage is like over there.

I hope you received my last letter all right as I have not received a reply yet but I suppose you'll have received it all right.

Well I'm sorry I can't say much more as time is limited and there is nothing to write about. Give my love to all at home – June and little 'Teddy', and remember me to Molly and Sid, and let Betty know if you can as I have lost her address.

Well so long for now, keep smiling and don't worry. Your loving son, Ray. Xxxxx

Ray's prophecy was wrong, however: when Nora read his letter, he was not, in fact, 'over there'. As we have seen the 1st Airborne Division was exasperated throughout the summer of 1944, by proposed operations being repeatedly cancelled, some at the last minute. On Saturday, 16 September 1944 (although incorrectly dated '1943'), Ray wrote what would be his last letter home to 'Dear Mother':

Just a line to let you know that I received your letter on Wednesday. We have been on a 36 hour pass since then but it was too short a time to get home on. We all thought we were going to get another four or five days, but it was cancelled and we had to be satisfied with 36 hours.

Well I'm glad that the money has come through for you but I suppose it will still be a week or so until you get it.

Has Betty been home on leave yet, or is she expecting any soon? I hope she gets it.

Well the weather here hasn't been bad at all here for the last week or so. What has it been like at home?

I hope you are all well at home as I am still in the best of health. Well I reckon I'll have to finish now as it is tea-time and I'll have to rush to get my tea.

So good-bye for now.

What Ray could not say, was that the whole 1st Airborne Division was abuzz with activity. After sixteen cancelled operations, doubtless many considered proceedings with a 'Here we go again' shrug of the shoulders – but this time, there would be no cancellation.

By necessity, on Sunday, 17 September 1944, the Reconnaissance Squadron was conveyed to Arnhem in two groups: thirty-nine jeeps and two 20mm Polsten guns were flown from Tarrant Rushton to LZ 'Z' in twenty-two Halifax/Horsa combinations; the main body of the unit flew in Dakotas from Barkston Heath, near Grantham, Lincolnshire.

ARNHEM 1944

Troopers McSkimmings and Barlow shared the same Dakota, the latter inquiring whether his friend was wearing the body armour they had recently been issued: 'Too true', Ray replied, 'in fact I've got too sets on, one front and one back, I don't want any stray bullets up my arse as we go over!' According to the Squadron's War Diary, the sky over the LZ was 'full of Dakotas – streams of coloured parachutes in the air'. The two pals dropped on LZ 'X' at 1406 hrs, as Arthur Barlow recalled:

> Mac jumped No. 3, after me, over Renkum Heath, and as we struggled out of our parachute harnesses he shouted across 'Are you OK, Art?'
> 'Yes, OK', I shouted back.
> As he walked away, he turned and called 'See you later'.
> 'On the bridge!' I shouted back.
> Who could then foretell the events of the next few days?

Who indeed?

The 1st Airborne Reconnaissance Squadron, however, had been trained, as the unit designation implies, in probing ahead of the main force, gathering and passing back information regarding the enemy's deployment, disposition and intention. It was untrained, though, for the task now ahead: an assault on a specific objective against unknown forces. Major Gough's argument that his squadron would be better employed scouting ahead of the 1st Parachute Brigade's three battalions was rejected by Brigadier Lathbury. Nonetheless, the mood was confident and optimistic, the Squadron proud that it had been chosen to spearhead the way to Arnhem Bridge – and expecting, according to Gough, to meet 'only a few old grey Germans and a few ancient tanks and guns'. What could possibly go wrong?

By 1445 hrs, all battalions had rendezvoused, the 2nd and 3rd Parachute Battalions and supporting troops moving off at 1500 hrs, 1st Parachute Battalion at 1530 hrs. Ten minutes earlier, however, General Urquhart was for some reason told that the Squadron had lost its transport and so would not be dashing for the Bridge as planned. This was not the case, although it had taken longer than anticipated to form up all the jeeps required for this proposed *coup-de-main* assault. It was true, however, that the four jeeps of 9th Field Company Royal Engineers (RE), which were to join Gough's force, had landed not as intended on LZ 'Z' but on 'S', and so failed to turn up. It would not be until 1540 hrs that 'Freddie Gough's Specials' moved out. Arthur Barlow:

> We were at the RV [rendezvous], waiting for the jeeps. Lieutenant Bucknall was very impatient; he knew we should be first off . . . Bucknall was very impatient; his language would not be printable. He was furious. So, he took the second jeep, turning the driver out and taking the wheel himself, and telling me to stay behind and wait for the No. 1 jeep. We were at least half an hour late. Bucknall set off, bumping along the road to Wolfheze, and went out of sight. It was four

or five minutes until the other jeep turned up and we followed, with Lance-Sergeant MacGregor in charge. The other sections followed us; they had all assembled properly and had moved off at proper intervals, within hand-signalling of each other, but Lieutenant Bucknall's jeep was five minutes ahead of us and out of sight.

We met no military along the way to Wolfheze, just civilians waving to us from windows or gardens; we didn't stop to speak to anyone. We weren't worried about encountering any resistance; we had been told there would be little opposition. We were hoping that it would be quiet like that all the way through to the bridge. We went over the railway crossing at Wolfheze and turned right, down a track alongside the railway. Then two things happened almost at once. We heard heavy firing from in front, where we assumed the first jeep was, and, at the same time, we were fired on from the railway embankment up the road to the right.

Up ahead, Lieutenant Bucknall's jeep had been hit by some of SS-*Sturmbannführer* Sepp Krafft's men: SS-*Hauptscharführer* Wiegand – a tough veteran of many battles – had included a heavy machine-gun section in his reserve platoon, which he located on both sides of the track – Johannahoeveweg – taken by Bucknall and the Reconnaissance Squadron. Looking east along the track, towards Oosterbeek and Arnhem, in the squadron's direction of travel, Wiegand positioned some of his men to the north side of it, hidden in trees, and others on the south side, high up on the railway embankment immediately east of a culvert. Major Gough's men speeding towards this danger, were oblivious of the threat ahead. The time was now about 1600 hrs.

The firing heard up ahead by Trooper 'Art' Barlow was *Hauptscharführer* Wiegand's men letting fly at the Lieutenant Peter Bucknall's jeep: all its occupants, including the impatient young officer, so keen to press on, were killed. Next in the Germans' line of sight was Sergeant McGregor's jeep, in which travelled Trooper Barlow:

> Reg Hasler was driving and immediately stopped the jeep, which had taken a direct burst of machine-gun fire across the radiator. Jimmy Pierce, Tom McGregor and myself ran to the road verge on the right-hand side of the jeep. Dicky Minns, Hasler and 'Taffy' Thomas were to the left of the jeep and partly beneath it. Heavy machine-gun fire continued. Minns, being more exposed, had his hip shattered and other wounds, and lay on the road, bleeding profusely, calling for help. Thomas was hit in the foot, while Hasler was hit in both legs and unable to move. On our side of the road, McGregor was to my left, about four or five feet away. He raised himself up on his hands to have a look around and died immediately, falling flat on his face without making a sound, killed by a burst of machine-gun fire in the face and chest. I could have reached out and touched him, and did so later, shaking his shoulder and saying 'Come on, Mac'.

The infamous railway culvert at Wolfheze, where elements of 1st Airborne Reconnaissance Squadron were ambushed, suffering fatal casualties – fortunately Ray's friend, Trooper Arthur Barlow, survived, albeit wounded and captured. (Author)

Further shots were exchanged, Trooper Barlow being hit by one round on his Sten's cocking mechanism, another in the thigh. Eventually one of the survivors waved a white handkerchief. A German NCO with a perfect command of the English language came and took them prisoner. Arthur Barlow's baptism of fire was over – just a few hours after landing in Holland.

Major Gough withdrew, but communications difficulties frustrated attempts by General Urquhart to contact him and vice-versa. Consequently, Gough, having driven around unsuccessfully looking for the General, decided to make his own way to Arnhem Bridge. Meanwhile, according to Martin Middlebrook, this left the 'bulk of his unit to return lamely to the divisional area, not to be employed again that day in any useful role, and losing its commander for the rest of the battle'. SS-*Hauptscharführer* Weigand, had he known it, had prevented the proposed *coup de main*. Having withdrawn to Wolfheze, at 1830 hrs, the War Diary records, the squadron was relieved by men of the Glider Pilot Regiment, moving into the 'Divisional area' at 1900 hrs, spending the night holding the 'west flank of the Divisional area'. Trooper Ray McSkimmings was amongst the 'C' Troop survivors of that fateful day, during which he had seen bullets fly in anger and men wounded and killed for the first time. How he felt can only be imagined, his friend, 'Art' being missing, fate unknown. Fortunately, Arthur Barlow would survive his wounds and time as a prisoner of war, but these first few hours were a salutary lesson to the uninitiated of the true, uncompromising and violent, nature of war.

The following day, at 0630 hrs, whilst the other troops were engaged on reconnaissance duties, 'C' Troop, after its battering at Wolfheze, dug in on the east side of the landing ground north of the railway line, ready for arrival of the second lift. The Troop's War Diary succinctly describes events:

0700 – Positions of defence adopted. Snipers become troublesome, patrol sent to squash them.
1000 – Four snipers caught, very frightened.
1100 – Planes overhead which are taken to be ours. Bursts of cannon fire dispels all beliefs of friendly aircraft. The *Messerschmitts* use plenty of ammunition but inflict no damage.
1200 – Strong attack comes in on Lt FOULKES and his Section. Attack held and eventually beaten off. Two OR casualties.
1230 – *Messerschmitts* give another display of aeronautics.
1400 – Supply drop. Plenty of flak.
1500 – Germans send over a barrage of mortar and shell fire supported by MGs, which make it impossible to get out onto the LZ.
1900 – Troop withdraws to 1 Airlanding Brigade HQ 683785. The night spent there.

The following day, 19 September 1944, would be somewhat more active for 'C' Troop. At first light, the troop's jeeps were out, reconnoitring the area of Reijers Camp and Amsterdamseweg, the main road leading into Arnhem north of the railway line and 1st Parachute Battalion's initial route of march. In the vicinity of Peijesheise, at the Amsterdamseweg, the troop was 'heavily mortared', as a result of which Captain John Hay, 'C' Troop's commander, withdrew his men to Wolfheze. The jeeps travelled independently, some cautiously probing along through the woods, others belting down the main road at high speed. Having safely rendezvoused, at 1015 hrs, Captain Hay decided to again head towards the Amsterdamseweg, travelling off-road. This was already a dreadful day of battle, the Division's forlorn attempt to reinforce Lieutenant Colonel Frost's small composite force at Arnhem Bridge concluding in virtual annihilation in western Arnhem. Increasingly, German reinforcements were arriving in the Arnhem sector, including armour – and the Amsterdamseweg was one of the most important arterial routes into the city. 'C' Troop's journey along the edge of woods, away from open ground, led them just south of Planken Wambuis, on the Amsterdamseweg. *En-route*, several German prisoners were taken, searched, and sent back towards the divisional area. The troop pressed on, along a woodland track which was hard-going. Passing beneath a culvert, with evidence that someone had only very recently vacated the location, suggesting that the troop's progress may have been observed by the enemy, Lieutenant Pearson climbed a tree. From this vantage point he could clearly see that, according to John Fairley, 'as far as he could see, enemy armoured vehicles were moving slowly from the West in a direction of Arnhem'. Behind them, the woods likewise betrayed the ominous sound of troop movements. It was clear that 'C' Troop was within a huge concentration of German troops heading towards Oosterbeek and Arnhem. It was an unenviable position. Another problem was that the patrol had ventured beyond the range of the Squadron radio net, meaning that this critical information could not be immediately or easily shared.

By 1200 hrs, 'C' Troop was hidden along the Amsterdamseweg, slightly east of the Planken Wambuis restaurant. According to the War Diary, at that point in time things were 'Very quiet'. Then, just 200 yards away, a party of Germans crossed the road, followed by several more. Clearly, 'C' Troop was in the midst of a hornet's nest. The options available were limited to say the least. Captain Hay could perhaps have re-traced his steps southwards, through the woods, but detection and engagement by infinitely stronger German forces was a near certainty. The only other alternative was to 'Bash on Recce', hell for leather, down the Amsterdamseweg towards Arnhem, at high speed, hoping no road blocks existed and to re-gain the Wolfhezerweg a mile away, and the Divisional area beyond. Whilst Captain Hay discussed all of this with his officers and senior NCOs, the decision was made for them when the Polish lift arrived on LZ 'L', east of Wolfheze. Immediately, the woods through which the troop had only recently passed, was alive with the thump of mobile flak guns, which had since invested the area. A southerly withdrawal, therefore, was no longer any kind of option. Captain Hay, however, realised that the gliders' arrival was actually to his advantage, given that the Germans would be preoccupied with engaging this third lift, and the din of battle would disguise the noise of his speeding jeeps. The high-speed dash was the only choice.

According to Robert Hilton's recently-published unit history (see Bibliography), there were six jeeps involved, led by Captain Hay, who was driven by Lieutenant Pearson. Jeep No. 4, driven by Lance-Sergeant Christie, carried Lance-Corporal Palmer, and Troopers McSkimmings, McCarthy and Cook, all of 'C' Troop's HQ Troop. The men got ready, the jeep-mounted Vickers machine guns ready to fire, along with the recce men's Brens and Stens. At Captain Hay's command, the drivers engaged gear – and the race began, setting off at 50mph.

For the first half-mile all went well, the road passing through largely open heathland. Then the woods thickened on both sides of the road. A group of six British airborne men were spotted at the roadside as the desperate convoy flashed by, probably prisoners, then the lead jeep suddenly weaved all over the road – ambush! With Germans pouring small arms and machine-gun fire from both sides of the road, Captain Hay's jeep ran off the road, smashing into a tree. Stopping was not an option: the remaining jeeps raced on, the occupants desperately returning fire. Sergeant Christie kept going, Corporal Palmer swept the woods with his Vickers; in the back, Trooper McArthy banged away with his Bren, whilst, back-to-back, Troopers McSkimmings and Cooke emptied their Stens into the roadside enemy. Later, Cooke remembered that there were 'hundreds of them, laid three deep on each side of the road'. Christie could have 'spat on the Gerries, they were so close'. Cooke also described what happened when the jeep ahead was hit: 'It was like all hell let loose, I saw Mr Pearson's jeep go right up in the air. It must have been hit by a shell, because it just blew up and bits of it landed all over the place.' Christie hurtled through the danger at 70mph. A tree barred the way forward, Christie making a split-second decision to drive over the thin end – which worked.

At some stage in this maelstrom of shot, shell, noise and smoke, Trooper Ray McSkimmings was killed. A burst of machine-gun fire had passed over Cooke's head to hit the taller lad from Carlisle (who was 5ft 10in tall). From his injuries, it was obvious that the cheerful young northerner had died instantly. Christie raced on, at last reaching the Wolfhezerweg junction, and, pedal still to the metal, and going flat out, swung the jeep into the junction. As he straightened up, the driver heard something crash onto the road. Looking around, he saw only two men, who confirmed that McSkimmings had been killed and fallen from the speeding vehicle. Accepting Cooke's assurances that Ray was already dead before falling from the jeep, Christie put his foot down and continued to safety. In front was Sergeant Fred Winder's jeep and crew, none of whom, remarkably, had been hit. As the firing started, jeeps five and six, seeing what was happening, had sped off the road, dismounted and evaporated into the woods.

The two surviving jeeps driven by Winder and Christie entered the divisional area, turning left, passed the dead German General Kussin on the Utrechtseweg, and continued eastwards a few hundred yards to the Divisional HQ at the Hartenstein Hotel. The War Diary reported that 'Two jeeps containing seven ORs – the remnants of "C" Troop – have appeared at Rear HQ. This very bad news indeed.' It most certainly was. Some thirty men of 'C' Troop had set off that morning – all but seven, including the Troop Commander, were either dead or missing. The survivors were, Lieutenant-Quartermaster Tom Collier, said, not surprisingly, 'very, very shaken. I remember sitting them down with their backs to some iron railings and pumping rum and strong tea into them.' Captain Allsop, whose Squadron HQ was located at the nearby junction of Utrechtseweg and Bredelaan, knew that this meant 'C' Troop had ceased to exist. The survivors, therefore, were absorbed into HQ Troop.

Lieutenant Hubert Pearson, Troopers Ray McSkimmings, Fred Brawn and James Salmon were all killed in the ambush. They were buried in a temporary military cemetery near Ginkel Heath, beside Verlengde Arnhemseweg, before interment at the Arnhem-Oosterbeek War Cemetery on 15 August 1945. Their comrades fought on, the 1st Airborne Reconnaissance Squadron losing a total of thirty men killed in action.

The first notification Mrs Nora McSkimmings received that her eldest son was

One of the Reconnaissance Squadron's jeeps on the Amsterdamseweg, after the ambush which claimed Trooper Ray McSkimmings' young life. (Imperial War Museum)

missing was a hand-written letter from Lieutenant John Wadsworth, of HQ Troop, who won an American Bronze Star at Arnhem, dated 3 October 1944:

> I regret to inform you that your son is missing. He went out with his Troop on a deep recce of the main road NW of Arnhem. The Troop ran into an ambush and were subjected to heavy machine-gun fire. Only two of the eight [author's note: there were six] jeeps returned. This is hope, and we all pray, that your son is a prisoner of war but I am afraid I cannot tell you whether this is so or not. We are doing everything possible to check upon what happened and should any further information come to light I will let you know straight away.
>
> Meanwhile, if there is anything we can do to help you in any way, please do not hesitate to ask us.

On 9 October 1944, the War Office wrote officially to confirm that '14583993 Trooper McSkimmings. R.' was missing, having been 'known to be wounded on the 25 September 1944 in the North-West Theatre of War'.

Eventually, the administrative process caught up, as survivors returned. By 11 October 1945, there was no doubt of Ray's fate, leading to issue of a Death Certificate.

RAYMOND MCSKIMMINGS

Official notification of death had been received the previous month, leading to a notice being published by Mrs McSkimmings in the local paper. On 17 September 1945 – one year after Ray had parachuted into Holland – his former headmaster at Creighton School, Mr T.H. Bainbridge, wrote to Nora, 'on behalf of the School': 'It was with deep regret that I read the sad news about Raymond. We remember him as an intelligent youth, keen, alert, and cheerful. We mourn with you his passing, and trust that memories of his fine life will help to sustain you, and that strength will be given to you in your time of sorrow.'

The plot containing Trooper McSkimmings' original field grave in a temporary military cemetery near Ginkel Heath, beside Verlengde Arnhemseweg. (Imperial War Museum)

ARNHEM 1944

Trooper McSkimmings' original metal grave-marker at Oosterbeek - note incorrect spelling. (Ted McSkimmings)

The annual pilgrimage to Arnhem-Oosterbeek became a primary date in the McSkimmings family calendar – the family seen here at Ray's graveside in 1959. (Ted McSkimmings)

RAYMOND MCSKIMMINGS

A day later, a letter followed from Mr James Young, Secretary of Harrison & Hethrington, Ray's former employer:

It was with deep regret that the announcement contained in the local press on Saturday last was received at this office.

May I, on behalf of the Directors and Staff of the Company, convey to you our very sincere sympathy in the loss of your son, Raymond.

During the short period he served with us, he endeared himself to his colleagues with his cheery disposition, and I can assure you his ready smile will be missed by the rest of the staff for a long time to come.

Today, Ray's brother, Ted, and his wife, Shirley, proudly keep the memory evergreen :

The late Arthur Barlow remembering his friend, Trooper Ray McSkimmings, 1984. (Ted McSkimmings)

Trooper McSkimmings' grave at Oosterbeek today. (1.B.17). (Author)

There were seventeen years between Ray and me, so I was only two when he was killed and therefore have no personal recollection of him. It is nice, however, that he has referred to 'Little Teddy' in one of his surviving letters. Our two sisters are now deceased, Betty passing over in 1983, June two years later. Our mother died in 1998, aged ninety-three, having outlived three of her children – it shouldn't be like that. Of course Mum was adamant that I would not serve in the armed forces, which is understandable, but in any case I just missed National Service.

Mum was passionately committed to keeping Ray's memory alive. We first went out to Arnhem on one of the first annual pilgrimages, after which Mum went annually with other mothers who had lost sons at Arnhem, usually Mrs Smith, whose son was killed with one of the parachute battalions. Now that Mum has gone, we keep up the tradition. I think that the deep bond of friendship between the Dutch people and we British is an incredible thing – we have maintained a close friendship over many years with Riet van Mullen and family, for example. The children still placing flowers on the graves every year is just incredible. It is very important to us to know that this tradition will continue. We went over for the 40th anniversary, and met a veteran paying his respects at Ray's grave. This was his friend, Arthur Barlow. We just hugged each other and broke down. We stayed in close contact with Arthur until he died in 2003. There was a real bond there.

Trooper Raymond McSkimmings was amongst the youngest British airborne men to die at Arnhem – but in truth, at nineteen, he was just a boy.

Ted also shared a recollection of something his mother once said: 'I just wish I could dream about Ray, but I never have.'

Not content with taking sons, war, it seems, even steals dreams.

Chapter 7

Private Percival William Collett, 2nd (Airborne) Battalion, The South Staffordshire Regiment

Lightly-armed airborne troops, unsupported by heavy weapons and armour, rely upon speed and surprise; having dropped eight miles from the bridge, however, owing to distance, poor intelligence, loss of surprise and the rapid reaction of SS-*Sturmbannführer* Krafft in particular, only Lieutenant Colonel John Frost's 2nd Parachute Battalion and supporting divisional troops reached and seized the northern end of Arnhem Bridge. As we have seen, the advance of 1st Parachute Brigade's two other battalions, 1st and 3rd Parachute Battalions, swiftly became blocked by the enemy, it ultimately proving impossible to substantially reinforce Frost. Things, however, would get no better.

The air component of the operation had insisted on dropping and landing General Urquhart's division over two days – thus compounding the loss of surprise. The drop and landing zones also had to be secured on the first day by Brigadier R.H.W. 'Pip' Hicks's glider-borne 1st Airlanding Brigade – and held until the second lift arrived on Monday, 18 September 1944. Consequently, Hicks's three fighting battalions, 7th (Galloway) King's Own Scottish Borderers, 1st Border and 2nd South Staffordshires, were unable to move off with 1st Parachute Brigade, but stayed put. This substantially weakened the force trying to reach Arnhem Bridge on the first day, and it was that day, and the first few hours of it, when the Germans were confused, which offered any realistic chance of reaching and securing the prize with a substantial force.

Whilst the immediate German reaction to the landings was set back by 3rd Parachute Battalion eliminating General Kussin, the Arnhem *Stadtkommandant*, the British were in no better position. Due to the breakdown in radio communications, in an attempt to ascertain exactly what was happening up front and urge his troops on, General Urquhart had sallied forth in a jeep, meeting and going on with Brigadier Lathbury, commanding 1st Parachute Brigade. The problem with this was Urquhart's instructions that should he himself become a casualty, Lathbury was to take over the Division. At dawn on Monday, 18 September 1944, General Urquhart and Brigadier Lathbury remained with 3rd Parachute Battalion, which pushed on to reinforce Lieutenant Colonel Frost at the bridge. Taking the lower road through Oosterbeek, Lieutenant Colonel Fitch's men, with Lieutenant Cleminson's 'B' Company once more up front, made good progress for two and a half miles, reaching the Rhine Pavilion, a large building near the Rhine, beyond the Oosterbeek-Laag station. Cleminson had made great progress but was ordered to halt and await the remainder of the Battalion. Debate continues as to whether the advance should have pressed on, and Cleminson's opinion was that it should have. The Germans, however, noting this hesitance, brought up armour and, also firing from the south bank, pinned down Fitch's men – some of whom had linked up with 1st Parachute Battalion and were trying to push along the Utrechtseweg.

All of this time, both General Urquhart and Brigadier Lathbury were stuck with 3rd Parachute Battalion, the General unable to direct the overall battle. It was clear that they both needed to return to Divisional HQ at the Hartenstein Hotel in Oosterbeek. Around 1600 hrs, Fitch's entire group started to leave via the back gardens of the houses they had taken refuge in – finding only one way open: north, into the maze of narrow streets adjacent to the St Elizabeth Hospital. The General, Brigadier and his Intelligence Officer, Captain Willie Taylor, however, set off alone. Looking on, Lieutenant Cleminson realised that they were going the wrong way, and joined them to provide some protection. Every junction was under fire, Brigadier Lathbury becoming a casualty when shot in the leg and spine. Having dragged the wounded Brigadier into 135 Alexanderstraat, the General shot a German passing the other side of a ground floor window with his revolver. With no option but to leave Brigadier Lathbury, the three survivors then sought refuge at 14 Zwarteweg (now known as 'Urquhart House'), just beyond the junction with Nassaustraat. Unfortunately, a German self-propelled gun, supported by infantry, then stationed itself outside the building – forcing the three fugitives to hide in the attic. At the bridge, 2nd Parachute Battalion continued to hold on, but the effort to reach them this day had failed. Moreover, not only was the divisional commander now in hiding, where he would remain for twelve hours, incommunicado, but his nominated successor had been wounded and captured.

General Urquhart's succession plan was for divisional responsibility, in the event of Lathbury's incapacity, to pass to Brigadier 'Pip' Hicks of the Air Landing Brigade, and if necessary thence to Brigadier 'Shan' Hackett of 4th Parachute Brigade. At Divisional Headquarters in Oosterbeek, General Urquhart's Chief of Staff, Lieutenant Colonel Charles MacKenzie, knew the time had come to put that succession plan into action. With General Urquhart *and* Brigadier Lathbury out of contact and God alone knew where, MacKenzie sped off from the Hartenstein Hotel in a jeep, bound for the landing grounds and to inform Brigadier Hicks of his new responsibility. Having to still maintain the drop and landing zones for the second lift, which had been delayed due to fog over England, Hicks's deputy, Colonel Hilaro Barlow, assumed command of the Airlanding Brigade and awaited arrival of the much-needed airborne reinforcements. At 0915 hrs, Brigadier Hicks arrived at Divisional HQ.

Deployment of Lieutenant Colonel Derek McCardie's 2nd South Staffords, part of the Airlanding Brigade, had been split over the two lifts. Whilst 60 per cent of McCardie's force had arrived with the first lift, the remainder were awaited with the overdue second drop. With 2nd Parachute Battalion requesting urgent reinforcement, the game plan had clearly changed. The plan for 1st Parachute Brigade to reach and take Arnhem Bridge on the first day had failed. With only Lieutenant Colonel Frost's small force desperately holding on to that objective, capture of the high ground north of Arnhem, as originally envisaged, was no longer an option – reinforcing 2nd Parachute Battalion at the Bridge was now the priority. Consequently, recognising this changed and urgent scenario, Brigadier Hicks decided to detach McCardie's men and send the 2nd South Staffordshires to join 1st Parachute Brigade's continued push to reach Arnhem Bridge. Hicks decreed that upon arrival, the rest of McCardie's men would move off and join their battalion in Arnhem.

At 1030 hrs on Monday, 18 September, some 420 South Staffords left their positions at Wolfheze, shortly after which their column was strafed by enemy fighters. The appearance of the *Luftwaffe* was an uncomfortable surprise for the airborne troops, given the impression of Allied aerial superiority, which had gone a very long way towards defeating the Germans in Normandy. In his diary, Captain-Reverend Wilfred Chignell, Chaplain to 2nd Glider Wing, wrote that 'German fighters have been over – we nearly mistook them for our own and went out to wave and cheer, only to hustle back quickly when we saw the black crosses . . . The German fighters shot-up the LZ only about ten minutes after my little party and I left it. Another thirty Me 109s have been over and shot up our positions but there were no casualties.'

Air Vice-Marshal J.E. 'Johnnie' Johnson, the RAF's officially top-scoring fighter pilot of the Second World War, commented: 'The *Luftwaffe* soon sorted itself out after Normandy and still had plenty of fighters and fighter-bombers with which to attack our lightly armed airborne troops.' Although enemy air opposition on the first day had been negligible, with only between fifty and seventy-five sorties being flown against the strong protective Allied fighter screen, from 18–25 September 1944, practically the whole German air effort in the West was diverted against the airborne landings, the defence of the Reich becoming a secondary consideration. Reinforcements were committed to the battle from the strategic fighter defence of Germany, some 320–350 German single-engine fighters, almost double the force in the immediate area of the Allied landings. Bad weather, unsuitable airfields and shortage of fuel, however, restricted the enemy fighter effort to some 250 sorties per day, but the long-range bomber force re-entered the fray for the first time in a fortnight, contributing 100 sorties over the two nights when operations were possible. The *Luftwaffe*, however, would not play a prominent part in the German success at Arnhem, but the reaction achieved was the first sign of the remarkable recovery mentioned by Johnnie. Nonetheless, the *Luftwaffe*'s rapid and aggressive reaction was unanticipated by Allied planners.

Having also been made to abandon the more direct route and use the lower road through Oosterbeek, seven and a half hours later McCardie reached St Elizabeth Hospital, linking up with the pitiful remnants of 1st Parachute Battalion. Originally, the second lift had been scheduled for take-off at 0700 hrs, but low-lying cloud delayed this until 1045 hrs. The remaining 40 per cent of Lieutenant Colonel McCardie's 2nd South Staffords were lifted from Broadwell in forty gliders, all but one of which landed without mishap at LZ 'S' by 1530 hrs. Amongst them was Private Percival William Collett.

Born on 28 August 1922, 'Percy' Collett, the son of William and Janet, hailed from Stoulton, a small village just outside the West Midlands city of Worcester, near the sleepy country town of Pershore. Having achieved 'Educational Grade "D"' at what is now Pershore High School, Percy worked as a 'General Labourer' before enlisting, aged eighteen, at Worcester in the Royal Warwickshire Regiment on 15 April 1941. On that day, Private Collett was posted to The Drill Hall (demolished in the 1980s to make way for 'social housing') in Cromwell Road, Malvern Link, also in Worcestershire. Percy then joined the Regiment's 70 (Young Soldier) Battalion, comprising volunteers aged below twenty and therefore too young for conscription. Part of the 47 (London) Infantry Division, these young soldiers remained in England, engaged upon Home Defence, throughout the war.

A week after enlisting, Private Collett was punished at Gosport with 168 hours detention in the 'Unit Detention Room' for 'misconduct': 'failing to comply with an order given by his superior officer and using abusive language to an NCO'. Over a year later, on 17 June 1942, Private Collett was 'attached 2nd Battalion South Staffordshire Regiment', to which unit he was formally transferred the following day.

In October 1941, the 2nd South Staffords had become part of the new 1st British Airborne Division, as glider-borne infantry belonging to what was initially the 1st Airlanding Brigade Group. Although glider troops were not volunteers as such, like parachutists, the very nature of flying to battle dictated a higher fitness requirement – and not all existing 2nd South Staffords were found suitable. These men were swiftly reassigned, and the battalion began training in earnest for glider operations. This process, therefore, had already begun when Private Collett arrived in June 1942. On 28 November 1942, however, the young soldier was confined to barracks for fourteen days following 'Conduct to the prejudice of good order and military discipline'.

On 16 May 1943, Percy and his battalion embarked at Liverpool on HMT *P74*, bound for North Africa, disembarking at Oran in Algeria ten days later and joining the

Private Percy Collett, 2nd (Airborne) Battalion, The South Staffordshire Regiment. (Eunice Collett)

PERCIVAL WILLIAM COLLETT

8th Army. In North Africa, the 2nd South Staffords trained on American Waco gliders towed by C-47s, in preparation for the invasion of Sicily – Operation HUSKY. This was subdivided into four tactical operations, two of which, Operations LADBROKE and FUSTIAN, involved 1st Airborne Division. Brigadier Hicks's 1st Airlanding Brigade, including the 2nd South Staffords, was tasked with LADBROKE – capturing the Ponte Grande Bridge and Syracuse. From their airfield near Souss on 9 July 1943, this involved a flight of some 350 miles, turning on Malta, before the Wacos were released 3,000 yards off the enemy coastline and at a height of 3,000 feet. In the event, strong winds blew many glider and tug combinations off course, and anti-aircraft fire panicked some inexperienced tug pilots into releasing their charges too early. Consequently, a number of gliders landed in the Mediterranean, whilst those making landfall were scattered. 'A' and 'C' Company, however, in Horsa gliders, reached and captured the Ponte Grande Bridge. For the fiery young Private Collett, serving in 'A' Company, this was a baptism of fire indeed. Ultimately Syracuse was also taken, but at a high price for Lieutenant Colonel McCardie's South Staffords: of forty-eight officers and 768 men who participated in LADBROKE, only nineteen of the former and 269 Other Ranks survived. 19 August 1943, however, saw Private Collett in trouble again and 'awarded Field Punishment' for being drunk; after the experience of LADBROKE, however, who could blame him?

Due to heavy losses, the 2nd South Staffords did not take part in the invasion of Italy, but were sent to Taranto by sea, as reinforcements, on 12 September 1943. After further fighting, as infantry, on 27 November 1943, the battalion embarked for England, arriving on 10 December. Seventeen days later, Private Percy Collett married Edna May Brookes in their home village of Stoulton, Worcestershire.

Now, the 2nd South Staffords began rebuilding and training once more, at Woodhall Spa, ready for the liberation of enemy occupied Europe. Along with the rest of 1st Airborne Division, however, they were held in reserve whilst 6th Airborne Division gained the glory in Normandy. Marriage, though, clearly did not placate young Percy, who was fined four days' pay for being Absent Without Leave between 2359 hrs on 25 June and 1015 hrs on 26 June 1944. Another offence of being 'AWOL' occurred 15 September 1944, for which the following day our errant private was fined another day's pay and placed under 'Open Arrest'. With sixteen cancelled operations before MARKET-GARDEN, and the battle raging on the Continent, frustration throughout 1st Airborne Division was high, the maintenance of good order and discipline being an increasing problem with some highly-strung troops. Nonetheless, two days later, Private Collett was in a Horsa glider bound for LZ 'S' – still under open arrest. Safely down near Wolfheze, the newly arrived South Staffords rapidly formed up and moved off in the direction of Arnhem. 'A' Company led the way, including Private Collett in Lieutenant Alan Barker's No. 8 Platoon. By nightfall, 'A' and 'D' companies had joined those South Staffords from the first lift on the Utrechtseweg, near the St Elizabeth Hospital. There they remained for the night, amidst the dreadful noise of battle, awaiting dawn and a fresh attempt to reach Arnhem Bridge. The question on the minds of every British soldier at Arnhem, regardless of rank, was 'When will XXX Corps get here?'

By now, the Germans had a very clear plan: isolate and destroy Frost's men at the bridge, and prevent the British from reinforcing his beleaguered 2nd Parachute Battalion. On 18 September, two British parachute battalions, advancing on a front just 200 yards wide, had failed to penetrate the hastily-established but ever-strengthening German defences – and following arrival of the second lift, SS-*Obersturmbannführer* Walter Harzer, commanding 9-SS *Panzer* Division *Hohenstaufen* knew that another effort would be mounted; it was his job to resist the expected British attack. North of the railway line, looking down on what was soon to become a scene of carnage, *Kampfgruppe* Gropp was located with 20mm flak. *Kampfgruppe* Möller blocked the Utrechtseweg, and, closer to the river, *Kampfgruppe* Harder barred the Onderlangs. Harzer was also reinforced by army, air force and navy personnel. Across the Rhine, the vengeful remnants of *Hauptsturmführer* Viktor Gräbner's reconnaissance unit – badly mauled by Frost's men the previous day, their commander being amongst the fatal casualties – were ready and sited around a brick works opposite the Onderlangs, with their 20mm and 37mm flak weapons. Moreover, six even heavier guns, 75mm flak guns of 4./RAD-*Flak-Abteilung* 216, were situated in the adjacent Meinerswijk Polder. This meant that the British faced not only a substantial force ahead but also overpowering fire from heavy weapons on both flanks.

The British plan was for the 2nd South Staffords to advance along the Utrechtseweg, past the hospital, and push on, always push on, into Arnhem, covered by the 4th Parachute Brigade's 11th Parachute Battalion, which had arrived with the second lift. 1st Parachute Battalion would attack along the Onderlangs, the lower road. Unfortunately, the German positions ahead were unknown, any nocturnal reconnaissance having been prevented by enemy snipers and patrols.

At 0400 hrs, the British attack went in, the South Staffords initially making good progress for some 700–900 yards along an undefended section of road, reaching the town's museum (inexplicably described as a 'monastery' by the Battalion's War Diary). All hell, however, had by now broken loose. 'A' Company's 7, 8 and 9 Platoons took shelter in three large houses opposite the museum, in that order, from left to right, dislodging the existing German occupants in the process. From the rear of these buildings the South Staffords had a good field of fire towards the railway and houses beyond from which fire poured down.

At 0600 hrs the fighting waned, as both sides rested, providing an opportunity for reinforcements to be brought up. Half an hour later, by which time the Onderlangs attack had failed and was already falling back, the Germans resumed firing with an even greater intensity – concentrating on 'D' Company and the South Stafford mortar positions located around the Museum. Withering fire of all calibres poured from *Kampfgruppe* Gropp's northern position, making any further advance impossible: it was a massacre.

The domed building is Arnhem Museum, erroneously referred to as the 'Monastery' by British troops, scene of dreadful fighting on 19 September 1944, as 4th Parachute Brigade and other elements of 1st British Airborne Division fought desperately, but unsuccessfully, to reach and reinforce Lieutenant Colonel Frost at Arnhem Bridge, a mile away. To the south, the river Rhine can be seen, the road running parallel to it being the Onderlangs (see Chapter 8). A few hundred yards along the Utrechtseweg, on which the Museum is located, to the west is the St Elisabeth Hospital. To the north, across the railway line, are houses on higher ground, from which the Germans poured fire, and from the south bank. 7, 8 and 9 Company of the 2nd South Staffordshire's 'A' Company, took refuge in three houses opposite the Museum. (Gelders Archief)

The view across the Onderlands and river Rhine from the Utrechtseweg, opposite the hospital, showing the brickwork site from which relentless fire pounded the British airborne troops. (Author)

ARNHEM 1944

As Major Robert Cain, commander of the South Stafford 'B' Company wrote, '20mm and machine-gun fire was incessant, ricocheting off buildings all around us'.

Significantly, *Sturmgeschütze-Brigade* 280 was *en route* with seven StuG III self-propelled assault guns and three StuH 42 *Sturmhaubitze* self-propelled assault howitzers. Previously, this armoured unit had fought extensively in Russia before re-fitting in Denmark. Whilst proceeding to reinforce German units defending Aachen, 280 was diverted to Arnhem, and these tracked vehicles now ominously clattered into the battle up the Utrechtestraat, towards the museum and hospital.

By 1000 hrs the British attack was all but spent, Lieutenant Colonel McCardie captured and Lieutenant Colonel Fitch dead. The survivors of this deadly maelstrom were either rounded up and taken prisoner, or streamed back towards Oosterbeek. It was the turning point in the battle, the final attempt to relieve 2nd Parachute Battalion still gallantly and courageously hanging on to the northern end of Arnhem Bridge.

Lieutenant Alan Barker's No. 8 Platoon invested this building, from which Private Collett sallied forth to fetch PIAT ammunition from the Museum – but was cut down and killed in the process. (Gelders Archief)

The same house on the Utrechtseweg today. (Author)

Private Percy Collett did not survive the arrival of *Sturmgeschütze-Brigade* 280, the presence of which tipped the balance firmly in Harzer's favour (had it ever been in doubt). Initially buried at the Moscowa General Cemetery in Arnhem, the 21-year-old married glider soldier from Worcestershire was later reinterred at the Arnhem-Oosterbeek War Cemetery. It would be many months, however, before his wife and family received confirmation of his fate.

On a Sunday in 1945, a memorial service for Percy Collett took place at Stoulton Parish Church. The glider soldier's widow laid flowers on the village war memorial in memory of her husband. His platoon commander, Lieutenant Alan Barker, had survived the massacre at Arnhem and was captured by the Germans; although repatriated, he was unable to attend the service but sent a letter which was read to the congregation by Rev T. Morgans:

Percy was at all times a good and loyal soldier and eventually died to save my life.

After a considerable pounding at Arnhem, when all our nerves were badly shaken, he volunteered to come with me and attempt to destroy a tank. The ammunition for the gun was some yards away and without thought for his own personal safety he moved forward to get it. He was very badly injured whilst doing so and died shortly afterwards.

Only those who were at Arnhem can know what it was like to go forward alone in such terrible fire, and I have no hesitation in saying that Percy was as brave as any man who gave his life that day.

As I am unable to attend the memorial service, I would be grateful if you could make clear his bravery to those who knew him.

Further comment would be superfluous.

Private Collett's grave at Oosterbeek today. (15.C.9). (Author)

Chapter 8

Privates Gilbert Anderson and Harry Jenkin, 11th Parachute Battalion, and Private Gordon Best, 1st Parachute Battalion

Lieutenant Colonel George Lea's 11th Parachute Battalion, a component of 4th Parachute Brigade, was lifted from Saltby at 1100 hrs on Monday, 18 September 1944, in thirty-three aircraft of the American 314th Troop Carrier Group – destination Ginkel Heath, DZ 'Y'. Amidst heavy flak and with several German machine guns sweeping the DZ with fire, the 11th Parachute Battalion dropped onto a 'hot' DZ, before lying up in the extensive woods to the immediate south-east of Ginkel Heath. The British paratroopers immediately took forty German prisoners, such was the extent of the enemy's presence in the area. Owing to General Urquhart being missing, Brigadier Hicks had taken over the Division; Brigadier Hackett discovered that plans had changed: Hicks had decreed that his 11th Parachute Battalion, being closest, by a small margin, to

DZ 'Y' at Ginkel Heide, north-west of Wolfheze, where 4th Parachute Brigade dropped on 18 September 1944. (Author)

Arnhem, was to follow the South Staffords, coming under command of 1st Parachute Brigade, and push on towards the Bridge. At dusk, the Battalion moved off, with 'A' Company leading the way to Arnhem, eight miles distant. With the leading Company's No. 2 Platoon was 21-year-old Private Gilbert Anderson.

Gilbert Anderson was the second son born to Thomas, a Scottish 'assurance agent', and Elizabeth Anderson of 34 Stamford Road, Mossley, a small town in Tameside, Greater Manchester, on 14 July 1923. Gilbert joined Thomas, his elder brother by four years (later a prisoner of the Japanese on the horrendous Burma Railway); four years on, Christina followed but sadly died a year later; Gordon completed the Anderson children in 1934. The family subsequently moved to 25 Ash Street, then 24 Marsden Road, Blackpool, Lancashire. Gilbert, a keen musician who enjoyed piano, attended St George's School, leaving, aged fourteen, on 16 July 1937. The following year, his former headmaster, Mr M. Satterthwaite, provided Gilbert the following reference:

Private Gilbert Anderson in 1943, in which year he joined the 11th Parachute Battalion. (Tanja Anderson)

> Gilbert Anderson left this school in July 1937, having passed all the standards under my supervision. I found him more interested in the practical side than reading or written work, and he produced some creditable work in art and handicraft. He was always honest and reliable, and showed a very willing disposition. I can recommend him to any occupation of a practical nature.

Gilbert, by religion a 'Salvationist', first worked in a cotton-spinning factory, Robert Hyde Buckley & Sons in Mossley, before the family moved to Blackpool and he became a milkman, working for CWS Dairies, a subsidiary of the Cooperative Group. On 22 July 1941, however, a week after his eighteenth birthday, the 5ft 9in tall milkman enlisted at Preston into the 70th Battalion, the Border Regiment. In June 1940, when Britain was threatened by invasion, the 8th Border Regiment recruited young soldiers, aged sixteen to eighteen, the battalion being engaged on Home Defence. Three companies then became the 70th 'Young Soldiers' Battalion, also committed to defending Britain. 3606646 Private Anderson completed basic training at Camp Hadrian, an annex of the regimental depot located at the castle, near Carlisle. Interminably boring coastal and airfield defence duties in Scotland followed. On 18 June 1943, Private Anderson for some reason transferred to the 5th East Lancashires, also engaged on home defence. Almost immediately, Gilbert was sent on a gas training course at the Chemical Defence Experimental Station, Porton Down, Wiltshire. Clearly these duties were not what Gilbert had in mind, however, because on 4 August 1943, he answered the call for volunteers and joined the Army Air Corps, attending No. 78 Course at the Depot and

Airborne Forces School at Hardwick Hall, Chesterfield, for parachute training. For some unknown reason, Gilbert was re-coursed, joining No. 80 Course, but broke his leg, presumably in a landing accident, and was then admitted to Ward 9 at Manchester Military Hospital. Undeterred, between 29 November and 13 December 1943, Private Anderson was back at Hardwick Hall, on Course No. 93, which he successfully completed. In January 1944, the 4th Parachute Brigade returned from Mediterranean service, Gilbert joining 'D' Company of the 10th Parachute Battalion. By August, he was serving with 11th Parachute Battalion, which was billeted in villages around Leicester. On 17 August 1944, Private Anderson was 'Deprived ten days by CO for insolence and insubordination to an NCO'.

Returning to the violent events of 18 September 1944, 11th Parachute Battalion, led by 'A' Company, reached Divisional Headquarters at Oosterbeek's Hartenstein Hotel at 1900 hrs. There, Lieutenant Colonel Lea was ordered by Brigadier Hicks to continue into Arnhem, link up with the South Staffords and, together with other divisional troops, force a way through to relieve 2nd Parachute Battalion and supporting units at Arnhem Bridge. At 2230 hrs Lea's men moved off, meeting Lieutenant Colonel McCardie's 2nd South Staffords in Arnhem's western limits. The plan involved McCardie pushing along the top road, the Utrechtseweg (also known as Bovenover, the high road), whilst Lieutenant Colonel Dobie's 1st Parachute Battalion advanced along the Onderlangs, the

Private Gilbert Anderson (right) and pals whilst serving as 'young soldiers' aged between sixteen and eighteen in the Border Regiment. (Tanja Anderson)

parallel lower road running alongside the river Rhine. 11th Parachute Battalion was to follow Dobie. At first light, it could clearly be seen that the Onderlangs was open, coverless ground, saturated by fire from the brickworks on the far bank. Lea therefore decided to advance following the South Staffords along the top road, then before the Museum, cut down through the steep wooded ridge on his right to a rare patch of cover on the Onderlangs. This, he hoped, would bring his battalion up to the 1st Battalion's left-rear. By 0630 hrs, the push by the 1st (and remnants of the 3rd) Battalion had failed. At 0900 hrs, the South Staffordshires having been halted at the Museum, the assault guns of *Sturmgeschütz-Brigade* 280 appeared and swung the battle irrevocably in the Germans' favour. Fire still poured from the brickworks, preventing the intended push along the Onderlangs. Withering fire also pulverised the British from above and beyond the railway line. As explained in the previous chapter, the proud advance to relieve 2nd Parachute Battalion, still desperately clinging on to the northern end of Arnhem Bridge, had degenerated into a massacre. Somewhere in that maelstrom of shot and shell – it is not known how or where – Private Gilbert Anderson lost his life.

After the attempt to seize Arnhem Bridge failed, amongst the prisoners taken by the Germans was Roman Catholic Father Danny McGowan of 133 Parachute Field Ambulance. McGowan had dropped with 4th Parachute Brigade on 18 September 1944, but was captured two days later when the medical dressing station he was providing ministry at was overrun. Thereafter the brave priest continued to tend the wounded and even managed to move freely about the Arnhem and Oosterbeek area, working with a Dutch Red Cross man to gather food and medical supplies – and bury the dead. Between the period 28 September – 6 October 1944, McGowan and his Red Cross friend buried many of the dead, and recorded details of hasty field graves. On 2 October 1944, Father McGowan – who would receive a Military Cross for his efforts – reported having buried the following British airborne casualties at 'Park Onderlangs, East of St Elizabeth Hospital, Arnhem, Holland':

The Onderlangs below Arnhem Museum, looking west, back along this long coverless road towards the Utrechtseweg. (Author)

View from the Utrechtseweg, opposite the St Elisabeth Hospital, over the wooded escarpment known as the 'Dell', immediately west of the Museum. On the Rhine's far bank the brickworks can be seen, and, beyond the newer Nelson Mandela Bruug, the all-important Arnhem Bridge. (Author)

Looking east, uphill along the Utrechtseweg towards the St Elisabeth Hospital and down the Onderlangs, towards the Rhine. (Karen Sarkar)

Best, G, 1463210, 1st Parachute Battalion.
Younger, J C, 4916025
Rehill, B, 2937117, 11th Parachute Battalion.
Parkes, G, 491797, 2nd South Staffords.
Unknown, no discs
Wright, P, 140491, 2nd South Staffords.
Anderson, G, 3606646, 11th Parachute Battalion.
Gordon, O, 4690230, 1st Parachute Battalion.
Ashdown, G, 5883315, 11th Parachute Battalion.

Father McGowan's report is very specific, providing information of both service number and identity, confirming that Private Anderson was buried beside the Onderlangs. Later that month, the 21-year-old paratrooper's parents received official notification that their second son had been killed in action.

After the war, No. 37 Graves Registration Unit and No. 80 Graves Concentration Unit were responsible for exhuming the dead from their original field graves around Arnhem and concentrating these casualties for re-interment in the Arnhem-Oosterbeek War Cemetery. Curiously, however, although clearly recorded by Father McGowan as having been buried in 1944, Private Gilbert Anderson's name will not be found engraved on any headstone there – much to his family's distress.

What of the others mentioned in Father McGowan's report?

Of Private Best, like Private Anderson, there is now no trace. No record of a 'J.C. Younger' has ever been found in casualty records, and it is not known where at Oosterbeek, or even if, the completely unidentified body from Onderlangs was buried. The other casualties on Father McGowan's list were all buried at Oosterbeek in Plot 19, rows A and C.

Private Gordon Best, 1st Parachute Battalion, and Rita Best. (Andy Wilkins)

GILBERT ANDERSON, HARRY JENKIN AND GORDON BEST

On 11 December 1946, the War Office wrote to Mr and Mrs Anderson regarding an unidentified British paratrooper interred at Oosterbeek, Plot 15, Row C, Grave 19. These remains, the letter noted, were of a man 5ft 9in tall with brown hair. Private Anderson was of that height and hair colour. However, four red chevrons stitched on to the casualty's battledress, indicating 'four years' service in His Majesty's forces', meant that this was not Private Anderson, who had only served for three. Mr and Mrs Anderson were asked whether they could 'agree' these details with 'what you remember of your son', because if so, 'it is proposed to accept this grave as that of your son'. Unfortunately, for the reason explained, Mr and Mrs Anderson did not accept that this was Gilbert – and there, for many years, the matter lay. Private Anderson's younger brother, Gordon, coincidentally married a Dutch lady and has lived in the Netherlands for many years. To both Gordon and his daughter, Tanja, identifying Gilbert's last resting place has taken on a deep meaning. It is something that both, and the wider family, feel must be done.

Given that the Netherlands was both occupied and fought over during the Second World War, human remains are still discovered from those tumultuous times. In January 1945, such was the scale of fighting that the Dutch formed the Recovery & Identification Unit (RIU). Part of the Royal Netherlands Army, the RIU, according to its commanding officer, Captain Geert Jonker, still works 'on around forty cases annually and is responsible for the recovery and identification of missing Dutch civilians and military personnel (both Allied and German). This is still something that the Dutch government considers both a duty of care and a debt of honour. Tens of thousands of bodies have been recovered and identified since our Unit's inception.' Indeed, Geert has been extremely successful in recovering and identifying, or identifying those already buried as 'unknown', from the great airborne battle at Arnhem. Research by Geert confirmed that the grave 19/C/16 contained the remains of 'a private, the Parachute Regiment', whose body had been recovered from beside the river at Onderlangs. Could this be Private Gilbert Anderson?

The problem is that Private Gordon Best of 1st Parachute Battalion, also buried by Father McGowan at Onderlangs, is also 'missing'. Best was married to Rita, was twenty-three, born on 30 January 1921, to Pickard and Anne Best from Cleckheaton, Bradford; he was 5ft 8in tall. However, the exhumation report, preserved amongst Commonwealth War Graves Commission (CWGC) records, only mentions that the occupant of 19/C/16 was a Parachute Regiment private, making no mention still by the casualty buried as 'unknown' by Father McGowan, the fate of which is uncertain. These remains could also have been exhumed in 1945, and interred at Oosterbeek, possibly in 19/C/16. Who could this have been?

Of all the casualties from that dreadful day's fighting beside the Rhine, Private Harry Jenkin, also of the 11th Parachute Battalion, has never been found. Indeed, as Geert Jonker put it so well, it is 'as if he perished into oblivion'. Harry William Jenkin was born on 16 June 1920, the son of Frederick, a coal merchant, and Leah Jenkin; he was one of four boys, the family living at 2 Church Lane, Boldre, near Lyndhurst in Hampshire's picturesque New Forest. The diminutive van driver, 5ft 1½in tall with dark brown hair, enlisted, aged eighteen, joining the Hampshire Regiment on 25 October 1938, at Bournemouth. Serving at home until 24 July 1939, as war with Germany loomed large, Private Jenkin journeyed with the regiment's 1st Battalion to Egypt the following day. He subsequently also served in Palestine and Malta. On 25 May 1943, however, he volunteered for the Army Air Corps, joining the newly formed 11th Parachute Battalion in Palestine. Having successfully completed parachute training, Private Jenkin, wearing the coveted red beret, returned home on 6 January 1944, marrying Elizabeth Mary Ancliffe on the 29th of that month. His month-long disembarkation leave over, Harry re-joined the 11th Battalion in Leicestershire, but on 8 August 1944, he was 'awarded ten days by CO and fined one day's pay' for having been 'AWOL' for '23 hours 46 minutes'. On 18 September 1944, he parachuted onto Ginkel Heath – a day later he was dead. Intriguingly, his Army Service Record states that Private Jenkin was 'known to have been wounded' and was 'presumed' to have 'died of wounds on or shortly after 19 September 1944'. This suggests that although

Private Harry Jenkin, 11th Parachute Battalion, and Elizabeth Jenkin. (Angie Jenkin)

he was reported 'missing', rather than having 'perished into oblivion', someone witnessed and reported the young paratrooper's fate. It is possible, given his unit and this recorded information, that Private Jenkin was killed during the same action in the Bovenover-Onderlangs area as Privates Best and Anderson, and could have been the 'unknown' buried by Father McGowan beside the Bovenover-Onderlangs. For these reasons, therefore, Private Jenkin could also be a contender for occupancy of 19/C/16.

In the immediate aftermath of battle, and indeed into peacetime, chaos reigned – especially on the European mainland, given the scale of reconstruction required and volume of displaced people. Some 35–40 million people, soldiers and civilians, are believed to have perished in Europe between 1939–45. Hastily dug and recorded field graves were sometimes lost when markers became weathered and faded, identities disappearing, or such graves sometimes lost completely when ground was re-fought over. Explosive and efficient modern means of killing also dictated that sometimes there was simply nothing left to identify of an individual – or even find. Over-stretched, under-resourced and poorly trained Grave Registration Unit personnel had the unenviable task of exhuming field burials and organising re-burial in communal, formal war cemeteries. Often records were incomplete, illegible, and owing to the scale of the task offset against available time and resources, understandably mistakes were made. Although, therefore, we know for certain that Father McGowan buried both Privates Anderson and Best in 1944, this may explain why they have no known grave at Oosterbeek. It is assumed that somehow either the graves' identifications were lost between October 1944 and exhumation in 1945, or, although less likely, identification details were somehow lost between Onderlangs and internment at Oosterbeek. Captain Jonker comments that 'The main issue, in my opinion, is that in 1945–6, the GRU and GCU apparently did not have the 1st Airborne Division's casualty lists and burial records at their disposal; they did not know, therefore, who those killed or missing in action were, or who had been interred in field graves. In the case of the Onderlangs graves, they did not know who had been buried there by Father McGowan. If they had, they might have somehow identified more bodies as there would have been specific, known, candidates. They could, for instance, have checked for matches with Army Dental Records.' Whatever happened, the fact remains that these two young paratroopers had known graves in 1944 – but did not from 1945, onwards. Given the circumstances and chaos involved, this is far from such an isolated case.

The same scenario, of course, arose after the First World War. In those days, unlike today, casualties were rarely returned home, the volume of dead and modes of transport available making that impossible. Consequently, for those families whose loved ones were found and buried in a named grave, these were in 'a corner of a foreign field', inaccessible to many, or only rarely, due to cost and distance. In order to compensate for this lack of a local grave, therefore, war memorials, inscribed with names of those who had so proudly marched to war but failed to return, sprang up in communities all over Britain and in the Allied lands beyond. This gave way to annual, ritual, collective mourning, with services of remembrance held at these shrines and symbolic gravesites. Similarly, the grief of millions of families whose loved ones had no known grave was assuaged through imposing memorials dedicated to the missing, such as the Cenotaph, tombs of unknown warriors, and the Menin Gate. It simply was not practical, governments argued, to search for the missing, of whom in most cases identification was impossible, and the task of reconstruction was more pressing. Memorials to the missing, therefore, were intended to provide families closure in a dignified but practical manner. This mode of commemoration and remembrance, in fact, continued after the Second World War, the names of those missing from the battles in Arnhem and Oosterbeek, for example, being inscribed on Groesbeek's cenotaph to those who perished in the area but have no known grave.

Today, advances in forensic science, such as DNA comparison and isotope analysis, make possible the identification of skeletal remains – the fusion of history and science returning long-lost identities. In 2003, for example, a pipeline laid near Vimy Ridge uncovered the remains of a soldier identified as Canadian from his tunic buttons. Three years' combined effort by historians, anthropologists, genealogists and scientists led to this casualty's identification. Key to the process was DNA, the genetic material existing in most living cells. A comparison with a potential living relative found by genealogists confirmed the remains to be those of Private Herbert Peterson, a 21-year-old from Alberta. In 2007, the Petersons were, at last, able to bury Herbert in France alongside his comrades. Since that time, DNA comparisons have identified a number of servicemen, from both world wars, whose remains have been discovered in recent times – and even those of an English medieval king, lost since 1485.

However, up until now it has not been permitted to take DNA samples for comparison from the actual grave of an 'unknown', due to the CWGC policy of non-disturbance. Arguments against doing so are manifest, not least because, identified or otherwise, the individual concerned has been appropriately respected, buried, and is at rest. Disturbance, therefore, may seem inappropriate. However, are those buried as 'unknown' really 'resting in peace'? Not so far as many of their families are now concerned, given that DNA comparison could bring, at long last, real closure. Memorialisation alone, therefore, may no longer be enough. The Anderson family is very much a case in point.

Private Gilbert Anderson's brother, Gordon, entirely supported by his daughter, Tanja, is determined that one day her uncle's remains will be identified. Tanja says:

> My uncle, Gilbert, came to the Netherlands as a soldier to fight and help to end the war with Germany. I am sure that he and his comrades believed that the war would be over by Christmas 1944. They all knew the risks involved but, of course, they all wanted to survive and return home to their families. They didn't know what hell they were being sent into.
>
> At the end of 1945, however, the War Office sent the most terrible message to our family: 'Gilbert is missing in North West Europe', and, later, 'Gilbert was killed in action in North West Europe'. Gilbert was gone but nobody knew where his remains were.
>
> My grandmother, Elizabeth Anderson, did everything she could to find information; she wanted a grave for her son. She wanted to know what had happened to him. She wrote letters, attended commemorations in the UK and in the Netherlands. The first thing Thomas [Gilbert's elder brother] did upon return from a Japanese prison camp was write to the War Office for information about his lost brother. Aunty Leah [sister of Elizabeth], also tried to obtain information from the War Office.
>
> My father, Gordon, came to the Netherlands as a boy with his parents to attend commemorations; in 1953, Gordon came to live in the Netherlands and married my Dutch mother, Beppie. He then began doing everything possible to find his missing paratrooper brother. His wife and children knew that he had to

go to Arnhem to find Gilbert. He wrote letters, talked to veterans, authors, and historians. He bought books, maps, drawings, went to museums and attended a special meeting at Aldershot. He even corresponded with Father McGowan. No positive result was forthcoming.

One day, Gordon took his mother to Onderlangs and pointed out the place where he thought Gilberts field grave was located. Elizabeth cried and laid flowers. They did not know then that the field grave had been exhumed, and that Gilbert had been very likely put to rest in an 'unknown' grave at Oosterbeek War Cemetery.

In 2010, I had a talk with Gordon about his brother. He told me about his research and his dream. He dreamed that eight men emerged from a hole in the ground. Six walked away and two stayed behind. One of the two men was Gilbert, trying to tell Gordon something. But the dream was silent and Gordon had the feeling that he was watching the scene through a window. The scene was Onderlangs. Gordon talked about his research and the despair of not finding useful clues at all.

I felt his pain, grief and despair. I promised to do everything possible to help him, to find the grave and a headstone named Gilbert Anderson. A promise easily made but difficult to keep. I never knew that it would be this hard. First I started to read the personal letters Gilbert had written to his parents and little brother. The letters were from a nice young man. I started to search the internet. I corrected details on photos and information on different rolls of honour. We requested the Army Service Record from the MOD, and put Gilbert's letters into a timeline. This gave the letters context, and they became my guidance. I did everything I could to find information: wrote to Gilbert's former school, to the Salvation Army, to Members of Parliament (about Gilbert's effects and personal belongings). I became member of different online enthusiast forums and bought books. I made contact with the Dutch Red Cross, and with historian and author David van Buggenum in Arnhem. David, who is one of only two permit holders authorised to use a metal detector in the Renkum municipality for the purpose of locating unmarked field graves, brought the case of Gilbert to the attention of Dutch army officer and Arnhem historian Colonel Gerrit Pijpers, and Captain Geert Jonker, commander of the Royal Netherlands Army Recovery and Identification Unit (BIDKL). Gerrit Pijpers and the Dutch Red Cross requested that the BIDKL investigated Gilbert's case. At the same time, I came in contact with Geert Jonker on the ww2talk forum. These people helped me all they could. They gave me information, were honest about the slim chances of finding Gilbert, and were very patient in answering all of my many questions.

Every time I think there is no information to be found, or that I have tried everything, something happens. I do not how this works, but I am sure that Gilbert is not at peace because we, his family, are not at peace (it is not a religious thing, more a feeling or state of mind). My father and other family members, like a cousin in New Zealand (who has memories of Gilbert), still suffers the grief of this loss. So, I still have to go on and continue to do what I can. It will never come to the point that I will say to my Dad 'Sorry, but I cannot keep my promise'.

All the actions of Gilbert's mother, brother, aunt, cousin, the Dutch Red Cross, the BIDKL and others have led to the point where we think that Gilbert is buried in a particular war grave at Oosterbeek. Only DNA comparison will confirm whether Private Gilbert Anderson is at rest in grave 19/C/16.

Indeed, Gordon and Tanja feel very strongly that as the evidence available suggests that the occupant of 19/C/16 is very likely either Gilbert, Private Gordon Best, Private Harry Jenkin (who was perhaps the unknown body with no discs), or, as Captain Jonker says, 'possibly the obscure JC Younger', a DNA comparison should be allowed by the CWGC. This, they argue, would not require an exhumation, but a probing rod pushed into the sandy soil which would collect the necessary sample. Captain Jonker adds that 'In theory, this could be done, but ideally a 7 cm sample from a long bone, preferably a femur, would be required, in addition to a non-carious, unrestored, dental element'. Nonetheless, the family of Private Jenkin also supports the concept of a DNA comparison. Sadly, Private Best, although a married man, died childless, and no living blood relatives have yet been found. To strengthen the argument for such a test, ideally approval of the Best family would also be helpful. Nonetheless, either way, the Andersons would at least discover whether or not this is Gilbert – and may possibly find the closure they so desperately seek.

These matters, however, are far from simple, as Captain Jonker explains:

On 22 November 1944, the War Office still considered Gilbert Anderson to be a prisoner. Maybe no-one actually saw him killed; he is not mentioned in the post-war enquiries.

As for 4916025 Younger JC, my theory is that this could be a soldier of the 2nd South Staffordshire Regiment. The number block '491' was allocated to this Regiment. Only three missing Staffords have army numbers in this block: 4917909 Bates F (19-9), 4917787 Fellows JG (19-9) and 4917905 Gater SE (20-9). The latter's seems to come closest. Stan Gater is known to have been killed near the Museum when a shell hit a handcart containing mortar bombs. Of course, there is always the possibility that there actually was a '4916025 JC Younger', who was not at Arnhem personally but some item of his kit – like a belt or cross straps – was. There is a precedent of South Stafford burials at Onderlangs: 4917974 Private George Parkes, for example, who is on Father McGowan's original list, and, although not on that list, Major Philip Wright. I see many misinterpretations of discs in GRU/GCU records. The mistake in the

Army number of Private Parkes being a good example. These mistakes were caused by two things, mechanical and biological: discs were affected by war damage, by decomposition of the body, by blood, by fire, by acidic soil.

We must also remember that both physically and mentally this was hard, gruesome, work for the GRU/GCU people: investigating decomposing bodies, searching for discs, AB-64s, and personal effects. It is well-known that some of the personnel involved were hard drinkers – a coping mechanism. It is clear, however, that even though unpleasant and stressful nature of their work is appreciated, some of their reports are sloppy and leave room for improvement – especially in the not so straightforward cases and unknowns. Indeed, we now know how much depends on the quality of their work. It should have been a great help, for example, when all dental charts had been established by dentists; GRU/GCU personnel, however, could hardly be expected to understand whether a 'missing' dental element had either been lost post-mortem, extracted, or caused by peri-mortem trauma, was rudimentary, was impacted, unerupted, etc. So, all these years later, we must be aware of the circumstances at the time and records we now have to work with.

Why, some may ask, is this so important, so many years later? The missing are, after all, remembered by name on local memorials and specific monuments. Tanja Anderson explains why:

> I believe that every soldier who goes to war, fighting for freedom and peace but who ends up wounded, captured or killed, should be treated with all possible respect by both his own country and that where the battle took place. Their field graves should be protected against grave robbers; their remains should be identified and buried in an individual grave with a named headstone. They lost their most important possession: their lives. When a soldier is killed, their families suffer a terrible loss. They need a grave not only to grieve at but also to take away their sorrows and worries. They need something to confirm that their loved ones are not coming home anymore. Before a soldier was sent to battle, they used to write a farewell letter. When a father or mother receives this final letter they have reason to worry and fear that the most terrible official message follows: killed in action. But when a soldier is missing or ends up in a unknown grave, the suffering of these families goes on and on and on and on. That is why I want DNA comparison on grave 19/C/16 and, if necessary, other graves – to give the soldier respect deserved and his family's suffering.

Perhaps, if ever this case is officially considered by the CWGC, and policy permits a DNA investigation, this moving letter, written recently by Gordon Anderson to his deceased brother, should be read:

Mrs Anderson, Private Gilbert Anderson's mother, with his younger brother, Gordon, remembering their 'missing' loved one at the Airborne Cemetery. (Tanja Anderson)

Gordon Anderson is unable to accept that the authorities cannot do more to identify his 'missing' brother. Research indicates that grave 19/C/16, at which Gordon is pictured here, which contains the remains of an unknown airborne soldier, could well be either Privates Anderson, Jenkin or Best. All three families require a DNA test, but this is contrary to CWGC policy. How reasonable this is, given advances in forensic science, is for the reader to decide. (Tanja Anderson)

GILBERT ANDERSON, HARRY JENKIN AND GORDON BEST

It is very strange writing this over you, my brother. Strange because I hardly had the time to get to know you better. In the time that I came to know you, I was really too young to realize what was happening all around me. In that time, you were already in the army but when you came home on leave you left very vivid memories with me.

Those memories were all quite short. You always let me empty your kit bag and took care to put something in it for me right at the bottom. When the sirens sounded, we would go to the back door and pretend to shoot them German planes down, and you would tell me some of the things you and your pals had done in training. Boy oh boy, you made me feel as if I was as big as you!

Even after you had left us to go to Arnhem, you tried to help me. Strange but you must have been watching over me because you contacted me in my dreams by 'Onderlangs' in Arnhem, trying to reassure and guide me. I still feel that you are watching.

After a while I did not know what further steps I should take in my search for you and then all at once more family and friends joined me. I do feel that you know this already.

You might be listed as 'unknown' but, Gilbert, you are definitely not forgotten.

The names of Privates Anderson, Best and Jenkin all appear on the memorial at Groesbeek to the many 'missing' from this theatre of war. For their families, those engraved names on that symbolic cenotaph are their only form of closure. No grave for them to weep at. No grave for 'Flower Children' to place floral tributes every September. Just names engraved in cold stone far away. Whether that will ever change currently remains a matter of conjecture.

Chapter 9

Private Patrick Taylor, 156th Parachute Battalion, and Private Albert Willingham, 10th Parachute Battalion

The selection of landing sites so far from the 1st Airborne Division's objective was the RAF's decision, dictated by the need to avoid flak concentrations and because of heavily-wooded countryside around Arnhem. That the division was dropped over two days was also an air decision, due to there being insufficient aircraft to transport the entire division in one lift. As we have seen, this meant that the three battalions of the Air Landing Brigade had to remain at and maintain the drop zones until after the second lift on 18 September 1944, leaving only the three parachute battalions of 1st Parachute Brigade to fight their way through to Arnhem Bridge – eight miles away. Although Brigadier Hicks was forced to revise the original plan due to 1st Parachute Brigade's failure to reach Lieutenant Colonel Frost at the bridge, sending the 2nd South Staffords into battle at Arnhem, the other two battalions of his Air Landing Brigade had to stay put. By this time fighting had broken out for possession of the landing grounds, and so 4th Parachute Brigade, comprising 10th, 11th, and 156th Parachute Battalions, had the unenviable task of dropping onto a 'hot' landing zone. Brigadier John 'Shan' Hackett commented that:

> In retrospect, it was crazy for my Brigade to drop on the second day with all surprise gone, but we realized that we had to get into the battle after all these cancellations. You can't go on doing that to troops of quality. They were so good, so fit, so keyed up, so keen to get on, that you had to get into the battle at almost any price. So, shortcomings in the plan were readily forgiven so long as we could get there.

There was also a third glider lift expected north of the river on 19 September 1944, bringing in elements of the Polish Independent Parachute Brigade Group, the drop of the remainder of which, south of the river, near Driel, had been postponed by a further day owing to bad weather – yet another major setback for the airborne troops holding on gallantly at Arnhem Bridge. The third glider lift would also bring in attached 4th Parachute Brigade units. It was hardly an ideal scenario.

Geoffrey Powell, a company commander in 156th Parachute Battalion and later a respected commentator on the battle, suggested in his excellent book *The Devil's Birthday* that it may have actually been advantageous not to have a second lift at all, because without the need to maintain the landing grounds for two days, both 1st Parachute Brigade and Air Landing Brigade, six fighting battalions in all, would have been available to take Arnhem Bridge on 17 September 1944. Be that as it may, a second lift there was.

The 10th Parachute Battalion had been raised in Egypt on 1 January 1943, comprising volunteers from the 2nd Royal Sussex Regiment, with Lieutenant Colonel K.B.I. Smyth commanding. 11th Parachute Battalion followed on 4 March 1943, and by September 1944 was commanded by Lieutenant Colonel George Lea DSO. Recruitment, however, was difficult for this new unit, due mainly to a lack of volunteers owing to the extent of casualties, and because 10th and 156th Parachute Battalions took precedence. Nonetheless, an influx of personnel from 1st Special Air Service Regiment, which was reducing establishment, and the successful work of recruiting teams addressed this issue. Both new battalions, in fact, were built around the existing 156th Parachute Battalion, which had been raised in India during 1941, before joining the two new battalions at Kabrit, in Egypt, in 1943; the 156th would be taken to Holland by Lieutenant Colonel Richard des Voeux. Brigadier Hackett's 4th Parachute Brigade was, however, the least combat experienced of the 1st Airborne Division's two parachute brigades. Both 10th and 156th Parachute Battalions had participated in the seaborne landings at Taranto, Italy, but only 11th Parachute Battalion had dropped into action, on 14 September 1943. On that occasion, Lea's men dropped on and secured the Greek island of Kos. Afterwards, 4th Parachute Brigade returned to England and began training for the 'Great Adventure' – the Allied liberation of enemy-occupied mainland Europe.

General Urquhart's plan was for 4th Parachute Brigade to arrive in Holland on Monday, 18 September 1944, immediately striking eastwards along the Amsterdamseweg to link up with elements of 1st Parachute Brigade between the main roads out of Arnhem to Apeldoorn and Ede. The original idea was for 2nd and 3rd Parachute Battalions to push on into Arnhem, whilst 1st Parachute Battalion secured and held the high ground and arterial roads north of the city – where 4th Parachute Brigade was to meet them and extend the defensive ring. Before the second lift even arrived, however, that plan had by necessity been revised. The urgent need to reinforce Lieutenant Colonel Frost's 2nd Parachute Battalion at Arnhem Bridge had seen 1st Parachute Battalion abandon its attempt to reach the high ground objective. The 4th Parachute Brigade was badly needed to bolster efforts to reach the all-important bridge, the crescendo of which would begin around 0400 hrs on Tuesday, 19 September. Moreover, due to General Urquhart being cut off from his Division and in hiding, following a failed attempt to get through to Frost, Brigadier 'Pip' Hicks of Air Landing Brigade was now commanding the Division. Owing to the urgent need to reinforce the small force at Arnhem Bridge, Hicks had not only reduced his force defending the landing grounds by sending the South Staffords into Arnhem, but had also decided to detach 11th Parachute Battalion upon arrival to join the effort attempting to reinforce Frost. None of this, owing to the breakdown in communications, was known to Brigadier Hackett, who was still awaiting his brigade's flight to Holland. The original plan was for the second lift to take off at first light on 18 September 1944, but in the event low-lying cloud over England delayed this for four hours. Eventually, at 1120 hrs, 4th Parachute Brigade was at last on its way.

The Germans, of course, anticipated the arrival of reinforcements, so the drop zones were by now the scene of fighting. Without news of when the overdue second lift would arrive, the landing grounds were grimly held in the face of increasing enemy opposition – including a strafing attack by a whole *gruppe* of German fighters. Fortunately, when the second aerial armada did arrive from England, the Me 109s were refuelling and rearming at their bases in Germany. In anticipation of the likely direction of approach, however, German flak defences had been increased accordingly – easy enough to do, given the volume of vehicles available toting anti-aircraft guns of varying calibres. Whereas the first drop had gone entirely to plan, achieving surprise and without mishap, these were very different circumstances. The first aircraft to arrive, flying slow and straight, from a direction of Nijmegen and passing over a mobile, *ad hoc* flak concentration, were two American troop-carrying C-47 groups. In the van, droning ponderously towards DZ 'Y' at Ginkel Heide, north-west of Wolfheze, at 1500 hrs, was 156th Parachute Battalion.

Major Geoffrey Powell stood in the doorway of a C-47, preparing to jump, when:

> Suddenly the flak was real. As I looked back down the line, the plane just behind seemed to lurch to one side, a bright red spot on its port wing glowing in the sunshine before it spread in a sheet of flame towards the fuselage. Then the nose of the plane dipped, and it disappeared from view. No. parachutes appeared. I knew that it carried men from the Battalion, and tried to stop speculating who was inside it.

The stricken aircraft, hit at 1345 hrs near Nijmegen, was C-47 'Skytrain' 43-15180 (A-31, chalk number 619), of 50 Troop Carrier Squadron, 314 Troop Carrier Group, of the 9th American Air Force's 52 Troop Carrier Wing based at Saltby. Aboard were an American crew of six, the pilot being Captain Leonard Ottoway, and eighteen paratroopers: half of 156th Parachute Battalion's Medium Machine-Gun Platoon. With his port engine and fuel tank ablaze, Ottoway – the holder of the Air Medal with two Oak Leaf Clusters – fought to maintain control and crash-land beside the Bonegraffseweg, between Ochten and Dodewaard, twelve miles south of Oosterbeek. Tragically this courageous act was all for nought: upon impact the C-47's undercarriage collapsed and the machine exploded. There were no survivors. Amongst the dead was nineteen-year-old Private 14640602 Patrick Taylor of Malvern Link, Worcestershire.

Born on 5 April 1925, to William and Caroline Taylor of 37 Quest Hills Road, Malvern Link, Worcestershire, 'Pat' was one of a large family and initially enlisted in his local Worcestershire Regiment. Earlier in 1944, however, he had volunteered for and successfully completed parachute training before joining 156th Parachute Battalion. Before leaving for Arnhem, Private Taylor had returned home on leave. His younger brother, Rob, however, was suffering from a contagious disease and in quarantine: 'Pat couldn't come in to see me, but I stood at the window and waved to him, as he stood in his red beret and battledress at the bottom of the drive. He was my hero and I was ever so proud of my paratrooper big brother. It was the last time I ever saw him.'

One of the British paratroopers, Private Thomas Stevens, was thrown clear during the explosion, but was mortally injured; with a broken back and dreadful burns, he died the following day. Under supervision of Dr van Driel, the bodies were buried adjacent to the crash site. Due to the fire, none could be individually identified, but the head count later confirmed that all present aboard the 'Skytrain' were accounted for. After the war, the co-pilot, Captain Herbert Pluemer Jr, was 'repatriated to New Jersey', whilst his crewmates were reinterred at the Ardennes American Cemetery at Neupre-Neuville. All eighteen paratroopers were buried together at Jonkerbos War Cemetery, near where they died, in a mass grave. Their individual headstones are all inscribed 'buried near this spot'. More recently, movingly, the Dutch have erected a memorial at the roadside, remembering these young sky soldiers who came to free them from Nazi oppression so long ago.

Private Patrick Taylor, 156 Parachute Battalion. (Rob Taylor)

Soon after the war, a Corporal F. Scrivens, then living in King's Heath, Birmingham, wrote to the authorities concerning Private Taylor's fate:

> When I landed on the ground I looked in the air for a moment or two, I saw the engine of one of the planes coming along the DZ catch fire, the plane continuing on its flight, the fire getting worse. It then occurred to me that I had not seen anyone jump; the plane was coming down fast and was only about 100 feet up when I last saw it. When we assembled at the DZ I heard that it was one of our 'S' Company planes. Later I was told that it was the MG Section plane, of which Section Private Taylor was a member. I knew Taylor slightly as is natural as my family belong to Malvern and one likes to meet anyone from the home place.
>
> I gave the above information to Mrs Taylor because according to her daughter a chap had been to their home and said he saw Private Taylor on Arnhem Bridge on the Friday following the start of the operation. Seeing that I belonged to 156th Parachute Battalion myself I knew that we never got to the bridge, especially the MG Section.

ARNHEM 1944

The memorial at Ochten, commemorating all who perished on 18 September 1944, when Dakota chalk number 619 of the 9th American Air Force's 52 Troop Carrier Wing crashed in flames in the field behind. Six American crewmen and eighteen British paratroopers of 156 Parachute Battalion's Medium Machine-Gun Platoon lost their lives as a result – including nineteen-year-old Private Taylor. (Marcel Boven)

Although all those who died in the Ochten crash were found, individual identification proved impossible. All are buried together at Jonkerbos, near Nijmegen, but who is beneath which stone is unknown – hence the inscription of Private Taylor's headstone. (Author)

PATRICK TAYLOR AND ALBERT WILLINGHAM

Uniquely in this book, Private Taylor is not buried at the Arnhem-Oosterbeek War Cemetery – but the loss of Captain Ottaway's aircraft and half of 156th Parachute Battalion's Medium Machine-Gun Platoon, was very much a portent of what was to follow for 4th Parachute Brigade and, indeed, the outcome of Operation MARKET-GARDEN.

As the Allied armada held course and droned on to Ginkel Heide, however, Major Geoffrey Powell prepared to jump:

> I never saw the red light turn to green . . . I was out of the door . . . I looked up at a sky choked with hundreds of parachutes, most of them patterned in green and brown camouflage, but others a galaxy of colours, red and orange, purple, blue and yellow, vivid against the scattered white clouds. Every moment more aircraft arrived to disgorge their cargoes into the crowded air. Then I noticed the humming. We were being shot at from the ground. There were *Boche* on the dropping zone. Something was badly wrong.

'Badly wrong' was right. Unbeknown to Brigadier Hackett, Brigadier Hicks, in General Urquhart's enforced temporary absence, now commanded the division; although senior to Hicks in the Army List, Hackett was a cavalry commander, whilst Hicks was an infantryman and therefore possessed more experience relevant to the operation in hand. Moreover, Hicks had been on the ground since the first lift, whereas Hackett had not. Understandably, Brigadier Hackett was especially unhappy that the battalion he was to lose had been pre-selected without reference to himself. Although feelings certainly ran high, it is likely that certain accounts are exaggerated of just how heated the brigadiers' meeting at the Hartenstein Hotel really was. Indeed, Brigadier Hicks, agreed to modify the plan to fight through to Frost by accepting the frustrated Brigadier Hackett's proposal: 4th Parachute Brigade, minus 11th Parachute Battalion but instead with the King's Own Scottish Borderers within the battle group, would strike out along the Arnhem-Utrecht railway line to seize the ridge at Koepel (where the Arnhem-Oosterbeek War Cemetery is now located). Whilst 1st Parachute Brigade continued to attack via the main Utrechtseweg into Arnhem, the idea was that 4th Parachute Brigade could open up a new sector through which reinforcements might reach 'Johnny at the Bridge'. Nonetheless, the commander of 4th Parachute Brigade considered it a 'grossly untidy situation'.

Although Brigadier Hackett scheduled his composite brigade's attack to start before first light the following morning, Lieutenant Colonel des Voeux pushed on well into the night with 156th Parachute Battalion, the lead company of which halted in woods near the Dreijenseweg, just a mile short of the Koepel objective. Ahead, unbeknown to the paratroopers, was *Sperrline*-Spindler, by now a substantial and well-equipped enemy force largely comprising men of the 9-SS *Panzer* Division. Unable to outflank the Germans, Des Voeux's lead company, commanded by Major Geoffrey Powell, withdrew and settled down for the night as best they could. What lay ahead for 156th Parachute Battalion would be bitter fighting, with many casualties, in those leafy Dutch woods.

At 1100 hrs on Monday, 18 September 1944, following a three-hour delay due to bad weather, some 550 men of Lieutenant Colonel Ken Smyth's 10th Parachute Battalion had departed RAF Spanhoe, near Rutland, bound upon the 'Northern Route' for DZ 'Y' at Ginkel Heath. Having made most of the flight at 1,500 feet, the American Dakotas dropped to 500 feet before running in over the DZ in the face of increasing flak: two of 10th Parachute Battalion's C-47s were hit before reaching their objective. Most reached Ginkel unmolested, but on the ground the Air Landing Brigade's 7th King's Own Scottish Borderers were hotly engaged with SS-*Wach Bataillon* 3, most personnel of which were Dutch and Ukrainian Nazis. This 600-man strong unit provided guards for concentration camps in the Netherlands; recruitment standards were low and training poor, and these men had blood on their hands: from the end of June to beginning of September 1944, SS-*Sturmbannführer* Paul Helle's men had murdered several hundred prisoners at Vught. In the Arnhem battle, Helle would lose 200 men, whilst a further 200 deserted. This SS formation, therefore, was not of the same quality as Krafft's men or, indeed, those of *Hohenstaufen* and *Frundsberg*. The Germans, however, were increasingly reinforcing Arnhem with miscellaneous units, including airmen and sailors pushed into an infantry role due to a lack of aircraft and vessels. Ideal troops they may not have been, certainly nowhere near the standard of elite paratroopers, but there were many of them, with plenty of weapons and ammunition.

By the time of the second drop, SS-*Sturmbannführer* Helle's somewhat dubious unit was threatening certain of the proposed rendezvous points for the 4th Parachute Brigade. Unlike the previous day when 1st Parachute Brigade achieved complete surprise, Brigadier Hackett's men leapt out onto what was a 'hot' DZ. Amongst those of 'Chalk 673' was Private Albert Willingham, a veteran of 10th Parachute Battalion who was, according to his family, 'a most unlikely hero'.

Albert Willingham was born in Portsmouth, Hampshire, on 30 June 1915, the son of George Henry, a stoker on HMS *Inconstant* and a veteran of the Battle of Jutland, and Rose Willingham, of 24 Ethel Road, Kingston. The Willinghams were Roman Catholics, and Albert was one of eleven children born to this working-class couple, two of whom died at an early age. Growing up in the hard environment of Portsmouth between the wars, in a large sporting family, Albert was a fighter, developing an interest and ability in boxing, which would lead to a friendship with the famous boxer Jack Dempsey. After leaving Portsdown School, Albert became a farm labourer at Denmead. In search of a better life he wanted to join the Royal Navy but was rejected, his late sister Eva recalled, due to a 'hammer toe', a condition in which a toe is bent downwards, usually due to ill-fitting footwear. This, however, seems unlikely, given that Albert enlisted, aged nineteen (not sixteen, as previously believed and published elsewhere), into the Dorsetshire Regiment at Portsmouth on 9 July 1934. According to his description on his enlistment papers into the Regular Army, 5725153 Private Albert

Rose and George Willingham, the parents of Private Albert Willingham, 10th Parachute Battalion. (Kim Hymers)

A young Albert Willingham (left), with friend in 'civvies' before the war. (Kim Hymers)

Willingham was A1 fit, 5ft 5in tall, weighed 118lbs, had a 'fresh' complexion and brown hair. Albert was now set on the path which would lead to Oosterbeek, ten years later.

Having joined the 2nd Battalion, Private Willingham served at home between 9 July 1934 and 9 March 1936, when he went to Palestine (where he 'forfeited seven days' pay' for an unknown misdemeanour on 24 October 1936). On 2 January 1937, the 2nd Battalion returned home, and on 9 March 1937, Albert was posted to the 1st Battalion, leaving with his new unit for India the following day. There, on 30 October 1937, Private Willingham represented his Battalion in an army boxing bout, winning a silver cup as

Private Albert Willingham served in Palestine with the 2nd Dorsets 1936/37, where this photograph was taken. (second left, rear row). (Kim Hymers)

runner up. On 16 June 1939, 1st Battalion was deployed from India to the Mediterranean island of Malta, where, with the 2nd Devonshires, the Dorset men garrisoned the island. Malta was, of course, the key British base in the Mediterranean, from where the Royal Navy and RAF disrupted the supply route of Rommel's much-vaunted *Afrika Korps*. Consequently, the little island was besieged, subjected to sustained air attacks which, according to one RAF fighter pilot survivor, 'made the Battle of Britain look like child's play'. In an experience which still has currency today, as it does in Arnhem and Oosterbeek, Allied servicemen and Maltese civilians endured this violent onslaught and associated deprivations together. Ultimately Rommel was defeated and the Germans pushed out of North Africa, lifting the dreadful siege which won the rocky island fortress a unique George Cross. Private Willingham was there throughout, but was not with the 2nd Dorsets when Sicily was invaded in July 1943: on 7 May 1943, he transferred to the Army Air Corps and became a paratrooper. After qualifying as a parachutist at RAF

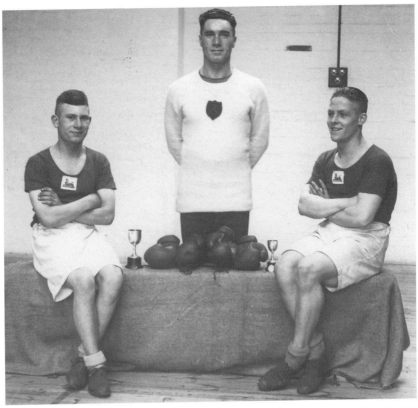

Private Willingham, having transferred to and represented the 1st Dorsets in a boxing bout he finished as runner up, India, 30 October 1937. (Kim Hymers)

Kirbrit in Egypt, on 40 Parachute Course, Private Willingham was posted to join 10th Parachute Battalion, also in 'British North Africa', on 2 August 1943.

On 9 September 1943, 10th Parachute Battalion was detailed to participate in Operation SLAPSTICK, an attempt to hide from the Germans the main location for the Allied invasion of Italy at Salerno. SLAPSTICK was the seizure of the Italian ports at Taranto, Bari and Brindisi – but by sea, not by air. Only 10th and 156th Parachute Battalions were available for the 4th Parachute Brigade

The boxing trophy Private Willingham won in India. (Author)

contribution to this effort; fortunately, the landings were unopposed but battle was soon joined. Later tasked with taking the airfield at Gioia del Colle, thirty miles inland, near the town of Castellaneta, 10th Parachute Battalion was engaged by enemy *Fallschirmjäger* who blocked the way. The subsequent successful assault claimed the divisional commander's life. Two days later, 10th Parachute Battalion reached Bari and Brindisi, playing no further part in operations and was withdrawn back to England. Private Willingham, however, remained in Italy – in hospital. According to Albert's sister Eva, he had been 'badly injured by an Arab who crept up on him with a knife in the darkness and drew a lot of blood. He was sent back to England and his wound was still weeping when he persuaded the Army to let him take part in the greatest airborne operation of the war – Arnhem.' His Service & Casualty Form (Part One), however, clearly states that Private Willingham was admitted to 133 Parachute Field Ambulance Unit on 16 September 1943, having been 'wounded in action', but the nature or circumstances of the wound are unrecorded. It is likely, however, that he was amongst the five Other Ranks of 'B' Company wounded in Gioia, fighting against German paratroopers, that day. Whatever the wound was, it was sufficiently serious for him to be transferred to 95 General Hospital on 23 October 1943, where he remained until embarking for England on 26 December 1943, arriving on 5 January 1944. Back home, Albert re-joined 10th Parachute Battalion, serving in HQ Company. Before leaving for the Netherlands on Operation MARKET-GARDEN, Albert went home to Portsmouth on leave, as his Eva later recalled: 'He must have had a premonition. When I went to kiss him goodbye, he cried. I said "What's the matter?" He said "I won't be coming back this time".'

Private Willingham, however, survived what was his first combat jump, under fire, on 18 September 1944. Others were not so lucky. Green smoke guided the new arrivals towards their new rendezvous point. SS-*Wach Bataillon* 3 continued to pour fire onto the position, until Major Peter Warr's 'B' Company overran the enemy. Lieutenant Colonel Smyth's men then dug in, whilst he awaited further orders from Brigadier Hackett, who, as we have seen, was dealing with a changed situation and had received new instructions from Brigadier Hicks. Subsequently Brigadier Hackett's revised plan was for

Private Willingham whilst serving on Malta with the Dorsets. (Kim Hymers)

11th Parachute Battalion to come under 1st Parachute Brigade's command, 156th to move into 11th's position and lead 4th Parachute Brigade into Arnhem via the railway line, and for 10th Parachute Battalion to 'hold firm area "Rendezvous Wood"'. As the brigadier later wrote, 'The 10th were firm . . . being attacked from time to time in a desultory manner and incurred casualties. My intention was to move the Brigade less 11th Battalion towards the centre of Divisional activity as quickly as was compatible with the retention of its coherence.' Heavy casualties, though, delayed the move off until evening, 10th Parachute Battalion pushing on at 1900 hrs. Although hoping to reach Arnhem by midnight, at dusk Smyth was ordered to halt for the night before reaching the all-important railway line. Early the following morning, 10th Parachute Battalion moved forward towards Koepel, to the north of 156th Parachute Battalion and therefore became the most northerly and exposed British unit striking towards Arnhem.

Private Albert Willingham, 10th Parachute Battalion. (Rosy Tee)

The plan was for 156th Parachute Battalion to take and hold the Lichtenbeek woods whilst 10th Parachute Battalion held the main Ede-Arnhem road (Amsterdamseweg), protecting the former's left flank. With Lichtenbeek secure, the parachute battalions could then take the 'Koepel' high ground – so-called after a tea house on the site. The Germans, however, had other ideas. This, the Dreijenseweg, a connecting road between upper Oosterbeek and the Amsterdamseweg, was now a substantial blocking line. That imposed by SS-*Sturmbannführer* Krafft along the Wolfheze road on the first day was immediate but understandably comparatively weak – although nonetheless very effective. This line, however, was a formidable obstruction to 4th Parachute Brigade's intended route of march towards Arnhem. The Germans knew full-well that Lieutenant Colonel Frost must not, under any circumstances, be significantly reinforced at Arnhem Bridge. The equally determined airborne troops likewise appreciated the urgency of reaching Frost's gallant but beleaguered force – and it was here and now that the matter would fatefully be decided. The German advantage, of course, was heavy weapons, a plentiful supply of ammunition – and armour. And amongst these German troops were *Waffen*-SS veterans of extensive combat experience who provided a backbone of steel to the enemy's defence.

Having reached the main road, 10th Parachute Battalion needed to take the Amsterdamseweg-Dreijenseweg crossroads – which is where the real trouble started. The Dreijensweg is a long, straight road, with woods either side, stretching from the Amsterdamseweg south to upper Oosterbeek railway crossing. At the crossroads is located the Leeren Doedel Hotel, taken over by the Germans as a field headquarters and aid post, the Dreijensweg being the substantial blocking line imposed by SS-

Obersturmbannführer Ludwig Spindler – a collection of various units now fighting as *Kampgruppe* Spindler. Around the crossroads guns of 9th SS *Flak-Abteilung* were located, and armour, including tanks and self-propelled guns, prowled menacingly up and down the road, determined to prevent the British crossing the Dreijensweg and making any further progress towards Arnhem.

Up ahead of 10th Parachute Battalion were two mobile flak guns, *Flakpanzer* IV *Möbelwagen*, a 3.7cm Flak 43 gun mounted on a *Panzer* IV chassis, also of *Hohenstaufen*'s SS-Panzer-Flak-Abteilung 9. Firing high-explosive shells, one of these rapidly knocked out Lieutenant Colonel Smyth's jeep as his battalion came under fire and was forced to take cover in the wood on the road's southern side. With 'A' Company providing protection to the northern flank, the remainder of 10th Parachute Battalion headed eastwards through the wood, reaching the edge of it – where, within sight of the Leeren Doedel Hotel and the Dreijenseweg, the German defenders opened heavy fire. There was no chance of crossing the open ground ahead, so the paratroopers shrank back into the woods, only to suffer a bombardment by artillery and mortar rounds. Private Willingham and 10th Parachute Battalion HQ Company were further back, their rear protected by 'S' Company. The battalion dug in, but HQ Company was soon probing forward, trying to find out what was happening up front.

Lieutenant Colonel Smyth received warning of yet another threat – thirty half-tracks full of *panzergrenadiers* approaching his position from a direction of Arnhem. The Germans deployed and swept the area with fire, forcing HQ Company to go to ground and dig in. The situation was getting worse by the minute – and 156th Parachute Battalion was unfortunately faring no better. The woods offered little real cover, and the open ground ahead was impossible to cross. Casualties mounted. 10th Parachute Battalion had no armour or artillery support, so Lieutenant Colonel Smyth responded with his 3in mortars, sited near Battalion HQ. The tragedy is that the Light Regiment's guns, sited around the Ter Horst house and Old Church in Lower Oosterbeek, were easily within range – but could not be called into action owing to the breakdown in radio communications. The only weapon capable of engaging armour was the PIAT, but ammunition for that contraption and Smyth's mortars soon ran short. The troublesome *Möbelwagen* were still an issue, advancing from a pumping station at the crossroads and firing into the trees, causing air bursts which rained down deadly splinters. It was a mess. Nonetheless, the paratroopers fought back as best they could, with grenades, the PIAT and mortar fire – but this was unsustainable given the pressure being brought to bear by 9th SS.

Free from his attic incarceration, General Urquhart was back on the move and visited Brigadier Hackett's HQ near the railway embankment. It is important to appreciate that this high sided obstacle is substantial, and, in 4th Parachute Brigade's area, can only be negotiated by vehicles at three points: the storm-water culvert below Wolfheze, where the Reconnaissance Squadron's jeeps had been ambushed, and the crossings at Upper Oosterbeek and Wolfheze. 4th Parachute Brigade was vulnerable due to mainly being north of the railway line, whilst the remainder of 1st Airborne Division was to the south, between the railway and river. The Germans were in possession of the railway crossing at Oosterbeek, and self-propelled guns and other tracked armoured vehicles were being drawn to the area like moths to a flame. Around 1500 hrs, Brigadier Hackett received the disconcerting news that more enemy troops were approaching from the west – which would cut off his brigade from the division. By now, the Germans had formed substantial composite battle groups, *Kampfgruppen*, and this latest threat from the west was significant: *Kampfgruppe* Von Tettau – which was of divisional strength. There was now no option but to withdraw 10th Parachute Battalion to Wolfheze, just over two miles away, given that the Germans already held the closer point at Oosterbeek, at the southern end of the Dreijensweg. Smyth was to hold the Wolfheze crossing until 4th Parachute Brigade was safely over it. With Von Tettau approaching from the west, there was a degree of urgency attached to 10th Parachute Battalion disengaging and covering the distance to Wolfheze. With his men still heavily engaged, at least one company being overrun by tanks, Lieutenant Colonel Smyth ordered 10th Parachute Battalion to withdraw from contact and retreat towards Wolfheze, there being no question, such was the pressure, of awaiting the cover of darkness. As Smyth retreated back along the Amsterdamseweg, SS-*Sturmbannführer* Krafft's men – who had caused so much trouble on the first day – attacked from the north, whilst *Kampfgruppe* Spindler pursued them from the east. The fighting – hand-to-hand and at the point of the bayonet – was evil, and further casualties mounted. As Brigadier Hackett wrote, 10th Parachute Battalion consequently became 'disorganised'. Things were about to go from bad to even worse.

To reach Wolfheze, it was necessary for 10th Parachute Battalion to cross several open fields, which, inevitably, were raked by German machine guns. To contextualise this trauma, Dutch fields are typically much bigger than English meadows, and these around Johannahoeve were no different – a fearful proposition to cross under fire. Having inevitably sustained more casualties, the survivors eventually reached the comparative safety of the woods around Johannahoeve. En route, along the railway line by Wolfheze, was where Captain Lionel Queripel was last seen, whose example had been an inspiration: his 'signal act of valour' – one of many – earning the 24-year-old a posthumous Victoria Cross. Beyond the trees at Johannahoeve, however, was more fire-swept open ground. By now, the exhausted men were crossing part of LZ 'L', east of Wolfheze. There, men of the King's Own Scottish Borderers still patiently waited in anticipation of the long overdue third lift – gliders bringing in the jeeps and anti-tank guns of General Stanislaw Sosabowski's Polish Independent Parachute Brigade. Already assailed by the enemy, without radio communications and no means of knowing when or even if the overdue third lift would arrive, the Borderers had no option but to hang on. The problem was exacerbated by 4th Parachute Brigade's retreat under fire to Wolfheze, the enemy hot on their heels and thereby bringing even more German troops

The field and woods near Johanna Hoeve, through which men of 4th Parachute Brigade made their fighting withdrawal. (Author)

The straight Dreijenseweg, running from northern Oosterbeek to the Amsterdamseweg, along which the Germans placed a blocking line 156th Parachute Battalion was unable to penetrate. (Author)

Airborne marker commemorating the battle fought on the Dreijenseweg by 156th Parachute Battalion. (Author)

and vehicles towards LZ 'L' – threatening to overrun the field. And then the gliders arrived.

As the unescorted Stirlings released their charges, a *schwarm* of Me 109s appeared, shooting up the defenceless Horsas approaching LZ 'L'. Attacked by Me 109s and fired upon from the ground, miraculously, although a number of gliders were hit, only one was destroyed. As the gliders descended below the treeline, they were, in fact, relatively safe from flak owing to the guns being unable to depress sufficiently. On the ground, a Polish correspondent, Swiecicki, saw the woods surrounding LZ 'L' 'erupt in fire. Everything – mortars, machine guns and even individual rifles.' Brigadier Hackett later wrote that the 'enemy reaction was instantaneous and violent'. Strafed by German fighters, those who landed safely struggled to get their equipment unloaded as German troops attacked. 4th Parachute Brigade, already relentlessly pursued by Krafft and Spindler, now had to cross this inferno, also being engaged by Marine *Kampfgruppe* 642, *Kampfgruppe* Bruhn and *Bataillon* Eberwein as it fought its way through to Wolfheze. Upon reaching the village, the paratroopers were doubtless relieved to find it largely unoccupied by the enemy. The survivors of 10th Parachute Battalion numbered less than 100 men, along with some from the 156th and other units. Fortunately, there was no further enemy attack that evening, and the Brigade's vehicles all arrived safely via the culvert. In just twelve dreadful hours, 4th Parachute Battalion had lost half its strength – and twenty-nine of the fifty-four dead were from 10th Parachute Battalion.

Private Albert Willingham was amongst the survivors of 19 September 1944 – a disastrous day, on which the fate of the Battle of Arnhem had hung in the balance but ultimately swung, irretrievably, against the 1st Airborne Division. 1st Parachute Brigade's brave effort to push on along Tiger Route to 'Johnny at the bridge' had ended in a massacre; 4th Parachute Brigade's attack had been violently repulsed, the parachute battalions involved also decimated. Furthermore, the enemy was in possession of the supply drop zones and enjoying extra rations from England – delivered at great cost in life by the RAF – but General Urquhart's men were not, therefore, being sustained with further ammunition, food or medical supplies. Lieutenant Colonel Frost still held the northern end of Arnhem Bridge, however, and the bulk of Urquhart's force, unable to penetrate the German blocking line and reach Frost, would soon be concentrated within a thumb-shaped defensive perimeter at Oosterbeek, from the southern side of the upper Oosterbeek railway embankment to the Rhine. It was clear that there was now no question whatsoever of reinforcing John Frost at Arnhem Bridge – a bitter pill for all involved and not least General Urquhart: 'It was an awful conclusion to come to: it meant the abandonment of those men at the Bridge who had endured the most terrible battering. But with the weak force I had left, I could no more hope to reinforce Frost than reach Berlin. Clearly the Germans now controlled every route into the town and Bridge. They were being strengthened almost hourly, and their Tiger tanks were causing havoc. Already the best part of four battalions in the town had ceased to exist.' In due course, the General would 'order Hackett to forget the ultimate idea of pressing into the town, but to bring his brigade, or that part of it which survived, into positions on the north-east side of our area. At all costs, we now had to concentrate on holding a perimeter which would form a small bridgehead north of the Neder Rhine once XXX Corps caught up with us. It was essential now to save what we had left.'

Fortunately, the Germans did not, for some reason, press home their attack on Wolfheze that evening or during the night. Having found some respite from the fray north of the railway line, Brigadier Hackett now had to get his battered remnants from their current comparatively safe harbour into the divisional area at nearby Oosterbeek. Between his position and the British western flank, however, was the Bilderberg woods, surrounding the Hotel Bilderberg and from which Krafft's men had engaged 3rd Parachute Battalion after the first drop. The Germans were wide awake by now and in close contact. Just west of the Hotel, at the junction of the significant Breedelaan and Van Tienhovenlaan, Hackett's column was checked and halted by strong opposition. Less than a mile to the east, along the nearby Utrechtseweg, was Divisional HQ at the Hartenstein Hotel – so near and yet so far. The 4th Parachute Brigade group was mortared and shelled by the much-feared six-barrelled *Nebelwerfer*, known as 'Moaning Minnie' on account of the high-pitched shriek accompanying each round. At mid-day, Lieutenant Colonel Smyth was wounded in the leg and arm, but pressed on. Brigadier Hackett found the enemy too strong ahead of him, so was unable to fight his way the short distance south to the Utrechtseweg, but found a weak spot in the woods to the east. His Brigade Major, Major Dawson, skirmished ahead in that direction, 'killing a number of Jerries'. 156th Parachute Battalion, or what was left of it, was to hold the position whilst 10th Parachute Battalion tried to get through eastward.

Eventually, after more casualties which included the gallant brigade major, Brigadier Hackett ended up taking refuge in a depression, now known as 'Hackett's Hollow', to the east of the Hotel, on the eastern edge of the Bilderberg woods adjacent to Valkenburglaan and opposite Sonnerberglaan, which leads directly to the Hartenstein. Just a few hundred yards across Valkenburglaan, to Brigadier Hackett's east, was the 1st Border Regiment's positions, which formed the western flank of the British perimeter. For several hours, the 4th Parachute Brigade survivors sheltered in the hollow, under fire. Major Geoffrey Powell of 156th Parachute Battalion decided that 'The men were finished . . . They were passed defending themselves'. Brigadier Hackett, having conferred with Major de Gex of the Royal Artillery, knew that 'the enemy was apparently determined to liquidate our positions before dark and was now pressing even more than ever'. Major Powell was astonished when the Brigadier ordered his exhausted men to make a bayonet charge, to break through the enemy position and reach safety. Major Powell 'bawled' at his men to 'follow me', adding that

The trees around 'Hackett's Hollow' still bear the scars of war. (Author)

Having withdrawn under fire to Wolfheze, in an attempt to gain the British defensive perimeter around Oosterbeek a number of 4th Parachute Brigade survivors, led by Brigadier 'Shan' Hackett himself, gathered in what is now known as 'Hackett's Hollow' in the Bilderberg woods. From there, the Brigadier himself led a bayonet charge through the shocked Germans, safely reaching the British lines. The author gives scale in this photograph of the 'Hollow' in 2016. (Karen Sarkar)

it was better to be killed going for the bastards than lying in that bloody ditch . . . No one hesitated. Then men rose to their feet . . . Sergeant Weiner broke into a scream of rage, harsh and furious. The yell spread down the line. Too heavily laden and too tired to sprint, we lumbered forward towards the enemy in a sort of jog-trot. Now I was careless of everything. We did not stand a chance, but this was the right way to go. This was the proper way to finish it all. Nearly hysterical now with rage and excitement, I heard my own voice joining in the screaming.

The famous 'MDS' crossroads in Oosterbeek, looking towards Arnhem, with the Schoonoord on the right-hand side and the Hotel Vreewijk opposite. Annastraat is next on the right after the Schoonoord. (Author)

Faced with the somewhat terrifying sight and sound of a hundred or so desperate, filthy, angry and vengeful paratroopers, the German line broke; Major Powell: 'We had done it! We had driven the enemy out at point of bayonet! This was the ultimate in war!' One hundred yards ahead, Brigadier Hackett and his men reached an orchard, through which, still a fearful sight, they passed safely, having suffered few casualties, to the Border Regiment position. It is likely that Private Willingham was with this exhausted but ferociously brave group – and had survived yet another ordeal by combat.

Brigadier Hackett immediately reported to General Urquhart at the Hartenstein, who ordered the 4th Parachute Brigade survivors to assume responsibility for the eastern side of Oosterbeek the following morning. Major Peter Warr led 10th Parachute Battalion from the Hartenstein grounds, moving through the streets and gardens until checked by a German machine gun at the junction of Annastraat and the Jagerspad – just south of the Utrechtseweg which runs through Oosterbeek central and 200 yards or so east of the Café Schoonord. The Schoonord, located on the southern side of the Utrechtseweg, at its crossroads with Pietersbergscheweg to the south and Stationsweg to the north, had become a Medical Dressing Station, as had the Hotel Vreewijk opposite, on the northern side of the Utrechtseweg. It was crucial that the essential facilities at the 'MDS Crossroads' on the perimeter's eastern boundary were defended – which was now the job of the sixty or so 10th Parachute Battalion survivors.

By now, the Germans had pushed on from Arnhem into Oosterbeek, thanks to the arrival of *Sturmgeschütz* Brigade 280's self-propelled guns, which supported *Hohenstaufen*'s assault-pioneers. Warr's men, however, drove the Germans out of houses around the junction of Annastraat and the Utrechtseweg, rapidly occupying these defensive positions. Lieutenant Colonel Smyth set up his HQ at 2 Annastraat, just off the junction with the Utrechtseweg, so into this house, as a member of HQ Company, Private Albert Willingham fatefully went. The overall perimeter, stretching from the railway line in the north to the river in the south represented a vertical thumb-shape, whilst the area now occupied by 10th Parachute Battalion protruded from it and has been likened therefore to a 'sore thumb'. This protrusion into an area heavily infiltrated by Germans was very vulnerable, being subject to attack on at least three sides.

It is essential to understand that Dutch civilians had not been evacuated in advance of the airborne landings, due to the operation's need for surprise. After the euphoria of

House of horror: 2 Annastraat, in the cellar of which wounded British officers and Dutch civilians took refuge. (Author)

what appeared to be their moment of liberation turning to disappointment, the inhabitants of Arnhem and Oosterbeek took shelter in their cellars – whilst above them the battle raged. Ans van Wijck: 'In those days I was ten years old, living in Oosterbeek. My father worked as the local police station's caretaker, in which building we lived. During the fighting, we stayed in the cellar there, together with some policemen and their families, who did not have cellars and who went to the police station with their wives and children.' For Ans, like most local civilians, the terrifying battle is remembered as a virtual troglodyte, subterranean existence. Living close to 2 Annastraat, at 160 (now 178) Utrechtseweg, Corrie Tijssen remembers that 'the battle was horrendous, the terrible noise, the dreadful suffering'. 2 Annastraat was the home of a Dr Onderwater, in whose cellar sheltered various civilians, including the Voskuil family. Their ordeal, however, was far from over.

The 10th Parachute Battalion force, with no friendly troops in the houses adjacent to them, must have felt somewhat vulnerable and isolated. The night of 20 September 1944, however, passed reasonably quietly, but the following day the Germans stepped up their efforts to re-take Oosterbeek – which had now degenerated into a terrifying, devastated urban landscape – even known by the Germans as the *Hexenkessel* ('Witch's Cauldron'). There still being no sign of relief from XXX Corps, with the paratroopers increasingly, desperately, short of food, sleep and ammunition, it was inevitable that eventually the well-armed and supported enemy would prevail. At 2000 hrs, a strong attack by infantry and armour was unleashed on 10th Parachute Battalion, from its rear, the south, and east. StuGs, unmolested, liberally shelled the houses gloriously defended by Smyth's men, who had no means of resisting such a determined armoured attack. Each house was systematically destroyed. Falling back from house-to-house, Major Warr led a spirited defence until 2 Annastraat was the only building not yet overrun. HQ Company had no option but to get out as the Germans concentrated their attack on their position. Major Warr was badly wounded whilst attempting to leave, so was taken down into the darkness of 2 Annastraat's cellar. Lieutenant Colonel Smyth was likewise hit whilst trying to cross the narrow road, and joined Major Warr. It is likely that Private Willingham was involved with carrying one or both of these fine officers down to the cellar's comparative safety, for he too found himself in that dark, damp, overcrowded place as a self-propelled gun began pumping shells into the building. Then, German infantry attacked, engaging those 10th Parachute Battalion survivors still alive and above ground in hand-to-hand fighting.

In 2 Annastraat's cellar, Mrs Bertje Voskuil was amongst the twenty Dutch civilians who had taken refuge there. An English-speaker, Mrs Voskuil had interpreted for the badly-wounded Lieutenant Colonel Smyth and Major Warr; she described the almost unimaginable scene and unfolding drama:

> They brought Peter Warr down and laid him on the ground in front of me; I was sitting with my son [Henri] on a bench. Peter Warr had been hit in the thigh; it

was very painful. Sometimes he was unconscious and at others he was awake, grumbling and swearing – he had every reason to. I remember him saying 'Oh for a pint of beer'. Then they brought Lieutenant Colonel Smythe down, badly injured. He was also unconscious some of the time, but when awake kept repeating 'Where am I?' I tried to explain, that he was in Holland, at Oosterbeek, and that it was in the war, but he didn't understand. I think he had been shot in the stomach. There was a lot of blood, but it was so dark, with only one candle in the cellar, that you couldn't see properly.

Then I heard them fighting in the house above us – shots and screams; they made all kinds of noises when they were fighting, just like animals. Then the door burst open and the Germans came in. A British soldier jumped in front of Peter Warr and I, with his back to the Germans. Then there were two terrific explosions – German grenades. The British soldier was hit in the back and fell forward, over me: he was dead.

Many of the people in the cellar were wounded. I was hit in both legs and my hearing was affected – and still is. The candle was blown out by the explosions. I felt down for my nine-year old son; I felt his body; he didn't move, and there was a lot of blood. I thought he was dead, but he was still alive, hit by splinters in his stomach and face. He regained consciousness the next morning and made a full recovery. My husband was hit in the hand and knee. Major Warr was badly hurt again, in the shoulder. He had been hit when he raised himself up on his elbow when the Germans came in and called out to them that he and his men were surrendering.

There was a tumult. You have no idea how much people scream in such circumstances. Then a German officer called out to me 'Do you speak English?' I said I did, and he told me to translate quickly, to tell the English that they had fought gallantly and behaved like gentlemen, but they must surrender now and hand over their weapons, helmets and ammunition, also their watches and identification papers.

I asked someone to take the soldier's body off me, because he was bleeding all over me. I had some suede shoes on, and his 'life blood' on the floor was so thick that the shoes were stained so badly that I threw them away. One of the British soldiers near me had his rifle and was so nervous that the butt was rattling on the floor. You get beyond fear when things get so bad; I was icily cold when I was translating for that German, although I believed my son was dead. Perhaps it was utter despair, because a year before I had lost my younger son from a blood disease.

Colonel Smyth regained consciousness and asked to see the German commander. He came down – a dreadful looking man with a monocle on a ribbon and with his hair parted in the middle. He asked me what 'that man' wanted. I was so furious that I said the Colonel, stressing *the Colonel*, needed a

The cellar of 2 Annastraat, into which a German threw a grenade. (Author)

doctor. The German officer went away, but a good doctor came, so probably it was only the appearance and manner of the German officer that was so unpleasant.

The British soldier who had selflessly given his life to save others was Private Albert Willingham – whose prophecy that he would 'not be coming back' had sadly been fulfilled.

Both Lieutenant Colonel Ken Smyth and Major Peter Warr MBE were taken into captivity by the Germans. 10th Parachute Battalion's commanding officer lingered on in this world until he died of his wounds in Apeldoorn on 26 October 1944; he received a mention in despatches. Major Warr recovered at the Luidina Hospital in Apeldoorn and survived the war, receiving a well-deserved DSO for his brave example and leadership at Oosterbeek; he died in 1982.

Dr and Mrs Voskuil and their young son survived. In 1946, the Voskuils celebrated the birth of another son, Robert – a brother for Henri. Fittingly, today Dr Robert Voskuil is an internationally recognised expert on the great airborne battle of September 1944, heavily involved at the Airborne Museum – situated at the reconstructed Hartenstein Hotel – and President of the Arnhem Fellowship.

PATRICK TAYLOR AND ALBERT WILLINGHAM

The remains of Private Albert Willingham, whose identity was unknown to whoever buried the brave Hampshireman, were first laid to rest in the garden behind 2 Annastraat. His shrapnel-torn helmet was left on the wooden cross marking his grave, and on a nearby wall directions were written to the grave of an 'unknown' British soldier, killed at 2100 hours on 21 September 1944. After the war, Private Willingham was reinterred at the Arnhem-Oosterbeek War Cemetery. His headstone, however, records his age as having been thirty, but he was, in fact, twenty-nine years young when he shielded Mrs Voskuil, her young son, and Major Warr from that fateful German grenade. Like so many at Arnhem, his brave and selfless deed went unrecognised.

Mrs Bertje Voskuil, whose life Private Willingham sacrificed his own to save, taking the grenade's full force himself. (Dr Robert Voskuil)

Mrs Voskuil's young son, Henri, also saved by Private Willingham's selfless, courageous, humanitarian sacrifice. (Dr Robert Voskuil)

Private Willingham's field grave in the garden of 2 Annastraat. (Kim Hymers)

Private Willingham's original grave marker at Oosterbeek. (Kim Hymers)

Understandably, the Willinghams, a close family, were devastated by their loss. Mr Willingham died in 1952, his widow, Rose, after suffering serious depression, followed him in 1977 – the same year, coincidentally, that the film *A Bridge Too Far* was released. Before her death, Mrs Willingham, along with two of her daughters, namely Maisie and Eva, went on a pilgrimage to Oosterbeek and visited Albert's grave. There they met another survivor of 2 Annastraat's cellar, a Mrs Schute, who told Eva that 'My brother caught the grenade and had part of his body blown right out. She took me to the house where he was killed but I couldn't go in. She said that my brother was kind and had grown a moustache, which made him look handsome. Mrs Schute told me the strange thing about where Albert was first buried, in the garden, is that nothing will ever grow there, it just goes black.' Mrs Schute had, in fact, written to Albert's parents on 4 October 1946:

> I live in Oosterbeek, near Arnhem. I was there too in September 1944. During the battle my husband, children and I had to leave our house and shelter in the

cellar of a friend of ours, a doctor. Colonel Smyth, Major Peter Warr and chaps arrived at that house. After some days, the situation for the English soldiers was hopeless. The Germans came with hand grenades and a lot of English boys were killed or wounded. My husband and I were wounded too. One of the soldiers killed had the name Willingham.

After our liberation, we came back to Oosterbeek and I found in the doctor's garden the grave of Private Willingham. My children and I looked after the grave there and after it was moved to the British War Cemetery. We put flowers on the grave, bringing fresh flowers every Saturday or Sunday. I would like to have a photograph of Private Willingham and to know his family. Please write to me. I will write back and may be able to tell you something of Private Willingham's last days.

Unfortunately, no further correspondence survives between the Willinghams and Mrs Schute.

Sister Eva paid her respects at her brother's grave on nineteen separate occasions, such was her affection for him: 'Albert was not frightened of anything, or of dying. He used to say, "What will be will be". It is wrong, though, after what he did, that he did not get a medal or even spoken about in Britain. I think he should be honoured in some way. You would expect them not to forget men like Albert. He gave his life to the army. Giving his life to save others was typical of him.' During the research for this book, taking into account how Albert's family feels, I inquired of Lieutenant General Sir John Lorimer, Colonel Commandant of the Parachute Regiment, whether there was any possibility of recognising Private Willingham's sacrifice with a posthumous award. Unfortunately, for a variety of reasons this is not possible; Sir John, however, wrote that

Your letter concerning Private Willingham has reached far and wide. Lieutenant Colonel James Loudon, Commanding Officer of 4 PARA, gave a particularly moving speech at the Ginkel Heath commemorations this year (2017), where he told the story of Private Willingham, as an example of one of the many unsung acts of heroism that occurred in September 1944 . . . I understand that Lieutenant Colonel Loudon has discussed the matter with his successor, Lieutenant Colonel Andrew Wareing, and they intend to commemorate Private Willingham's sacrifice.

That is good news indeed, and it will be interesting to see, in due course, what shape this proposed commemoration takes.

The Dutch have not forgotten Private Willingham either. Robert Voskuil is acutely aware that, albeit indirectly, he owes his life to Albert Willingham, as, more directly, did his parents and brother. This story, I think, as much as any, is a memorial to the shared suffering endured by airborne warriors and civilians alike during those few hellish days in that now far-off autumn of despair. Significantly, until 2016, Private Albert Willingham's headstone at Oosterbeek incorrectly recorded his age as thirty, as does other CWGC records. Provision of his birth certificate to the Commission, however, provided irrefutable evidence that the selfless paratrooper was, in fact, twenty-nine. Having the facts correctly recorded was important to his family, so it was pleasing to see a cleaned and corrected headstone had been arranged in time for the September 2016 commemorations. As Albert's nephew's wife, Kim Hymers, said 'That means a lot to us, and makes us think that perhaps Albert and what he did still means something even after so long, and that he isn't forgotten'.

What now remains: Private Willingham's Italy Star, 1939-45 War Medal, and ribbons to the France & Germany Star and 1939-45 Defence Medal. (Author)

Private Willingham's birth certificate conclusively proved his age to have been twenty-nine, the CWGC correcting the headstone. (27.A.10) in 2016, upon receipt of irrefutable evidence provided by the author. (Author)

The final lines of this chapter go to Albert Willingham's late sister, June: her tribute to beloved 'Alby':

> In Flanders field the poppies grow
> Where so many young soldiers sleep.
> Such a vivid crimson
> So many, Alas I weep
> One who sleeps with you,
> I love as no other
> Forever in my heart
> You see he is my brother.
> Sleep on dear ones,
> You are precious in God's sight.
> Sleep on your peace is won.
> I'll join you at night
> Not in a Flanders field.
> But where night meets day
> We will walk together
> Forever and a day
> In the light of God's glory
> Things we will understand
> life's bitter-sweet mysteries
> in God's promised land.

In May 2018, the author delivered Private Albert Willingham's medals and other personal possessions to the Airborne Museum, Oosterbeek, kindly loaned by the family for the exhibition based on this book at the Airborne at the Bridge Museum in September 2019. The artefacts were accepted by Dr Robert Voskuil, the Museum's highly respected Archivist, President of the Arnhem 1944 Fellowship – and whose mother's and brother's lives were saved by Albert's sacrifice. Robert is pictured here with Albert's boxing trophy during what was a deeply emotional moment connecting past and present.

Chapter 10

Lieutenant Peter Brazier and Staff Sergeant Raymond Gould, Glider Pilot Regiment

It is no exaggeration to say that men of the Glider Pilot Regiment were a rare breed. Although the unit was comparatively short-lived, 553 Glider Pilots made the ultimate sacrifice – 229 of these so-called 'Total Soldiers' losing their lives during the Battle of Arnhem.

It was the Russians, in fact, who first recognised the potential benefits of a glider-borne force, creating in 1935 a unit of troops conveyed by gliders. The following year, the Poles inaugurated their parachute detachment, and the French in 1939. Although officially prohibited from having an air force by Article 198 of the Versailles Treaty, in 1924 a secret German military flying training school was established at Lipetsk, in Russia, far from prying Western eyes – which closed down in 1933 when Hitler came to power, determined to bin the hated Versailles *Diktat*.

Whilst contemplating their forthcoming aggressive expansionist foreign policy, the Germans fully recognised the strategic potential of airborne warfare. Consequently, *Luftwaffe Oberst* Kurt Student became the visionary and driving force behind Germany's airborne force. On that fateful day when Hitler unleashed his *Blitzkrieg* against the West, 10 May 1940, Student's glider troops achieved an inspirational victory on their first mission by landing on and capturing the strategically key Belgian fort at Eben-Emael. Parachute and glider landings followed in the Netherlands, providing irrefutable evidence of the value of Student's new force.

Inspired by Student's forward-thinking success, on 22 June 1940, the British Prime Minister, Winston Churchill, decreed that a force of 5,000 airborne troops should be raised in Britain, including both parachute and glider troops. The idea was that gliders would be towed by conventional powered aircraft, then cast-off at an appropriate juncture to continue, silently, to the prescribed landing zone. The gliders largely used operationally by the British were the ubiquitous Airspeed Horsa and the huge General Aircraft Limited Hamilcar, both capable of transporting troops, small vehicles and guns. The creation of this new British glider-borne force, however, was a most complex matter, it being unclear, for example, as to whether pilots should be drawn from the RAF or Army. One thing not in dispute was the fact that glider pilots, being expected to land 'dead stick' in unfamiliar territory, sometimes in low-light conditions, needed to be experienced flyers. Once on the ground, the glider pilot was redundant in an aviation sense, so also needed to be a competent infantry soldier, trained in the use of various weapons and tactics. And so was born the concept of the 'Total Soldier'.

The Army Air Corps was born on 24 February 1942, the '1st Glider Pilot Regiment' being the new formation's first unit. Personnel were to be, like paratroopers, volunteers from amongst already serving soldiers throughout the army. Successful applicants spent their three-week probationary period at the Regimental Depot at Tilshead airfield, on Salisbury Plain. Those who passed were then posted to No. 16 Elementary Flying Training School (EFTS), at Burnaston, near Derby, where they earnt their wings flying powered aircraft such as the De Havilland Tiger Moth. Afterwards, half of the newly-qualified pilots went to No. 1 Glider Training School (GTS) at Thame, the rest to No. 2 GTS at Weston-on-the-Green. Thereafter it was off to either 101 Glider Operational Training Unit (GOTU) at Kidlington, or 102 GOTU at Shobdon. A rigorous syllabus was applied, involving flying Hotspur gliders on tactical exercises and at night. The instructors were all experienced pilots, including, at Shobdon, Flight Lieutenant Mike Bush DFC, who had flown Hurricanes during the Battle of Britain and later in Russia: 'The glider pilots worked very hard, and were keen to get the opportunity to prove themselves in battle, which in due course they most certainly did.'

Ronald Owen Johnson had joined the TA in early 1939, being commissioned into the Essex Regiment in September 1943. In December that year, he volunteered for the Glider Pilot Regiment:

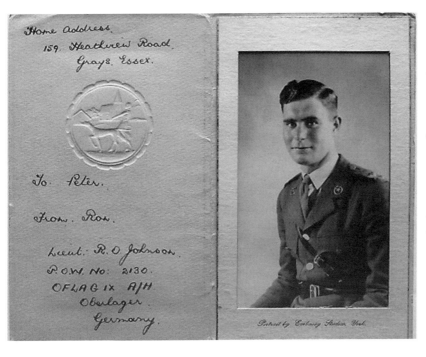

An official wartime photograph of Ron Johnson, sent to his cousin and Godson, Peter Bodell, by his father, Carl Owen Johnson, providing Ron's postal address whilst a POW in Germany. Ron had not personally seen this photograph until 2019! (Christine Campbell).

ARNHEM 1944

I did my elementary flying training on Tiger Moths at RAF Clyffe Pypard in Wiltshire. From there I trained on the Hotspur glider at Stoke Orchard and Horsas at Upper Heyford. The training was shortened by then and were rushed through in a hurry. As a newly qualified pilot, I then joined 'E' Squadron at Down Ampney as a 2nd Lieutenant in April 1944. There were six of us, five glider pilots and an admin officer, sharing a Nissen hut right by the church. Amongst our company was Lieutenant Peter Brazier, an experienced pilot, who was highly regarded. When I got there, I particularly remember, he made me feel very welcome. I always felt very friendly towards Peter. Although I only knew him from April to September 1944, in that short time I came to regard him as a close friend. I liked him very much.

Peter John Brazier was the eldest son of Jonathan Philip and Mabel Alice Brazier, born on 22 January 1922, of 'Thatchholme', in Conway Road, Bromsgrove, Worcestershire. Known by his middle name, Philip, Peter's father was the grandson of Jonathan Brazier, who was, according to the family historian, Alan Richards, '. . . the archetype of the Victorian entrepreneur who rose from humble surroundings in a court or alley of nailers by self-help to become one of the biggest employers in Bromsgrove . . . He was industrious and the far-sighted founder of a family firm which has left a widespread imprint on Bromsgrove and its district.' The 'firm' was a building company, which, between 1850 and 1990 heavily contributed to the built environment of Worcestershire. Jonathan Brazier's sons, John and Albert, succeeded him in directing J & A Brazier Ltd, which it became in 1919. Their sons took over in due course, until in the 1960s, Jonathan Brazier's great-grandsons, including Roger Brazier – Peter's younger brother – became the firm's final directors, selling the business in 1990.

The Brazier family story represents a perfect example of the fact that divided though British society was between the wars, socially and economically, it was possible, through initiative and hard work, to rise in status. In the wake of the First World War, Britain experienced privations caused by the Great Depression, resulting in widespread unemployment highlighting the disparity in the distribution of wealth. Indeed, Charles Loch Mowat described the 1930s as 'gloomy', a 'devil's decade'. According to Branson and Heinemann, in 1937, 35.7 per cent of the population earned £2 10s per week; 37.8 per cent earned between that amount and £4; 21.3 per cent earned between £4 and £10, but only 5.2 per cent earned over £10. The lowest wage earners represented 4,318,000 families, whilst the top earners amounted to only 635,500. Although social classification is not solely decided by income, these figures nonetheless illustrate the gap and division between classes. Mowat, in fact, concluded that there were 'several Englands' between the wars, and that 'their differences had never been so sharply drawn'. In 1933, the celebrated novelist and broadcaster J.B. Priestley made his 'English Journey', finding 'four Englands': the southern counties of the guide books, the industrial north with many cold and silent furnaces, the prosperous Home Counties, and the 'England of the dole'.

Phillip Brazier, a director of the family building firm, with his sons, Roger (left) and Peter, on a pre-war seaside holiday. (Christine Campbell)

Given the family firm's success, the Brazier family, however, was very firmly located in the top 5.2 per cent of British society's socio-economic pyramid.

Education, in fact, was the key to advancement, but the quality of schooling was entirely dependent upon the ability to pay fees. The top 5.2 per cent sent their children to independent fee-paying schools known as 'public schools'. The middle class, however, were expanding, and recognised the benefits provided by this elitist educational system: in 1914, there were 22,000 public-school pupils, increasing to 82,000 by 1930. Most public-school pupils boarded. Collectively, such 'seats of learning' were considered 'training grounds for leaders of the nation'. Indeed, in 1931, it was estimated that 76 per cent of 691 holders of 'high office' in the church, state and industry were educated at public schools. Unsurprisingly, universities too were largely the preserve of the wealthy. Again, figures illustrate the rise of the middle class: between 1925 and 1926, there were 29,275 undergraduate students in Britain; by 1939, that figure had risen to 50,000. Again, however, funding opportunities were limited (emphasising the Tate brothers' achievement in securing Cambridge scholarships, see Chapter 2), meaning that students were reliant upon their families' ability to pay fees. This, therefore, secured the upper echelons of education for the socio-economic elite. Moreover, not only was society sharply divided socially, economically and educationally between the wars, it was also heavily sexist: in 1925, for example, of the 29,275 university students, only 8,376 were female. To get on in Mowat's 'devil's decade', therefore, it clearly helped to be male and from a family of means.

The success of J & A Brazier Ltd, meant that the family could afford private education, their chosen seat of learning being Bromsgrove School, the local independent school founded in 1553. Indeed, the firm built most of the school buildings between 1880 and 1986. Significantly, in 1930, the Braziers were awarded a contract to build the school's War Memorial Chapel. Philip Brazier, Peter's father, oversaw both the first phase in 1931, and the final works in 1960 – by which time the project had a personal significance. The chapel was a memorial to Bromsgrovians who had lost their lives during the First World War, then the Second. During the First, Philip had lost a cousin; in the Second he would lose both son and a nephew. The chapel also commemorates the seventeen Brazier boys who attended Bromsgrove School between 1897 and 1986.

Peter Brazier attended Bromsgrove School between 1935 and 1939, where he achieved his School Certificate 'A', having spent five years in the OTC. This is significant. The Certificate 'A' was awarded to those who had passed the OTC's examination based upon a military syllabus. All public schools, from 1905 onwards, had OTCs. During the First World War, those armed with their Certificate 'A', a good school report and an application endorsed by any colonel, were entitled to a commission as of right. Such a system preserved commissions for the 5.2 per cent, and little had changed by the outbreak of the Second World War. By that time, Peter had gone up to Birmingham University as an undergraduate engineering student. On 24 September 1940, however, he abandoned his studies and enlisted, in Birmingham, as Sapper 1896774 Peter John Brazier of the Royal Engineers. Giving his occupation as 'student', age 'eighteen years and eight months', religion as Church of England, the new recruit was described as having a 'fresh' complexion, brown eyes and hair, 5ft 11¾in tall, and weighing 159lbs. The Medical Board passed Sapper Brazier as Grade I, 'Fit for general service at home and abroad'.

Peter's entry to the army was deferred, however. Although posted on 4 October 1940, to No. 4 RE Training Battalion (TB), Colchester, this was a technicality only. In reality, he was returned to Birmingham University to study land surveying at the Survey Training Centre (STC). Sapper Brazier 'arrived from Birmingham University STC' on 1 April 1941, joining 'D' Company of No. 3 RE TB at Ripon. On 28 May 1941, he was posted to 141 Officer Cadet Training Unit (OCTU) RE, at Aldershot, two months later re-mustering as a 'Pioneer E III'. On 14 November 1941, Pioneer Brazier was 'discharged having been appointed to a commission'. His 'military conduct' was recorded as 'Very good. His military conduct and efficiency is such that he has been

The Braziers were a well-off, privately educated, middle-class family: Peter Brazier (centre) pictured here before the war at the family home, 'Thatcholme' in Bromsgrove, with his cousins Dr David Brazier and Monica Paul. (Christine Campbell)

selected for a commission.' 2nd Lieutenant Brazier RE was then posted to No. 10 TB RE. The young officer subsequently attended and passed the Motor Transport (Officers) Course at Ripon, and a Wireless Telegraphy course at Dorking. Clearly home service in the RE was not to Peter's liking, however: he volunteered for and was accepted by the Glider Pilot Regiment, the 1st Battalion of which he joined at Aldershot on 20 August 1942 (this being before re-organisation into wings and squadrons in January 1943). On 24 September 1942, 2nd Lieutenant Brazier was posted to the 2nd Battalion, at Tilshead; a week later, he was promoted to full lieutenant.

On 20 January 1943, Lieutenant Brazier arrived at RAF Clyffe Pypard for elementary flying training on single-engined powered aircraft. Passing the course and winning the coveted flying brevet, Peter's next stop was No. 4 GTS, Kidlington. Although undated, on a 'Sunday', Peter wrote home, as he often did, to 'My dear Ma and Pa':

2nd Lieutenant Peter Brazier, having been commissioned into the Royal Engineers in 1941. (Christine Campbell)

> Thanks for the telegram and log-book, but most of all for the way you have always looked after us and given us the best possible education and bringing up to prepare us for the years to come. As I said before, if the next 21 years are as successful as those that have already, you will never hear me utter a single word of complaint. I only hope that you both have no regrets as to what you have done for us. I can promise you that I really do appreciate the schooling and the happy home life which I have always been lucky enough to enjoy.
>
> This place is quite nice and very handy as there are two bus and one train services within five minutes of the place, and Kidlington village and Woodstock are both very close . . . I had my first trip up on Friday and very much enjoyed it. As far as we can see, there is very little to this gliding game, which is if anything easier than ordinary flying. The drome is very near Blenheim Palace, over which we fly every time we go up, and only about four miles from the centre of Oxford.
>
> We get one day off a week, Saturday one week and Sunday the following, so will not be able to get home very often I am afraid. As we have only just got here, we are not having a day off this week.
>
> We went to the local cinema last night, which is about 25 minutes walk away, and saw Fred Astaire and Rita Hayworth in a film called 'You'll Never Get Rich', over which we had a very good laugh.
>
> We work the same system here as at Clyffe Pypard, working the morning and flying in the afternoon, then vice-versa the following day. We have got a fairish syllabus of ground subjects, but they are not far advanced on those we have already done. The course will take about ten weeks if the weather is reasonable, more if not, but with any luck ten weeks should suffice.
>
> The trouble here is that a lot of time is wasted pulling the gliders, after they have landed, back to the take-off point. The tug takes you off and you keep behind and slightly above so as to get out of the slipstream of the propeller. When you are ready, you release the tow rope and glide down. It is a grand feeling when you are on your own and surprising how far you can go without losing too much height.

No. 11 Course, 4 Glider Training School, Kidlington, 1943. (Christine Campbell)

Having enjoyed gliding over Oxfordshire, Lieutenant Brazier passed the course and became a fully-fledged 'Total Soldier', moving back into the 1st Battalion; action would shortly follow.

When the Allies finally defeated the *Afrika Korps* in North Africa, where the fighting concluded on 13 May 1943, it was already decided the Allied armies in the Mediterranean theatre would next invade Sicily, thence Italy. Churchill had insisted that the Sicilian operation should take place in or very soon after June 1943. The Glider Pilot Regiment found itself training and making preparations to join 1st Airborne Division in North Africa, in order for its fifty fully-trained crews to participate in the forthcoming invasion. The regiment's commanding officer, Colonel Chatterton, and advance elements of his regiment arrived in North Africa in April. On 10 June 1943, Lieutenant Brazier disembarked in North Africa, travelling sixty miles inland to Tizi, where the Division was concentrated with the American 51st Wing, Troop Carrier Command. The 51st flew C-47 Dakotas, which would tow the gliders into action. The gliders available were mainly American Wacos. The plan was for the British 8th and

Lieutenant Peter Brazier (right) pictured with an unknown army officer, also a pilot, location unknown. (Christine Campbell)

American 7th Armies to invade southern Sicily by sea. The British effort at Cap Passaro was to be led by Brigadier 'Pip' Hicks's 1st Air Landing Brigade, flown into battle by the Glider Pilot Regiment. Hicks was to take and hold the Ponte Grande Bridge over the Anopo Canal, before moving on, if possible, to seize Syracuse. This, Operation LADBROKE, was to happen on the night of 9/10 July 1943. The following night, gliders were to land anti-tank guns in support of Operation FUSTIAN, the 1st Parachute Brigade attack on Primosole Bridge. Beforehand, Chatterton's pilots, including Lieutenant Brazier, had to convert to the Waco, with which they were unfamiliar, and the tug pilots needed to practice towing and releasing gliders. There was little time for this.

The Dakotas at this time had yet to have armour plate and self-sealing fuel tanks fitted, making them extremely vulnerable. Consequently, the Americans insisted upon releasing the Wacos 3,000 yards before reaching the Sicilian coast, to ensure avoidance of the German coastal flak batteries. There would be little science attached to calculating what was a critical distance, this being guesswork only. In the event, probing German searchlights and alert flak emplacements panicked the tug pilots, who released their charges in excess of the agreed 3,000 yards – making landfall impossible. Most gliders consequently went into the sea, the few crossing the coast being scattered over a distance of twenty-five miles. Over half the tugs failed to reach the 3,000-yard mark, over half the American-towed gliders ended up in the 'drink', and only 34 per cent reached Sicily. Somewhat surprisingly, Ponte Grande was nonetheless successfully captured. Churchill, however, called the outcome a 'disaster'. General Browning, commander of all British airborne forces, was unmoved, commenting that: 'The results achieved in this, our first glider landing, do not shake my confidence . . . Troops carried by glider . . . can carry with them a more liberal supply of ammunition, transport and comparatively heavy weapons' (compared to parachutists). Undoubtedly, lessons had been learned, but the cost was high: 300 men had been drowned; fifty-seven glider pilots lost their lives. Fortunately, Lieutenant Brazier was not amongst the dead or missing on this occasion, his baptism of fire, regarding which he wrote home about, in somewhat sanitised terms:

> I expect you have been wondering what has been going on during the last few days, but we have just returned from a rather hectic operation. You will be pleased to know that I am absolutely unscathed, although God alone knows why. It is very nice to come back and find comparative comfort and good food again, and to wash up and step into clean clothes. One thing I can say is that we were the first troops to open the Second Front. I expect you will know as much about Sicily from your papers as I do, by the time this reaches you.

After the Sicilian adventure, the glider pilots returned to North Africa, where they were able to train on Wacos. Further, undated, letters followed:

> Well, in spite of the conditions out here I am still very much alive and kicking. We left our first port of call about a week ago and after doing escort to some German officers. We arrived here to join the lads who came out earlier on. This place is a kind of semi-desert with a few trees here and there and a sun which is rather too hot . . . We had a treat this morning and were allowed to pay to visit a mobile bath unit, which travels around the countryside and fixes up showers for the troops for a few days before moving on. It is very nice to feel clean again, for a short time at any rate . . . The war in this part of the world is going fairly well and I understand the Russians are still doing their stuff.

The subsequent invasion of Italy on 3 September 1943 was an amphibious operation, British airborne troops landing by sea at Taranto and being used as infantry. 'Total Soldiers' though glider pilots were, and able infantrymen indeed, they were nonetheless specialists in short supply. For that reason, Chatterton's men were wisely used in non-combatant roles. Peter wrote home from Italy:

> I am afraid it is some time since I last wrote, but we have been on the move and we have only just had time to write now. As you have probably guessed by now we have gone over to Italy, this time as a seaborne division, instead of our proper method of travel . . . The climate and general conditions are if anything a good deal better than North Africa, which by now I have seen pretty thoroughly.

Between 31 October and 3 November 1943, the young glider pilot was admitted to No. 98 General Hospital, although it is not known why; Peter does not mention this in letters home. On 26 December 1943, he embarked for England, the Glider Pilot Regiment returning to bases in the West Country. Back in England, Lieutenant Brazier served with Major B.H.P. Jackson's 'E' Squadron, of Lieutenant Colonel J.W. Place's No. 2 Wing, based at RAF Down Ampney, near the Cotswold capital of Cirencester in Gloucestershire. Down Ampney was one of a group of three airfields dedicated to air transport, the other two being RAF Broadwell and RAF Blakehill Farm. All three were constructed to accommodate air transport squadrons of 46 Group, Down Ampney opening in 1944. The airfield had three concrete runways with fifty hard-standings and two Type T2 aircraft hangars. A small village of only thirty-three inhabitants, service personnel were accommodated in temporary Nissen huts. The base was home to two RAF squadrons, 271 and 48, operating the C-47 Dakota. A busy and perilous time lay ahead for Down Ampney's aircrews.

The experience gained in combined operations during the Mediterranean campaigns would now prove invaluable to the planning of the 'Great Adventure': Operation OVERLORD, the long-awaited Allied invasion of enemy-occupied Europe. It was clear that any undertaking would have to initially rely heavily upon airborne troops to pass over Hitler's much-vaunted Atlantic Wall, rendering the defences impotent, capture key objectives and establish a bridgehead perimeter. With this in mind, glider training increased in intensity, by November 1943 exercises being successfully undertaken involving up to forty gliders. Methods for marshalling and setting formations off on the right course were evolving, and tug pilots gained experience of towing and releasing their unpowered charges. Planning for D-Day continued throughout the late winter and spring of 1944, every detail meticulously considered. During the final weeks before the Allies set foot once more on French soil, training increased further still. Whereas 1st Airborne Division had fought overseas whilst 6th Airborne Division had remained at home in reserve, vice-versa would apply for the forthcoming invasion – much to the 1st's chagrin. There was, however, a role for the glider pilots – and these were exciting times indeed.

    The overall air plan, Operation NEPTUNE, required 5th Parachute Brigade to drop north of Ranville on the night of 5 June 1944, seize the Orne and Caen Canal crossings (for which a coup de main party of six Horsa gliders was to be used), clear and secure the surrounding area and finally hold the landing zones ready for Operation MALLARD to touch-down on the evening of D-Day. MALLARD was a significant undertaking, 143 Horsas and 30 Hamilcars from 'A', 'B', 'C', 'E' and 'F' squadrons flying to LZ 'N' near Ranville, and a further 80 Horsas from 'A', 'C', 'D' and 'G' Squadrons alighting at LZ 'W', just inland of Sword Beach, collectively conveying the main body of 6th Air Landing Brigade. With the initial airborne operations and seaborne Allied landings having been successful, so to was MALLARD – which made history in that this was the first time an armoured formation had been flown into battle, a distance of 200 miles. Because further airborne operations were expected, however, all participating glider pilots were returned to England as soon as possible. Ron Johnson remembers that 'Unfortunately I can't "shoot a line" about Normandy because our Squadron Commander held me back as Duty Officer at Down Ampney! Very disappointed, of course, but Peter went to Ranville with the rest of "E" Squadron'. For the 22-year-old Lieutenant Peter Brazier, what the feeling was like of having participated in such an historic event can only be imagined. The official account of British airborne operations during the Second World War, *By Air to Battle*, succinctly appraised the contribution made by glider pilots on Operation MALLARD: 'The success of this operation is the best tribute to those who had first shown on the dusty fields of Sicily what skill and gallantry can achieve in the handling of a new and hazardous vehicle for the carriage of troops into battle.'

    The summer of 1944, however, would be one of anti-climax and frustration for the 1st Airborne Division, whiling away their time at home in reserve whilst 6th Airborne grabbed the action and glory. Peter's letter to his brother, Roger, written from Down Ampney on 'Wednesday 20th' (presumably June, July or August of 1944), is revealing:

Thanks for the letter and glad to hear everything is OK with you.

I, quite frankly, am bored to tears at the moment, just filling in time doing nothing of any use. I had a day off Sunday last, so we went up to Tewkesbury and had a very boozy day and had tea with Aunt Maud.

Geoff Smith flew off from here for Normandy, I hope nothing untoward has happened to him.

I wish to God we could get over there!

I haven't been up home for ages now, I think the last time was at the beginning of March. I have been trying for ages to get a 48, but have not succeeded as yet.

As we have already seen, the other issue, apart from inactivity, negatively affecting General Urquhart's troops in England was the succession of cancelled operations. Airborne operations, especially large-scale ones, are incredibly complicated affairs, so this was a stressful time for the Glider Pilot Regiment in England. Attached to the Regiment were two 'Sky Pilots', namely the Reverend George Pare, chaplain to No. 1 Wing, and the Reverend Wilfred 'Chig' Chignell of No. 2 Wing. 'Chig', based at No. 2 Wing HQ at Broadwell, near Burford in Gloucestershire, kept a diary, providing an insight into the feelings of the time (the extract reproduced here with kind permission of the Reverend Mike Vockins):

By now the Second Front was becoming very active and mobile. This meant that many air-landing schemes were planned, only to be dropped because the ground troops were advancing so fast. Between D-Day and MARKET-GARDEN, no less than sixteen of these abortive schemes were planned, and some were only cancelled a few hours before take-off. This was very exhausting and frustrating to the airborne troops, not least the Glider Pilot Regiment, whose chief responsibility was to plan the actual ferrying of non-parachutists to the selected site.

On Friday, 15 September 1944, Peter wrote what no-one knew at the time would be a poignant last letter home, from the Officers' Mess at RAF Down Ampney. His frustration regarding cancelled operations and inability to get back into the war is again evident:

We have been having a very busy time, as usual, waiting for something to happen. I doubt now if it ever will. We had a day off yesterday, so I visited Cheltenham and Tewkesbury. We did not visit Aunt Maud as there were rather a lot of us. I hope, but somehow doubt, to come on leave when Roger has finished his course; perhaps that is wishful thinking. We spend most of our time playing cards and an old game called 'Monopoly', which we used to play about ten years ago. Well, I will now close, love, Peter.

ARNHEM 1944

As we have seen, Operation MARKET-GARDEN was launched on Sunday 17 September 1944. Both Lieutenant Peter Brazier and 2nd Lieutenant Ron Johnson of Captain A.A.R. Oxenford's No. 25 Flight, E' Squadron, however, were on the second lift, flying Horsa gliders in on Monday 18 September 1944. Peter was first pilot on Horsa Chalk 848, his second pilot being Sergeant Maurice Hibbert. Their load was an unusual one: an Airborne Bulldozer (Clark Air Tractor Crawler), used for creating temporary airstrips, a Matchless motorcycle, a standard airborne trailer and personnel from 261 (Airborne) Field Park Company, RE. Aboard Chalk 848 was sapper Sergeant Mervyn J. Potter:

> In order to load the bulldozer into the glider, a specially designed loading ramp was necessary. This was designed and made under my personal supervision in our Company workshops. This was carried around from one planned and cancelled operation to another, in the same Bedford 3-tonner as the bulldozer. From the very first planned and cancelled operation with which our detachment were concerned, I knew that we would not be able to take this 'special ramp' with us on an operation, so other means had to be found to unload the bulldozer. I decided that the easiest and quickest way to achieve this was by using small charges of explosive, to blow away the landing supports and struts of the glider, to settle her on her belly. My idea was presented to the Commanding Officer of 9th Field Company, RE, and he rapidly gave permission. So, from this time on I carried in my Airborne smock two small charges of gelignite, detonators and safety fuses for this purpose.

Delayed by four hours due to bad weather over England, 'E' Squadron was at last on its way and bound for LZ 'X', near Wolfheze.

Ron Johnson remembered:

> Before take-off at Down Ampney, the gliders were massed together and hooked up to our Dakota tugs and all ready to go. If you tried to do this individually, of course, it would take all day to get them off. Each tug and glider combination is ready to go, one after the other, so you get into a stream. From Down Ampney we went over Hatfield, across to Aldburgh, in Suffolk, on the Northern Route, going across to the Dutch islands, along to 's-Hertogenbosch. You could see the tugs and gliders in the streams for about 100 miles ahead, it was the most impressive sight that has stayed with me forever. As we went over, there were two gliders down in the sea, and I remember the sheer feeling of elation when we reached 's-Hertogenbosch, because this was my first time going into action and when we went over 's-Hertogenbosch I knew we were going to get there. Before then, in a glider, you could never be sure whether you were going to get shot-up en route by flak or a German fighter.

PETER BRAZIER AND RAYMOND GOULD

Getting cast off from the tug is the delightful part. We were taught on powered aircraft, of course, but I didn't much like it, but I loved glider flying. It suited me for some reason, I don't know why. When we were cast off, we were at about 2,500 feet. In still air, a Horsa, as a rough guide, will go about three miles per thousand feet, but you don't get still air in reality, you get cross winds and so on, and it isn't like flying a sailplane which can ascend on thermals. You tried to keep height, see where you wanted to come down and do so with full flaps. The descent is a very steep angle indeed. When I was at Netheravon, I was out for a run along the towpath one morning when a young Spitfire pilot came up and said he'd always wanted a flight in a glider and could I arrange him a trip? So, later that day, we took him up. We got cast off at about 2,500 feet, near the edge of the airfield. I took the glider up to the stall, then put it nose-down, coming down very steeply, and put on full flaps, which are like big barn doors, to reduce speed. You come down almost like a lift! Now, you're in charge of the controls, you're trained for it, you know exactly what you are doing and what's happening. This young Spitfire pilot was stood in the cockpit doorway, all the way down. I levelled out and landed. When we stopped, he was ashen, and said 'I've never been so scared in all my life, I'd never do that again!'

I said 'Well, if you could take me up in your Spitfire, you'd be able to frighten me to death!"

Of course, he was used to being in control of a powered aircraft, which is a very different experience and what he had been trained for.

On 18 September 1944, I was the second pilot, Sergeant R Wade being first pilot. This was because my training had been rushed through, and Sergeant Wade was a more experienced pilot. Flying a Horsa, being towed, is very tiring, because you have to concentrate constantly on being at the right distance behind the tug – no automatic pilot in a glider, you have to fly it all the way. On a three-and-a-half-hour flight, say, you would need two or three pilots. In the event, we landed in soft ploughed fields near Wolfheze without incident.

The No. 2 Wing War Diary noted that at '1415 – Flak much heavier and number of aircraft were shot down'. Staff Sergeant Reg Grant, also of 'E' Squadron, described the scene: 'The Germans, expecting reinforcements, and helped by the delay, had by now brought up anti-aircraft guns, so some of the gliders and Dakotas carrying paratroopers got a very hot reception. The LZ was covered in smoke, the enemy having set fire to the grass and gorse upwind of the area. Some of the glider pilots, unable to see the ground until they were about fifty feet above it, landed very fast, hitting all kinds of obstacles.' Two hundred and ninety-seven gliders had headed for Arnhem, of which, for a variety of reasons, twenty-four failed to arrive, including fourteen forced down prematurely by flak. Two hundred and twenty-four had been allocated to LZ 'X', of which 189 arrived at the correct site, amongst them Lieutenant Brazier and Sergeant

Hibbert, who put Chalk 848 down on LZ 'X' without drama. Sergeant Potter then immediately set about unloading the glider:

> Using our explosive method, the bulldozer and all our other gear was successfully unloaded without damage to anyone or anything (except the glider). The explosives were attached to the struts in such a way that the detonating wave was away from the fuselage in order that no damage would be sustained to the fuselage or its contents. Bear in mind that our trailer, apart from other engineering equipment, contained a large quantity of explosives.

From 1500 hrs onwards, the newly-arrived glider pilots sought out and gathered in their squadrons, ready to move off. Lieutenant Colonel Place's No. 2 Wing was ordered, via Wolfheze, to a small area of high ground in woods of the Ommershoff estate, a few hundred yards north of the Hartenstein Hotel, where Divisional HQ was located, and slightly to the west, right on the western edge of Oosterbeek's built-up area. With no further aerial reinforcements to accommodate, 1st Air Landing Brigade had at last been able to relinquish the drop and landing zones, moving into Oosterbeek. Whilst the 2nd South Staffordshires were detailed to join the parachute brigades' push into Arnhem, the Border Regiment and King's Own Scottish Borderers also joined the Oosterbeek defensive line. The glider pilots were required to plug the gap left by the South Staffords being re-deployed to Arnhem. To the immediate south of Place's pilots was the 1st Border Regiment, whose companies were thinly spread from there, straddling the Utrechtseweg and continuing right down to the Westerbouwing and Driel ferry on the Rhine. To the immediate north was the 21st Independent Parachute Squadron and 4th Squadron RE, with the 7th King's Own Scottish Borderers occupying positions from west to east across what was effectively the top segment of an oblong-shaped perimeter, immediately south of the arterial railway line. Other units then held the line southwards, to the riverside polder east of the church at Lower Oosterbeek. Remarkably, given the battle's fluid ebb and flow over the days ahead, Pace's men fought throughout in more or less the same positions, given some minor adjustments dependent upon enemy pressure.

At 1900 hours, No. 2 Wing at last moved off from the LZ, 'E' Squadron leading, followed by 'C', Wing HQ, and 'F' Squadron. The column marched down from Wolfheze, turning left into the Utrechtesweg, passing the wrecked car and bodies of General Kussin and his companions, and eastwards towards Oosterbeek. After a few hundred yards, beyond the Koude Herberg crossroads and just before the Hartenstein, the glider pilots turned north, shortly occupying their allotted position in the line, where they dug slit trenches. Wing HQ moved into a large house on the edge of the built-up area. According to the No. 2 Wing War Diary, the glider pilots spent a 'disturbed night with considerable firing coming from the direction of railway line, but no attack developed'.

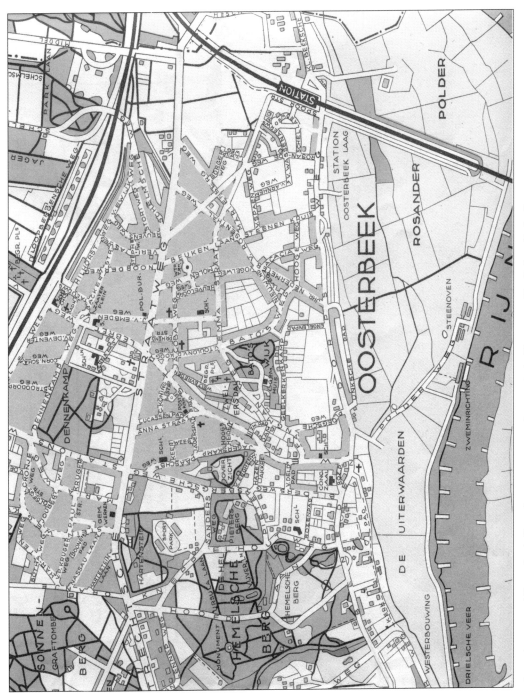

A wartime map of Oosterbeek (for colour version see plate section). (Courtesy of Dr Robert Voskuil)

ARNHEM 1944

The following morning, Father 'Chig', a Worcester man, did his rounds of the squadrons, during which the positions were strafed by Me 109s for thirty minutes. 'Chig' found himself sharing a slit-trench with another Worcestershire man: Lieutenant Peter Brazier. The padre later wrote that 'Quite early on in the battle, I was sharing a slit-trench with him while Me 109s were strafing us. Peter was quite unconcerned, cracking jokes with his men in nearby trenches.' With No. 2 Wing preparing to defend the western boundary of the British position, and No. 1 Wing gathered about and providing defence for Divisional HQ at the nearby Hartenstein, Messerschmitts aside, the battle proper had yet to reach them. That was taking place north of the railway line, as 4th Parachute Brigade attempted to fight its way eastwards into Arnhem, and likewise further east along the Utrechtseweg. As we have seen, this forlorn effort to reinforce Lieutenant Colonel Frost ended in disaster, the survivors streaming back into Oosterbeek. At 1600 hrs, the third lift, bringing in elements of 1st Polish Parachute Brigade Group, arrived, the landing zone a battlefield and under fire. With some understatement, the No. 2 Wing diarist recorded that 'The situation for the first time appeared a little difficult, and orders were issued for a fairly small perimeter to be held by the Division'. Wing HQ had by now moved to 17 Hartensteinlaan, at the end of the road on the north side of the common across the Utrechtseweg from Divisional HQ. 'Chig' wrote that 'We were warned, during the evening, to expect a large German attack from the north, which was our area together with the King's Own Scottish Borderers. As a result, there was little attempt at sleeping. "E" and "F" Squadrons, who had withdrawn to the woods and houses just north of Wing HQ, had a pretty busy time.' Soon, the battle would arrive in Oosterbeek – with ferocity.

On the evening of Monday 18 September 1944, *Panzerjager-Abteilung* 657's *Panzer-Kompanie* 224, commanded by *Oberleutnant* Alfred May, part of a German coastal defence formation, was allocated to Division von Tettau, which was responsible for attacking the western side of the Oosterbeek perimeter. 224 was equipped with captured French Char B1 tanks, the 75mm guns of which had been replaced by flamethrowers, the tanks re-designated *Flammpanzer* B2 (f). May's tanks arrived from Ypenburg airfield near The Hague during the afternoon of 19 September. Von Tetta deployed gave three *Flammpanzers* to the Dutch Nazi SS-*Standartenführer* Hans Michel Lippert, under whose command were SS battalions Helle, Eberwein and Schulz. These units were to attack from the west – against the line thinly held by the 9th Field Company RE, 4th Parachute Squadron, 'A' Company of 1st Border and 'E' and 'F' Squadrons. No. 2 Wing War Diary reports that on the morning of 20 September, 'enemy pressure increased greatly . . . "F" Squadron was forced out of its wood by a much superior force of SS troops supported by self-propelled guns. They retired with considerable losses to Divisional HQ. Heavy pressure also forced us to relinquish our hold on high ground at 689789, "E" Squadron withdrawing into wood 694792, joining with the Independent Parachute Company and the composite body moving south to join the Border Regiment.'

In his diary, 'Chig' wrote that 'We seem to have had a fair number of casualties. Briscoe and Brazier of "E" Squadron both put up a magnificent show – being cut off, they called their chaps and simply charged right through the enemy.' Later, Major Jackson, 'E' Squadron's commander, spoke of how 'two flights . . . had been heavily attacked and after a stiff fight against overwhelming odds, during which they were cut off from the main Allied position, they decided to break out. This they did in a gallant dash through the enemy lines, giving Jerry everything they had as they came through, and succeeded in regaining the main position which was strongly held.' In his unpublished notes, 'Chig' also recorded that '"E" and "F" Squadrons had had a pretty busy time', and that 'Wednesday morning brought a renewed attack on our front. I had my first sight of a German tank, like a pre-historic monster, slowly approaching part of "E" Squadron. It was knocked out by a PIAT gun after what seemed an endless wait as it came nearer and nearer and at last within good range.' In reality, whether this was really a 'tank', a self-propelled gun or some other tracked armoured vehicle it is impossible to say – but no known German loss on this day can be attributed to this entry. Nonetheless, in a subsequent report in Bromsgrove School's magazine, 'the Adjutant' of Lieutenant Brazier's unit writes that 'On one occasion, alone with an infantry anti-tank projector, he stalked a tank, waited until it was twenty yards from him and then destroyed it'. Whether this was one and the same incident referred to by 'Chig' cannot be confirmed – but must be considered a distinct possibility. On the other hand, without sleep, proper food or water, and under fire, how sure were men when finding a more peaceful moment to write-up records and diaries that events were remembered accurately and on the right day? Frequently, survivors have admitted to it all becoming 'a bit of blur'. Moreover, in the confusion of battle, doubtless men, with various weapons, fired at the same target, perhaps oblivious to the other's presence or involvement, meaning that a target could be claimed destroyed by multiple soldiers (as is proven to happen in an air battle). So just how accurate the written record is, really is a matter of conjecture which will doubtless vex historians forever. At 1500 hrs that day, the remnants of 'F' Squadron moved into a wood to plug the gap between 'E' Squadron and the Border Regiment. Also at 1500 hrs, one of the flamethrowing tanks trundled down Sonnenberglaan towards the Utrechtseweg – and was promptly destroyed by a 17-pounder of 2nd (Oban) Anti-Tank Battery. Simultaneously, another clanked east along Utrechtseweg, supported by SS infantry – and was knocked out by a Border Regiment 6-pounder outside the Koude Herberg Inn. If Lieutenant Brazier did knock out a tank that day, it was not either of these *Flammpanzers*, assuming that 'Chig' was correct when recording that the action took place that particular morning.

The following day was more of the same: the usual 0600 hrs mortar barrage, followed by various probing attacks by SS and other troops supported by armour. After the enemy brought up a self-propelled gun into the wood, 'E' Squadron was pushed out, re-locating to the corner of Hartenstienlaan and Oranjeweg, on the left flank of 'F' Squadron. On 'E' Squadron's left was 'A' Company of 1st Border, and to 'F' Squadron's right, in Paul Krugerstraat, the King's Own Scottish Borderers. In the afternoon, 'F' Squadron counter-attacked and drove the Germans further back into the woods. Mortaring, however, according to the No. 2 Wing War Diary, was 'severe', causing 'considerable casualties'. On 22 September, Brigadier Hicks sent a message confirming that 'We're up agin it'. Heavy shelling and mortaring continued throughout the day, but the glider squadrons held firm, By 23 September, the Wing diarist increased the status of the enemy's bombardment to 'intense', adding that 'Stocks of food and water very low. Many casualties.' Sadly, 22-year-old Lieutenant Peter Brazier would be amongst them – but, as is so often the case, confusion abounds regarding the date and circumstances of his death in action.

The CWGC records Peter Brazier's death as having occurred on '23/24 September 1944'. According to the Arnhem Roll of Honour, his field grave was located '100 metres North of the Hartenstein Hotel' – which would be on the common across the road, where the Airborne Memorial now stands. After the battle, it was Father George Pare whose records included reference to Peter – his hand-scribbled notes recording that his information concerning the deaths of both Staff Sergeant Gould and Lieutenant Brazier was 'via Briscoe'. This was Lieutenant R.W. Briscoe, also of 'E' Squadron. Back at Down Ampney, we know from survivor Ron Johnson that Briscoe was a hut-mate of Peter's and his, so would have known Peter well. Moreover, 'Chig's' record of 'Briscoe and Brazier' having charged through the enemy together places them in the same area. It may well be, that Lieutenant Briscoe buried Staff Sergeant Gould, who was killed and buried near Sonnenberg House, and Lieutenant Brazier, passing that information to Father Pare. What is in dispute, however, is the date of 22 September 1944 – which I believe to be erroneous.

On 16 June 1946 – less than a year after the battle – a survivor, Sergeant J.R.V. Davis, wrote the following letter to the 'E' Squadron Adjutant at RAF Down Ampney:

> With reference to your letter regarding S. Sgt Gould. The only information I have is as follows: On the morning of the 25th, we were holding a position with Lieutenant Brazier, linking up with the machine-gun post and a company of the Border Regiment. A flame-throwing tank overran our position, followed by another of French design. S. Sgt Gould and myself remained in position until the tanks got behind us and cut us off from our own troops. We decided to try and get through to re-join them. In doing so, we came under machine-gun fire from one of these tanks at very short range.
>
> S.Sgt Gould, who was in front, appeared to have been severely wounded by this burst. I was also wounded, in the back and arm. From the position in which I fell, I called to S.Sgt Gould and received no reply. I attempted to get to him but was unable to do so as he lay in the open in direct view of the tank. As far as I could see he was without doubt killed (I was only a matter of ten yards away).

Staff Sergeant Percy 'Nat' Gould. (Dave & Sally Hayward)

Percy Gould (centre, rear) 'capturing a German soldier' during training, probably when serving with the Royal Artillery in 1940. (Dave & Sally Hayward)

I could make no further attempts to get to S.Sgt Gould as I was again wounded myself by a grenade from the tank.

With regard to Lieutenant Brazier, all I can tell you is as follows: He, when the tanks first appeared, tried to get to Sqn HQ for a PIAT. He did not reappear and as far as I can gather was also killed in doing so.

I have already given this information to a person who was inquiring regarding missing personnel immediately upon my arrival in England.

Many years after the event, Mr Davis recorded the following of his experience:

As I am now in my eighties, I am afraid my memory is not very good. However, I was second-pilot to Staff Sgt Gould – known to us all as 'Nat Gould'. We took off from Down Ampney on the second load – think it was a Sunday, and were part of 'E' Squadron. Our load consisted of a small bulldozer and a section of men.

ARNHEM 1944

Davis and Gould, however, were on the second lift, on Monday, 18 September 1944, and the only bulldozer carried to Holland was by Lieutenant Brazier, so that detail is also incorrect. Mr Davis continued:

> We landed quite near to other gliders – rather late as our tug was unable to keep up with the others. We found that we had to saw the tail off with a bit of a battle going on around us. From there on it's all a bit hazy. I can remember we then took up a position on the outside perimeter and had several moves. On one occasion we moved at night, holding the tails of each other's jackets. As I had the Bren, we were usually positioned on the outside of our platoon – this gave us a lot of mortar fire and the Bren jammed up with soil etc. However, eventually we had a flame-throwing tank attack our trench. 'Nat" decided it would be better to move back into the woods. It seemed to be quiet and the tank had moved on. Not to be – he was in a dip with machine-gun barrels just showing over the top. He opened fire, killing 'Nat'.

Staff Sergeant Gould's Glider Pilot's flying brevet brooch. (Dave & Sally Hayward)

Staff Sergeant Raymond Percy Gould was a married man and father. Born on 4 May 1921, son of Percy and Ivy Gould, of Harrow, Middlesex, 'Nat' was an eighteen-year-old shop assistant when he enlisted at Roxeth in the Territorial Army, Royal Engineers, on 2 May 1939. When Britain mobilised for war, Sapper Gould was called to full-time service on 24 August 1939. On 1 August 1940, he was transferred to the Royal Artillery as a gunner with the 58th (Middlesex) Searchlight Regiment. During the forthcoming aerial Battle of Britain and the subsequent Blitz, this unit contributed to the defence of East Anglian airfields and the industrial East Midlands. Whilst serving as a gunner, 'Nat' married Jenny See at Hendon on 16 August 1941. The couple's home is recorded as having been at 15 Chippenham Gardens, Kilburn, NW6; the Goulds would be blessed with one child, a daughter, Sally. Still serving at home, on 7 August 1942, having volunteered, 'Nat' transferred to the Army Air Corps and Glider Pilot Regiment. Successfully passing his *ab initio* and glider pilot training, Sergeant Gould's flying brevet was awarded on 13 March 1943. Three months later, on 17 June 1943, 'Nat' was off with the Glider Pilot Regiment to North Africa, participating in the invasions of Sicily and Italy before returning home on 10 December 1943. On 18 September 1944, Staff Sergeant Gould and Sergeant J.R.V Davis flew to Holland; the latter's account continues:

The Flammpanzer destroyed in Sonneberglaan on 20 September 1944. (Dr Robert Voskuil)

Sonneberglaan in 2017. (Author)

I hit the ground – a bullet through my rump, which was bleeding badly. After lying dead for ages, I eventually crawled out of its sight, and found another small trench where I could push my bottom against the side to try and stop the bleeding. There were lots of mortars firing everywhere and something fell out of the tree and dropped behind me. I put my hand behind and found a German stick bomb. I threw it as quick as I could but it went off just in front of my face. As I'd covered my eyes with my right arm, it took most of the blast. I lost all use of my right shoulder and arm, and all feeling. In fact I thought it was blown off. In fact, the bits of the grenade had cut some nerves and blocked the main cerebral artery. When I had come to my senses I saw a Red Cross man going in and out of a door, so I upped and walked towards this. There was deuce of a battle going on and a lot of shouting to get down.

Anyhow, I had some attention to my wounds and found several others, including a German in the cellar. He had been put outside as dead but had been seen to move so brought back inside.

That night the Royal Army Medical Corps [RAMC] orderly told us that the withdrawal was happening that night. Unfortunately, I couldn't go as I had temporarily lost use of my legs, caused by shock. Next morning, I and the others were picked up. In fact my pick-up was a private car. Eventually I went to a barracks and after a few days put on a train to a small hospital near Munich. This was a convent with the Sisters of Mercy and the Matron still there. I stayed there until we were brought back by the Americans when the war ended.

Again, the only problem, with both the 1946 and later accounts is with the date of 25 September 1944.

Once more, the CWGC is noncommittal regarding the exact date of Staff Sergeant Gould's death, recording this as '23/25 September 1944'. No, 2 Wing's War Diary, however, records that, on 24 September 1944, 'In the afternoon, a combination of shelling, mortaring, self-propelled guns and a flame-throwing tank forced us to abandon the wood. The survivors took up positions in the houses across the road, covering the exits from the wood. No. reinforcements could be obtained.' The War Diary for 25 September 1944, concerns only orders and events concerning the evacuation, which took place, under fire, that night. By his own admission, Sergeant Davis was badly wounded and in shock. Had he mistaken the date, even in 1946, so soon after events, it would be both unsurprising and understandable.

From the evidence available, my conclusion is that both Lieutenant Brazier and Staff Sergeant Gould were most likely killed on *24* September 1944. Indeed, shortly after 'E' Squadron's survivors returned to England and Lieutenant Brazier's status was confirmed as 'killed in action', in his letter to Peter's parents, the 'E' Squadron Adjutant, Lieutenant Glynn Jones, who also shared the hut at Down Ampney with Lieutenants Brazier and Briscoe, and 2nd Lieutenant Johnson, wrote that 'The last time he was seen was on

The green opposite the Hartenstein mansion, now the Airborne Museum, in the streets and woods beyond which Lieutenant Peter Brazier and Staff Sergeant 'Nat' Gould fought – and died. (Author)

Sunday, September 24th, going forward into a wood armed with a PIAT gun, intent on knocking out a tank. Throughout the entire operation he carried himself with great dash and gallantry, and was in every way and an example to us all.'

This statement is consistent with Sergeant Davis's recollection that Lieutenant Brazier went to fetch a PIAT. It is likely, then, that Peter reached Wing HQ, collected a PIAT, and was killed stalking the *Flammpanzer* which had attacked his men. What remains unknown is who last saw him alive, stalking the tank.

Of the young subaltern, the commanding officer of No. 2 Wing wrote that 'Peter behaved with splendid gallantry and devotion to duty and at all times showed a grand spirit. He saved more than one nasty situation by his coolness, courage and great fighting spirit. He was one of my most promising young officers, and lived up to our valuation of him when his example and courage were most needed.'

On 10 May 1945, Lieutenant Brazier's name was amongst those published in the *London Gazette* of the officers and men Mentioned in Despatches for their 'gallant and distinguished service in North West Europe'.

1944, in fact, had been a cruel year for the Brazier family: Peter's cousin, Captain Edward Sydney John Brazier was also killed in action that year, whilst serving in Burma with the Worcestershire Regiment. Fortunately, Peter's brother, Roger, survived his service as a naval officer during the Battle of the Atlantic, and cousins, Ted Meredith, a Spitfire pilot, and his army officer brother Ray, also returned safely. After the war, as an aside, Roger travelled to Arnhem to find his beloved brother's grave – and met Richenda, who would become his wife, on the 'boat train' at Liverpool Station, London. Both were travelling to the Hook of Holland via Harwich, a journey Roger Brazier would never have made had Peter not been killed at Oosterbeek. Roger's daughters, Rachel, Christine and Vanessa, are acutely aware that if not for their uncle's death in action, they would not be here.

Lieutenant Brazier's original grave marker at Oosterbeek. (Christine Campbell)

Lieutenant Brazier's headstone at Oosterbeek today. (21.A.18). (Author)

Staff Sergeant Gould's original grave marker at Oosterbeek. ((27.B.9). (Dave & Sally Hayward)

Staff Sergeant Gould's headstone at Oosterbeek today. (Author)

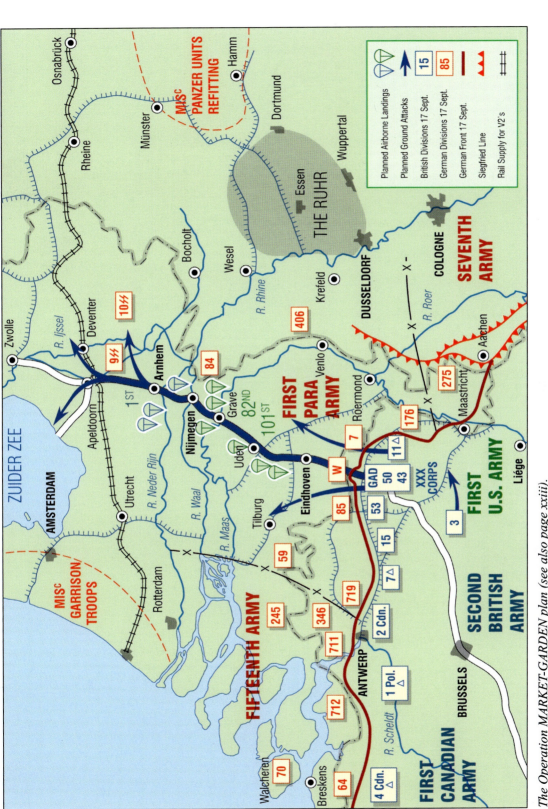

The Operation MARKET-GARDEN plan (see also page xxiii).

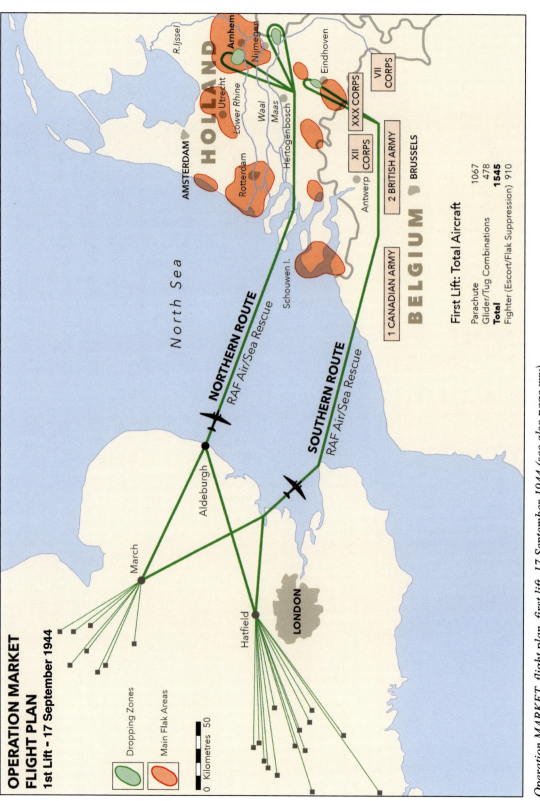

Operation MARKET flight plan, first lift, 17 September 1944 (see also page xxv).

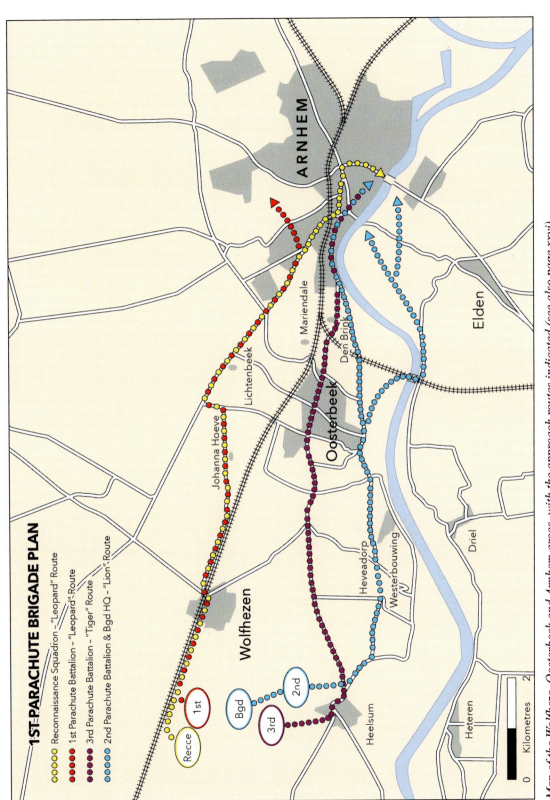

Map of the Wolfheze, Oosterbeek and Arnhem areas, with the approach routes indicated (see also page xxvi).

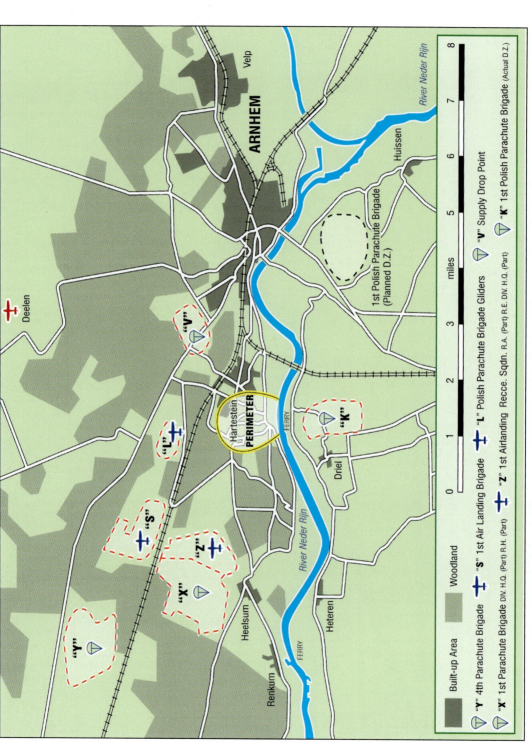

Location of the landing and drop zones for Operation MARKET GARDEN (see also page 9).

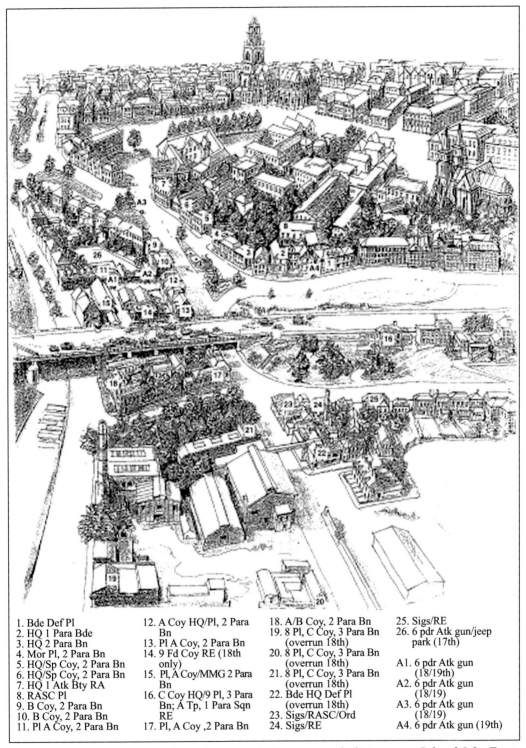

1. Bde Def Pl
2. HQ 1 Para Bde
3. HQ 2 Para Bn
4. Mor Pl, 2 Para Bn
5. HQ/Sp Coy, 2 Para Bn
6. HQ/Sp Coy, 2 Para Bn
7. HQ 1 Atk Bty RA
8. RASC Pl
9. B Coy, 2 Para Bn
10. B Coy, 2 Para Bn
11. Pl A Coy, 2 Para Bn
12. A Coy HQ/Pl, 2 Para Bn
13. Pl A Coy, 2 Para Bn
14. 9 Fd Coy RE (18th only)
15. Pl, A Coy/MMG 2 Para Bn
16. C Coy HQ/9 Pl, 3 Para Bn; A Tp, 1 Para Sqn RE
17. Pl, A Coy, 2 Para Bn
18. A/B Coy, 2 Para Bn
19. 8 Pl, C Coy, 3 Para Bn (overrun 18th)
20. 8 Pl, C Coy, 3 Para Bn (overrun 18th)
21. 8 Pl, C Coy, 3 Para Bn (overrun 18th)
22. Bde HQ Def Pl (overrun 18th)
23. Sigs/RASC/Ord
24. Sigs/RE
25. Sigs/RE
26. 6 pdr Atk gun/jeep park (17th)
A1. 6 pdr Atk gun (18/19th)
A2. 6 pdr Atk gun (18/19)
A3. 6 pdr Atk gun (18/19)
A4. 6 pdr Atk gun (19th)

Dispositions of 1 Parachute Brigade Group under the command of Lieutenant Colonel John Frost, CO of the 2nd Parachute Battalion, as on Monday, 18 September 1944 (see also page 27).

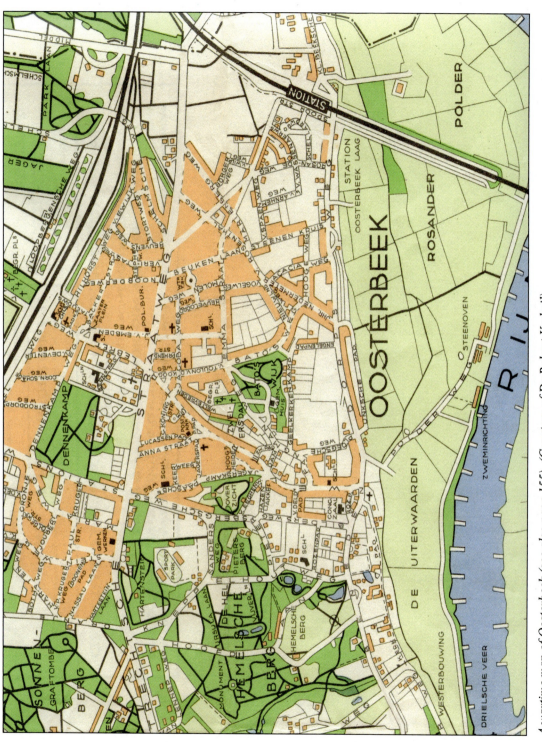

A wartime map of Oosterbeek (see also page 155). (Courtesy of Dr Robert Voskuil)

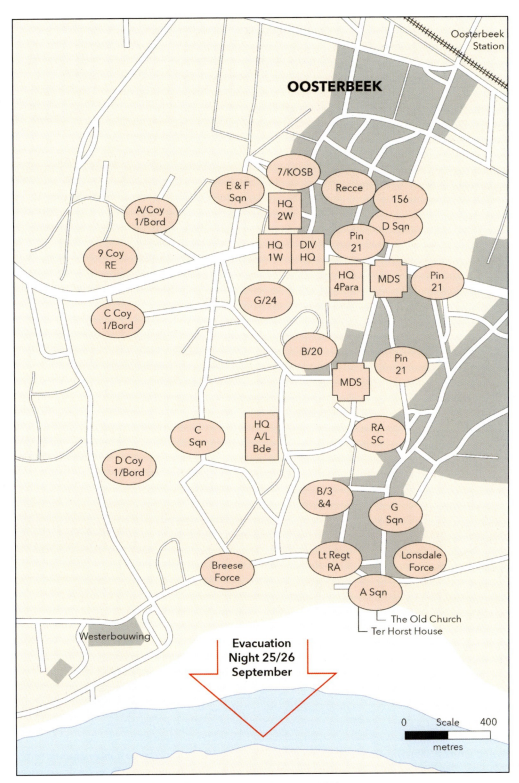

Unit dispositions in the Oosterbeek area (see also page 292).

The Cross of Sacrifice at the Arnhem-Oosterbeek War Cemetery, immaculately maintained by the Commonwealth War Graves Commission and a deeply moving place of pilgrimage for visitors the world over.

It was, not uncommonly, some months before Peter's death was official and published. On 25 September 1945, his parents received this letter, from a Betty McLeod of Hull:

> It was with deep regret that I read today in the 'Daily Telegraph' of the official notification of the death of your son at Arnhem.
>
> At that time, my husband and I were stationed at Down Ampney, and it was my pleasure to work with 'E' Squadron, Glider Pilot Regiment, as a clerk, and my husband serviced the gliders. We both knew Peter very well, and I can honestly say for both of us that he was one of the nicest boys we could hope to meet. In RAF slang, 'a smashing type'. We watched the gliders go out and as men came back in twos and threes, we looked for Peter, and everyone was fed up when he didn't come back and I must confess that I hoped that one day the news would come that he had been made a prisoner.
>
> Nothing I can say will, I know, take the place of your son, but I thought that perhaps this tribute from a stranger to you, may lessen the grief.
>
> May I also say, in conclusion, that I never heard anyone say they disliked Peter, and in an assembly of men of all types, that is a very high tribute. For myself, I would say I found him charming, interesting to talk to and full of fun. He often used to come into my office to chat when he hadn't much work to do, and when one meets so many different people in the forces, it is a refreshing change to find someone whom you instinctively like.
>
> Please accept this token of sympathy from my husband and myself, who are proud to call Peter a friend.

'Chig' said simply that 'Peter was a grand boy, a really fine and courageous leader adored by his men'.

On this occasion, the last line goes to Ron Johnson, ninety-six years young at the time of writing, who survived being wounded twice himself at Arnhem, and suffered the privations of being a prisoner of war: 'I have thought about Peter often over the years. What a waste'.

Chapter 11

Staff Sergeant Eric 'Tom' Holloway MM, Glider Pilot Regiment, and Lieutenant Ian Meikle, 1st Airlanding Light Regiment, Royal Regiment of Artillery

Whilst 'E' and 'F' Squadrons of the Glider Pilot Regiment's No. 2 Wing fought tenaciously to hold their line north-west of Divisional HQ, elsewhere in the Oosterbeek perimeter, other Glider Pilot Regiment units fought with similar bravery and determination. Amongst their number was Staff Sergeant 'Tom' Holloway of 'G' Squadron.

Eric John Holloway was born on 1 February 1920, to Henry Ernest Holloway, a builder, and his wife, Sarah Elizabeth. The latest addition to the Holloway clan was the youngest of nine children, and entered the world at the family home in Cranbury Avenue, Eastleigh, Hampshire. Later, the Holloways moved to 25 Factory Road, Eastleigh, where the youngest Holloway lived for most of his short life. His niece, Peggy, remembers that:

> I used to see him a lot, he was such fun to be with, so popular, everyone always wanted him at their house at Christmas. In those days, we used to go to the 'Saturday morning flicks' at the local cinema; there he was very taken with a particular actor, Tom Mix, who played the hero in numerous cowboy films between 1909 and 1935, always running around pretending to have two revolvers and saying he was Tom Mix, kept on and on about it. So, that is why everyone called him 'Tom', nobody referred to him as 'Eric'. Tom had a happy life, really, he loved dancing and having fun. He had a shock of very fair hair, so his other nickname was 'Snowball'.

Tom was educated at Chamberlayne Road and Toynbee Road Boys' Schools. He was a sportsman, playing right-half for Eastleigh Corinthians Football Club, and was a member of the victorious team which won the Eastleigh Benevolent Cup in the last season of peace. He was also a diving champion at Eastleigh Swimming Club. After leaving school, Tom became a machine shop apprentice at Southern Railway. Aged seventeen, he moved on to become a trainee civil engineer working on the Winchester by-pass. On

The Holloway family, Eric, known as 'Tom' Holloway second left, front row. (Don Holloway)

18 April 1940, however, the twenty-year-old Hampshireman enlisted into the Welch Regiment as an infantry soldier. Posted to 305 Infantry Training Centre, on 22 June 1940, Private Holloway was for some reason transferred to the 8th Royal Warwickshires. Promotion to Lance-Corporal followed on 6 July 1940, and a move to 143 Infantry Brigade HQ on 2 September. There, on 26 April 1941, unusually, Tom reverted to the rank of Private 'at his own request'. Thereafter Private Holloway was in succession attached to No. 2 Technical Training Centre, No. 12 Field Hygiene, and 'G' Branch Training Establishment, Royal Army Ordnance Corps (RAOC). On 7 May 1942, Tom was transferred to the HQ Intelligence Section, but clearly none of this was to his liking: on 15 June 1942, he volunteered to join the Glider Pilot Regiment. Having successfully passed all flying training, receiving the 'Army Flying Badge' on 11 January 1943, on 16 June, Sergeant Holloway went to North Africa, disembarking ten days later and subsequently participating in the invasions of Sicily and Italy. On 9 December 1943, he returned home to be promoted Staff Sergeant on 29 December. On 5 May 1944, however, Tom broke his right leg in unrecorded circumstances whilst 'On duty but not

to blame'; he was admitted to the RAF hospital at Wroughton, near Swindon, until discharged on 13 May. Whether he participated in any of the following month's D-Day-related operations is unrecorded.

Staff Sergeant Holloway was a member of 10 Flight, commanded by Captain Maurice Priest, in Major Bob Croot's 'G' Squadron, based at Fairford in Gloucestershire, a component of Lieutenant Colonel Ian Murray's No. 1 Wing. 'G' Squadron was scheduled to fly in the second lift to Arnhem on Monday, 18 September 1944. Due to arrive in Holland at 1000 hrs, the lift was delayed for five hours owing to fogbound English airfields. Eventually, Brigadier Hackett's 4th Parachute Brigade dropped on Ginkel Heath, to the north-west of Wolfheze, and shortly afterwards 275 Horsa, fifteen Hamilcar and four Hadrian gliders descended on LZs 'S' and 'X'. Tom's second pilot was Staff Sergeant Mark Leaver, the pair flying one of fifteen 9 and 10 Flight Horsas, towed by 260 Squadron's Stirlings. The flight to LZ 'X', just west of Wolfheze, in Chalk 1003 lasted three hours and ten minutes, Holloway and Leaver landing safely late in the afternoon. The latter recalled that 'apart from light flak over various parts of Holland, the flight was fairly uneventful'. Chalk 1003's load was Sergeant Flower and five men of No. 2 Detachment, 261 (Airborne) Field Park Company, RE, their jeep – and a trailer full of explosives bound for Arnhem Bridge.

Staff Sergeant Eric 'Tom' Holloway – awarded a posthumous Military Medal for his efforts protecting gun positions in Oosterbeek. (Dave Baverstock)

After unloading, Staff Sergeant Leaver recalled that:

> We made our way to Wolfheze, where we received orders to make our way to the bridge in Arnhem, via Oosterbeek and lower road near the river. We made good progress until rounding a bend in Klingelbeekseweg, running into heavy fire from the junction with Utrechtseweg, where German tanks were located. We did as speedy an about-turn as possible with a jeep and trailer, managing to return back around the bend just as the Germans spotted us and brought their heavy guns to bear.
>
> As there was no other way available, we decided to wait near the green adjacent to the railway station at Den Brink (now two private houses and actually Oosterbeek-Laag), until reinforcements arrived. After dusk, we had several skirmishes with German patrols but held our position.
>
> At about midnight on 18 September, and after hearing a lot of heavy firing coming from the other side of the railway line, we heard quite a large group of men marching along the bottom road from the direction of Oosterbeek, approaching our position. We issued a challenge and were very relieved when it turned out to be the South Staffords. We advised them of the position and

decided that we would continue on to the bridge at first light. This we did, but made little progress and were taking a lot of casualties.

On that fateful day, 19 September 1944, the courageous effort to reach and reinforce the small British garrison desperately clinging on to the northern end of Arnhem Bridge ended in failure – with high casualties. Moreover, with the arrival in Arnhem of *Sturmbrigade* 280's ten StuG III self-propelled guns, the battle swung inexorably in the enemy's favour, it being clear that there could be no further attempt to reinforce Lieutenant Colonel Frost and his small detachment at Arnhem Bridge. Consequently, as previously explained, the survivors of this forlorn attempt were ordered to form a defensive perimeter around Oosterbeek. No. 1 Wing had moved into the grounds of the Hartenstein Hotel, securing the area and thus enabling Divisional HQ to function there. 'G' Squadron's 9 Flight was tasked with providing protection for a battery of 75mm pack howitzers belonging to Lieutenant Colonel W.F.K. 'Sheriff' Thompson's 1st Air Landing Light Regiment RA. The six troops of Thompson's three batteries had occupied positions around the old church at lower Oosterbeek, firing in support of Lieutenant Colonel Frost at Arnhem Bridge – Target 'Mike One'. 10 Flight, however, was not deployed as a unit but dispersed as reinforcements for the other squadrons.

During the afternoon, many of those who survived the failed attempt to get through the enemy's blocking line near the St Elisabeth Hospital on the outskirts of western Arnhem, streamed into lower Oosterbeek. The commander of 'G' Squadron, Major Croot, organised these men into a defensive line on the perimeter's eastern side, stretching north across the polder from the Rhine to the Benedendorpsweg road. Staff Sergeants Holloway and Leaver, having been unable to get through to Arnhem Bridge with their RAOC comrades and explosives, were amongst the arrivals in lower Oosterbeek sometime that day. All troops in this south-eastern sector of the perimeter became known as 'Thompson Force', after the most senior British officer responsible for that area. Subsequently, Thompson entrusted his south-eastern defence to Major Dickie Lonsdale, second in command of 11th Parachute Battalion – and so was born 'Lonsdale Force'. However, as Lieutenant Mike Dauncey of 'G' Squadron's No. 9 Flight, who had not been involved in the earlier effort on Arnhem, later wrote 'We were in buoyant mood; the real battle had yet to start for us'. Having successfully blocked the way to Arnhem Bridge, however, *Kampgruppen* Möller and Harder were now ominously pressing westwards, bent on the airborne men's destruction.

By Wednesday, 20 September 1944, the 1st British Airborne Division found itself moving towards fighting an entirely defensive battle. As more German reinforcements arrived in the area, the enemy was able to concentrate mortar and artillery fire on the relatively compact perimeter, following this up with repeated attacks from armour supported by infantry. According to Staff Sergeant Leaver (who has referred to 'Eric', but for the purposes of consistency changed here to 'Tom'): 'Tom and I occupied the rear bedroom of the second house in a row at the back of the laundry, our position facing

Defending the Oosterbeek perimeter. Private Barr (drinking) and Lance Corporal Wilf Pridmore, both of Support Company, 1st Border Regiment, pictured in a foxhole on 20 September 1944. (Historic Military Press)

Men of HQ Company, 1st Border, pictured in foxholes in the Van Lennepweg gardens, 22 September 1944. (Historic Military Press)

over open land towards Arnhem . . . we had now been joined by a Bren gun team.' This house would have been at the southern end of Ploegseweg, to the immediate west of which was located the Van Hofwegen laundry. This sector, extending north to Fangmanweg and west to Weverstraat, was occupied by elements of the 2nd South Staffordshires, led by Major Robert Cain, whose men had deployed around to defend the Light Regiment's gun positions. The pressure exerted on the beleaguered British was relentless. *Kampfgruppe* Spindler attacked over the railway and through the culvert on Benedendorpsweg. This infantry attack was easily repelled by Vickers medium machine-guns, but not so easily dealt with were the StuG IIIs roaming about the parish. To the perimeter's east, 21-year-old Sergeant Jack Baskeyfield of the South Staffords' Anti-tank Platoon Support Company distinguished himself by destroying a StuG on Benedendorpsweg, and a mobile flak vehicle near the railway bridge, after which the German attack faltered and withdrew – buying time for the airborne men behind his position to organise a defence. Sadly, the brave young man from Stoke was killed during the action – for which 'signal act of valour' he was awarded the Victoria Cross.

When recounting his recollections many years later, Staff Sergeant Leaver recorded that the following events had occurred on '20 September 1944'. That, however, cannot be correct, as is so frequently the case. The events described undoubtedly occurred on Thursday, 21 September:

> During the morning, we spotted a German squad of about eight men setting up a mortar position about 400 metres to our left. We opened fire and cleared the site. There was no time for congratulations for from where the mortar had been appeared a Tiger tank, which wasted no time in demolishing our position, causing us to evacuate at very great speed. We then crossed the road at the back of the laundry under cover of a phosphorous grenade. We were then very lucky to get across the road without casualties, as a few minutes later a self-propelled gun with infantry support came down the road towards the laundry. With the assistance of Major Cain and his men, plus gunners from the 75mm howitzer site, this menace was suitably dealt with. We then occupied a house at the side of the laundry, adjacent to the gun battery.
>
> Early in the afternoon we were up in the front bedroom with an officer from the gun battery. We were feeling a bit hungry, so I volunteered to go down into the cellar at the rear of the house where there was quite a supply of bottled fruits and vegetables. Whilst making my way with some speed down the stairs (as the front door was missing and the stairs had previously been under fire), there was a very loud explosion in the front bedroom which blew me down the last few steps. I returned through the mother of all dust storms to the front bedroom where I found the artillery officer dead and Tom badly peppered with shrapnel from an 88mm airburst shell fired by a self-propelled gun situated on the other side of the open space to our front (the shell had entered through the bedroom window).

ARNHEM 1944

Major Cain wrote that 'There was a self-propelled (SP) gun which came every morning and afternoon and shelled us. I had been using a PIAT against it at a high angle. I had a gunnery officer in a house observing for me.' This was Lieutenant Ian Meikle, the Gun Position Officer of the adjacent 'B' Troop battery. Major Cain continued:

Ian Miekle. (Janice Chapman)

I fired about fifty bombs from this weapon, which blew my left eardrum in. I could not hit the gun. I doubled across the road with the PIAT and two bombs. There was a little house there with a shed. I looked round and saw the SP with a chap standing up in it. I put my head around the corner, and saw the man looking straight at me. I fired a bomb at the thing and it went off underneath it. His gun was swinging round on me, so I went back into my trench. I had just got over the road when he blew the shed right out of the ground, so it was very lucky I went back. After that, I did some more indirect firing with Ian Meikle, until he was killed. He was shouting instructions to me when the chimney pot from the house he was in fell into the trench I was in. The other man in the trench got out screaming and scrambling. I told him to come back, but he would not and I never saw him again. A rifle in the trench was trapped and the chimney pot, which was very solid, landed just near my leg. Luckily the PIAT bombs were not touched. Just after this, the tank came up the road. The chaps told me about it. I crept to the corner and there it was coming up the road. I put a bomb into the PIAT and fired at the tank. The range was about a hundred yards. I think it must have struck the track. The tank fired immediately in my direction, and this raised a huge cloud of dust and smoke. As soon as I could see the outline of the tank, I let it have another. This also raised a lot of dust again. The tank gun fired straight down the road. Then I loaded again and watched, and through the dust I saw the crew of the tank baling out. I had a couple of Brens on the road and told them to keep up continuous fire. I shouted out to the two field guns to get a gun up. I went round to get a nearer shot round to the left, and I met the crew. They were lurking further down the road behind the tank. They opened up with *Schmeissers*, but I got my men onto them and they were killed. Accidentally, the laundry had been burnt down, and I had a narrow shave. I threw a grenade, which hit the rafters and came straight back at me. I flung myself into the red-hot ashes, the grenade went off, but I wasn't touched. The tank crew was eliminated. Dickens and an officer on the spot told me this. The last bomb I fired (the sixth) went off in the PIAT, which was very near to my face. I had bits of stuff in my face and two black eyes. It blew me over backwards, and I was blind. I was shouting like a hooligan. I shouted to someone to get on the PIAT as there was another tank behind. I blubbered, yelled, and used some very bad language. They dragged me off to the

Regimental Aid Post (RAP) but I came back in about half an hour. Major Alan Bush of 3rd Parachute Battalion had taken over from me, so I reported to him and said 'I am no good, I am done'.

For this and other 'signal acts of valour' during the Battle of Arnhem, Major Robert Cain was also awarded the Victoria Cross; uniquely, of the five Arnhem VCs, he survived the experience. On 2 November 1944, the War Office published details of the award:

Lieutenant Ian Meikle, who spotted from a first-floor room in a building on Ploegseweg, Oosterbeek, for Major Robert Cain, who stalked the troublesome enemy self-propelled gun with a PIAT. Cain was later awarded a VC – the only VC to survive the battle. Lieutenant Meikle and Staff Sergeant Holloway were fatally wounded when the StuG III shelled the house they were in. (Janice Chapman)

In Holland on 19 September, 1944, Major Cain was commanding a rifle company of the South Staffordshire Regiment during the Battle of Arnhem when his company was cut off from the rest of the battalion and during the next six days was closely engaged with enemy tanks, self-propelled guns and infantry. The Germans made repeated attempts to break into the company position by infiltration and had they succeeded in doing so the whole situation of the Airborne Troops would have been jeopardised.

Major Cain, by his outstanding devotion to duty and remarkable powers of leadership, was to a large extent personally responsible for saving a vital sector from falling into the hands of the enemy.

On 20 September, a Tiger tank approached the area held by his company and Major Cain went out alone to deal with it armed with a PIAT. Taking up a position he held his fire until the tank was only 20 yards away when he opened up. The tank immediately halted and turned its guns on him, shooting away a corner of the house near where this officer was lying. Although wounded by machine gun bullets and falling masonry, Major Cain continued firing until he had scored several direct hits, immobilised the tank and supervised the bringing up of a 75mm howitzer which completely destroyed it. Only then would he consent to have his wounds dressed.

In the next morning, this officer drove off three more tanks by the fearless use of his PIAT, on each occasion leaving cover and taking up position in open ground with complete disregard for his personal safety.

During the following days, Major Cain was everywhere where danger threatened, moving amongst his men and encouraging them by his fearless example to hold out. He refused rest and medical attention in spite of the fact that his hearing had been seriously impaired because of a perforated eardrum and he was suffering from multiple wounds.

The StuG was destroyed, albeit too late to save Meikle and Holloway, and is pictured here, in Ploegseweg, in 1945. (Dr Robert Voskuil)

Another view of the Ploegseweg StuG. The young Dutchman is considering a British mortar round! (Dr Robert Voskuil)

On 25 September, the enemy made a concerted attack on Major Cain's position, using self-propelled guns, flame throwers and infantry. By this time the last PIAT had been put out of action and Major Cain was armed with only a light 2" mortar. However, by a skilful use of this weapon and his daring leadership of the few men still under his command, he completely demoralised the enemy who, after an engagement lasting more than three hours, withdrew in disorder.

Throughout the whole course of the Battle of Arnhem, Major Cain showed superb gallantry. His powers of endurance and leadership were the admiration of all his fellow officers and stories of his valour were being constantly exchanged amongst the troops. His coolness and courage under incessant fire could not be surpassed.

Again, however, there are certain inaccuracies in the citation: the action described on 20 September 1944 is that which, as previously explained, actually occurred the previous day (it is likely that this was Staff Sergeant Leaver's point of reference many years later). Also, the enemy armoured vehicle destroyed was not a 'Tiger' tank but the second of the two StuG IIIs lost by *Sturmbrigade* 280, this one in Ploegseweg.

Staff Sergeant Leaver continues regarding events following the shell exploding in the bedroom occupied by Lieutenant Meikle and Staff Sergeant Holloway: 'I called for medical assistance from the artillery battery. This came very quickly. We got Tom to Kate ter Horst's house by the church, which was now a Medical Aid Post.' Another glider pilot, Sergeant Bob Shipley, was also wounded but helped to carry Lieutenant Meikle on a mattress to the Ter Horst house. Inside, the scene must have been horrific. With scant medical supplies and basic facilities, with the Ter Horst children sheltering in the cellar, over 350 men, it is said, were treated by hard-pressed medical staff at the beautiful former rectory. Kate, however, had selflessly thrown open the doors, her acts of kindness towards the terribly wounded airborne men inspirational. Famously, the so-called 'Angel of Arnhem' also read passages from the New Testament to the wounded and dying men, including, appropriately, Psalm 91: 1-7:

> Thou shalt not be afraid for the terror by night;
> Nor for the arrow that flieth by day;
> Nor for the pestilence that walketh in darkness;
> Nor for the destruction that wasteth at noonday.
> A thousand shall fall at thy side,
> And ten thousand at thy right hand;
> But it shall not come nigh thee.

Sadly, neither Staff Sergeant Holloway or Lieutenant Meikle survived that day, 21 September 1944 (although the former's headstone incorrectly records his death as having occurred on 18 September 1944). Both were amongst some fifty British soldiers buried

Lieutenant Meikle and Staff Sergeant Holloway were taken to Kate ter Horst's nearby home, inundated with casualties and in use as a Regimental Aid Post. Sadly, both died there, and were buried in the garden. (Ter Horst Collection)

The western end of the Ter Horst house pictured in more peaceful circumstances in 2016. (Author)

An airborne soldier's grave outside the Ter Horst house. (Gelders Archief)

in Kate ter Horst's once tranquil garden; in 1946, they would be interred at the Arnhem-Oosterbeek Cemetery.

On 18 October 1944, the award of a Military Medal was approved for Staff Sergeant Tom Holloway; his citation read:

> During the period 18 – 25 September 1944, Staff Sergeant Holloway commanded a Section in a house in the area of Oosterbeek. He showed great courage in patrol work. When the enemy launched their first big attack against the gun positions he kept up effective fire with a Bren gun throughout the time the house was being demolished by a self-propelled gun at point blank range. By remaining at his post he was largely responsible for breaking up the enemy attack. His complete disregard for his personal safety saved what might have been a serious break-through by the enemy.

Tom's young niece, Peggy, remembered that

> When Tom was killed I was fourteen. We both had birthdays in February and the last time I saw him alive he said 'When this is all over we'll have a joint party with lots of food, we won't ask anyone else we'll just eat the lot ourselves!' After the war, the 'Flower Child' who had adopted Tom's grave came to stay with my grandmother, Tom's mother, but neither could speak each other's language – nonetheless, there was a bond there, difficult though communication between them was.

Staff Sergeant Mark Leaver continued fighting with Lonsdale Force until evacuated across the Rhine on the night of 25/26 September 1944; he died some years ago.

Arguably, Lieutenant Meikle also deserved a medal, but, like so many others, his deeds went unrecognised. His involvement in the destruction of the Ploegseweg StuG III and subsequent death is well-known – but, like most other casualties featured in this book, little or nothing personal has ever been previously published regarding the man himself.

Ian Ormiston Meikle was born on 16 August 1920 (coincidentally, the day I am writing this would have been his 97th birthday), at Upminster in Essex. His father, Ormiston, was Scottish, his mother, Phyllis, English. The family lived at 'High Trees', Butts Green Road, Hornchurch, Essex. The family was well off, Mr Meikle owing a heating business. Like the Bromsgrove Brazier building family, this enabled the Meikle children to attend public school. Ian and his younger brothers, David William and Colin Campbell, were all sent to board at Wycliffe College, at Stonehouse in Gloucestershire. Afterwards, Ian went up to Cambridge University, where, on 2 October 1939, the nineteen-year-old student attended No. 6 Reception Unit and enlisted. The student's height was recorded as 5ft 6in, his complexion fair, hair light brown and eyes brown.

Another StuG destroyed in Oosterbeek also remained in situ on Benedendorpsweg for long after the war, this one knocked-out by Lance Sergeant Jack Baskeyfield – who was awarded a posthumous VC. This photograph looks west, towards the Old Church and Baskefield's position near Acacialaan. (Dr Robert Voskuil)

The Benedendorpsweg StuG, looking east. (Dr Robert Voskuil)

The same view in 2017. (Author)

ERIC HOLLOWAY AND IAN MEIKLE

Although the Meikle family was Church of England, he gave his religion as 'agnostic'. Afterwards, Gunner 939022 IO Meikle, who could read, write and speak French fluently, was transferred to the Territorial Army Reserve, RA. On 20 June 1941, Ian was discharged after one year and 282 days of service, with a record of 'very good', having been granted 'an emergency commission'. Where 2nd Lieutenant Meikle was posted, or the units he served with prior to Arnhem is unfortunately not recorded in his Army Service Record. From letters home, however, we know that he served in North Africa and Italy. On 14 June 1943, he wrote an incredible letter to his parents, six typewritten foolscap pages, after Rommel's defeat in North Africa, describing in detail his experiences with 'Z' Troop, 1 Battery, Royal Horse Artillery. From this letter, we know that Ian fought at El Alamein, El Hamma, and throughout the Tunisian campaign. One interesting experience, relevant to this book, in many ways, he described after one occasion on which the 'troop had been shelled to hell'; Ian was ordered to bury Bombardier Hickmott. His CO had left with the troop's last gun, and Ian found that his own trucks had also left:

So, there I was, with not a soul in sight, with a shovel and a dead body. Still, I applied the tests to see if he really was dead (there wasn't much doubt about it, as he must have had pretty nearly a direct hit, and was bit of a mess), and then got down to it and dug a nice, deep, grave. It was sandy soil, and nice sort of digging, but it was rather a nasty business getting the body in. However, I managed it, and had just finished filling up the grave, when up came the Battery Captain, who had been sent to look for me. We fixed up some sort of cross, then he took me back in his truck to the Troop. We quickly found a new area, and for the rest of this day blazed away merrily without a shell in return.

Gunner Ernest Hickmott was thirty-three, killed on 22 July 1942, and now lies in the British War Cemetery at El Alamein.

Ian's letter concluded that:

The first and most important lesson is that even in the stickiest position you are pretty safe if you have your wits about you. In our troop of about sixty men, we had one killed, eight wounded, and five damaged by being run over, falling off trucks, or suffering from nerves. Of the wounded, four have already re-joined us, and most of the rest are back soon. The reason for low casualties is not that we weren't in dangerous places, for actually we were almost always the most forward of all the artillery, being right up with the tanks and infantry, it was simply that every officer and man had some previous experience of battle, and knew how to look after himself. Deep slit-trenches are dug at every opportunity, without any orders needed. Gunpits are deep and strongly made; trucks move quickly and with big intervals by day, and closely and with no lights showing by night. Officers out as observers never get out of their armoured cars or tanks, which insures them against anything but a most unlucky direct hit. And if we get in a position where we are shelled heavily, we move out like greased lightning. Another thing is that men can go for a surprising length of time without sleep or proper meals, and still do great things at the end of it. I saw this at Alamein, but it was brought home even more strongly here.

Having fought in the Western Desert, it was next stop Italy. Between 6–17 March 1944, however, Lieutenant Meikle, having volunteered for the airborne artillery, made the required number of jumps at the Parachute Training School, Ringway, and won his wings. Clearly, this was another intrepid scholar who revelled in being at the sharp end.

Creation of an effective airborne force, of course, required not just paratroopers or glider-borne infantry, but supporting divisional troops of all kinds, from provost companies to medical units and everything in between. Airborne troops are lightly armed, so whilst able to carry the small 3in mortar, this was insufficient fire power. The answer was the American 75mm pack howitzer, which could be glider-borne and jeep-towed, batteries of which could provide substantial supporting fire to airborne troops. To achieve such an airborne deployment of artillery, the 1st Airlanding Regiment, RA, was formed on 6 February 1943. The regiment would subsequently support 1st Airborne Division in North Africa, Sicily and Italy. Back in England, the gunners were based around Boston in Lincolnshire, where events were awaited. When Operation MARKET-GARDEN was planned, it was decided that the RA contribution would be in the shape of the Light Regiment, two Anti-tank Batteries and a Forward Observation Unit, all under the overall command of Lieutenant Colonel Robert Loder-Symonds. Lieutenant Meikle was Gun Position Officer in Captain John Walker's 'B' Troop. Meikle, five other gunners, a jeep and trailer were flown from Harwell to LZ 'Z' on the first lift, 17 September 1944, in an 'A' Squadron Horsa, serial number RN581, towed by a 570 Squadron Stirling. The glider's pilots were Staff Sergeant Freddie Chapman and Sergeant Bob Shipley. After landing, the, following morning the pair accompanied the gunners as part of the Glider Pilot Regiment detachment ordered to provide local security for the Light Regiment. This explained why Shipley was also wounded by the shell which fatally wounded both Lieutenant Meikle and Staff Sergeant Holloway, the latter glider pilot having joined the effort to protect the all-important gun batteries after the failed attempt to reach Arnhem Bridge on 19 September.

On 1 October 1944, the commander of 'B' Troop, Captain John Walker, who had returned from Arnhem to England, wrote to Ian Meikle's father:

It is with many regrets that I write to you to tell you that your son Ian was killed in action at Arnhem. This was a bitter blow to us, and to me especially since I had known him for a very long time as we were at Hollingbury Court School together. Up until his death he was doing splendid work, and was by his own example an inspiration to the men under his command; I myself was his Troop Commander, and he was good a right-hand man as I would ever wish to have, both in action and in barracks. If there is anything that I can do for you in helping you in any way to sort out any of his Army affairs, then do not hesitate to let me know and I will do all I can for you.

With deepest regrets, I am yours sincerely.

Having already lost one son, the effect of reading Captain Walker's words must have been devastating.

On 13 October 1944, Mr Ormiston Meikle received official notification of his eldest son's death from the War Office:

In confirmation of War Office telegram dated 9 October 1944, I am directed to inform you, with an expression of deep regret of the Army Council, that a report has been received from the Military Authorities in North West Europe that your son, Lieutenant IO Meikle, Royal Artillery, was killed in action on the 21 September 1944.

Sadly, it was not the first such letter received by Mr Meikle: on 8 October 1943, another son, Sergeant David William Meikle, a bomb aimer, was killed when the 90 Squadron Stirling he was flying in, EF426, crashed near his unit's home airfield at Wratting Common. All aboard were killed except the rear gunner, David lingering in hospital until succumbing to his injuries on 12 October. The 21-year-old was buried in Cambridge City Cemetery.

On 26 October 1944, John Sibley, nephew of the Meikle brothers' former headmaster at Wycliffe College, wrote to Mr Meikle:

I was terribly sorry to hear about Ian. His last letter to me was marked with the censor's stamp and I consequently gathered that he must be in a transit camp; only a day or two after I received it we heard about the Arnhem landing and I knew he would be there or in one of the other parts of Holland where our airborne troops landed. It was so like him to take part in this most daring and unhappily most tragic of all our deeds in this war, although in the North African campaign he had seen more and harder service than most of his contemporaries, he was not satisfied with what he had done but felt compelled to join the most daring and dangerous branch of the Army – or any service; his record makes those of us left behind ashamed that we have done so little ourselves.

As you know, he was my friend at school and my best friend at the University. There he was quite the best English scholar of his year; not only his First (which he would undoubtedly have repeated) but his wide knowledge and penetrating judgement of matters quite outside the scope of the Tripos convinced his acquaintances of this.

We valued him chiefly of course for something much greater and deeper than any learning or kindred accomplishment. Like his brother, we knew of him that he would always be, with typical unselfishness, wherever the danger and need were greatest.

We will never forget him. Please tell me if there is anything, howsoever little, I can do to help you in any way at this dreadful time.

In a letter dated 16 November 1944, to Mr W.A. Sibley, headmaster of Wycliffe College, near Lampeter, Mr Meikle wrote that 'Ian was looking forward to spending another year or two at the University before settling down to a job of work. Education was his choice, and if there is a more interesting vocation than education, I have yet to hear of it.' Mr Meikle also wrote of his third and youngest son, Colin, training overseas to be a pilot in the RAF: 'Ian and David are sadly missed at "High Trees" and now our only hope is that Colin will be spared to us. He has now taken to gliders, and is enjoying the training very much – far more than his parents.'

On 18 March 1945, Lieutenant Bob Woollacott, a member of the 1st Airlanding Light Regiment's 'B' Echelon (Seaborne), wrote to Mrs Meikle:

I have always regretted not paying you a visit after the Arnhem business – when I received a letter recently from Mrs Johnson it served to rub the whole thing in with a vengeance. I know, however, that Captain Walker of Ian's Battery had written you and after writing to the families of score upon score of my men, I felt that writing to you might serve only to deepen the tragedy. How wrong I was I can only judge now in the light of new experience.

I campaigned together with Ian for several months in Italy, and living and working at his side I soon grew to admire his sterling qualities. We were great friends, but when upon returning to England I was transferred to one of the other batteries, it was not so easy to see each other except at Mess. His was a great loss to us all – liked as he was by both officers and men, he had a rare sense of humour and made friends very easily.

His personal gallantry and endeavour in the midst of a battle where great deeds were the order of the day was quite outstanding. In the words of a Gunner from his own Troop, 'He died a gallant death, every bit a hero'.

Lieutenant Woollacott's letter was another fine tribute to Ian and kindness to his parents. Another bitter blow to them, however, loomed large on the horizon.

Tragically, the Meikles' sole surviving son, Colin, would not be 'spared': on 6 June 1945, whilst the war against the Japanese still raged, the aircraft he was ferrying whilst serving with 307 Maintenance Unit at Lahore, India, crashed. Flight Sergeant Meikle, twenty-one, was buried many miles from home, in Delhi War Cemetery.

After the war, on Sunday, 1 December 1946, Jeanne, the teenage daughter of the blacksmith, Breman, of 175 Bendendorspweg, Oosterbeek, wrote to Mr Meikle, her letter arriving out of the blue and providing an insight into the perimeter battle:

> You'll be surprised to receive a letter from a complete stranger, but I'll tell you why I write. First, allow me to introduce myself. My name is Jeanne Breman, I am nearly eighteen years, and I go still to school.
>
> Your son, Lt IO Meikle, was with us during the terrible days of September 1944. We had many English soldiers in our house, garden and cellar. We made many friends, for the soldiers were all such good and kind boys. Your son came often in the cellar to see us and check that we were alright. We had a talk with him then. He was a very good man, for his soldiers and for us, and I cannot tell you what it was to hear that he was killed. 23 of our good friends killed with him and were buried in our garden. Your son not, because they took him to the hospital, three minutes from our home, when he became wounded and also there he was buried.
>
> After being evacuated for more than eight months, we returned to Oosterbeek. The graves of the boys were covered with grass. I cleaned them all and every night laid fresh flowers on the graves. In September 1945, men of the Airborne Cemetery came to dig up the boys and took them away to the cemetery. They are lying there now, all together. The children of Oosterbeek take care of the graves. Every child has a grave adopted. I don't know who takes care of your son's grave, but I often go to the cemetery to put flowers on the graves of our friends.
>
> You'll be wondering how I got your address. I was in England this summer, where I had a lovely time. I stayed with a family in London, and I told them about the battle at Oosterbeek and Arnhem, and I also told them about the boys who were killed. I gave them the list with all the names of the boys and they sent it to the War Office at Liverpool. Some time ago I received a letter from the War Office, with the list and next-of-kin of each soldier. I sent this letter to the War Office and they sent it to you. I hope it'll find you in the best of health.
>
> I have a father, mother, and a little sister of 13 years, no brothers, and I am very sorry for not having one.
>
> I'll close my letter now, hoping you don't mind my liberty of writing to you. I hope you can understand my English.
>
> Mam, Dad, Roelie (that's my little sister) and myself send their very kindest regards and best wishes to you.

Again, this is clear evidence of the shared experience between the Dutch civilian population and airborne soldiers during this dreadful battle. It is also further evidence of Ian's character and contribution, in addition to being an early indicator of the lasting

David Meikle.

Colin Meikle, an RAF flight sergeant and pilot, would be killed in a flying accident in India in 1945. (Janice Chapman)

Tragically, the Meikle family lost all three sons during the war. This is Flight Sergeant David Meikle's grave, killed on an air test in a Stirling bomber and buried in Cambridge. (Darrell Graham)

All five Meikle children: Colin, David, Janice, Ian, and April. Only the girls survived the war. As Janice says, for her, 'it was like growing up with a ghost family'. (Janice Chapman)

Phyllis and Ormiston Meikle, pictured after the war. Mrs Meikle believed their cause just and was remarkably not bitter about her sons' loss. (Janice Chapman) bond between the British and Dutch people. The letter also confirms the debt the Dutch feel they owe, and how deeply this experience of war affected and defined the lives of those who survived. There is no doubt whatsoever that Ian Meikle was a truly exceptional individual, a gifted scholar, leader and brave soldier. Jeanne Breman's letter also suggests that he was a humanitarian.

Although, tragically, all three Meikle brothers perished in the Second World War, their two sisters, April and Janice, survived. At first, April went into a closed order of nuns, but later became an Oxford scholar; she died, recently, in her nineties. The youngest Meikle child, Janice (now Mrs Janice Chapman), is the sole survivor – and tells us a little more:

Staff Sergeant Holloway MM's headstone at Oosterbeek today. (3.A.15). (Author)

> The boys were all happy at Wycliffe College. After Ian's death, we received a letter from the headmaster about how brilliant Ian was; he wrote poems. He was a bit of a rebel, though, and didn't like the bull attached to soldiering, and nor did he like Field Marshal Montgomery, under whom he had served in the 8th Army in North Africa and thought a 'peacock'. Ian was a quiet person – but very stubborn.
>
> Given that we had already lost David and Ian, my younger brother, Colin, did not have to go, but was determined to also do his 'bit'. David, I remember, didn't like being a bomb aimer, though, and had a premonition of his own death.
>
> Our mother was a remarkable person, warm, and kind, and never let the tragedy destroy her life. She was not bitter and often spoke of the boys a lot, but not in a morbid way. We had Jewish friends and she thought the cause in which her sons had died was a just and necessary one. After the war, my brothers' friends were always welcome at our home, and often called in for advice (or to borrow money!). Post war, my parents used to go skiing in Switzerland with a German couple (he had been a submarine commander). People were aghast and could not understand how she, a mother who had lost three sons during the war, could even contemplate being friendly to Germans. 'Why not?', she used to answer, 'They also lost two sons'.
>
> For me, being the youngest and having only known my brothers for a comparatively short time, it was like growing up with a ghost family.

Lieutenant Meikle's headstone at Oosterbeek today (2.B.11). (Karen Sarkar)

Chapter 12

Sergeant George Thomas, 1st Airlanding Anti-Tank Battery, Royal Regiment of Artillery, and Sergeant James Sharrock, Glider Pilot Regiment

Airborne warfare dictates that paratroopers drop behind enemy lines, relying upon surprise and speed to reach, seize and hold their prescribed objective before rapid relief by ground forces. Given the nature of their arrival in hostile territory, paratroopers are by necessity comparatively lightly armed. The parachute battalions, for example, had only hand-held PIATS with which to fight tanks – and a limited supply of ammunition to do so. The three glider-borne Airlanding Battalions, however, provided more substantial anti-tank capability in the form of three dedicated platoons armed with the Ordnance Quick-Firing 6-pounder 7 cwt anti-tank gun. The ubiquitous '6-pounder' was the British army's primary anti-tank weapon of the war, having first seen action in at Gazala in North Africa during May 1942. However, as the Germans introduced bigger and more heavily armoured tanks during the following year, including the Panther and Tiger, it was found that the 6-pounder was ineffective against these metal monsters' frontal armour, but could still cause damage to the more thinly-armoured sides and rear. The British response was the Ordnance Quick-Firing 17-pounder anti-tank gun, introduced in 1943. This 76.2mm (3in) gun, with armour-piercing discarding sabot (APDS) shot, could penetrate the armour of even the much-vaunted King Tiger, which weighed seventy tonnes and was protected by up to 185 mm of frontal armour. The sabot round was a spin-stabilized armour penetrating projectile with a rock-hard tungsten carbide tip, making the 17-pounder a significant threat. The British Airborne Division was fortunate to have two Airlanding Anti-Tank Batteries, each with, in addition to their 6-pounders, two troops of 17-pounders. This weapon would give the Germans a vicious surprise at Arnhem. Commanding one of those 17-pounders, in Lieutenant J.T. Lewis's 'D' Troop of 1st Airlanding Anti-Tank Battery, was Sergeant George Thomas.

George Edward Thomas was born at Lydbrook in Gloucestershire's picturesque Forest of Dean, on 23 June 1910, to George Edward, a stone mason, and Mary Elizabeth Thomas. George became a coal miner, mining the small coalfield beneath the Forest. Aged eighteen years and eleven months, however, on 10 June 1929, George enlisted in the regular army at Bristol. He was recorded as being 5ft 8in tall, having a 'fresh'

GEORGE THOMAS AND JAMES SHARROCK

A young George Thomas pictured when a gunner, shortly after joining the Royal Artillery between the wars. (Margaret Davies)

complexion, brown hair and blue eyes. Passed 'Physically fit in every respect for service', the young man from Lydney was now 794078 Gunner George Edward Thomas of the Royal Artillery. And so began a journey that would take the former miner on many adventures overseas. On 22 November 1930, Gunner Thomas embarked for India, the Jewel in the British Empire's crown, where he remained, amidst the heat, spices and completely alien culture, until returning to England on 15 January 1932. Whilst serving at home, on 9 August 1933, the 23-year-old gunner, stationed at Somme Lines, Catterick Camp in North Yorkshire, married twenty-year-old Frances Margaret Sutton, of 65 Christchurch Street, Greenwich, London, the youngest daughter of retired Major Arthur Sutton, who had won a Military Cross in the First World War. The ceremony took place at Greenwich Register Office. Frances moved from London to set up home at 70 High

Street, Cinderford, also in the Forest of Dean. In due course, George and Frances would have two daughters, Margaret, born in 1933, and Maureen in 1936. By the time George's second daughter was born, he, now a Bombardier, had completed the six years he had signed on to serve the colours, leaving regular army service on 10 June 1935. As per the conditions of his engagement, George was then transferred to the Army Reserve List for a further six years. This provided a fully-trained body of men for recall to the colours in time of emergency – which, sadly, was only a few years away.

Gunner George Thomas with his wife, Frances. (Margaret Davies)

In the autumn of 1938, Hitler made his first overt move against an independent state, demanding that Czechoslovakia's western border region – the Sudetenland – should be annexed to the Reich. At Munich on 29 September 1938, the Prime Ministers of Britain, France and Italy agreed to this concession in return for a guarantee of 'peace in our time'. The following March, the Czech government was induced to ask Germany for military protection from Poland, Hitler's troops subsequently completing the occupation of Czechoslovakia without firing a shot. Hitler's true intentions were now clear, and the Western powers stepped up their lacklustre efforts to re-arm. Owing to the 'Danzig Corridor', a strip of land severing Eastern Prussia from the Reich and ceded to Poland at Versailles in 1919, Poland was now vulnerable. Europe stood on the brink of another war. In March 1939, Britain and France held army staff talks agreeing that in the event of hostilities, Britain and France would stand shoulder-to-shoulder. It was decided that Britain's contribution to any Continental fighting would comprise a ground expeditionary force and an Advance Air Striking Force (AASF). On 29 March, the British Cabinet ordered that the Territorial Army (TA) be doubled in size. The Military

Training Act was passed on 27 April, as a result of which some 200,000 men aged between twenty and twenty-one years old registered for military service. That month, the Secretary of State for War declared that the British Army numbered 224,000 regulars, 325,000 Territorials, and 96,000 Territorials in anti-aircraft units. Significantly, in April 1939, Britain pledged to assist Poland militarily in the event of an attack by Germany. Political difficulties existed with the Netherlands and Belgium, however, both of which countries were determined to remain neutral unless their borders were attacked. No. staff planning, therefore, took place regarding the Belgian or Netherlands army's integration into an Allied force, or, indeed, the defence of those countries. Escalating events since Hitler came to power in 1933, had the whole world on the edge of its seat, and doubtless, like countless other reservists, family man George Thomas looked on with grave concern.

On 1 September 1939, the storm broke: Germany invaded Poland following a fabricated act of 'Polish aggression'. On that day, without further ado, 3,000 reservists were recalled to the colours – amongst them Bombardier Thomas, who left his beloved wife and daughters to re-join the RA and become a member of the BEF, commanded by former Grenadier, General The Viscount Gort VC. Two days later, Hitler having ignored the ultimatum by Britain and France to withdraw his troops from Poland, Britain and France declared war on Germany: the storm had broken. The BEF, comprising 160,000 men, began moving to France on 10 September, Gunner Thomas proceeding overseas on 2 October.

Poland soon fell to the German invaders, but the BEF sat and waited in trenches and other prepared defences along the Franco-Belgian border. It would be a hard winter, known variously as the '*Sitzkrieg*' or 'Phoney War', in which nothing much seemed to happen. Certainly, the much-feared so-called 'Knockout-blow' from the air had failed to materialise, and so the world still held its breath. On 10 May 1940, the Germans achieved complete surprise and invaded the West. Airborne landings in the Netherlands and Belgium preceded tanks and infantry supported by aircraft, this new aggressive and mobile strategy – *Blitzkrieg* – shocking the Allied command system. The Belgian King called for help, leading to the BEF executing Plan 'D', advancing to the River Dyle in anticipation of the main German attack coming through Belgium as in the Great War. This entailed the BEF leaving its carefully prepared defences and pivoting forward sixty miles into Belgium across unfamiliar ground and without ammunition dumps. Whilst the Allies' attention was firmly focussed in that direction, however, Hitler's Army Group 'A' was meanwhile executing a perfectly camouflaged *Schwehrpunkt* (point of main effort), some forty miles further south: through the supposedly 'impassable' Ardennes poured the majority of German armour, outflanking both the much-vaunted Maginot Line and Plan 'D' in the process. Almost immediately, therefore, the BEF was in great danger. Given the Belgian army's collapse to Gort's north, and the *panzers* soon on the Channel coast at Boulogne, the BEF was in great danger of envelopment. Gort's force was then forced to fight an orderly withdrawal, from one river or canal to the next – which it did tenaciously but for which has never had due credit.

By 26 May 1940, however, it was clear that France and Belgium were lost, and so the reluctant decision was made for the BEF to retire upon and evacuate from the port and beaches of Dunkirk. By 3 June 1940, the evacuation was complete. According to War Office figures, 211,532 'fit men', 13,053 wounded, and 112,546 Allied troops were rescued and brought safely to England, a total of 337,131. There is no question that Operation DYNAMO, as the undertaking was codenamed, was a miracle. Although the BEF's armour and heavy weapons had been left behind in France, had those men been captured Britain's position would have been more perilous still – and Hitler, with so many prisoners, would have had an unprecedented diplomatic advantage. The catastrophe that was the Fall of France is difficult to comprehend today. As Pilot Officer David Scott-Malden, a young Spitfire pilot, wrote in his diary 'France has fallen. Cannot yet conceive the enormity of it all.' Indeed, a little-known fact is that France was Europe's largest military power at the time – when France surrendered after just six weeks, therefore, the unthinkable had happened. Fortunately, amongst the exhausted British troops brought home from the shambles in France was Bombardier George Thomas.

Sergeant George Thomas pictured whilst serving in the Mediterranean Theatre. (Margaret Davies)

After Dunkirk, George Thomas served at home until 12 April 1942, on which day he embarked for North Africa. Subsequently, George served with the RA detachment in Italy, following the Allied invasion of 3 September 1943. There, on 3 November 1943, George was promoted to Sergeant. For some unknown reason three days later, he was 'severely reprimanded by CO'. Unfortunately, Sergeant Thomas's Army Service Record is scant, there being no detail regarding exactly which RA units he served with overseas – or when he volunteered and became an airborne gunner.

From letters written home from North Africa to his elder daughter, Margaret, what is clear that George Thomas was a devoted father and family man:

11 November 1942:
To Daddy's Darlings, Margaret and Maureen,
Just a line on this airgraph wishing you are all in the best of health. I am feeling fine myself, the only thing that is wrong with me is that it is very cold over here, and I cannot stand that, after Daddy being in India, then in the terrific heat of Africa, then land up in Italy where its as cold in November as it is in England. Wouldn't it be lovely to sit in front of the fire in Cinderford, with you and Maureen playing with your dolls, and Mammy and me cuddling up to the fire.

Never mind, sweethearts, those days will come again, and we will make up for the past four years that we have been separated through this hard war. Well God bless you and Maureen, give my love and kisses to Mammy, Nanny and Granddad. What do you call Granddad these days, you haven't told me in your letters, do write and tell me. All my love, Daddy xxxxxxxxxxx

In an undated letter to Margaret, addressed to 'Daddy's Pet', George wrote:

Just a few lines my little sweet to let you know that Daddy is 2000 miles away. I am always thinking of you and of Maureen. Now, I haven't bought anything as yet for your little sister, only the ring of which I sent, but if you get this before Maureen, come along, tell her that there is one on the way. Well Daddy's darling, accept all my love and kisses, also give some to Maureen and some big hugs to Mammy, give some to Nanny and Granddad, and don't forget the cat! I hope you pass your exam so that you get into high school. Well, Daddy will close now, all my love and kisses to you and Maureen.

11 October 1943:

To My Daughter Margaret,
Just a few lines my sweetheart to let you know that Daddy is keeping safe and well, and I hope to have confirmation of winning your scholarship, now mind you do because I want to hear of you going to high school, and I am sure you would like that as well. As a matter of fact, I would like to see you going. As soon as this war is over, I hope I shall get the chance. Well, I have sent you a very nice Christmas box. Whether you will get it by then I don't know, but I have given it two months', so if you don't get it you must blame Mr Hitler! You don't like him, do you. Well Daddy's little darling I shall have to close now as its tea time and because of this noisy here. I also want to write to Maureen, as it's her birthday on the 20th of the month. God bless you, Maureen, Mammy, Nanny and Granddad, your Daddy.

Sergeant Thomas returned to the UK on 6 January 1944, subsequently spending a short period of leave with his beloved family before his Division stood idly by whilst 6th Airborne Division won the glory in Normandy. After the exasperation of sixteen cancelled operations, eventually emplaning for Operation MARKET-GARDEN, which went ahead, was a welcome prospect of action before it was all over.

Sunday, 17 September 1944, found Sergeant George Thomas commanding a 17-pounder gun crew in 'D' Troop: Bombardier J. McCullock, and Gunners V. Barnett, R. Hare, K.R. Pitman and Purnell. Thomas's crew, gun and towing vehicle, an adapted Morris Commercial, were loaded, at Tarrant Rushton airfield, east of Blandford Forum in Dorset, into one of the huge Hamilcar gliders. This aircraft, Chalk 320, of the Glider Pilot Regiment's No. 1 Wing's 'C' Squadron, would be flown by Staff Sergeant 960077 Stanley 'Pong' Waring (who had himself, coincidentally, enlisted in the RA during 1940) and Sergeant 3606728 Jim Sharrock of No. 6 Flight, and towed to Holland by Halifax LL355 of 298 Squadron. Whilst the more numerous Horsas could accommodate the 6-pounder anti-tank guns, the much bigger Hamilcars were required to transport the longer 17-pounders and their heavier towing vehicles.

The 298 Squadron Operation Record Book reported that for the Halifax crews, 'Final briefing was held at 0830 hrs and the crews were out at their aircraft by 0930 hrs. The take-off was at 1020 hrs and it was a reasonably good take-off, wind being light from the north, cloud about eight-tenths at 2,000 feet . . . The weather over the target was fair but hazy and all of the gliders were seen to land safely. Little or no flak was encountered and no aircraft were damaged.'

Aeronautics magazine's Air War Correspondent, Robert Montgomery, was aboard LL355:

> 'Rope tightening . . . rope tightening . . . rope tightening . . . rope taut'. It was the tail gunner's voice talking over the intercom to the skipper of Halifax 'G' for George. Standing behind him I glanced forward to see the flight engineer helping push the four throttle levers right through the gate, and then, with maximum boost, we were roaring down the two mile runway. We gathered speed slowly and glancing behind I could see the Hamilcar airborne. We were half way down the runway when we hit a bump and became airborne too, but it was only for a short while and once more we were trundling along with the boundary fence rushing towards us. We cleared it with inches to spare and set course for the first leg of our journey to Holland.
>
> We were climbing slowly and with difficulty for we had an overload of petrol and our Hamilcar was loaded with a seventeen-pounder gun, its truck, ammunition and crew of eight. After half an hour or so the navigator warned the pilot we were approaching 'high ground' – it was only 800 feet high, but a danger to us. I was now sitting in the second pilot's seat and next to me the pilot was literally struggling with the controls. It was all he could do to keep the combination flying and to make the climb was blacksmith's work. The sweat was literally pouring off his face and cascading like a waterfall over his moustache. It was no joke and as we flew along we gradually got into a stream of other aircraft and gliders so that very soon the whole sky seemed full of bombers and Hamilcars and Horsas and then a few Wacos appeared and passed below us. Our speed had now increased to 135 miles an hour and we had struggled up to 1,200 feet.
>
> Below us it was Sunday morning and we could see little knots of people gazing up at us and I could imagine them saying what a fine sight it was. Little

did they realise the struggle we were all having. As we passed out over the North Sea with Ordfordness to starboard, we joined the main stream and now tugs and gliders stretched before us and behind us as far as the eye could see. It was truly a magnificent sight. The weather was perfect and a thin layer of cloud at about 2,000 feet was ideally suitable for the operation. In the aircraft, it was hot and the blue sea looked almost inviting.

Soon we saw our first casualties. Three Horsas were down in the drink and their tugs were speeding home, but there was nothing we could do for the swimmers. It was a full-time job seeing to it that our Hamilcar didn't join them. It was now a case of flying in 'rough air" all the time. The slipstream was terrific and my pilot – Squadron Leader Bob Imber – was still going through the actions of an all-in wrestler.

As we approached the coast of Holland I started to wonder exactly what type of a fool I was. I recalled the briefing officer's remarks about the terrible amount of flak through which we would have to fly, unless the bombers and fighters had already knocked it out. According to him, the trip was 'suicidal' unless they had done their job well. Crossing the coastline, we could see before us a vast area of flooded land making the country unrecognisable from the map. Below us a couple of flak ships were blazing but apart from this there was no sign of the enemy.

As we got deeper in there was still no sign of flak but below us now we could see our fighters – Typhoons, Mustangs, Spitfires and Mosquitoes – swooping down on the villages and beating up the railway lines and roads. If there were any strong flak positions remaining they were brave men if they fired, for no sooner had they done so they were shot to pieces. Above us there were our aircraft weaving in and out of the clouds and when patches in the clouds thinned we saw the Dakotas which had dropped the first paratroopers hurrying on their way home.

North-east of Tilburg we turned for our run in and soon the glider pilots were warned that they had ten minutes more before the landing zone. Just before the River Waal passed below us they were given the five-minute warning and then the 'second river' was coming up. At the time, I was treating this river as just another landmark – in actual fact it was the Rhine.

Over the intercom the pilot told the glider to cast off. There was a jerk – the pilot twirled the tail trim wheel vigorously and we started to climb. To the starboard was the village of Oosterbeek and beyond it Arnhem. Below us were rows of gliders very nearly as orderly as they had looked before take-off except for one or two which had piled up in the wood.

We flew for two minutes or so before we could drop our rope. In front of us the air seemed to be full of trailing ropes and the rear gunner, 'Dagwood', was kept busy telling us how our own Hamilcar was faring and that the rope should not be dropped yet. Eventually we dropped our rope, and knowing that our glider was safely down we climbed steeply into the clouds, up through them and out into the sunshine.

It is hard for those who were not there to imagine the intense relief that the crew feels when the job is finished. At once the intercom was full of voices congratulating the pilot on his fine show, and we were all inwardly grinning to ourselves. For the pilot, the dropping of the load meant bodily as well as mental comfort, for he could now fly a relatively lightly loaded aircraft. Even the Halifax seemed to have taken on a new lease of life and no longer wallowed or refused to answer her controls promptly.

The flight home seemed uneventful and apart from some flak in the distance nothing to worry about. Over the North Sea the air was still full of aircraft going both ways, and on the surface of the water, the Horsas were still floating and Air Sea Rescue launches were rushing towards them. When we reached our base, we had to queue up for a short time before landing, but we were soon down and it was good to hear that there had not been a single casualty from our group . . . For myself I count it as one of the greatest privileges of my life that I was able to fly with the first wave of gliders on that historic Sunday.

When landing on LZ 'Z' at 1400 hrs, according to one of those aboard, Gunner Ronald Hare, the heavy Hamilcar hit the ground hard, then bounced back into the air, came to earth again, hitting a tree, before eventually grinding to a halt. Sergeant Thomas, however, was frustrated to discover that the heavy landing had smashed his towing vehicle but managed to enlist the help of a Universal (Bren) Carrier driver who had landed nearby. At the Light Regiment's positions near the LZ, it was decided to move 3 Battery to a new location on the polder immediately west, south and east of Oosterbeek Church – putting Arnhem Bridge within range. This was on Lion Route, the lower road which 2nd Parachute Battalion and other divisional troops had taken to successfully reach Arnhem Bridge. This was, however, before formation of the Oosterbeek defensive perimeter, meaning that the guns would be isolated in land unoccupied in strength by the Division. Consequently, it was decided that Major Bob Croot and forty glider pilots would accompany the gunners to provide local protection. It is highly likely, therefore, that Sergeant Jim Sharrock, who had flown in Sergeant Thomas, was amongst them. It was also agreed to that two 17-pounders of 1st Airlanding Anti-Tank Battery would also accompany 3 Battery, being deployed to defend the approaches. These were the guns commanded by Sergeant Thomas of 'D' Troop and Sergeant Bower of 'P' Troop. At first light on Monday, 18 September, the party set off, reaching the church in Benedensdorpsweg without incident. Upon arrival, Sergeant Thomas lost no time in positioning his gun alongside the church's north wall, facing east towards Arnhem. The defence of 3 Battery was a crucial role, because its gunners were in direct contact with Major Denis Munford at Arnhem Bridge, who was accurately directing their fire in support of the hard-pressed airborne troops fighting desperately to retain hold of the northern end of the all-important road bridge.

On 21 September, the Light Regiment's batteries were heavily mortared from dawn onwards, the precursor to *Kampfgruppe* Harder's attack from the east, across the railway line. Sergeant Thomas's gun was in action, firing at the advancing enemy, whose attack was repulsed. Gunner Hare recalled that their gun 'put four rounds into a pill box on the railway embankment'. The pressure increased all around what was now the Oosterbeek perimeter – known as the *Hexenkessel* or 'Witch's Cauldron' by the Germans. Persistent attacks were made by enemy armour, supported by infantry, the mortar barrage and shelling taking a heavy toll. According to Lieutenant E.E. Shaw MC of 'C' Troop, on 22 September, he became separated from his men and instead joined up with Lieutenant J.T. Lewis's 'D' Troop. Later, he recalled (in *The Gunners at Arnhem* by Peter Wilkinson MC) that there was a 'tank alert'; as he made for Sergeant Thomas's gun, it received a direct hit. Both 34-year-old Sergeant Thomas and 25-year-old Bombardier John Jack McCullock were fatally wounded. Gunner Hare recalled that Sergeant Thomas had been hit by a large piece of shrapnel, seriously injuring his shoulder areas. He then helped to take his gun commander to the nearby home of Kate ter Horst, fearing that Thomas's wound was so bad 'he wouldn't see morning'. Both Sergeant Thomas and Bombardier McCullock did indeed succumb to their wounds – although, as is so often the case, when is unclear.

As we have already seen, the human memory is fallible, and arguably even at the time, through the fog of war, survivors did not always correctly record the days on which certain events occurred. On 19 October 1944, the War Office, however, wrote to Mrs Thomas, regretting to inform her that George had been posted 'missing' on 26 September 1944, it being 'known' that he had been 'wounded on the 21st September 1944 in North West Europe'. On 12 September 1945, a further letter arrived from the War Office, ending months of uncertainty and confirming that 'reports have been received from members of the unit who state that your husband was seriously wounded by a mortar bomb. In view of this information and of the lapse of time during which no news which would indicate that Sergeant Thomas survived has been received, the Department has reluctantly and with deep regret reached the conclusion that he succumbed to his wounds.' It is likely, therefore, that Sergeant Thomas and Bombardier McCullock were mortally wounded by a mortar bomb on 21 September 1944. When they died is unclear, but would have been sometime between then and when the Germans overran the Ter Horst house on 26 September 1944 – by which time the Division had evacuated back across the Rhine. Neither wounded man was alive or captured at that time, having been buried in Kate's garden. Whilst they may have 'succumbed' to their wounds on that day, equally the date could be arbitrary; we will never know.

Back in Cinderford, the Thomas family was devastated, not least George Thomas's eleven-year-old daughter Margaret and eight-year-old Maureen. Times thereafter were hard for Frances as a single parent and war widow, but Mrs Thomas won the respect of

ARNHEM 1944

Sergeant Thomas's 17-pounder anti-tank gun, knocked-out beside the Old Church on Benedendorpsweg.

The author stands in for Sergeant Thomas's gun, 2017. (Karen Sarkar)

The Airborne Cemetery at Oosterbeek shortly after construction in 1945; Sergeant Thomas's grave is indicated by a 'X'. (Margaret Davies)

all, bringing up her daughters and working at the Gloster Aircraft Factory at Brockworth in Gloucestershire; Mrs Thomas never remarried. In 1991, Margaret visited her father's grave at the Arnhem-Oosterbeek War Cemetery, where Sergeant Thomas had been interred in 1945. Travelling from Wales on the same coach was, coincidentally, an Arnhem veteran from Cardiff, Lance-Corporal J.T. 'Hank' Harding, formerly of 11th Parachute Battalion's 'B' Company PIAT section. The old man explained that after the effort to reinforce Lieutenant Colonel Frost at Arnhem Bridge failed on 19 September 1944, he had withdrawn along the river road into lower Oosterbeek, finding himself at the old church. There he met Sergeant Thomas and crew, who he helped re-position their 17-pounder. The kindly sergeant gave the young paratrooper 'some bully beef and a fag' before sending him on his way. 'Hank' then fought throughout the rest of the battle with Lonsdale Force, defending the Light Regiment's guns and maintaining the perimeter. Sergeant Thomas's small act of kindness was clearly something the veteran never forgot. Whilst in the Airborne Cemetery, Margaret also met another veteran, Gunner Stan Wrightman, who knew Sergeant George 'Chippy' Thomas well. Margaret heard how Stan's twenty-first birthday had been spent in an Oosterbeek cellar, to which he had been directed by Sergeant Thomas after being wounded; it was there that the young gunner heard that 'Chippy' had been killed. It was heart-warming for Margaret to hear from Mr Wrightman how her father was 'always talking about his family and was like a father-figure to the rest of us'. In 2005, Margaret

Sergeant Thomas's headstone at Oosterbeek today (3.A.18). (Author)

Bombardier McCullock's headstone at Oosterbeek today (2.B.15). (Author)

Sergeant Thomas's gun is one of two displayed outside the Airborne Museum at Oosterbeek – the damage to it all too evident. (Author)

GEORGE THOMAS AND JAMES SHARROCK

Margaret Davies, George Thomas's proud daughter, displaying her father's medals in July 2017. Sadly, Margaret passed away in August 2018, so did not live to see this book published - but did read and approve this chapter in draft. (Karen Sarkar).

Sergeant Thomas's medals and airborne insignia: 1939-45 Star, France & Germany Star, North Africa Star, Italy Star, Defence and War Medals. (Karen Sarkar)

and her mother made another pilgrimage to Arnhem; it would be Frances's last visit to her husband's grave: Mrs Thomas died the following April, her ashes later buried in George's grave. Love, they say, never dies.

So, what of the glider pilots, Staff Sergeant Stanley 'Pongo' Waring and Sergeant Jim Sharrock? The former was safely evacuated across the Rhine on the night of 25 September 1944, and survived the experience. Nobody knows, it seems, what became of Jim Sharrock – except that he perished in what had become a vortex of violence and destruction at Oosterbeek.

James Johnson Sharrock was born on 6 April 1923, the son of Thomas William and Elizabeth Ellen Sharrock. 'Jim's' formative years were spent living at Common Street, in the small mining community of Hart Common, in Westhoughton,

Sergeant Jim Sharrock. (Parnel Seabrook)

Lancashire. Jim's second cousin, Parnel Seabrook, describes more of the family background:

> In the terraced houses and cobbled streets of Hart Common, Jim was surrounded by his mother's family during those early years. His grandmother, aunts and uncles all lived 'on't common' (on the Common) and would all have spoken in the distinct old Lancashire accent used in the town, particularly by the men of the family, that could be separated from surrounding towns by the locals. His best friend was his cousin Jim Williams, also named James Johnson after their uncle James Johnson Roberts who had been killed in action during the Battle of the Somme, age eighteen. Johnson was their grandmother's maiden name and it was used down the generations as a middle name for several of the boys born into the family.
>
> Jim was the eldest of four children and would have attended the small school at Hart Common along with many of his family and friends from the small community. Sadly, his mother, 'Nelly', died on 4 February 1935, of acute bronchitis, aged forty-one. Jim was almost twelve and his youngest sister just three years old at the time. By 1939, Jim's father, Bill, listed as a 'public works contractor', was living with another woman, as man and wife, with his four children and her son; they married in 1941. It is also believed that at some stage he was a policeman. It is also well-known within the family that Bill was an abusive husband and father, who beat and humiliated his wife and children. Jim's cousin, Lucy, has some nice memories of Jim. He and her brother, Jim Williams, used to take her to the fair during Westhoughton Wakes, swinging her between them. She loved the pair.

On 21 August 1941, Jim Sharrock, a 'loom sweeper', enlisted into the TA at Bolton. Although allocated to the 70th Border Regiment, Jim's 'Embodiment', however, was deferred, it not being until 16 September 1942, that he joined the 4th East Lancashire Regiment, serving at home. On 15 November 1943, having volunteered, Private Sharrock was posted to Hemsby and the '2nd Glider Pilot Regiment'. Having successfully passed flying training, on 26 March 1944, Sergeant Jim Sharrock was posted to No. 2 Wing, Glider Pilot Regiment. Flying the great Hamilcar glider, it is likely that he joined 'C' Squadron on Operation MALLARD to Ranville on the eve of D-Day, 6 June 1944. Before Operation MARKET-GARDEN, Sergeant Sharrock went home on leave. His cousin, Mavis, remembers him visiting her home, 'lifting me onto his lap and telling me that he would be coming back'.

As is so often the case, little or no evidence exists to confirm what happened to 21-year-old Jim Sharrock, another who, to all intents and purposes, simply disappeared. His name is remembered on the Groesbeek Memorial, just one of forty-six other glider pilots still 'Missing in Action' from the Battle of Arnhem. What evidence there is

'B' Section of 'C' Squadron, pictured by a Hamilcar glider at Tarrant Rushton on 15 July 1944: second from left: Staff Sergeant Leonard Wright; fourth left: Sergeant Jim Sharrock; fifth left: Staff Sergeant Stanley Waring; seventh from right: Lieutenant Thomas Goodman; third right: Sergeant Jack Barnes; second right: Sergeant Robert Simpson, all of 6 Flight. (Parnel Seabrook)

The huge Hamilcar glider. (RAF Museum)

regarding the date of his loss is quite specific, though: according to both his Army Service Record and Service & Casualty Form, Sergeant Sharrock was killed in action on 22 September 1944 – although the location and circumstances are not noted. The CWGC also records the same date of death. A glider pilot veteran, Len Wright, stated many years later than Jim was killed on a patrol 'in the woods', which may or may not have been the case. It is possible that Sergeant Sharrock remained with Sergeant Thomas and his gun throughout, and was killed in action fighting with Lonsdale Force near the old church at lower Oosterbeek a day after the mortar 'stonk' that mortally injured Sergeant Thomas. Equally, he may have lost his life elsewhere in Lonsdale Force's south-eastern sector of the perimeter, defending the Light Regiment's guns with Major Croot's glider pilots.

Whatever the point of fact, Sergeant Jim Sharrock has no known grave – and his family therefore has been denied closure. There are 1,773 British, Commonwealth, Polish and Dutch servicemen buried in the Arnhem-Oosterbeek War Cemetery – of which (at the time of writing) 245 remain 'Known unto God'. Five of that number are known to be glider pilots; there may well be more amongst those listed simply as 'Army Air Corps'. Two of the five, a Staff Sergeant (3.A.1), and a Sergeant (3.A.2 were first buried in front of the Hartenstein Hotel; another Sergeant's field grave was 100 yards west of it (3.B.2). According to the headstone of grave 16.A.17, the occupant is a

The graves of two unknown glider pilots at Oosterbeek, one a sergeant; who can say whether this is Sergeant Sharrock, or one of many other missing glider pilots? (Author)

'private' of the Glider Pilot Regiment. This cannot be correct, however, because all aircrew, including glider pilots, held at least the rank of sergeant. Grave 30.B.10 is that of a glider pilot with an undetermined rank. Where the field burials were of the latter two casualties is unknown. It is possible that Sergeant Jim Sharrock is, like so many others, buried as 'unknown' at the 'Airborne Cemetery'. Without any substantial evidence regarding the circumstances or location of his death, however, and because the CWGC will not share field burial exhumation reports with the public, which may reveal other clues, there are no open avenues of inquiry. Whether he is one of the unknown burials identified as glider pilots, or amongst the anonymous Army Air Corps 'unknowns', is impossible to say – but is certainly a possibility.

Many years after Jim was reported missing, his cousin Margery, now eighty-six, recalls that when the sad news was received, she had to go on a bus ride to tell an aunt, because 'everyone else was too upset to do it'; Margery was then thirteen years old.

Amongst Jim Sharrock's clinical Army Service Record is a pro-forma letter dated 21 June 1945, sent from Army Records in Edinburgh to Jim's father. This document lists items of Jim's personal property being returned to his next of kin: a pair of cricket boots, a table tennis bat, and two torches.

Sometimes, there are just no words.

Chapter 13

Sergeant Thomas Watson, 1st (Airborne) Battalion, The Border Regiment

Thomas Watson was born on 20 June 1916, into a working-class family in the mining village of Cowpen, Blyth, Northumberland. One of eight children, his father, Joseph, was a coal trimmer; his mother, Agnes (née Dalziel), a Scot from Moniaive, Dumfriesshire, worked as a cook. On 18 April 1940, as Britain's darkest hour fast approached, Thomas Watson, then a 23-year-old van driver, enlisted as 3662924 Private Watson of The Border Regiment, an old Line regiment with a proud history, the recruiting area of which being, as the name suggests, the border lands of England and Scotland. At 5ft 10in tall with blue eyes and fair hair, his religion recorded as Church of England, the young 'Geordie' marched off to war and the Infantry Training Centre (ITC) at the Regiment's Carlisle depot.

Having successfully passed his infantry training, Private Watson was posted to join the Border Regiment's 1st Battalion at Crook, south-west of Durham, on 21 June 1940. At that time, the 1st Border was re-building to strength after the Fall of France and Dunkirk evacuation, receiving many replacements. On 1 July, the battalion moved to Prudhoe, where Private Watson clearly impressed, because on 21 July he was promoted there to lance corporal. In September, after an invasion scare, the Battalion moved to Hampshire. At Kingsclere on 1 October 1940, Watson was promoted to corporal. Two months later the battalion was on the move again, this time to Welwyn Garden City, Hertfordshire, joining 31st Independent Infantry Brigade. In February 1941, another move followed, to Crickhowell in South Wales, where 1st Border began training in mountain warfare, particularly regarding using pack animals for transportation, guided by experienced Indian Army mule handlers. 1st Border, however, was not destined to fight in mountain air: in September 1941, it was decreed that the battalion would join, together with the brigade's other battalions, the new 1st Airborne Division's 1st Airlanding Brigade Group – and be flown to battle in gliders. As we have seen with other units, those men with no desire to fly or parachute into battle were given the choice for reassignment; Corporal Thomas Watson was not amongst them, and an airborne warrior he consequently became.

In December 1941, the new Airborne Division was based on Salisbury Plain, 1st Border at Barton Stacey, near Winchester, again in Hampshire. Tragedy struck, however, when volunteers were required for a glider flight testing for airsickness at Ringway,

THOMAS WATSON

near Manchester: the Hotspur glider crashed, killing six men and injuring both the pilot and the Glider Pilot Regiment's first CO. It was an inauspicious start, but training continued in earnest, welding the 1st Airborne Division together into an effective fighting force. In October 1942, 1st Parachute Brigade had gone overseas, to North Africa, seeing heavy fighting; it was to join them that the remainder of the division, including 1st Border, embarked, Sergeant Watson – having been promoted again on 30 March 1943 – leaving from Liverpool for foreign shores and uncertainty on 17 May 1943.

Sergeant Thomas Watson, 'B' Company, 1st Border Regiment. (Irene Thomson)

Nine days later, 1st Border disembarked at Oran, Algeria, finding a somewhat different culture and climate to the North of England. There, training moved on apace in preparation for the invasion of Sicily. 1st Border, on the night of 9/10 July 1943, was to participate in Operation LADBROKE, tasked, with other glider-borne elements, with seizing and holding Syracuse. As we have seen in previous chapters, many gliders were in the event cast off too soon, landing in the sea with high casualties. Of the seventy-two gliders transporting 1st Border, for example, forty-two came down in the 'drink'; only twenty landed on Sicily, and only five of those within five miles of the objective. Too widely dispersed to concentrate in force at intended rendezvous points, 1st Border parties instead harassed and confused enemy units, spreading confusion and panic amongst the Italian troops, which, it was officially concluded, significantly contributed to the enemy's surrender. Sadly, however, the Airlanding Brigade and Glider Pilot Regiment sustained 605 fatal casualties during the operation – a tragic 300 of which drowned before ever having the chance to fight. Once more, therefore, 1st Border found itself rebuilding to strength, back in North Africa. On 11 September 1943, 1st Border joined in with the 1st Airborne Division's contribution to the seaborne invasion of Italy, landing at Taranto and pursuing the retreating Germans up the Adriatic coast. 17 November saw the Battalion's return to North Africa, sailing for England in the *Duchess of Bedford* on 28 November. This voyage was not uneventful: *en route* to England, the *Duchess* rammed another troopship, the *Monarch of Bermuda*, which required repair at Gibraltar. The *Duchess* limped home, however, arriving in Liverpool on 9 December. According to Sergeant Watson's Army Service Record, he 'Disembarked UK' two days later, the 1st Border travelling by train to Woodhall Spa in Lincolnshire. Having left behind no known written account, what Sergeant Watson's personal experience of the airborne operations and fighting was in Sicily and Italy is unknown – but he survived.

On 7 June 1944, the day after the greatest seaborne invasion of all time landed in Normandy, 1st Border moved to Bulford in Wiltshire. There the Battalion continued training, the unfolding campaign in Europe requiring the 1st Airborne Division to be ready for rapid deployment. Again, as we have seen, whilst 6th Airborne Division won their spurs in Normandy, the 1st stood idly by, desperate for action and exasperated by sixteen cancelled operations. All that, however, was to change: on 16 September 1944, all ranks of 1st Border were briefed regarding Operation MARKET-GARDEN, and Burford Camp locked down for security reasons. This time there would be no cancellation. Along with the two other airlanding battalions and supporting troops, 1st Border's job was to land on 17 September 1944, securing and holding the landing grounds for 4th Parachute Brigade's drop and subsequent glider lifts north of the Rhine and north-west of Arnhem.

The 1st Border War Diary tells us that at 0700 hrs on Sunday 17 September 1944, the Battalion 'embussed for the airfields with the exception of one rifle platoon and five glider loads of the Transport Platoon not due to leave until 18 September; Battalion strength 41 officers and 754 Other Ranks'. At 0945 hrs, the 'First glider took off from Broadwell, followed by "C" Company and BB Mortar Platoon from Blakehill Farm. Good flying weather, with slight ground mist'. 'All gliders less six landed safely' at 1315 hrs, the diarist continued, 'with one exception in which one man was injured, but load was taken out undamaged. Uneventful flight with light flak and small arms fire directed against aircraft when nearing LZ at 6581. CO's glider did not arrive.' The flight, however, had been anything but uneventful for Sergeant Watson, the commander of 'B' Company's 14 Platoon.

Sergeant Watson and certain of his men were bound for LZ 'S' at Reijers Camp, immediately north of the railway line near Wolfheze, in Horsa glider, Chalk 161, towed by a 575 Squadron Dakota. At the glider's controls was Lieutenant Colonel John Place, CO of the Glider Pilot Regiment's No. 2 Wing. Second pilot was Lieutenant Ralph Maltby, the Wing Intelligence Officer. Half an hour before reaching the LZ, a startled passenger in the glider's rear suddenly shouted that the aircraft's tail was coming adrift! Private Johnnie Peters relayed the message to Lieutenant Colonel Place. Lieutenant Maltby went aft to investigate, returning to his seat and confirming that all was well, the glider having been harmlessly spattered by light flak. Place then gave Maltby control, enabling the former to check his map. At this time, Private Johnnie Peters inquired of Sergeant 'Tommy' Watson how long it would be until landing; it was Maltby who replied: 'Fifteen minutes'. It was exactly 1300 hrs when the Horsa was hit by flak again, according to Place 'a tremendous bang right in the cockpit'. The glider had been squarely hit over s'Hertogenbosch, by a high explosive anti-aircraft round. Lieutenant Maltby slumped in his seat, hanging on his straps. Place 'shouted for somebody to come forward and see what could be done for Ralph . . . the platoon sergeant poked a startled head into the cockpit. I told him to try and get Ralph back on the floor of the cockpit, but before he could do so, Ralph was dead.' That 'platoon sergeant' was Sergeant Watson – who himself suffered a head wound whilst the glider was under fire. Private Peters, and doubtless other passengers, was perturbed, wondering what their fate might be should the sole surviving pilot also be killed or incapacitated – there was no-one else aboard, of course, capable of landing the aircraft. Fortunately, notwithstanding being raked by machine-gun bullets whilst steeply diving earthwards to land, wounding the Scout Section's Bren gunner, Private Hughes, in the knee, Lieutenant Colonel Place put the Horsa down safely. The dead second pilot was buried alongside the road near the farm at Reijerscamp. For Sergeant Watson and 14 Platoon, it was a portent of things to come.

Safely on the ground, there was no time to dwell upon the traumatic events of only a few minutes previously. Men gathered together into their units at pre-determined rendezvous points, in 1st Border's case the LZ's south-western corner. 'B' Company were tasked with blocking the Utrecht road heading through Renkum to Arnhem. 'D' Company was to close the road from Bennekum at Heelsum. 'A' Company remained in the area of the LZs, watching the all-important railway line running between them. 'A' Company's role was to move eastwards, to the south-west of Wolfheze, to block any enemy approach from the east. Having furthest to travel, Major Tom Armstrong lost no time in leading 'B' Company off. According to the War Diary, whilst en route to Renkum, 'B' Company 'captured three marines and two MG34s in railway station at Buunderkamp. Otherwise no opposition' (there was no such station at this location, so this must have been some other railway-related installation). It is likely that the enemy 'marines' were from 10 or 14 *Schiffstamm-Abteilung*, a German *Kriegsmarine* (navy) unit. A number of these units were formed, in which sailors were trained to fight as infantry. Amongst them was *Bootsman* Helmut Jensen, a despatch rider with 14 *Abteilung*, based north-east of s'Hertogenbosch. Astonished, he had watched 'the sky darkened by an enormous fleet of aircraft towing gliders . . . Confusion reigned'. At Renkum, 'B' Company invested a brickworks close to the Rhine, spending the night either in buildings or slit-trenches. A German patrol was heard approaching during the night, but seen off with a volley, after which all was quiet.

Already, however, the airborne troops were contained within a ring of Krupp steel. To the west, *General die Infanterie* Hans von Tettau, charged with defending a sector along the Waal, hastily formed an ad hoc battle group – *Kampfgruppe* von Tettau, drawing upon units already under his command, from coastal defence units further afield, and other units sent to reinforce him. Collectively, Von Tettau's command was subordinated to General Willi Bittrich's II SS *Panzer Korps*. Because of the temporary nature of Von Tettau's formation, and given how many more reinforcing German units would arrive in the Arnhem area during the battle's course, it is impossible to provide a comprehensive order of battle for *Kampfgruppe* von Tettau. What is known, however, that to the north was SS-*Wach Bataillon* 3, a 600-strong unit of Dutch and Ukrainian Nazis, with SS-*Bataillon* Eberwein in support. Von Tettau's centre was the responsibility of airmen, like their sailor comrades, converted to infantry and formed into several battle groups – backed up by the combat veterans of SS-*Bataillon* Schulz. To the south, the two *Kriegsmarine* units, 10 and 14 *Schiffstamm-Abteilung*, completed Von Tettau's western-based forces.

Schulz's SS men cleared Renkum of British occupation early in the morning of Monday, 18 September 1944. 10 *Schiffstamm-Abteilung* was tasked with evicting 'B' Company from the brickworks. Their attack was surprisingly determined, considering the sailors' overall lack of combat experience. The 1st Border War Diary reported that at 0700 hrs 'B' Company '. . . after inflicting some casualties, were heavily mortared and all vehicles were destroyed by 1400 hours'. In truth, the sailors substantially outnumbered 'B' Company, which had no option but to disengage and withdraw – a very difficult manoeuvre when in contact and under fire. This, however, was successfully achieved, the Company moving east towards Castle Doorwerth, although forced to leave behind all 'supporting arms' except 'Vickers machine-guns, which were carried out'. At 1700 hrs, 'B' Company was 'held up by mortar fire but eventually passed through "C" Company'. By then, the second lift had arrived, releasing other 1st Border elements, which moved south-east to join the battalion.

By 0515 hrs on the morning of Tuesday, 19 September, all companies were dug in, forming the western British line of defence from just north of the Utrechtseweg in Oosterbeek, to the Westerbouing, the high bluff overlooking the Rhine (much more of which later). 'A' Company was the northernmost 1st Border company, straddling the Utrechtseweg opposite the junction with Van Lennepweg, a short distance west of the Hartenstein Hotel and on the road's southern side. On the north side of the road, a Vickers medium machine-gun was located, connecting 'A' Company with engineers and glider pilots defending the north-western edge of the newly-formed perimeter (see Chapter 10). There was also a Border 6-pounder anti-tank gun further forward along the Utrechtseweg, looking east towards the Koude-Herberg crossroads. A few yards to the east of the Van Lennepweg/ Utrechtseweg junction, the Hoofdlaan joins the Utrechtseweg, just after the former's junction with Van Lennepweg (an 'L' shaped road). 3 Hoofdlaan was selected as the Regimental Aid Post (RAP) – a considerable distance to bring a casualty, uphill, through woods, or a road swept by fire, from company positions further south – 'B' Company was the furthest away from this essential medical facility: 1,300 metres. Battalion HQ was established at 3 Van Lennepweg – close to Divisional HQ at the adjacent Hartenstein Hotel, but, again, a long way from most companies. Opposite the 1st Border HQ and in the woods, a 3in mortar crew, commanded by Corporal Jim McDowell, provided fire support to 'C' Company – dug in along Van Lennepweg, and 'D' Company. The latter was dug in along Van Borsselenweg, the arterial road running south off the Koude Herberg crossroads to the Westerbouwing. The Koude Herberg, and therefore the Van Borsselenweg 'D' Company line, was several hundred metres further west along the Utrechtseweg from the junction with Van Lennepweg. This, therefore, put 'D' Company in a very vulnerable position, being isolated. Moreover, the distance from and nature of the ground to cover in order to reach the RAP, would soon make evacuating the company's casualties impossible. Disconcertingly, the closest friendly force was 'C' Company, to the north-east at Van Lennepweg and out of sight. This gap prevented mutual fire support, through which the enemy might pass. Indeed, the late Frank Steer summed up the 1st Border's position perfectly in his battlefield guide of the landing grounds and Oosterbeek (see Bibliography): 'The western perimeter was, really, a sieve through which the Germans

The Driel ferry seen from the Westerbouwing in 2017. (Author)

should have been able to walk almost at will. It was due to the tenacity, courage and fighting capabilities of the Border Regiment that they did not.'

The Westerbouwing is a wooded beauty spot some seven miles west of Arnhem Bridge. This is a rare area of high ground, commanding views over the Rhine above Heavedorp, of Arnhem to the east and over the river across Driel and as far as Nijmegen. Crucially, it was also the location of the Heavedorp to Driel ferry, although the boat had been beached by the Germans. Had that been appreciated and the ferry reinstated, General Urquhart would have had a practical means of moving troops across the river and, crucially, receiving reinforcements from the south bank. It was there, in fact, across the river at Driel, that the Independent Polish Parachute Brigade was scheduled to drop – but somehow had to cross the Rhine. That ferry would have provided the means, but, alas, as we will in due course see, that was not to be. The Westerbouwing was also the south-western base of General Urquhart's defences, barring the way along Benedendorpsweg to the area around the old church, where the Light Regiment's batteries were located. Van Borsselenweg, the southern arterial road leading off the Koude Herberg crossroads, travels downhill to the immediate west of a woodland brook, passing through 'D' Company's positions, to the Benedendorpsweg crossroads with Veerweg. There, the Veerweg continues south, a field east from the Westerbouwing, skirting the high ground and bending around to the west, following the river, to the ferry. A few hundred metres east along Benedendorpsweg from the Veerweg crossroads were the Oosterbeek gasworks, and at the western side of that field, on Benedendorpsweg, a large white villa known as 'Dennenoord'. This small but crucial area would soon become a bloody battlefield – and 'B' Company would be in the thick of it.

For once, excellent references exist regarding the deployment of 'B' Company around the Westerbouwing on 19 September 1944. The 1st Border War Diary and account by Canon Alan Green, commander of 'D' Company's 20 Platoon at Oosterbeek, published in the unit history *When Dragons Flew* (see Bibliography), provide an accurate picture. One of 'B' Company's platoons surrounded the restaurant, on the Westerbouwing's highest point, on the southern edge of the high, wooded bluff. A very

Looking west across the Van Borsselenweg/Benedendorpsweg/Veerweg crossroads, towards the Westerbouwing. (David van Buggenum)

Van Borsselenweg, approaching from the north, and Veerweg, running south to the Rhine, around the Westerbouwing feature, seen looking east along Bendendorpsweg. (David van Buggenum)

steep, cliff-like bank then swept away down to the river and ferry. Eastwards, a field fell away to the crossroads. The Company HQ and Aid Post were set up in a farmhouse situated at the Veerweg end of the field. Between the crossroads and river, along the Veerweg, the Company's other three platoons dug in. Arguably, the Westerbouwing, this unique feature, should have formed the base of General Urquhart's perimeter – instead of being vulnerable, lightly defended, on the western boundary. It is easy, however, to be wise after an event; as Robert Kershaw rightly argued in his account of the German perspective, *It Never Snows in September* (see Bibliography), General Urquhart had been 'trapped on ground not of his own choosing and was powerless to react'. Nonetheless, any German attack was likely to come from the west, so it is perhaps surprising that only one platoon was stationed around the restaurant, with the three others several hundred yards behind them, to the east.

At 1900 hrs, reports came in from the Reconnaissance Squadron that enemy forces were building up to the east, around Heelsum, suggesting an impending attack. At that time, according to the War Diary, 'All company positions were attacked . . . but all attacks were repulsed'. This may have encouraged 'B' Company's Commander, Major Tom Armstrong, to reconsider his earlier deployment. By 2245 hrs, Major Armstrong had dug in 11 Platoon north of the restaurant, along the Oude Oosterbeekseweg, the road running east to or west from Heavedorp, which joined Benedendorpsweg slightly north-west of the Westerbouwing feature. Sergeant Watson's men of 14 Platoon were divided, some dug in above the restaurant buildings, on the Westerbouwing bluff, facing west, whilst Corporal Ian Hunter's section covered the Veerweg, to the east, in line with the gasworks. 13 Platoon took up station on the bluff's southern edge, parallel with the Veerweg. One section, including a Bren gun team and a sniper, ensconced themselves along the track leading from the Veerweg to the river and ferry crossing point. 12 Platoon dug in to the left of Company HQ, in the field near the crossroads. The night, however, was fairly quiet, 'active patrols' returning with 'nothing to report'.

At 0600 hrs the following morning, 20 September 1944, the Germans opened up with the so-called early morning 'Hate', a fearful barrage of mortar bombs and other missiles, which was maintained, on and off, throughout the day. Whilst 'A' and 'C' Companies were heavily engaged to the north, the day passed surprisingly uneventfully, shelling aside, in the 'D' and 'B' Company areas. The night also passed quietly, with 'occasional mortar fire of nuisance value only'. This was soon to change – violently.

Kampfgruppe von Tettau was still receiving reinforcements throughout 20 September. Many, including the teenage soldiers of the *Luftwaffe* Herman Göring training regiment, arrived from northern Holland by bicycle. This unit had been taken over by a new *kommandeur*, *Oberst* Fritz Fullriede – who had won a *Ritterkreuz* fighting in North Africa with Rommel. Fullriede's job, together with his combat-experienced officers and NCOs, was to train teenage replacements for the *Reichmarschall's Fallschirm-Panzer-Division* 1 Hermann Göring, the vain Nazi chief's personal *panzer* division. Fullriede's command was of divisional strength: 1200 men, sub-divided into three training battalions, and several battle groups engaged on coastal defence – amongst them the 600-man strong 'Wossowski Battalion', commanded by *Oberleutnant* Artur Wossowski and comprising four infantry companies. Based at Katwijk ann Zee, Wossowski was ordered to Arnhem on 18 September 1944. Travelling on bicycles, the young Germans arrived in the Arnhem sector and spent the night of 19 September along the Ede-Arnhem road, north of the railway line. The following day, the unit moved across Ginkel Heide, scene of the previous day's second lift, but encountered no resistance so continued to Wolfheze. From there, the cyclists continued south, spending the night east of the Westerbouwing.

That morning, British resistance at Arnhem Bridge had been crushed, providing the Germans an opportunity for a command structure re-organisation and plan an all-out assault on the Oosterbeek perimeter. *Kampfgruppe* Von Tettau, therefore, was placed under the overall command of SS-General Bittrich, who subordinated tactical control to *Obersturmbannführer* Harzer. Bittrich ordered an assault of unprecedented fury against the besieged airborne troops to be unleashed at 0800 hrs on Thursday, 21 September 1944. The Wossowski Battalion faced 1st Border's 'B' Company, between the Rhine and Oosterbeekseweg/Benedendorpsweg, with SS battalions Schulz, Eberwein and Helle extending northwards along the western side of the British perimeter. The German attack was to be supported by the French-built *Flammpanzers* of *Panzerjäger-Abteilung* 657, *Panzer-Kompanie* 224 (see Chapter 10).

At 0530 hrs on 21 September 1944, the morning 'Hate' rained down once more upon the British perimeter – where casualties mounted and conditions were increasingly grim. That said, the airborne troops were stoic: whilst the Germans described the perimeter as a 'Witch's Cauldron', the British press reported a 'forest citadel'. At 0800 hrs, the Germans attacked, in strength, around all three sides of the perimeter. Surprisingly, the evidence confirms that the Germans had not grasped the Westerbouwing's tactical importance – perhaps explaining why this area was allocated to the inexperienced young *Luftwaffe* men. Wossowski's men, it seems, were unaware of what lay ahead. According to eyewitness evidence, the Battalion advanced towards the Westerbouing, through the woods, with no forward reconnaissance. Nonetheless, the *Flammpanzers* emerged from the trees on the Westerbouwing with scant warning – although the Wossowski Battalion was roughly handled by 14 Platoon when machine-gunned whilst forming up. For Lance-Corporal 'Ginger' Wilson of 11 Platoon, the German infantry appearing was 'like a crowd at a football match'. Faced with such an onslaught, Sergeant Watson immediately ordered Corporal Hunter's section from the crossroads to reinforce his precarious position on the hilltop. *En route*, Hunter met Major Armstrong, who directed him towards some mortarmen he believed were also in the field, to their right. Hunter found none but positioned his section in a trench, where machine-gun fire killed his

View west from the Westerbouwing, looking down the field across which 'B' Company, 1st Border, retreated and in which Sergeant Thomas Watson lost his life on 21 September 1944. (David van Buggenum)

View from the Westerbouwing height over the Veerweg, towards the railway bridge at lower Oosterbeek; the buildings of Arnhem can be seen on the horizon. This photograph clearly indicates the observation platform this feature provided. (Karen Sarkar)

lance corporal and destroyed the section Bren. A smoke grenade permitted Hunter's escape, but he found none of his section again.

Elsewhere, the flamethrowing tanks were engaged by PIATs – three were destroyed. As the sole surviving *Flammpanzer* retreated, a mixed bag of Bordermen counter-attacked. Corporal Hunter and Sergeant Watson ran forward together. Hunter gave Watson two German stick grenades. In front of them ran a German soldier, who repeatedly stopped and threw grenades at Hunter, who, his Sten jammed, returned them – killing the German. The enemy's fire, however, was so heavy that the counter-attack was thwarted, the survivors retreating back across the field towards the crossroads. Re-joining what was left of the Company, Hunter found a PIAT but was wounded by a mortar round whilst re-loading it. Ambiguously, Canon Green writes that 'Sergeant Watson was killed in this action'. Some have interpreted that to mean that the gallant Geordie was killed by a mortar bomb, which may or may not have been the case. Given the ferocity of the German attack, and firepower involved, he could equally have been killed by other means. As is so often the case, nothing, in the fog of battle, is certain. What we do know is that Sergeant Watson was buried along Veerweg, after being pushed off the Westerbouwing height. Corporal Hunter was more fortunate: he was carried by a comrade to the nearby aid post. As 'B' Company pulled back further still, to the gas works and Dennenoord house on the south side of Benedendorpsweg, and woods of the Hemelse Berg estate to the north, the now isolated 'B' Company Aid Post had to be abandoned; there was no choice but to leave the wounded to be captured by the enemy.

ARNHEM 1944

According to the War Diary, 'Officer Commanding "B" Company and a party of approximately two platoons in strength moved in the direction of the crossroads . . . all contact with them was lost. Nothing further was heard of this party for the remainder of the operation.' In truth, 'B' Company had been roughly handled: Major Armstrong was wounded and captured, WO2 Company Sergeant Major Alfred McGladdery killed, as were two platoon commanders, one being Sergeant Watson. After this action, 'B' Company was reduced to two officers and the equivalent in strength of a single platoon. The survivors, therefore, joined an *ad-hoc* battle group around Dennenoord, commanded by Major Charles Breese – known as 'Breese Force'. This formation held a strong defensive position at the perimeter's south-western base, whilst opposite, just 700 yards away, the similarly composite 'Lonsdale Force' held the Germans off in the south-eastern sector. The new position commanded good fields of fire, looking west, towards the Westerbouwing, across open ground – the Germans, for that reason, made no further heavy attacks on this sector from the west. The high ground, however, had been lost – and at a high price. The enemy, though, had far from had it all their own way. Four tanks had been lost in the battle for the Westerbouwing; later, *Oberst* Fullriede wrote that 'In the attack on Westerbouwing, the Wossowski Battalion lost all its officers except a *leutnant*, and half its other ranks. These casualties were due to a certain *Oberst* Schramm who was in command of this operation and forbade use of heavy weapons because he was afraid his own men would be hit. The idiot instead preferred to let hundreds of them die.' Three days later, Schramm was relieved of his command. Fulriede went so far, in fact, as to return 1,600 of his recruits to Germany, arguing that 'to send them into battle would have been infanticide'. Nevertheless, his Wossowski Battalion's victory at the Westerbouing was the outstanding success that day of the entire *Kampfgruppe* von Tettau.

Elsewhere that fateful day, 21 September 1944, the other Border companies were all heavily attacked, 'D' Company most heavily, suffering many casualties. Indeed, over the hours ahead, as the perimeter shrunk under the weight of German attacks, 'D' Company, in its vulnerable forward position along Van Borsselenweg, was completely cut off. On the morning of 26 September 1944, the survivors of 'D' Company would discover that during the night their Division had withdrawn across the Rhine

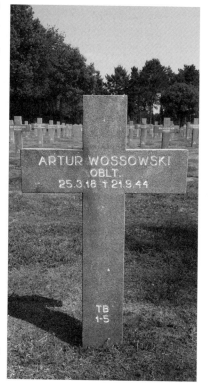

Oberleutnant *Artur Wossowski's grave at Ysselsteyn. (Marcel Boven)*

– but it had been impossible, without radio communication, for anyone to get through the woods and let them know.

It must be remembered that the 1st Border, along its thinly but tenaciously held line, suffered more casualties than any other battalion. The Arnhem Roll of Honour (2011) records that the 1st Border lost twenty-one men killed on 21 September 1944, and a total of 118 throughout the whole battle. Of these, it says, twenty-nine remain missing or unidentified. This figure, however, is now a little less, thanks to the ongoing efforts of Captain Geert Jonker and the Royal Netherlands Army Recovery & Identification Unit. In September 2016, for example, six 1st Border Regiment soldiers originally buried as 'unknown' at the Arnhem-Oosterbeek War Cemetery were identified as a result of this dedicated unit's efforts. As the unit history rightly states, 'The Battalion had fought well and had maintained the high standards of courage, discipline and honour with which the Regiment had always prided itself; it had also left, as in other wars, many sons of the Regiment on the battlefield'. Martin Middlebrook, as ever, succinctly contextualised the 1st Border effort: 'There is no doubt that the Oosterbeek perimeter could not have been held without the sturdy defence of the Border companies, and this should be recognized just as much as the 2nd Parachute Battalion's more spectacular action at Arnhem road bridge.' There could be no higher tribute.

Sergeant Watson's headstone at Oosterbeek today (18.B.13). (Author)

Memorial to the 1st Border Regiment at Westerbouwing today. (Author)

Back home, Sergeant Tommy Watson was mourned by his large family. Today, Tommy is remembered by someone he never met: his daughter, Irene, born in October 1944.

> My Mam, Jean Cran, was divorced with two children when she met my father in Aberdeen, when he was in Scotland on manoeuvres. She didn't know he'd been killed in action until six months later, when a friend of his wrote to her. Mam did not meet anyone else, and didn't speak much about my father because it upset her too much; in those days, these things were simply not talked about. Mam passed away in 1987. It was then that I decided to search for information about my father. I was really looking to fill in gaps in my family tree, but found some relatives, who provided me with the only known photograph of my father. I wish I had started it before, when I was stationed in Germany whilst serving in the Women's Royal Army Service Corps, because I would have been not far from where he was killed. More recently, however, I did have the pleasure of communicating with the sadly now late Johnnie Peters, who was in my father's platoon, and thought highly of him.

Sergeant Tommy Watson was clearly a highly competent and experienced soldier, and an exemplary NCO. Without doubt, Irene Thomson has a father to be proud of.

Chapter 14

Major Alexander Cochran and Private Samuel Cassidy, 7th (Galloway) Battalion, The King's Own Scottish Borderers

Like the Airlanding Brigade's two other battalions, the 7th (Galloway) King's Own Scottish Borderers belonged to a long-established regiment with a proud history. Raised initially by David Leslie, the 3rd Earl of Leven, on 18 March 1689, the 25th Foot owed is existence to a Dutch connection: this was the time of the 'Glorious Revolution', when the Protestant William of Orange, maternal nephew of the deposed and executed English King Charles I, laid claim to the British Crown. Leven was a 'Williamite', supporting the successful usurpation of the Jacobite King James II. In 1805, the 25th was allocated the Scottish Borders as its recruiting area, becoming known as the 25th (The King's Own Borderers) Regiment of Foot, and simply The King's Own Scottish Borderers in 1887. Thereafter, the 'KOSB' served in wars and stations throughout the British Empire. During the First World War, KOSB battalions had fought at Gallipoli and in France, before once more being dispersed around the world, from Ireland to India, between the wars. When the Second World War came, the 1st Battalion was the first to fight, in France and Belgium with the BEF, before evacuation via Dunkirk. The 7th Battalion was engaged upon mundane Home Defence duties, from the south-eastern approaches to the Orkneys. That, however, was to change in early December 1943, when, with another coincidental Dutch connection, the 7th sailed from Scotland aboard the *Amsterdam* – to join 1st Airlanding Brigade at Woodhall Spa, in Lincolnshire. After so many years of comparative inactivity, this was an exciting prospect indeed – although, as the War Diary, observed, 'it was doubtful if many of us had ever seen a glider'. Nonetheless, the transition to glider troops was achieved, and, at 1000 hrs on 17 September 1944, as the battalion diarist enthusiastically recorded, the 7th KOSB was 'Off at last' from Down Ampney and Blakehill Farm – bound for LZ 'S', north of Wolfheze – '. . . and our great adventure has started'. Sadly, it was a 'great adventure' from which few airborne Borderers would return.

At 1330 hrs on that first day, two miles from Wolfheze, the gliders carrying the 7th KOSB into battle were released to descend and land upon LZ 'S'. It was 'an impressive sight', the diarist wrote, 'seeing those dozens of gliders nosing their way in, but there is no time to watch as unloading has to be proceeded with at once'. As the parachute battalions of 1st Parachute Brigade and supporting troops struck out for Arnhem Bridge from their drop zones, 1st Airlanding Brigade's role was, according the 1st British Airborne Division's after-action report, '. . . to protect the DZ and LZ areas until arrival of the second lift on D+1, then to form a defence line of the western outskirts of Arnhem'. With local inhabitants 'delighted' at the would-be liberators' arrival, Lieutenant Colonel Robert Payton-Reid and his HQ Company, commanded by Major Alexander Verner Cochran, took stock: of fifty-six gliders, eight had failed to arrive and an anti-tank gun had been destroyed in a heavy landing, but overall the Battalion was substantially complete. At 1500 hrs, 'A' Company moved off to take up its allocated positions to the north, along the main Ede–Arnhem road – where it was attacked by a German 'armoured car' but in response 'inflicted several casualties upon the enemy and took a number of prisoners'. Other companies were deployed around DZ 'Z', ready to defend it for the next day's scheduled second lift. During the night, 'vigorous patrolling was carried out by all companies', but 'lack of communications proved a great drawback, both now and later. Owing to the thick woods, the wireless sets would not function over the distances between companies. Line was laid, but, being out of assault cable, was also unsatisfactory owing to distance and breakages.' The issues revolving around communications failure at Arnhem is well-trodden ground, General Urquhart himself having declared during the battle that this essential aspect of the operation was 'a complete failure' and that the 'radio sets were inadequate for their purpose, and that their effectiveness was further limited by the sandy, heavily wooded terrain'. This, however, Major John W. Greenacre argued in 2004, was 'substantially untrue'. The actual cause of failure, Greenacre opined, was not technical limitations or inadequacies, but more so that 'procedural errors and mishaps combined with

Major Alexander Cochran 7th (Galloway) Battalion, The King's Own Scottish Borderers. (Alec Colvin Smith)

Major Cochran's headstone at Oosterbeek today (20.C.7). The CWGC has accepted the author's evidence that Major Cochran was actually killed on 21 September 1944, and will correct the headstone accordingly. (Luuk Buist)

poor timing and in some cases just bad luck were responsible for the breakdown of the 1st British Airborne Division's internal radio communications during the Battle of Arnhem'. Be that as it may, the fact is that communications failed – with dire consequences for General Urquhart's division.

That night, 'A' Company was repeatedly attacked by a mobile flak vehicle, which shone a searchlight onto the British positions and 'then rained down cannon-shell and machine-gun fire into it, whilst their infantry infiltrated round it'. The company withstood this assault but was 'severely shaken'. Lieutenant Colonel Payton-Reid, however, was unaware of these attacks at the time, due to the communications failure. Nonetheless, it appeared that the wood north of the DZ was 'occupied by the enemy in some strength'. 'D' Company was despatched to seize the wood, via a settlement previously occupied by Captain Gourlay's platoon. This did not go to plan, owing to the settlement having already been overrun. 'D' Company bypassed the buildings, therefore, hurrying into the wood. Without communications, no information was forthcoming but the sound of gunfire confirmed a fierce battle was being fought. The only reserve available to Lieutenant Colonel Payton-Reid was seventeen men of Support Company, one of whom may have been Private Samuel Cassidy (of whom more later). Led by Major H.R. 'Glaxo' Hill, these men joined the fray, emerging two hours later having inflicted casualties upon the enemy, the major claiming 'two with his own rifle'.

By this time, the 4th Parachute Brigade's arrival was 'anxiously awaited'. Eyes anxiously scanned the sky, and ears strained to hear the approach of aero-engines. 'B' Company's anti-tank gunners on the main road had 'knocked out . . . at least six armoured tracked vehicles . . . their occupants eliminated by fire from medium machine-guns'. The second drop, however, was late – and without communications those on the ground had no idea when, or even whether, it would arrive. 'There followed now a difficult period during which the enemy pressed in on all sides. Steps were taken, using every man and weapon, to keep him in check and these were so successful that he eventually drew off the majority of his force northward. Therefore, when the parachute drop did eventually take place, between 1400 hrs and 1500 hrs, the DZ was completely clean and fire on it came from only a few isolated enemy weapons situated at a distance'. Safely down on terra firma, Brigadier 'Shan' Hackett, commander of 4th Parachute Brigade, 'specially thanked the CO for the protection provided'. The 7th KOSB had achieved its first task and been blooded at last. The safe delivery of 4th Parachute Brigade, however, had not been achieved without cost. Immediately prior to the drop, so intense was the fighting to clear the surrounding woods that even Major Cochran's HQ Company was 'actively engaged'. The CO's party came under 'enfilade machine-gun fire' on Ginkel Heath – Major Hill was 'shot through the head. His loss is a grievous one as he was a cool and courageous leader.'

7th KOSB was now given its next task – to proceed to the slightly higher ground at Johannahoeve, north of Oosterbeek, and secure LZ 'L' for the arrival of gliders bringing in Polish equipment the next day. After their first hot meal since landing the previous afternoon, the Borderers began their move, in the gathering gloom, at 1900 hrs. Proceeding north of the railway line, in a north-easterly direction, the route was found to be considerably congested owing to the various 'units and sub-units' of 4th Parachute Brigade also using the same line of march towards Arnhem. At 0100 hrs, 7 KOSB reached Johannahoeve, successfully seizing the farm buildings there but meeting 'stiff opposition from enemy machine-guns well dug-in, in fully prepared positions'. In the dark, it proved impossible to accurately locate these machine-gun nests, and after several casualties it was decided to discontinue the prospect of a nocturnal assault and instead dig in around Johannahoeve, Major Cochran establishing HQ Company in the farm buildings. By 0600 hrs on 19 September 1944, 'The situation . . . was well in hand and the Battalion suitably disposed . . . everyone was in very good heart'. 'Concentrated shelling', however, set the farm ablaze, and more casualties were sustained by the Me 109s' strafing attack (described elsewhere in this book). The 4th Parachute Brigade was by now head-to-head with the German blocking line, which it was unable to penetrate. Indeed, the advance was checked and, owing to the arrival of increasing German reinforcements, soon became a fighting withdrawal west through the woods (again, as described elsewhere in this book). Indeed, 7th KOSB received information of 'tanks and self-propelled guns approaching the locality – and our anti-tank guns are ready to receive them'. At 1400 hrs, the Polish glider lift arrived, 'greeted by heavy flak but little close-range fire'. The gliders 'appeared to land well', but losses were sustained by RAF aircraft making supply drops.

At this time, there was nothing to indicate that anything had gone especially awry. At 1500 hrs, however, Lieutenant Colonel Payton-Reid was 'called urgently to HQ 4th Parachute Brigade'. There Brigadier Hackett ordered an immediate withdrawal south of the railway embankment. During this fraught action, 'Battalion HQ and "D" Company laced into the enemy attack with everything they had and inflicted very heavy casualties on him. Major Cochran and Drum Major Tait, for example, each accounted for twenty Germans by Bren-gun fire. The enemy met such a devastating volume of fire, and suffered such casualties, that he was first checked, then held and finally drew right off.' Passing through the famous culvert beneath the railway, 7th KOSB reached the rendezvous in Wolfheze, from where, at about 1800 hrs, the battalion struck out for Divisional HQ at the Hartenstein Hotel in Oosterbeek. Reaching the British-held mansion as night fell, 7th KOSB was ordered to the north-western section of the hastily forced perimeter, to bolster the line already held by elements of the Glider Pilot Regiment, RE and 21st Independent Parachute Company. Lieutenant Colonel Payton-Reid chose a small wood immediately east of the pathfinders, which he and his second-in-command, Major Coke, set off to 'make a recce'. The location was found to be the 'grounds and gardens of two large houses . . . a well-defined and convenient area to occupy in the dark and covered the Battalion's allotted tasks'. By 0100 hrs on 20 September 1944, Major Cochran had led the battalion to and deployed it around its new defensive position: 'C' Company dug-in on the western side, partly facing north and south; 'D' Company held the rest of the northern boundary and entire eastern section; the weaker 'B' Company covered the southern sector. The mortar section was located within this circular defence, medium machine guns sited with 'D' Company, and anti-tank guns 'covered every face and road approach'.

'D' Company's position included the larger of the two occupied buildings – the Hotel Dreijeroord – dubbed the 'White House' by those who would soon defend it in earnest. This stood on 'dominating ground covering a crossroads at the north-east corner of the perimeter, but it, and the area around it, were clearly visible from the other houses outside the perimeter and also from the trees of the surrounding wooded area'. 'D' Company was bolstered by a section of glider pilots – commanded by 2nd Lieutenant Ron Johnson (see Chapter 10):

The battered Hotel Dreijeroord – dubbed the 'White House' by those who defended it – after the battle: more recently substantially demolished in spite of a high profile campaign to save the historic building.

Hotel Dreijeroord pictured in August 2017, shortly before controversial demolition work began. (Author)

Glider Pilot Lieutenant Ron Johnson, pictured at home in 2017, who also fought at the White House with the 7 KOSB. (Author)

During the move from Wolfheze on Tuesday night, my Section, being the last section of glider pilots on the move, got mixed up with the 7th KOSB. As a young 2nd lieutenant, I had a decision to make: either try and find our 'E' Squadron and where they had moved to, or remain with the KOSB. I made the decision to stay with the KOSB, so reported to their CO, and that is why we glider pilots came to fight for the rest of the battle at the so-called White House.

As Ron also said, 'Quite a lot would happen to us there, because as things turned out, the battle for the White House was intensely fought. A lot of people lost their lives there.'

The German pursuit of 4th Parachute Brigade had ended north of the railway, where the enemy stopped, probing cautiously forward and aware that Oosterbeek was potentially now a hornet's nest of besieged and angry airborne troops. That morning the Germans sought to locate the new British positions, and plan their next assaults, so the morning began comparatively quietly. Likewise, the British units sent out patrols to assess the enemy's disposition. By 0900 hrs, however, the enemy 'had become very active'. A 'strong enemy party' in the woods across from the railway line (close to where the Airborne Cemetery is today) posed a threat but was dealt with by mortar fire. The KOSB anti-tank section scored its first kill shortly afterwards, an 'armoured car' approaching from the north. A 'Tiger tank, towing flame-throwing apparatus' then appeared, which was knocked out, and its crew killed, by another KOSB anti-tank gun (this could not, however, have been a 'Tiger' in reality, because none were present at this time, so more likely a Char-B1 *Flammpanzer*). With the enemy now fully aware of the KOSB position, 'shelling, mortar fire and sniping . . . continued with ever-increasing violence throughout the day'. This 'violence' was firmly directed at the White House, leading Lieutenant Colonel Payton-Reid to evacuate his RAP to a safer house within the perimeter. Ron Johnson:

> The sniping was a real nuisance on that Wednesday. They were in one particular house opposite, and I remember saying to Des Page 'I'm going to have a go at them'. You have a choice, really, as a young officer: either you get a patrol together and take them, or use a PIAT bomb. I decided upon the latter. I crawled across, loaded a PIAT bomb, fired it into the house – and the snipers caused us no more trouble from that location after that!

During the early afternoon, a self-propelled gun, concealed from the KOSB anti-tank screen, pumped shells into the White House at close range. 'D' Company were forced to vacate the building, which was collapsing around them. Later, the evening was illuminated by burning buildings; the battered White House being an 'eerie place'. Ron Johnson:

> On that Wednesday night, one of the houses opposite our trench was hit and set ablaze, lighting up the sky. A young Dutch woman came out of the house and called out to our position, asking if she could come across the road to us. I yelled out in English, at the top of my voice, because I was the nearest officer to her, 'Stop firing! Stop firing!' She started to cross, then a machine-gun opened up and shot her down. She was lying in the road. Having giving her clearance to cross, I felt responsible, so still shouting 'Stop firing!', I went and picked her up, bringing her back and handing her over to Des Page. We never found out what happened to her, although we inquired after the war.

At morning 'stand-to', 0430 hrs on Thursday, 21 September 1944, the mortar and medium machine-gun sections responded to intelligence gathered throughout the night by KOSB patrols – and 'heavily engaged' locations known to harbour German troops. At 0630 hrs, the 7th KOSB stood-down to enjoy a hot meal, whilst the evacuation of wounded via two jeeps flying Red Cross flags, tentatively began. Respected by the enemy, the transfer of wounded to the Hartenstein and Tafelberg Hotel aid stations

After being wounded a second time, Lieutenant Johnson was treated at the Tafelberg Hotel, another important aid post and formerly Generalfeldmarschall *Model's HQ. (Author)*

continued throughout the day. From 0900 hrs onwards, however, the 'enemy commenced to be very active'. Snipers and shelling were a perennial problem; Ron Johnson:

> A mortar bomb landed in the trench next to mine, killing two KOSBs therein. I was hit by shrapnel in the head and in a bit of a mess, so at the RAP in the White House they had to take all of the stuff out of my head. I went back to my trench after that but must have been concussed, because I got out of my trench and went to the next one to see what I could do, but quite what I thought I could do I don't know. A sniper then put a bullet through my back! I was then sent to the better-equipped aid post at the Hartenstein, where the surgeon, Derek Randall, used penicillin on me, which was the first time it was used to treat a battlefield casualty. From there, I went to the aid station at the Tafelberg Hotel. As we drove up to it, I got one of the terrible shocks of the Arnhem battle: the garage doors were open and I could see that it was full of dead bodies awaiting burial. That has stayed in my mind ever since. When they moved me in, I was put upstairs and had a bed on the first day. My head was all bandaged, just holes for my mouth, eyes and nose, my arm was in a sling too. More and more wounded

came in so on the second night I was on the floor. Third night was even worse, I just had a stair to sit on. And that was how it was, until the place was eventually overrun.

At 1630 hrs on 21 September, Lieutenant Colonel Payton-Reid held an 'O' Group, reorganising his Battalion and arranging nocturnal dispositions. Major Coke having been wounded by a sniper the previous day, Major Cochran was now '2IC'. The 7th KOSB War Diary graphically describes the subsequent and very violent events that autumn afternoon:

> ... enemy activity increased and a very heavy mortar concentration was brought down on the position, many of the bombs falling within the perimeter. Finally, the CO decided to cut the conference short and see what was afoot. He found that the enemy, who had been forming up under cover in the woods to the north-east, was just starting an attack on our own position. This attack came in strongly, being made by fully a company of SS troops. The enemy got as far as the White House and the slit-trenches which we had vacated in that vicinity, but every move he attempted to make beyond there was frustrated by a deluge of fire from the Battalion. Every weapon was got into action, the MMGs, which simply belched forth unceasing fire, proving particularly effective. Once the enemy had been checked, the CO arranged a two-minutes 'crescendo', – 3-inch mortars on the woods, MMGs on the trenches, and anti-tank guns on the White House – at the end of which he led the Battalion in a bayonet charge which swept any remaining enemy off the field. The White House and nearby trenches were filled with the bodies of the dead Germans, with many more lying all over the open. The German attackers, except for those who had fled, were killed to a man. 'The battle of the White House', as this will be known, will live in the memories of all who took part in it. It came at a most opportune moment, so far as the Battalion was concerned, when everyone had reached a state of extreme exasperation at the continuous shelling and sniping. As a result, when the Germans showed themselves, the Borderers rose in their wrath and slew them – uttering the most blood-curdling howls meantime. The enemy were picked SS troops and put up a most gallant fight to the last, but they had taken on rather more than they had bargained for.

The bayonet charge cleared the Germans from the grounds, but at heavy cost:

> Our own losses were not light and included some of our best leaders. Major Cochran fell dead, with a dead German at his feet. Sergeant Graham, lion-hearted as ever, was killed in the midst of the fray... Our two days in the White House position were ones of strenuous fighting and cost us heavily in casualties, amongst whom were the following:

ARNHEM 1944

Killed: Major Cochran, Lieutenant Crighton, Lieutenant J Hunter.
Wounded: Majors Dinwiddie, Sherriff (twice)
Major Coke, Captains Coulthard and Bannatyne,
Lieutenants MacKenzie, Hannah, Kaufman and Sharples (who later died).

Sergeant Graham, who was well on the way to winning a VC, was killed. There were now no Company Commanders or Company Sergeant Majors (except CSM Swanston, who although wounded remained on) and few senior NCOs left in action.

According to one source (Robert Sigmond's *Off at Last*, see Bibliography), Major Cochran was killed by a sniper whilst standing next to Lieutenant Kaufman's slit-trench, refusing to take cover and maintaining that his behaviour would bolster the morale of his men. This, however, is inconsistent with the War Diary, which implies that the gallant major fell during the charge and in hand-to-hand combat. Indeed, according to Middlebrook, 'The body of Major Alexander Cochran was found on the hotel veranda with a revolver in his hand, lying head-to-head with a dead German officer who was holding a Luger pistol'. The gallant major's Army Service Record and Death Certificate, however, record his death as having occurred on 20 September 1944 (hence why the CWGC accept this date as accurate, which appears on Major Cochran's headstone) – but both the 7th KOSB War Diary and Major Cochran's obituary notice confirm that he was killed on 21 September 1944. There can be little or no doubt, I would suggest, that Major Cochran was indeed killed on 21 September 1944 – leading his men in vicious fighting in the White House's grounds. Originally buried in the Hotel's grounds, his remains were later interred at the nearby Airborne Cemetery (20.C.7). This would appear to be yet another case in which an administrative error was made – now difficult or impossible to correct.

The 31-year-old Alexander Verner Cochran – known to all in the Army as 'Bill' and to his family as 'Alic' – had an interesting background. Since the 1700s, the family home and estate was at Ashkirk House, Ashkirk, near Selkirk, in the Scottish borders. Army and naval careers were historically prevalent throughout the family. His father, Alexander Charles Purves Cochran, was a career soldier commissioned into the British Army in 1900, before transferring into the Indian Army (in which he served until retiring in the early 1930s as a Lieutenant Colonel). Alic's mother was Florence Edith Hurd Berthon, the daughter of General Thomas Berthon. Alexander and Florence married in Somerset during 1908, shortly after which they travelled to India. There, in 1911, the couple's firstborn died as a two-week old infant. Alic followed on 30 March 1913, born in Darjeeling, after which the young Cochran travelled around with his parents to his father's various postings.

In 1914, when the First World War broke out, Alic's father's regiment was garrisoned in Hong Kong, where, in Kowloon, he was joined by a baby sister, Daphne Alexine, in November. In February 1915, the regiment, complete with officers, wives and families, were loaded onto a captured German ship and taken to Marseilles where they disembarked. The officers set off for the Battle of St Julien, part of the Second Battle of Ypres; wives and families travelled on to Britain.

By the age of eight, Alic saw increasingly less of his parents, as they were in India and he was at school in England; he had also gained a second sister – Euphen Flora – who was born in 1917. During school holidays, he would spend most of the time with relatives, often his grandmother, and with his parents' friends, Will and Madge Ogilvie, who lived at Ashkirk. The Ogilvies had a son, George, who was a similar age to Alic, and the boys became firm friends. In 1927, Alic went to Wellington College where it was noted that he was a shy and mediocre pupil both in the classroom and on the sports field. He did, however, show an interest in the countryside and field sports, being a competent horseman and keen angler. Nonetheless, in 1930, he achieved credits in French, Mathematics and Mapwork in his School Certificate.

In 1931, Alic was accepted for entry to Sandhurst and commissioned in 1933, joining the 1st Battalion KOSB at Fort George. In 1936, he transferred to the 2nd Battalion, stationed in India, and soon joined the staff of HQ Southern Command India – a fairly comfortable posting in Poona, with most of the soldiering being ceremonial duties, although there was always the possibility of civil unrest. Field sports and game hunting were available, and working closely with the Governor of the Central Provinces, Sir Henry Twynham, generated many invitations to enjoy these pursuits. Working closely with the Governor also meant close contact with Sir Henry's family – in early 1942, Alic's engagement to the Governor's youngest daughter was announced: Captain Alexander Cochran and Penelope Hearson Twynam were married on 20 June 1942, at Christ Church, Pachmarhi, by the Bishop of Nagpur; a reception at Government House followed the ceremony. In 1943, Captain Cochran requested a transfer to Active Service, returning with his wife to England, where Alic joined the 7th KOSB. Promoted to Major and given command of HQ Company, like everyone else in the 1st Airborne Division, Alic was frustrated at having to stand idly by in reserve whilst the Normandy campaign was in full-swing. His nephew, Alec Colvin-Smith, comments that

> I have a letter from Alic to his mother in August 1944, expressing disappointment that after loading up for the Normandy invasion, they were 'stood down' as the Americans had beaten them to it [Author's note: this would be a reference to one of the sixteen operations cancelled prior to Operation MARKET-GARDEN]. Prior to the Arnhem lift, in a conversation with my father, he confided in his trepidation about going into action for the first time. His relationship with his father was definitely strained as my grandfather expected junior officers to obey his orders, but he had a much closer relationship with his mother. I don't think that my grandmother ever got over the death of

her son and when I was born, her first and only grandson, my mother received a letter of congratulations and suggesting that Alexander was a very good name for a baby boy.

At the time of Alic's death in action at Oosterbeek on 21 September 1944, his father, Colonel Cochran, was CO of the 2nd Battalion, Scottish Border Home Guard, to whom the Selkirk Home Guard detachment sent an expression of sympathy – one of many, no doubt, received. At Ashkirk Parish Church, the Rev. James Reekie spoke of Alic's loss:

> 'Let us always bear in mind', said Lord Roseberry when unveiling the memorial at Flodden Field, 'that heroes and heroism are visible and produced not in the splendour of triumph but in the anguish of adversity. The hero who most appeals to us is not the conqueror, but he who in the naked agony of catastrophe and despair rises superior to fate that leads captivity captive. It is to him that goes forth the eternal sympathy of mankind.' 'Tis thus we think and shall always think of Arnhem. In the glory and disappointment of that defeat, the King's Own Scottish Borderers had a share. So too did Ashkirk in the person of one of the officers of that regiment, Major Alexander Cochran, the 'young Laird', as we all knew him, whose death in action the whole community mourns. With our sympathy to his parents in their proud sorrow and to his widow in her early bereavement, we unite our thanks to God for the life and gallant services now ended here. But we like to think that the soldier's warfare is not warred until victory is won, that the spirits of those who fall keep leading the comrades they leave behind.

Another 7th KOSB comrade left behind was Private Samuel Paton Cassidy – although, not uncommonly, ambiguity exists regarding his date of death and last resting place.

Samuel Cassidy was born to an Irish father and a Scottish mother in Belfast, Northern Ireland, on 12 April 1920, his family living in the working class, Protestant Shankill Road area of the city in County Antrim – later synonymous with the so-called 'Troubles'. Little, however, is known of his early life, except that he had two older sisters, Sarah, known to all as 'Sallie', and Jean, and a younger brother, Charles. On 13 April 1939, Sam married an Irish girl, Mary Young, at Holy Trinity Church on Clifton Street, Belfast. The couple then moved to England, living at Sarehole Road, Hall Green, Birmingham, Sam working at a munitions factory. On 26 February 1942, Sam enlisted at Birmingham into the GSC, Territorial Army, and became Private 14207764 Samuel Cassidy (interestingly, upon enlistment he did not use his middle name of Paton). Just under 6ft tall, weighing 161lbs with brown eyes and black hair – Sam was known for his fiery Irish temper. Pregnant, Mary Cassidy returned to Shankill Road, where the couple's daughter, Elizabeth, was born on 26 October 1942.

As frequently occurred, Sam's joining was delayed, until 22 March 1942, when he was posted to No. 10 Infantry Training Centre. On 3 August 1942, Private Cassidy was transferred from the GSC to the 7th KOSB, with whom he would remain and make the transition to glider-borne soldier. Four days before his daughter was born, Sam was promoted to corporal – but for some unrecorded reason 'Reverted to Private' on 19 August 1943. Like many other members of the 1st Airborne Division, his Army Service Record indicates fines for going AWOL twice, for 23 hours 30 minutes on the first occasion and 8 hours the second. Sometimes, though, periods of absence were caused by disrupted transport. The trials and tribulations of wartime leave and travel are perfectly captured in an undated letter from 'Sammie' to his sister, Sallie; given the locations mentioned this must have been shortly before Arnhem:

Private Samuel Cassidy. (Paul Wright)

> Just a short note to let you know that I am back in my unit once again and everything is under control. Well, Sallie, when I left Charlie I got a Goddamned Yankee truck to a place called Witham. From there I went to Chelmsford by bus, and it cost me eight pence. Then I got from there to Hammersmith Bridge, as that was where they were going. I went into a boozer, had a few pints, and there was a jeep waiting to take me to a place called Newbury. Waiting on the other side of the road were a convoy of RASC trucks, going to my camp. I got off at the Guard Room. I arrived back in camp around 1230, so everything was OK. But I never told that I lost my pass while I was in London on Saturday night. I was just shaking in case some Military Police pulled me up. Anyway, they never. It wasn't bad, I enjoyed myself very much in the short time I was with you. I don't know as yet about the weekend. If I get to know I will send a telegram. I think this is all for now as I have a lot of work to do and have a letter to write home yet, to Mary. Give my regards to Charlie, also give Maureen a big kiss from me as she wasn't there when I was going back. Hoping to hear from you soon.

Mary and Betty Cassidy. (Paul Wright)

On 17 September 1944, as a member of Support Company, No. 1 Anti-Tank Platoon, Sam Cassidy was also 'Off at last'. According to all official records, the 24-year-old Irishman was killed on 21 September 1944; he has no known grave. In July 1945, however, information was received by the Casualty Wing, Infantry Records Office,

Perth, that a German record of field burials included reference to the fact that Private Cassidy had been buried in a 'comrades' grave' at 'Oosterbeek-Graf, Recterenstr. 12'. The White House is at Graaf van Rechterenweg 12. This evidence, therefore, suggests that Sam was buried in the mass grave in the Hotel's grounds. Clearly – as in the case of Private Gilbert Anderson – his identity was known when his remains were buried but somehow later lost. It is highly likely that Private Cassidy's remains were exhumed from the White House in 1945, but then buried as 'unknown' at the Arnhem-Oosterbeek War Cemetery. According to the Roll of Honour, twenty-one 7th KOSB casualties remain 'missing'. A search of the Airborne Cemetery confirms that of the many 'unknown' burials, seven are definitely King's Own – six of them privates. Whether one of them, or one of the unidentified burials whose units are unknown, is Private Cassidy, we will never know – but it is highly likely that 'Sammie' is amongst those 'Known unto God' at Oosterbeek.

So, what happened to Private Cassidy, and when? Roy 'Lofty' Tolhurst takes up the story:

> In 1999, I met Paul Wright, who, when visiting my home, spotted my copy of *Off at Last*, Dutch historian and specialist publisher Robert Sigmond's unit history of the 7 KOSB; Paul mentioned that 'my Uncle Sam, who was a King's Own Scottish Borderer, died at Arnhem'. After speaking to his mother, Paul confirmed that Sam's surname was Cassidy. We found reference in the book to 'Samuel Cassidy who accidently shot himself shortly after leaving the glider'. In April–May 2002, I invited Paul to join us on an Arnhem trip in my vintage ambulance, during which we visited the White House and placed a cross by a tree in the garden. Unbeknown to Paul, the placing of that cross would be the start of an incredible journey.
>
> The following year, another cross was placed by the tree in memory of Sam, and in 2004, Paul joined us for the sixtieth anniversary commemorations. On that occasion, he chose to lay a wreath in the garden of the White House, by the tree, which we planned to do on Sunday, 20 September 2004, after the cemetery service. As we were leaving the cemetery, however, we received a call from Robert Sigmund, who, when told about the wreath, suggested it was not laid until we had made contact with him as he would be in the Hotel, having lunch with some 7 KOSB veterans. Our arrival at the Hotel was announced, and Robert appeared with a small column of KOSBs and others; they stood in line by the tree. Robert suggested that Paul should say a few words, which, although unexpected, he did, explaining his personal connection to Sam Cassidy. The wreath was laid and the veterans showed their respect, as only they can for one of their own. We were all very moved.
>
> After the wreath was laid, Paul was approached by one of the veterans, John Crosson, who said 'Tragic wasn't it, what happened to Sam?' Paul explained

that although the story is weak he understood Samuel died on the DZ. 'No., no, no!' said John, 'He died not far from here!' and briefly gave his account. John expressed surprise that Paul knew so little about his Uncle Samuel, as he had been in touch with Samuel's granddaughter, Lynda Ross, for some years, who knew all the facts. So, Paul learned what happened to his Uncle and that he had a cousin living in Ireland. After returning home, Paul made contact with John, who kindly supplied a copy of his memoir, which includes reference to Sam Cassidy's unfortunate demise. It was evidence enough: Samuel was not killed on the DZ but during the fierce fighting around the White House on 21 September 1944. John also put Paul in touch with his new-found cousin. Paul joined us for another trip in 2008; another cross was laid. In 2009, the sixty-fifth anniversary year, Paul again laid a wreath at the White House, accompanied by seven 7th KOSB veterans who were Robert Sigmond's luncheon guests. Afterwards, the veterans, one of whom was Sam's Platoon Sergeant, George Barton, were leading a walk of the locality, which we were invited to join.

During the tour, on which the veterans provided a fascinating commentary, no mention was made of Sam Cassidy. On our return to the White House, Paul was approached by John Davidson and George Barton, and invited to accompany them to the very spot that Samuel died – the circumstances of which had yet to be properly explained to Paul. They walked together up Van Dedemweg to the junction of Cronjeweg and stopped. It was there, we heard, that a 6-pounder Anti-Tank gun, commanded by Lieutenant Hannah, was sited, which Samuel was in support of, looking down the road towards Stationsweg – where two German tanks were sitting. George Barton recounted how he had sent John Crosson down Cronjeweg to snipe from an upstairs window, down onto the enemy armour and hoping to draw them forward, towards the concealed anti-tank gun. The ruse worked. The first tank took the bait, advanced, was duly hit in the right-hand track and stopped. The second tank, supported by infantry, then started to withdraw. Sam, who was either lightly or unarmed, gave chase, and when close to a British position shouted for and was given a Bren. By this time, John Crossen had come down from his position upstairs, and was crouched in the drive of number seven. Moments later he saw Samuel in the road, in front of him. Sam aimed his Bren at the retreating enemy, pulled the trigger – nothing. It had jammed. Under normal circumstances a weapon should be removed to a place of safety and the blockage cleared, but this was obviously impossible in the heat of battle. Sam, therefore, banged the butt on the ground, which was a recognised procedure, but still the jam failed to clear. Furious, shouting and swearing, he banged it down again, harder – the gun went off. A round entered below his jaw and exited through the top of Sam's head. Death was instant. Naturally, it was assumed that he had been shot by a sniper. Sometime later, however, John Crosson returned to Sam's body, when it became evident that the fatal shot had come from his own Bren – killing him instantly. As the sad tale was recounted, Paul and the two veterans were standing at the gun position on the junction. They then walked along Cronjeweg to the very spot where Sam died. It was, naturally, a deeply moving moment for Paul in particular, who marked the spot and occasion by planting another cross.

Was Private Cassidy, though, really killed on 21 September 1944, as all official records state? It is widely believed, in fact, that his fatal accident actually occurred the previous day, which is consistent with this (previously mentioned) entry in the 7th KOSB War Diary:

> Later, another anti-tank gun, under Lieutenant Hannah, and escorted by a platoon of 'B' Company, went out to watch the road leading South from the road and railway crossing at 699791. Soon after it was in position, a Tiger tank, towing a flame-throwing apparatus, appeared and a spirited action took place. As a result of the courageous behaviour of our anti-tank gun crew, and of Corporal Watson and Private McWhirter in particular, the Tiger tank was completely knocked out and the crew killed.

Years later, even though the survivors had always known, Sam Cassidy's family at last has an account of their ancestor's demise. In all likelihood, however, Private Cassidy was killed on 20 September 1944, not the 21st as records state (ironically, Major Cochran's date of death is recorded as 20 September 1944, when it clearly occurred on the 21st). Whilst, as explained, in all probability Private Cassidy was buried at Oosterbeek as 'unknown', it is unlikely, unless the CWGC provides researchers access to exhumation reports, which it currently will not, any further progress will be made to identify exactly which grave is concerned. As always, some answers, but the big question remains: where is Private Cassidy's last resting place?

How fared the 7th KOSB during the rest of the battle? After the 'Battle of the White House', the 7th KOSB left the battered Dreijeroord Hotel, and moved to the perimeter's north-west corner. There the battalion fought virtually to a standstill, until the survivors were evacuated across the Rhine at 0200 hrs, 26 September 1944. According to the War Diary, 'Once on the other side it seemed one had reached a haven, and, despite mud and fatigue, all trudged the four miles to Driel with light hearts, if somewhat heavy footsteps. Near Driel, tea, rum and blankets were dished out, under excellent arrangements made by XXX Corps, and all were most acceptable . . . At Nijmegen, the survivors of the Battalion were welcomed by our own "Seaborne Tail" . . . soon refreshed, fed and sent to bed to enjoy their first real sleep for ten days.'

Only four 7th KOSB officers and seventy-two ORs were safely evacuated. One hundred and five Borderers were dead, fifteen more expiring from wounds whilst in captivity. 21 September 1944, was the day on which the battalion suffered its highest number of losses, twenty men, exceeded that day only by 1st Border which lost twenty-one. Indeed, as a result of this long-awaited 'great adventure', the 7th KOSB never fought again.

On 18 May 1945, the 7th KOSB held its first post-war reunion. Lieutenant Colonel Payton-Reid – awarded a DSO for his leadership at Arnhem – concluded his moving address with these simple words: 'May their memory never fade and their example remain our inspiration.'

Paul Wright lays a wreath commemorating his uncle at the Hotel Dreijeroord, with 7 KOSB veterans looking on. (Paul Wright)

Chapter 15

Gunner Thomas Stanley Warwick, 1st Airlanding Anti-Tank Battery, Royal Regiment of Artillery

According to Lieutenant John C Howe, 'The Battery Plan was quite straightforward: "A", "B" and "C" Troops were to support 1st, 2nd and 3rd Parachute Battalions; "D" Troop was to be deployed for protection of the Divisional Area, and "P" Troop was to be divided – two guns to follow 1st Parachute Battalion into Arnhem whilst the remaining pair were held in reserve at the Divisional Area.' Whilst the batteries mainstay was the ubiquitous 6-pounder anti-tank gun, 'D' and 'P' Troops were armed with the heavier and more dangerous 17-pounder. The total anti-tank gun allocation to 1st and 2nd Airlanding Anti-Tank Battery, Airlanding Brigade and the Polish Brigade was eighty-four anti-tank guns, of both types. As Lieutenant Howe later wrote, 'This would have been a formidable deployment around Arnhem Bridge, both north and south of it. This would have been possible had the entire lift gone on one day. However, it was spread over three days, and other events played their part.'

It was late on 16 September 1944, in fact, that the battery commander, Major W.F. Arnold, was notified that due to insufficient tug aircraft, the whole battery could not be lifted in one go: four gliders, carrying one gun each, had to hold back until 18 September. In the event, according to the HQ RA War Diary,

> One 6-pounder and two 17-pounder guns failed to reach the RV, the 6-pounder having landed about twenty miles short and two 17 pounders crashed on landing. The Brigade moved off with 'A' Troop under command of 1st (Parachute) Battalion, 'B' Troop 2 Battalion, and 'C' Troop 3 Battalion. Since this point, nothing was heard of Battery HQ or 'B' Troop except a report that the Battery Commander was at the Bridge at Arnhem. Of 'Z' Troop, the attached Troop, the Troop Commander landed short and joined up with the Americans. One gun was also lost, having landed on a Dutch island; the remaining three guns came under the Commander Royal Artillery upon arrival.

The HQ RA War Diary tells us that 'On D+2, all guns still in action and in Divisional HQ area were grouped under OC 17-pounder Group . . . As odd guns or detachments came to light they were placed in this group. Towards the end, this group controlled all the Anti-Tank guns in Divisional HQ area, which in fact was the whole of the north half of the bridgehead. Three 6-pounders and one 17-pounder were still in action when the withdrawal was ordered.' On this day, of course, the brave British attempt to reinforce Lieutenant Colonel Frost's small force at Arnhem Bridge ended in failure, the advance being halted by heavy machine-gun fire and armour at Arnhem Museum. The survivors streamed back into Oosterbeek, via the main Utrechtseweg and lower road. 'P' Troop had sent two guns with the force trying desperately to get through to Frost, one of which is known to have been commanded by Sergeant Tom Hughes, who engaged and destroyed a gun located on a Rhine barge; Hughes subsequently retreated along the lower road where his 17-pounder was later destroyed in the polder below the old church. The other two guns were held back to defend the Divisional HQ area. We know from Peter Wilkinson's account, *Gunners at Arnhem*, that the commander of 'P' Troop was Lieutenant T. Casey, and that his gun commanders were Sergeants P.H. Hughes, T. Neary and J. Bower, and Lance-Sergeant Meagher. According to the Dutch historian Eugenè Wijnhoud, from conversations with survivors, Sergeant Neary's crew – in which we will shortly become especially interested – comprised Bombardier R.A. Haslam, Gunners T.S. Warwick, J. Green and O. Higgins, Driver I. Lee and Lance-Bombardier J. Burbridge.

Gunner Stan Warwick. (Nadine Jeschko)

On 17 September 1944, 'D' and 'P' Troops of 1st Airlanding Anti-Tank Batteries were flown from Tarrant Rushton to Holland in eight Hamilcars of the Glider Pilot Regiment's 'C' Squadron of No. 1 Wing (see Chapter 12). Sergeant Neary's crew, 17-pounder gun and towing vehicle were flown to LZ 'Z' at Wolfheze on 17 September 1944, in Chalk 317, by Staff Sergeant John Bonome and Sergeant Geoff Higgins. The former remembered that:

> We took off in third position and almost from the start had problems with the tug aircraft, which needed the full length of the runway to get airborne, due to oil pressure problems. The pilot eventually regained our correct station in the main stream, as we approached the East Anglian coast, by an increase of speed, with the consequential stress on the tow rope, resulting in a loss of communications between glider and tug.
>
> During the flight over the North Sea, the fighter escort was

much in evidence and as we neared the Landing Zone saw no sign of opposition. Still in third position, we released ourselves from our tug and followed the other two Hamilcars in – one of which turned over on landing. I managed to reduce our landing distance by bouncing down hard before the trees at the top of the LZ, clipping a wing in the process.

All went well and the gun crew emerged unscathed – still no opposition to speak of. We glider pilots were instructed to remain with our gun crew until such time as we were relieved and flown back to England.

As we moved with the other 17-pounder gun crews to the assembly point, we met a number of Dutch people, some of whom were offering us fruit and drinks. We finally took up our defensive position at the southern end of the LZ, to await arrival of the second lift next day.

On Monday, 18 September, whilst awaiting the second lift, we received a visit from the *Luftwaffe*, who seemed to look on us as a target because the machine-gun fire came very close – fortunately causing no damage. They left, and then the second lift arrived, but this time they were heavily opposed.

No. sign of Sergeant Higgins and myself being relieved, so we remained with the gun crew who were now ordered to proceed towards Arnhem. We had difficulty in getting the gun over an embankment, but eventually managed to join the line of vehicles heading into Arnhem. I remember passing the German staff car which had been shot up earlier, on our way.

Eventually we reached our allocated position on the corner of Hoofdlaan and the Utrechtseweg, and set the gun up facing west, towards Utrecht, with our Bren gun positioned on the other side of the road. Having dug ourselves in, we awaited what might befall us. It seemed that we were to defend the Divisional HQ in the Hartenstein Hotel, about 200 yards to the east of us, and there we remained until the evacuation.

At 1700 hrs on 18 September 1944, the 1st Airborne Division HQ reported that 'Div HQ established HARTESTEIN 693784'. The beautiful mansion was a hive of activity, and an Aid Post was quickly established in the cellar. Around the picturesque surrounding deer park and woods, the glider pilots of No. 1 Wing dug in, providing security for the new HQ. Over the next few days, the full-weight of a furious German assault was brought to bear on what became a besieged perimeter. General Urquhart later wrote that 'In the "Cauldron" there were times when it seemed no living thing could survive above ground. The shelling and mortaring were kept up with a fury designed to bend the will of the little force now remaining.' John Bonome continues:

We had several casualties, including one of the Bren gun team and the sergeant in charge of the gun [Author's note: it was Sergeant Neary's gun at this location, where he was wounded, confirming that this was the gun and crew flown to

Gunner Warwick was last seen alive at the Aid Post operating at General Urquhart's HQ in the Hartenstein mansion at Oosterbeek, pictured here soon after the war. (Gelders Archief)

Holland by Staff Sergeant Bonome and Sergeant Higgins, and with which they remained throughout]. My second pilot, Sergeant Geoff Higgins, with one of the gunners, marched a couple of young Dutchmen to the Div. HQ, as we were suspicious of them. On one occasion, during a lull in the German bombardment, two trucks drove right past our positions, in the direction of Arnhem, at speed, when, too late, we saw they were filled with Germans! I don't know what became of them after that! News was passed to us by an artillery officer of events in other parts – not very encouraging, but at least we didn't feel isolated. Very rarely did we see others of the Division, or the Germans. I was, however, joined by another staff sergeant glider pilot who I knew and had been separated from his unit. Some members of the Polish Brigade also passed by us.

All the time we were subjected to mortar fire and snipers' bullets especially, as it seemed we were a prime target with the 17-pounder. On one particular occasion, we lost our towing vehicle to a direct hit, which caught fire, setting off our ammunition store. Soon after that, a mortar bomb burst near the edge of my slit trench, burying me. Geoff tells me that he dug me out and got me to the Aid Post, where I was sedated; I don't remember a lot after that. I didn't even know Geoff when he visited me some time later. I seemed to suffer from the blast, but was otherwise unhurt.

Sergeant Geoff Higgins recalled that on 23 September 1944,

The mortar fire came closer and this time it was mixed with the rather terrifying squeal of 88mm shells, some of which seemed to hit the trees above. There was nothing for it but to stay down in one's trench and hope for the best, for there was no enemy to engage. For how long the devastation went on I do not know, but as I remember it, it seemed like hours. The truck containing the ammunition and all the other equipment belonging to the gun received a direct hit and was soon ablaze. Ammunition was exploding, and it seemed this must be the end. However, there came a sense that the sound of explosions was receding and that the 88mm shells had become less frequent and more distant. So, I shook the sand, which had fallen from the sides of my trench, off my head and crawled out to see what had happened.

The towing truck was completely burnt out. The first person I looked for was John Bonome, my first pilot, but he was not about. Fearing the worst, I visited his trench. The other Staff Sergeant had gone and John was face down and quite obviously very distressed. I lifted him and found that he was very confused and obviously had no idea what was happening. As I had previously taken the Sergeant to the first aid post, I also took John there and handed him over to one of the orderlies.

According to notes recorded from survivors by Nigel Simpson, whose father served in 1st Airlanding Anti-Tank Battery, the 17-pounders in this area of the perimeter were commanded by Sergeant Masterson of 'D' Troop, who directed Gunners Leslie Larkin and Albert Cornwall Richardson to assist Sergeant Neary's gun. Both were originally members of Sergeant Fitchett's gun crew, which was destroyed when the Hamilcar carrying it turned over on landing. Sergeant Gentle's gun had also been wrecked on landing, so both these crews combined to fight as infantry and provide a reserve for the gun crews. A Sergeant Hardman stated that, during the bombardment referred to by Staff Sergeant Bonome and Sergeant Higgins, he jumped in a slit trench – finding both Larkin and Richardson dead within.

The scant evidence available, and as described above, indicates that this incident occurred on 23 September 1944. Gunner Larkin's date of death, according to the CWGC, however, was 21 September 1944; as we have already seen in previous chapters, the confusion and circumstances of battle frequently led to inaccurate records, which may be the case here. What we do know, though, is that Gunner Larkin's field grave was at map reference 693783, in a 'field west of the Hartenstein Hotel', and that after the war he was interred at the Arnhem-Oosterbeek War Cemetery (1.A.4). Gunner Richardson, a 27-year-old former bricklayer and married man from London, was, according to the Commission and his Army Service Record, 'killed in action' on '25 September 1944' (but, again, clearly this was not the case, 25 September 1944 being an arbitrary date); he remains missing. Gunner Stan Warwick, a member of Sergeant Neary's Hoofdlaan crew, is recorded as having lost his life on 23 September 1944, and is also still missing;

he was the only member of Sergeant Neary's original crew to die at Arnhem. Intriguingly, buried next to Gunner Larkin at the Arnhem-Oosterbeek War Cemetery (1.A.3) lies an unknown soldier.

From surviving exhumation records, Captain Geert Jonker of the Royal Netherlands Army Recovery & Identification Unit confirms that, in addition to Gunner Larkin, the following casualties were also recovered after the war from the burial site at 693783; in brackets appears the grave these unfortunates now rest at in the Arnhem-Oosterbeek War Cemetery:

- Corporal F.W. Grantham, 1st (Airborne) Divisional Field Park Company, Royal Army Ordnance Corps (1.A.2).
- Sapper H.A.M Cunningham, Royal Engineers – but there is no casualty of this name listed in the Roll of Honour – (1.A.5).
- Unknown Sergeant, Parachute Regiment (5.A.12).
- Sergeant D.F. Wilson, 3rd Parachute Battalion (5.A.13).
- Private R.J. Bass, HQ, 1st Airborne Division (1.B.7).
- Corporal B.H. Cope, 3rd Parachute Battalion (1.B.8).
- Sergeant T.A. Rubenstein, Glider Pilot Regiment (3.B.7).

Of particular interest, however, is that there was another unidentified body in this group – the unknown soldier who was buried next to Gunner Larkin in 1.A.3.

The exhumation report indicates that this unidentified casualty had dark brown hair, no identity discs, no personal effects, was clad in battledress trousers and regulation underwear; size 7 boots, no equipment. The laundry mark was 'J4187'. Gunner Richardson's Army Service Number was 14208187. Gunner Warwick's was 1427378. From their Army Service Records, Richardson was 5ft 6½in tall, Warwick 5ft 6in – both men could be expected to have size 7 feet. Richardson's hair colour is recorded as 'D/Brown', Warwick's 'Black'. What might confirm identity, either way, would be a comparison of dental records with details contained within the exhumation report. Unfortunately, Gunner Warwick's dental records have been destroyed. Whether Gunner Richardson's survive is currently unknown, but that information will hopefully be forthcoming one day. On balance, therefore, and also given that Larkin and Richardson were, it is believed, killed together, the body in 1.A.3 is, I would suggest, more likely to be Gunner Richardson than Gunner Warwick.

So, what happened to Gunner Warwick? Sergeant Higgins continues his recollections of events immediately after Sergeant Neary's gun was destroyed:

> I returned to the gun-site to see one of the gunners helmetless, wandering in the direction of the Hartenstein, somewhere in the area where the deer were kept. He was incoherent and when I went towards him I could see that he had been wounded. He had been hit on the side of his head and I applied two field

dressings and held them there as we set out for the Hotel. He quickly became less steady and as there was still evidence of mortar fire, our progress became more and more haphazard. I remember as one burst of firing that seemed quite near, I jumped into a slit trench. There was radio equipment and later on I became aware that we had made a brief call on a broadcasting unit. The gunner was almost out when we reached the door and was assisted by another soldier. After the gunner had been taken away, I sat down in the hallway.

During the short time I was there, I saw several wounded and also was aware that not far away a Padre was conducting a burial service for several casualties. I asked a passing orderly about the lad I had brought in. He said, 'He died, he was one of those being carried out'. I cannot be sure that this was so, but I then returned to the gun site where I was told by the bombardier that another soldier who had been occupying a larger trench with two others had been killed as a result of the blast. The gun had been hit on the shield, probably by an 88mm shell. It was fractured and bent.

Was Gunner Warwick the man Sergeant Higgins assisted and who died at the Hartenstien? If so, what happened to him? Is he buried at the Arnhem-Oosterbeek War Cemetery as 'unknown', or do his remains still lie on the battlefield, in some long-lost field grave? One day we may know the answer, but sadly, for Gunner Warwick's family, it is not this day. What we do know, *if* Eugenè Wijnhoud's identification of Sergeant Neary's gun crew is accurate, is that Gunner Warwick was the only member to lose his life during the Battle of Arnhem, adding circumstantial weight, if nothing else, to the possibility that it was he Sergeant Higgins helped all those years ago.

According to his Army Service Record, Thomas Stanley Warwick (known universally as 'Stan') was born to Wilfred Warwick and Lydia Poulson on 20 August 1920, at Eamont Bridge, Penrith, Cumberland. On 18 November 1938, aged eighteen years and three months, giving his occupation as 'farm labourer', Stan enlisted into the 'Regular Army' at Carlisle. He was, according to family lore, two years younger than stated, however, and this was his second attempt to join the army: on the first, his father, a gamekeeper and First World War veteran, found out and fetched the underage Stan back.

Upon enlistment, Stan became '1427378 Gunner Thomas Stanley Warwick, Royal Artillery'. Initially posted to 4/2 Training Regiment, where the new recruit was trained as an anti-aircraft gunner. On 25 July 1939, whilst serving with 6/2 Anti-Aircraft Regiment, Stan was posted overseas, to the British garrison at Gibraltar, where he was serving upon outbreak of war and remained for nearly three years. By 13 July 1942, Stan was an experienced gunner with 368th Heavy Anti-Aircraft Battery, on which date he arrived back in England. On 8 April 1943, Stan married Beryl Elsie Gough in Birmingham, the young couple setting up home at 234 Redditch Road, King's Norton; their daughter, Patricia, was born on 28 December 1943 – but Stan was again overseas by then. On 16 May 1943, Stan embarked for North Africa, serving there and in Sicily and Italy until landing back in England on 5 January 1944. Whilst in foreign climes, on 30 August 1943, Gunner Warwick was transferred to 1st Airlanding Anti-Tank Battery and became an airborne soldier. The record concludes that on 17 September 1944, he was flown to Arnhem by Hamilcar glider – and, according to the record, died there of wounds 'on or shortly after 23 September 1944'.

Things, however, get completely thrown out by a report on Gunner Warwick's loss in the local Eamont Bridge newspaper – which states that 'Official news has been received from the War Office by his wife and parents that Gunner Stanley Thomas Poulson Warwick of Eamont Bridge, died of wounds in a German hospital soon after being taken prisoner at Arnhem'. Having checked all the available records, Captain Jonker confirms no mention of Warwick at Apeldoorn, 'nor in the Lieutenant Colonel Martin Herford list, or those who died in captivity at Utrecht (German *Lazerett* 2/6/13), or in the Red Cross or Divisional casualty lists'. It is likely, then, that having been wounded on 23 September 1944, Gunner Warwick died in the basement of the Hartenstein Hotel, *perhaps* after the Germans walked in on 26 September, and hence reference to him having been a prisoner and dying in a 'German hospital'. That being so, it is equally likely that he was buried in one of the mass graves around the mansion and subsequently interred as 'unknown' at Oosterbeek. The problem is that, as in so many cases, sadly, the evidence available is incomplete and inevitably ambiguous.

Gunner Warwick is remembered on the Eamont Bridge war memorial at Penrith (note incorrect spelling of 'airborne'). (Nadine Jeschko)

There is, however, an interesting addendum to this story; Nadine Jesko:

Uncle 'Stan' was my late mother's brother. She often talked to us about him when we were growing up. They were very close amongst a family of nine children. I felt that I knew him. Mam always said that he was parachuted into Arnhem but murdered by the Germans, but we now know different. He was born and bred at Eamont Bridge in what was Westmoreland, now Cumbria. His mother was my grandmother Lydia Poulson, who I don't think was married to Stan's father, Wilfred Warwick. I know that Stan had a great singing voice, and a local doctor was so impressed that he was going to pay for him to have proper signing lessons when he came back from the war. Stan was married, to Beryl, and I remember a daughter being mentioned, but I didn't know anything about what happened to her or Stan's wife. When Mam passed away, about three years ago I was often thinking of Uncle Stan and so went on various websites to find out more. Two years ago, I just had to go to Arnhem, to see where he had fought and died. I wasn't really sure where, no-one really knew. I put a cross on the Airborne Memorial, and on other memorials too, with a photo of Stan from all his family in Cumbria. Two weeks later, the word 'Arnhem' caught my eye in our local paper's letters page, so I read it: the letter-writer was asking about the cross with Stan's name on it. Turns out that this was from Stan's daughter's husband – I was astonished! I called the number immediately and was soon talking to him, Wilf, and his wife, my cousin, Patricia. It turned out that they were in front of me at the Airborne Memorial – unknowingly I had waited for them to go before placing the cross and photo! Afterwards, whilst Wilf was in the Airborne Museum buying a book, his friend saw the cross and called him over. Wilf couldn't believe what he was seeing! He had to sit down! So, through all of this I have now met Wilf, Pat and their daughter. Amazing!

It is a fact that those who lost loved ones at Arnhem are bound together, connected by an invisible thread – which can ensnare the unwary when least they expect it . . .

The grave of Gunner Larkin at Oosterbeek (1.A.4); is the unknown soldier adjacent (1.A.3) Gunner Warwick or, more likely, Richardson – or neither of them? (Author)

Gunner Warwick's medals: 1939-45 Star, Italy Star, France & Germany Star, Defence & War Medals. (Nadine Jeschko)

Chapter 16

Corporal 'Joe' Simpson, Lance-Corporal Daniel Neville, Sappers Norman Butterworth and Sidney Gueran – and survivor, Lance-Sergeant Harold Padfield, 1st Parachute Squadron, Royal Engineers

Every year, surviving veterans still make their pilgrimage to Arnhem, there to maintain and nurture the long friendships made with the Dutch people, to meet old comrades – and to remember the dead. The emphasis of this book is, of course, on the individual stories of those who made the ultimate sacrifice – who have no voice – but we must not forget that survivors frequently carry with them the traumatic first-hand memories of combat. Today, this is widely understood as 'Post Traumatic Stress Disorder', which was unrecognised during the Second World War. Consequently, in 1945, survivors were largely left to deal with and reconcile their experiences alone and unsupported. Many I have spoken to over the years undoubtedly suffered from another condition, identified during the 1960s as 'Survivor Guilt'. In some cases, survivors remain haunted for a lifetime. One such was 1st Parachute Squadron, RE, survivor Harold Padfield, who sadly died in 2014. Well-known to Arnhem buffs and remembered with respect and affection around the world, Harold was a sergeant in command of men fighting at Arnhem Bridge, some of whom were killed in action or died later of wounds. As Harold's son, Dave, says, 'As their sergeant he felt totally responsible for these men'. As we will see, therefore, the story of Harold Padfield – a survivor – is inexorably entwined with that of 'Joe' Simpson, Danny Neville and Norman Butterworth, all of whom lost their lives either at or as the result of wounds sustained at Arnhem. This chapter is, therefore, unique.

When at Churchill's behest Britain forged an airborne force, it had soon become apparent that specialist engineers would be required to support glider-borne and parachute infantry troops. Consequently, the 1st Air Troop, RE, was formed, becoming 1st Parachute Squadron, RE, and declared operational in November 1941. The squadron comprised a headquarters section and three troops, 'A', 'B' and 'C', each commanded by a captain and sub-divided into two sections, which were commanded by a lieutenant, typically supported by a lance-sergeant, two corporals, four lance-corporals, and a compliment of ten sappers. Significantly, these troops were trained to operate independently if necessary, and were specialists in demolition, bridging, lifting, mine-laying and sabotage; they were also familiar with and able to use captured enemy weapons and equipment. In February 1942, 'B' Troop's commander, Captain Dennis Vernon, and a stick of airborne REs participated in Operation BITING, the audacious raid on Bruneval to steal parts a new secret German radar led by Major John Frost, then commanding 'C' Company, 2nd Parachute Battalion. On 30 October 1942, 1st Parachute Squadron embarked for North Africa. Sailing into uncertainty amongst the airborne engineers were Corporal 'Joe' Simpson, Lance-Corporal Daniel Neville, and Sapper Norman Butterworth.

William Leslie George Simpson – known to all as 'Joe' – was born in Chillaton, Tavistock, Devon, on 3 October 1914, the son of Walter Simpson and Mary Ann Routley. His daughter, Diana, adds that her father 'grew up with one brother and two sisters. When he left the village school he joined the local hunt as huntsman. Later, he moved to Market Harborough to continue his career with the Fernie Hunt. There, in 1938, he married my mother, Elizabeth Broughton; In 1940, we moved to Welford; I was two years old, and it was from there that he joined the army.' Indeed, on 7 February 1940, Joe enlisted in the Territorial Army, RE, being posted a week later as 1919427 Sapper W.L.G. Simpson to 689 General Construction Company, RE. On 17 March 1940, Sapper Simpson went out to France, serving with the ill-fated British Expeditionary Force until safely evacuated on 31 May 1940. Having served at home following the Fall of France, on 14 March 1942, having volunteered, Joe was posted to 1st Parachute Squadron, successfully passing his parachute training at Ringway on Course 11, between 6–18 April 1942. Having embarked for North Africa on 30 October, on 29 December, Joe was promoted to lance-corporal. Soon, he was to distinguish himself in battle – and was awarded the American Silver Star for gallantry; his citation reads:

Corporal Joe Simpson. (The late Diana Wright)

> .... for gallantry in action with the Army of the United States on 5 February 1943 near Djebel-Mansour, Tunisia. Reaching his battalion just as the order was given to withdraw, Lance-Corporal Simpson remained to assist with the destruction of equipment which could not be removed. He then single-handedly carried a wounded man through heavy enemy fire for a distance of two miles to a medical aid station. Later, while searching for more wounded men, he was

able to guide a party of stretcher bearers to safety. His courage and devotion to all were an inspiration to all.

His bravery was also recognised with a Mention in Despatches, gazetted on 23 September 1943, by which time Joe had been promoted to corporal. Having survived the fighting in North Africa, Corporal Joe Simpson – a brave and decorated airborne warrior – took part in the invasions of Sicily and Italy before returning home on 26 November 1943.

Daniel Neville was an Irishman, who entered the world on 5 June 1915, in Bedford, Listowel, County Kerry, in south-west Ireland, one of ten children born into the Roman Catholic family of Daniel Neville and Mary Murphy. 'Danny' attended Coolard National School at Lisselton, Listowel, County Kerry, until around the age of thirteen, after which time he became a carpenter. Today, only one of the Neville children survives, Nora Noonan, now aged ninety-seven, who was close to Danny and remembers growing up in between-the-wars Ireland as tough: 'there were many premature deaths, particularly from tuberculosis; our mother and two of her sisters died from the disease. As children, Danny and I were frequently at funerals, seeing people being buried, and played a childish game of burying things. I remember the two of us burying a hammer because to our child-eyes it looked like a body.' Catholics commonly believe that death is the passing from the physical world to the afterlife, where the deceased's soul will live on in heaven, hell or purgatory, depending upon the life they have led. It is also very important that the deceased has a known grave; sadly, morbid childish games would one day resonate where Danny Neville was concerned.

Lance-Corporal Daniel Neville. (David Noonan)

Before the Second World War, Danny journeyed from County Kerry to England, living at 65 Oxford Road, London W5, working as a carpenter. On 29 January 1940, however, he enlisted at Acton into the Territorial Army, RE, as 1911650 Sapper Daniel Neville. His Army Service Record describes the young Irishman as aged twenty-four years and seven months, 5ft 9½in tall, with grey eyes and brown hair, level of fitness 'Grade I'. Danny's nationality was recorded as 'British' – but Ireland was a troubled, divided land, as Danny's nephew, Kevin Neville, explains: 'At that time, to have a son in the British army was a no-no, after the history and civil war of 1916 to 1922. Our family did not, therefore, advertise Danny's position'. Inevitably known in the British Army as 'Paddy', Sapper Neville's first posting was to 691 General Construction Company, RE, with which unit he qualified as a 'Carpenter Joiner BIII' on 2 March 1940, and sailed for France and the BEF on 11 March. The German attack in the West, of course, came with unprecedented fury on 10 May 1940; interestingly, 691 Company disembarked at Southampton on 25 May 1940 – the day before Lord Gort's decision to retire on and evacuate from Dunkirk. Safely back in 'Blighty', Danny 'proceeded to rest camp Southampton', for an undetermined period before remaining with his unit on home service. By 28 November 1941, he was a 'Carpenter & Joiner BI'. More exciting things beckoned, though: on 1 September 1942, Danny volunteered to become an airborne engineer and joined 1st Parachute Squadron, successfully completing his parachute course shortly afterwards. On 30 October 1942, along with Joe Simpson, Danny embarked for North Africa, fighting there, in Sicily and in Italy, until safely returning to England on 10 December 1943, there to await events along with the rest of 1st Airborne Division.

Norman Butterworth was born in Oldham, Lancashire, on 1 December 1917, the son of William and Alice Butterworth. Little is known of his early life, but we do know from his Army Service Record that he was an electrical engineer who enlisted into the Territorial Army, RE, at Oldham, on 20 February 1941. Norman was a family man, having married Alice Lumbley in Oldham on 7 September 1940; the couple already had two daughters, Sheila and Patricia, with Carolynn following in 1943. First port of call for 2141624 Sapper Norman Butterworth was 'A' Company, 3 Training Battalion, RE. Upon completion of 'recruit training', Norman 'mustered as Pioneer RE EIII' and posted to 259 Field Company on 16 July 1941. Serving at home, he passed the electrical engineering course and re-mustered as an 'Electrician AIII' on 9 February 1942. Shortly afterwards, Norman volunteered for and was accepted by 1st Parachute Squadron, qualifying as a parachutist on 2 May 1942. Along with Joe Simpson and Danny Neville, he too left England, North Africa bound, on 30 October 1942. On 12 December, Norman wrote to 'Mother & Dad':

> Well I just don't know what to write about but as it may be a while before I have a chance to write again, I thought I may as well try to put a letter together. I have had no mail from anyone at home yet, that is what makes it so difficult to keep writing. I have wrote you a good few letters, the last two were dated 24 November and 17 December. I only hope you have been receiving them. I keep on asking if you received my Xmas card and the photos I sent, the reason being in case some of the letters don't get through. I am looking forward to the local paper, it will be real good to read something.

Although only the first page survives, the letter is interesting, emphasising as it does the importance of family contact through the erratic wartime postal service – something that with our modern instant communications we take for granted today. Regular letters from home were essential for good morale, and every effort was made to keep the mail coming. Sapper Butterworth saw action in North Africa, Sicily and Italy before also returning home to England on 10 December 1943.

Harold Padfield was born on 12 October 1921, at Holcombe, Somerset, the eldest of four children born to William James and Bertha Daisy Padfield. During the 1926 General Strike, however, the family moved to Kent, where Harold's father, a miner, found work at Tilmanstone Colliery, near Dover. The family lived in the village of

'B' Troop, 1st Parachute Squadron, RE, in Italy, 1943. At second left, first row sitting, is Sergeant Harold Padfield; Lance-Corporal Daniel Neville second left, front row; Sapper Norman Butterworth fifth from right, first row standing; Sapper Sid Gueran, same row, third right. (Airborne Museum Hartenstein)

Rear row, left to right: S. Gueran, N. Butterworth, W. Hurst, L. Williamson, G. Christie. Front row, from left: T. Gillie, unknown, S. Fleming, F. Navin. (Airborne Museum Hartenstein)

Elvington, the Padfield children attending the Elementary School there. In 1933, Mr Padfield, still suffering the after-effects of a gas attack during the Great War, had to stop his physically-demanding job at the coalface due to heart trouble. Times were hard. Surviving on 30 shillings a week, as Harold later wrote, 'We didn't have lots of things, but we always had a meal'. At Easter 1936, Harold left school and became a gardener at Lord Guildford's estate – but his sights were already firmly set on an army career.

Harold had already sat entrance exams at the Dover recruiting office, which he passed and chose to join the RE. As Harold said, 'It was Dad who talked me into it: he said I'd be better off joining the engineers because I'd learn a trade and that sort of thing. I decided to join the army because I didn't want to go into the pits.' So it was that on 7 September 1936, Sapper Padfield reported to Kitchener Barracks, Chatham, and joined 'M' Company Boys. This would become home, in fact, for

Harold Padfield serving as a warrant officer, after the war. (David Padfield)

the next three years. Harold, who had never been away from home before, later wrote that 'This was a time of great experience for me . . . Bugling, Fife Parades and Trade Training were the major activities to excel in until your eighteenth birthday: life was never dull. My trade training as a fitter involved spending twelve months on the bench; altogether you had to do 2000 hours before you could then move up to sapper training.' This was, of course, peacetime, fragile though that was; in wartime, the luxury of such comprehensive training was infinitely reduced. Harold would progress to sapper training in February 1940, at Shorncliffe, near Folkestone: 'Sapper training during the war had been reduced from nine to four months.' It was there that Harold and his young peers saw the effect of war for the first time, as the BEF's exhausted survivors arrived back in England via Dunkirk. As Harold said, 'This is when the gravity of being at war properly struck home'. In July 1940, Sapper Padfield was posted to 7th Field Company, RE, 'who had taken quite a bashing in the retreat to Dunkirk'.

Serving at home, training extensively, Harold Padfield was amongst those intrepid men who answered the call for volunteers to join the new airborne force: 'We applied not because we knew anything at all about parachuting, none of us did, it was more because we all felt that we were getting into a bit of a rut doing what we were doing – and this sounded an adventurous jump out of the rut!' Harold's application was successful and he consequently joined Course 40 at Ringway, 1–11 December 1942, qualifying as a military parachutist: 'In February 1943, word came that 1st Parachute Squadron needed reinforcement and so ten of us were on our way to North Africa.' There Harold would meet men with whom he would be inexorably connected for the rest of his life: including

SIDNEY GUERAN AND HAROLD PADFIELD

Joe Simpson, Danny Neville and Norman Butterworth. Like the others, Harold saw action in North Africa, Sicily and Italy before returning home for Christmas 1943. For some, it would be their last.

For Operation MARKET-GARDEN, as we have seen, the 1st Parachute Brigade's task, on 17 September 1944, was to seize and hold the main road bridge and nearby pontoon bridge in Arnhem, and take the railway bridge over the Rhine at lower Oosterbeek. It was reasonable to expect that the Germans would have set demolition charges on those objectives, which 1st Parachute Squadron, RE, was to deal with, striking out for their objectives with Lieutenant Colonel John Frost's 2nd Parachute Battalion via the lower, 'Lion', route. The lift of 1st Parachute Squadron is well described in a letter written fifteen months after the operation, to Mrs Butterworth, by the American pilot of Dakota 'U-Uncle' (unfortunately only the first page survives, so his name is unknown):

> Your husband and his unit parachuted from the American Army Air Force's Troop Carrier planes. He departed from the Barkston Heath aerodrome, located between Sleaford and Grantham, Lincolnshire, at approximately twelve noon. The total formation flighting from that field was seventy-two. Of that number, eighteen were operated by the 15th Troop Carrier Squadron of the 61st Troop Carrier Group. The squadron commander was Lt Col L.C. McMurbury of Texas. The take-off and flight of these planes (C-47 or Dakota) was an inspiring operation. The men, both previous to and during the flight, seemed to be in excellent spirits. The weather was clear and excellent for the landing of airborne troops. Flak and enemy opposition were moderate, though several of our ships were shot down and many others damaged, including my own. All ships arrived safely over the drop zone and the greater part of damage was done on the return flight. Before the men boarded the aircraft, tea was served. Tension and strain of the coming action was overcome and a jolly spirit existed between the Americans and English. Your husband's aircraft ('G'-George) was manned by Americans: two officer pilots, T/Sgt Engineer Weaver, and a S/Sgt radio operator . . . My ship, 'U'-Uncle, was parked directly in front of the ship 'G'-George, in which your husband was flown. I was talking with the pilots, Weaver and your husband an hour or so before take-off. I suggested that Weaver take a picture of your husband and me . . . just opposite 'G'-George.

As things turned out, Staff Sergeant Weaver's photograph would be the last ever taken of Sapper Norman Butterworth.

Harold Padfield was by now a 22-year-old lance-sergeant and section commander in Lieutenant 'Stiffy' Simpson's 'B' Troop; having landed in a tree on DZ 'X' near Renkum, he let himself down safely:

A remarkable snapshot showing Sapper Butterworth about to emplane for Arnhem, 17 September 1944. (Airborne Museum Hartenstein)

Gliders were coming in thick and fast, many with a horrible 'crunch', and there were hundreds of parachutists. At any other time, it would have been a sight to behold. I spotted the blue smoke for my rendezvous and ran over to join the rest of the stick. We collected our weapons and stores, then moved off towards Wolfheze. In battle, we carried our explosives and grenades on our person, so you made sure that the detonators were stored where you wouldn't fall on them.

Following the 2nd Parachute Battalion 'snake', 'B' Troop advanced towards Arnhem. Earlier, the mental hospital at Wolfheze had been bombed by the Allies, in the mistaken belief that the premises was occupied by German troops; now, the surviving patients wandered around the area, doubtless bewildered – a sight Lance-Sergeant Padfield described as 'strange and eerie'. As the airborne troops progressed through the party atmosphere of lower Oosterbeek, greeted by 'hundreds of Dutch with flags and bunting', the operation was about to suffer its first major setback: the railway bridge was blown up by the Germans just as elements of 'C' Company, 2nd Parachute Battalion, began to cross it. Further fighting around the Oosterbeek-Laag railway station followed, claiming the lives of the Gronert twins, and so it went on. 'B' Troop would not reach the environs of Arnhem via the low-road until 9 pm:

> . . . things were pretty lively, with fires lighting up the place. I had to get down to the river, find the pontoon bridge and check its suitability for use at a later stage. I took Danny Neville and Frank Navin with me. We found it about a mile downstream, minus its centre-section. We carried on for a further half mile and found the missing section, complete with explosive charges which we cut away and dumped in the river. We then made our way back to the main section which also had explosive charges fixed, so did the same with those. As we were coming away, a German soldier must have mistaken us for one of his own – poor chap . . . There seemed to be all hell being let loose at the bridge itself.

Lance-Sergeant Padfield and his section managed to safely pass under the bridge ramp, emerging on the eastern side and moving north a couple of hundred yards to a large, three-storey building adjacent to and overlooking the ramp. Lieutenant Simpson ordered Padfield to break into the building, which he did 'no bother'. As he searched the building, it became obvious that this was a school. This was, in fact, the Van Limburg Stirum School, a name now synonymous with the Battle of Arnhem Bridge. The engineers, comprising half of 'B' Troop, lost no time in preparing the building for defence, smashing windows to minimise the danger from flying splinters, and using the substantial furniture as barricades and cover. That night the small, besieged force commanded by Captain MacKay, was joined by 'A' Troop – including Corporal Joe Simpson. As Harold said, they were welcome 'extra hands to cover up top'. As dawn broke, the young sergeant toured the building, ensuring that his men had selected the best fields of fire:

Sid Gueran before volunteering for 1st Parachute Squadron. (Anne Wilton)

> I went to Sapper Sid Gueran and set him up on a desk, so he could comfortably sit and cover a vital area to the west, through a porthole window. I was telling him the area I wanted him to cover but couldn't understand why I wasn't getting a response. When I turned towards him, he was sat upright – shot through the mouth. It must have been a stray bullet because I certainly didn't hear anything. I got hold of Joe Malley, whom I had put in charge of this particular area, and we laid Sid out on the floor, making sure his dog tags were round his neck. So that was the end of Sid, and by 0900 hrs on the Monday morning, I'd had my first casualty. It was upsetting, to lose someone so early on, because you weren't trained to lose people or deal with it when you did. But, you just have to get on with it.

The ruined Van Limburg Stirum School after the battle – note the wrecked German half-track. (Gelders Archief)

Sidney Frederick Gueran was born on 2 October 1916, in Grays, Essex, the eldest son of Sidney Daniel Gueran, a Merchant Navy skipper from Deptford, and Florence May Ager. 'Siddy', as he was known in the family, had two younger brothers, Stanley and Norman, and two sisters, Constance Esther and Gwendoline Rose. The Guerans set up home in Ramsgate, Kent, which Sid's maternal niece, Anne Wilton, describes as 'a happy, busy, home, with dancing in the front room every Sunday afternoon, with all friends invited'. Sid and Stanley attended St George's Central School in Ramsgate, and were gifted sportsmen. Later, they worked together at Messrs Robert Brett of Canterbury, a builders' merchant. Whilst playing for Ramsgate Corinthian Cricket Club, Sid had won a coveted silver trophy for the season's top score of 100 not out. Aged eighteen, he joined Arsenal Football Club, playing for the 'Gunners' 'nursery side' at Margate, before signing, on loan, for Southampton Football Club. Three first team appearances followed for the 'Saints', but Sid, an inside-forward, was never to break into the big time – whilst playing for Exeter City, he retired in 1938. By then, Sid was working as a welder's mate, but on 17 April 1940, he enlisted in the Royal Engineers at Canterbury. According to his attestation papers, Sid was then aged 'twenty-three years and six months', 'five feet nine-and-a-half inches' tall, weighed 154lbs, had a 'medium complexion', 'blue-grey' eyes and brown hair. Sapper Gueran then served at home until 12 March 1943, when he embarked for North Africa, subsequently serving in Sicily and Italy. Whilst overseas, on 4 October 1943, he joined 1st Parachute Squadron, RE. Having qualified as a parachutist, Sid returned to the UK, disembarking on 9 December 1943.

SIDNEY GUERAN AND HAROLD PADFIELD

When the Second World War came, like countless others, the Gueran family was irrevocably broken up: whilst Sid served in the Mediterranean Theatre with 1st British Airborne Division, Stanley joined the RAF and was posted to the 'Forgotten Air Force' in the Far East; Norman worked on a farm, Constance stayed at home, and Gwen was evacuated to rural Staffordshire. Anne continues:

When Sidney was killed at Arnhem, my grandparents were devastated. Stanley, a leading aircraftsman, returned from India and Burma in 1945 – but died soon afterwards in Bishops Stortford Hospital, following a short illness arising from his overseas service, on 28 January 1945; he was twenty-five years old. Sid and May, my 'Nan' and 'Pop', never got over it. May didn't leave the house for a year and had a nervous breakdown. Their front room, where Sunday afternoons were previously spent dancing, became a shrine to

Sid Gueran's brother, LAC Stanley Gueran, who served in the Far East. (Anne Wilton)

The medals and photographs of former professional footballer Sapper Sid Gueran – still missing in action from the Battle of Arnhem. (Author).

Sapper Sid Gueran's sister-in-law, Jean, with his niece, Anne Wilton, pictured during the research process for this chapter. (Author).

Sadly, Stanley died in 1946, having returned home, following a short illness connected with his overseas service; he was buried at Ramsgate, Kent. (Anne Wilton)

their lost sons. It remained that way until they died, in 1983 and 1988 respectively. I can remember the striking black and white photographs of my uncles looking down on me from the tall wooden fireplace. I grew up living very close to Nan and Pop, and from my teenage years until Nan died, when I was thirty-four years old, I took her every week to Ramsgate Cemetery. We had permission to drive to Stanley's grave, my two young sons in their baby seats. The boys and I used to sit in the car for at least fifteen minutes every visit, whilst Nan spoke quietly to both her sons – because Sid had no known grave, Stanley's grave became a focal point and portal through which Nan spoke to both her boys. I could never hear what Nan said to them, in fact Nan and Pop said very little about them generally, such was the pain of their loss that they just couldn't bear to talk about Sid and Stanley. In 1951, when my parents got married, they honeymooned in Arnhem – and my Mum, Gwen, laid flowers on an unknown soldier's grave at the Airborne Cemetery, as a tribute to Sidney.

Gwen Titherington, Sid and Stan Gueran's sister, laying flowers at the grave of an unknown soldier at Oosterbeek in 1951. (Anne Wilton)

As Anne has said, notwithstanding Lance-Sergeant Padfield's efforts to ensure that Sid's body was identified, he is sadly yet another casualty with no known grave.

Returning to the Van Limburg Stirum schoolhouse that fateful autumn of 1944, the 1st Parachute Squadron War Diary describes events on the day Sapper Gueran lost his life, 18 September 1944:

0010 – A Troop and ½ B Troop reorganized in school beside Bridge under Command Captain Mackay.
0200–0300 – School attacked with grenades and machine-guns and made up charges. All attacks driven off.
0700 – Two machine-gun posts North of school engaged and knocked out; both crews killed.
0830 – Armoured column, 15 Vehicles – 5 Armoured cars, 10 Armoured Half-tracks, approach Bridge and attempt to pass. Engaged half-tracks. After one hour's engagement, 6 half-tracks are knocked out and by 1000 hrs all crews killed, i.e. 30.

This was, of course, the famous attack of SS-*Hauptsturmführer* Viktor Gräbner's *Hohenstaufen* SS-*Aufklärungs Abteilung* 9 (see Chapter 2). Lance-Sergeant Padfield's succinct account of this famous action conjures up graphic images:

> Three lorries approached the bridge from the South. We waited until they were well inside the net of troops around the bridge – then opened fire. Grenade and PIAT guns opened up from other areas, and those Germans who tried to escape their burning vehicles were mown down. Later that day, a convoy of trucks and half-tracks came from the same direction and met the same fate. There must have been a dozen or more. Three went over the embankment, others were burnt out and four came towards the school, all guns blazing. They were successfully put out of action and laid to rest at the side of the building.

After the decimation of Gräbner's once-proud column, there was a lull – but a mortar and artillery barrage soon followed, shelling becoming the 'main worry', again according to Padfield. Sapper David 'Tommy' Gray was the next of 1st Parachute Squadron to die, shot by a sniper.

The War Diary continues:

> 1000 – Lt Hindley's house attacked; Infantry and machine-guns. All attacks driven off.
> 1100 – Enemy launch full scale attack on X roads 30 yards South of school.
> 1300 – Bren Groups defending South side engaged. School Mortared for one hour.
> 1400 – Enemy infiltrate into houses opposite & set up machine-guns firing directly into eastern rooms. These are engaged and knocked out one by one by the eastern Bren Group, during the course of the afternoon.
> 1800–1930 – Desultory machine-gun & mortar fire.
> 1930 – Enemy set on fire with incendiary bullets two knocked-out half-tracks resting against the house in an attempt to fire the School. Fire-fighting parties keep flames in check until danger is past.
> 2000 – Germans fire 51mm mortar bombs directly through the northern windows from next house. Forced to evacuate rooms for one hour.
> 2100 – Enemy set on fire house next to school on North side, in a further attempt to fire the school. Fire-fighting parties move to roof & come under spasmodic machine-gun fire. There is a high wind blowing sparks & blazing fragments on to timber roof. All fires kept under control & finally doused by 2350.

Once more, darkness and the early hours of 19 September 1944 brought no respite:

> 0030 – Heavy attack on both North & East sides. Gren & rifle-grenades thrown & projected into all ground & first floor rooms. Enemy succeeding in getting a

machine-gun to ground floor window & spray room & hall. Enemy driven off by 0115. Ground floor rooms evacuated & barricaded up. Loopholes knocked in interior walls to cover individual rooms.

Lance-Sergeant Padfield took a Benzedrine tablet during the early hours of the Tuesday morning, then: '. . . all of a sudden, a grenade came in through a window. Sapper Butterworth immediately picked it up and threw it back out. I don't know what damage it caused outside, but Norman's swift action certainly saved us from disaster inside.'

0200 – Enemy attack S.W. corner of school with Anti-Tank 'bazooka'. Both South & East walls at first floor level at the corner, plus part of floor blown away. Enemy fail to follow up their advantage as defenders are stunned by explosions.

0300 – Enemy entirely surround School, talking & giving orders evidently under the impression the school is no longer defended. Estimated number 60 directly under windows. All unwounded men line 1st floor windows with two grenades each, together with all Sten-gunners & 6 Bren-guns. On the word of command, entire fire power, plus all grenades is let loose. Enemy retire leaving 30 dead, machine-guns, mortar, and Anti-Tank projectile.

0700–1000 – Enemy appear at X Rds, South with 3 Mk III tanks, & attack Sqn H.Q. & houses in vicinity. South face of School engage Infantry, heavy fire from tanks, with armour-piercing fire through S.E. corner.

1000 – Lt Hindley, Sqn HQ. knocks out a tank with Gammon bomb from above; tanks retire, leaving Infantry in house opposite South face of School.

1030–1200 – Enemy attempt to evacuate this position and are eliminated in twos and threes, 15 killed.

1200 – Enemy attempt to set up mortar, due North of School position: when in place this is eliminated and crew killed.

1230–1500 – Attacks renewed at X Rds with tanks & Infantry, Sqn HQ heavily engaged, South face of School also engaged. Enemy infiltrate into houses opposite East face of School, slightly North of yesterday's positions & engage East face with machine-guns. These machine-gun positions eliminated singly as for yesterday. During this period all positions under mortar fire, which has little effect save for 11 direct hits on the School.

1615 – Enemy set fire to block of houses opposite East face in an attempt to burn out Sqn HQ. Sqn HQ keeps fires under control till dusk.

1700 – Enemy fires block of houses opposite West face on other side of street also evacuate house opposite South face. Fire-fighting parties on roof to deal with sparks blown there in high wind. School only building in Bridge area not burning.

Worse, much worse, was to come – the defenders, now a mixed force of REs and fourteen men of 'C' Company, 3rd Parachute Battalion, were critically short of ammunition by this time, and – significantly – had no anti-tank capacity. The German forces fighting to regain control of Arnhem Bridge were controlled by SS-*Brigadeführer* Heinz Harmel, commander of the 9 SS *Frundsberg* Division. Harmel's troops, inevitably, comprised a composite force of his own *Frundsberg* men and *ad-hoc kampfgruppen*. On the evening of 19 September 1944, two Tiger tanks arrived in Arnhem – and were immediately allocated by Harmel to *Kampfgruppe* Brinkman. This was very bad news indeed for the British. The mighty, iconic Tiger always made an impact, on every battlefield from the Tunisian desert to Russia's frozen steppe. With its 88mm gun and substantial armour, the Tiger was a formidable opponent at the best of times, even for the 17-pounder-equipped Sherman Firefly – but it was impossible to fight back effectively against this metal monster with small arms. These particular Tigers were from *Schwere* (heavy) *Panzer-Ersatz-und-Abteilung* 500, and specifically from *Hauptmann* Hans Hummel's *Panzer-Kompanie* Hummel. Fourteen Tigers of this unit had been transported by rail from their base at Paderborn to Bocholt, but a line blockage dictated that the Tigers had to complete the last eighty kilometres by road: only two Tigers, commanded by *Leutnant* Knaack and *Feldwebel* Barneki, successfully completed the journey – and went into action immediately.

> 1900 – Mk VI Tiger Tank approaches up bridge ramp from North & engages NW corner of school at 30 yards range. NW corner blown away at 1st floor level, other shots right through School. Positions held.
> 1930 – Tiger Tank retires.

Elsewhere in the bridgehead, however, the airborne troops did still have a small number of 6-pounder anti-tank guns – one of which, commanded by Major Arnold, CO of 1st Airlanding Anti-Tank Battery, scored a direct hit on Knaack's turret, badly wounding two of his crew. The Tigers, however, would make their presence violently felt until the battle's end.

> 2100 – Fires on either side of Sqn HQ. out of control & Lt Hindley takes survivors to West side of Bridge to join remnants of 2nd Bn (Para).
> 2359 – Casualties during 19th in School: 12 wounded, Total Cas to date in School 2 killed 24 wounded.

Cries echoing around the blazing buildings of 'Waho Mohammet!' may have roused morale, but the men, without food, water, denied sleep, running out of ammunition, outnumbered and outgunned, were in an untenable position – with no sign whatsoever of the long-overdue relief by XXX Corps. The War Diary continues its grim account into 20 September 1944:

0700–0900 – Considerable Enemy activity at X roads 50 yards South of School. Individual sniping, no major attacks.

0915 – Enemy launch major attack with Tanks & Infantry support on Bridge; engage Infantry from South face of School.

0940 – Enemy capture Bridge & attempt to blow it.

1000 – Counter-attack by 2nd Parachute Battalion (remnants 50 strong) & Sqn HQ (6 strong). Lt Hindley & Sqn HQ remove charges.

1020 – Enemy re-capture Bridge & replace charges.

1100 – 2nd Parachute Battalion & Sqn HQ remnants (30 + 4) retake Bridge & remove charges.

1130 – All British resistance ceases. Lt Hindley, SSM, 1 Other Rank taken prisoner.

1400 – Germans move up a 'Tiger' tank & 105mm S.P. gun 80 yards from SE corner of School (now only building in British hands within 2 miles of Bridge).

1410 – Complete South face, SE corner, half East face blown away by heavy fire. School on fire in four places.

1430 – Fire out of control, two top stories entirely ablaze. Explosives & ammunition blown up. Capt Mackay orders evacuation of building to burnt out Library 30 yds North, Lt Simpson covers breakout with 4 Brens.

'A' Troop's Bren, covering the breakout, was fired by Corporal Joe Simpson, supported by Sapper Johnny Bretherton. On the trigger of 'B' Troops Bren was Lance-Corporal Danny Neville, assisted by Sapper Steve Carr. Brens could keep infantry back – but not 50-ton Tiger tanks. According to Padfield, 'Two German tanks were brought up onto the bridge and started to blast away with their 88mm guns. They had a direct hit on the front of the school and the roof was set alight. Joe Simpson and Danny Neville were killed . . . Joe and Danny were limbless bodies, otherwise everyone else was out.' Lance-Corporal Arthur Hendy, also of 'B' Troop, remembered things differently to Lance-Sergeant Padfield, however: 'We started pulling the rubbish and found Joe Simpson – as we pulled him clear, he was still grasping the Bren. I carried his upper body and Malley his feet, and laid him on the stairs. I took his helmet off but it was obvious he was dead. We then went to find Danny Neville, but there was so much debris we were unable to.' In a letter to Joe Simpson's brother, Mr W.C.R. Simpson, dated 23 October 1944, Captain Eric Mackay gave his account – and a third version of events: -

I am writing instead of Lieutenant Simpson as I was your brother's Troop Commander. I have not been able to get in touch with any of your family before, because all our records of next of kin were lost at Arnhem and the War Office have been very slow about replacing them. It is a big task as only three Officers and ten men got back, and four of these had to escape from Germany to do so.

SIDNEY GUERAN AND HAROLD PADFIELD

I can tell you practically everything about your brother as I was with him constantly during those three days and he died as I was carrying him. He did very well and I was going to recommend him for a DCM, but this is not an award you can have posthumously. The only one, apart from the VC, is a mention in dispatches and I have put him in for that.

Here is the story. After we dropped on Sunday 17th, we fought our way to Arnhem bridge. My Troop had an independent role. When we got to the bridge, so few people had managed to get to it (about 600) that everyone had to sit round it and defend it, irrespective of what arm of the service they were in. As you know this small force was never relieved and was constantly attacked until it was entirely eliminated on Wednesday Sept 20th, the day your brother was killed.

We took over a school just beside the bridge and your brother had charge of a first-floor room overlooking the road. On Monday, a column of armoured cars came over the bridge, attacked and your brother destroyed six of these together with their crews, two of them single-handed [Author's note: without wishing to detract from the bravery involved, this is unlikely; as has previously been mentioned in relation to this action, with so many airborne soldiers engaging the German column, it would have been impossible to definitively attribute specific casualties to any individual]. Well I won't go into further details, it is sufficient to say that during the next three days and nights we were continuously attacked by tanks, infantry, tank destroyers, self-propelled guns, mortars, machine guns, aircraft and Tiger tanks. There were two attempts to set the school on fire. Throughout all this, your brother held his positions with superb skill and courage, in spite of all his men being wounded, and took an ever-increasing toll of our attackers.

By midday Wednesday, everyone else round the bridge had been eliminated and the school was the only building holding out. They then brought up a heavy gun and systematically blew the school to pieces. I was within six feet of your brother, when a shell came into the room and a splinter struck him in the head. I was knocked out and when I recovered a few moments later I found the house was on fire. I had heard him cry out when the shell came in. I managed to get to him and found him lying unconscious on the floor. Not knowing how badly he was wounded I carried him to the head of the stairs, I had to lay him down for a minute as he was a heavy man and I found he was dead. I examined him and found he had this one wound in the head. It was a serious one and it is a marvel that he was not killed instantly. He probably died within two minutes of receiving it and would suffer no pain as he was unconscious all that time.

Joe, as we used to call him, besides being my best corporal, was a close personal friend of mine. He had been with me for 2½ years and we had shared many dangers and queer adventures. He had the courage of a lion and although he was twice decorated, he earned many more. He is a man I can never replace, men of his calibre are few and far between.

I would be grateful to you if you could send this letter, or a copy of it, on to your parents. There are none of Joe's friends left now, I and one corporal were the only survivors of my Troop, though many wounded were taken prisoner.

If you have any queries do not hesitate to ask and I will do all I can to answer them.

As elsewhere in this book, as Wim van Zanten, who 'adopted' Joe Simpson's grave, says, 'We have three versions of events; I doubt that we shall ever know which is correct'. Probably, I suspect, through the fog of war, a combination of all three recollections.

True to his word, Captain Mackay recommended Corporal Simpson to be Mentioned in Despatches:

During the operations at Arnhem Cpl Simpson held a position in a house beside the bridge. On 18 Sept 44 a column of Armoured Cars and Armoured Half Tracks came over the bridge towards his position. Cpl Simpson knocked out two Half Tracks by accurate shooting with his Sten gun, whilst himself under a hail of accurate machine gun fire. He was also instrumental in destroying a further three Half Tracks at a range of thirty yards.

On the night 18th/19th Sept 44 the room Cpl Simpson was commanding was heavily attacked by a German tank destroyer. Two walls and part of the ceiling were blown away. Everyone in the room was wounded. Cpl Simpson had three ribs broken and one eye completely closed. In spite of his wounds, he refused medical attention, and held his post for a further forty hours engaging the enemy with great ferocity and courage until finally he was killed. Cpl Simpson personally destroyed eleven of the enemy. His courage and fortitude were beyond praise.

Unfortunately, the 'Mention' was not forthcoming, because, as Captain Mackay later explained to Joe's mother, '. . . we have been restricted in decorations. This is really criminal as many more were earned.'

Corporal Simpson, father of a now six-year-old daughter, was buried in the wrecked schoolhouse. In 1945, however, his body was exhumed and interred at the Arnhem-Oosterbeek War Cemetery. Lance-Corporal Danny Neville, though, has no known grave – and neither do three more members of 1st Parachute Squadron buried within the demolished Van Limburg Stirum School. When Joe Simpson's body was exhumed, it was found in a group of other identified casualties – and an unknown body, subsequently buried as 'Known unto God' at Oosterbeek. The exhumation report concerning those anonymous remains is detailed regarding the individual's teeth and dentistry.

SIDNEY GUERAN AND HAROLD PADFIELD

Unfortunately, a request to the MOD for Lance-Corporal Neville's dental records, by Captain Geert Jonker of the Royal Netherlands Army Recovery & Identification Unit, revealed that these no longer exist – making a comparison and potential identification impossible. These remains could, of course, be those of any of the missing 1st Parachute Squadron men – or, indeed, those from other units, who may have ended up in the school during the chaotic final curtain. Yet again, we will never know. Undoubtedly, the reason so many of those killed at the schoolhouse – including Sapper Sid Gueran, who Lance-Sergeant Padfield had ensured was wearing his dog tags when laid out – have no known grave, is because identification was impossible owing to the school having ultimately been destroyed and gutted by fire. For Danny Neville's Roman Catholic family, however, the fact that he had no known grave was a particularly difficult scenario; his nephew, David Noonan, remarks that 'When we were children, my next younger brother, also called Danny, and I were always asked by Mum, Danny Neville's sister, to go the church on All Souls' Day [2 November] to pray for the release of Danny's soul from Purgatory. We said many "Hail Mary's" and another prayer I remember well: "Eternal rest grant unto them O Lord and let perpetual light shine upon them, may they rest in peace Amen". We did this for years and years – so I hope that he, for sure, got out a long time ago.'

Returning to the smoke and flame-wreathed, crumbling buildings around Arnhem Bridge on the afternoon of 20 September 1944, the ordeal was yet over for those who had survived thus far:

> 1445 – Wounded safely evacuated to next burnt out building where come under heavy MG & Mort fire. Cas have now risen to 4 killed, 35 wounded. Lt Simpson wounded & is ordered to surrender with the wounded by Cpt Mackay.

Lance-Sergeant Padfield:

> Twiggy Hazelwood was getting worse by the hour and sure enough another direct hit and the school was well alight. We got the wounded downstairs, and I went round all the rooms to be sure everyone was out . . . We tore down doors to put the wounded on and went out the way we had come in. As we made our way across a wall, we came under fire. John Bretherton was killed as he was getting over it. Twiggy got a machine-gun burst up the side of his body as we were lifting him over the wall, but he was still clinging on to life. We were all eventually over and the bank gave a little protection. One of the wounded was Major Lewis, who must have come into the building with a signaller on the first night; when he got wounded I don't know, but he was the Company Commander of 'C' Company, 3rd Parachute Battalion. The next twenty minutes or so were phenomenal. We were caught in an enfilade of fire and air bursts. Charlie Greer was hit by a stray bullet; it made a hole in his helmet but didn't mark his head.

Billy Marr had his pack severed from his back but without injury. The captain in charge of the school was of the view that it was every man for himself and in response some made off. However, the remaining survivors and wounded were ordered by Major Lewis to surrender. He said that we should all take pride in our performance. He then instructed us to take the bolts out of our weapons and throw them away. The weapons we left where they were. At my instruction Sapper Butterworth (who was further forward) put a white handkerchief on the end of his rifle and went forward waving it. As he was walking forward, a machine-gunner opened up and hit Norman in the legs. The German officer present immediately drew his pistol and shot the machine-gunner. After that, he told us to come forward, saying 'You are very brave but very foolish'. We considered we were unfortunate. We were then led off, with our hands up, through the streets of Arnhem and our wounded were taken off us. We were prisoners of war.

Norman Butterworth, badly wounded in both legs, was captured by the Germans and taken to St Joseph's Hospital at Apeldoorn – *Kriegslazarett* 4/686. On 9 October 1944, Mrs Butterworth received notification from the War Office that her husband was 'posted as missing on 20 September 1944' – but 'Believed prisoner of war (wounded) North West Europe'. From hospital, Norman was able to write home to his 'Dearest Wife and daughters' on 8 November 1944, explaining that

> I am doing fine, but I do get fed up with being in bed as it is nearly eight weeks since I was put to bed. I have had my leg in the air and about sixteen pounds of weights tied on to pull the bone the right length, and it gets me cheesed off. They are all decent chaps here, all very cheerful and looking forward to getting home soon . . . It is very cold here . . . We have English doctors and orderlies . . . Don't forget, Dear, to send plenty of cigs. We only get three a day so we are fairly short. Tell Pop to have a couple of pints for me.

On 20 December 1944, Norman wrote home 'Well Dear, I am still improving and getting better and better every day. I think I will manage to be sat up at the table for my Xmas dinner. I am hoping so anyway. I am just about fed up with being in bed, and I certainly never want to be in bed this long again. Still, it's no good moaning, there are lots of lads worse off than me.' There were no further letters, however – and no news of Norman would be forthcoming for months.

The war in Europe finally concluded in an overwhelming Allied victory on 8 May 1945 – but still there was no word from Norman Butterworth. Desperate, his wife wrote to the Royal Engineers Record Office in Brighton for news. The response, on 29 June 1945, confirmed that there was still nothing known of Norman's current status. On 17 July 1945, news from Brighton came at last – although not of the nature Mrs Butterworth welcomed: it had been confirmed that Sapper Norman Butterworth had died whilst a 'prisoner of war in German hands' on 27 February 1945. Nobody, though, seemed to know what had happened. Then, on 30 September 1945, Major G. Rigby-Jones of the Royal Army Medical Corps wrote to Mrs Butterworth:

> Your husband came under my care on 26 October 1944, at *Kriegslazarett* 4/686, Apeldoorn. He was doing quite well until early in February 1945, when he fell sick with *erysipelas* [an acute skin infection], which had become epidemic in the German hospital. From this he developed 'blood-poisoning' and died on 21 February 1945. I am sure that his death will come as a shock to you after he was doing so well. During the whole time he was a patient he was always cheerful and a constant source of encouragement to those around him. Allow me, for myself and on behalf of those who were prisoners with him, to express our deepest sympathy for you. If there is anything further that you wish to know, please do not hesitate to write to me.

Sapper Norman Butterworth's grave at Oosterbeek (18.C.9). (Author)

The grave of an unknown RE at Oosterbeek. 1st Parachute Squadron lost twenty-two men, ten of whom remain 'missing'. Whether this grave is that of Danny Neville or Sid Gueran, we will never know, but symbolically at least, it provides a focus for these families denied closure. (Author)

This, however, provides ambiguity over the date of Norman's sad death: was it 21 February 1945, as according to Major Rigby-Jones, or 27 February 1945, as per Royal Engineers Records? Either way, the 27-year-old Lancastrian was first buried at the Heidehof General Cemetery at Apeldoorn, then exhumed and interred at the Arnhem-Oosterbeek War Cemetery. Norman's death after being wounded whilst surrendering, and after recovering well in hospital, is especially sad. Left behind were a wife and three young daughters. One of them, now Patricia Crabtree, was only four years old when her father died, and given his long absences from home during the war, she has no recollection of him: 'After the war my mother married Corporal Jack Millard, 3rd Parachute Battalion, who was a friend of Norman's and had a few pints with him when on leave. My mother and Jack had a son, named Robert in memory of Jack's friend Robert, who was shot just after they had been captured by the Germans. Jack was a wonderful father to us all and much liked and respected by all who knew him.'

The story, though, was not yet over. Harold Padfield survived the privations of six months as a prisoner of war in Germany during that last winter of war. At the beginning of April 1945, together with Ted Laker, Harold escaped from *Stalag* XVIIC, near Innsbruck. Making their way across the Austrian mountains, the pair reached American lines at Zell-am-See, where they were introduced to fellow Operation MARKET-GARDEN survivor Major-General Maxwell D. Taylor, commander of the 101st Airborne Division, the so-called 'Screaming Eagles', who was awaiting *Feldmarschall* Albert Kesselring's formal surrender. Harold was repatriated soon after VE Day: '...we were given some kit, money and ration cards, and sent on leave. I arrived at New Milton Station quite bewildered. I arrived home and there was a large "Welcome Home Harold!" sign pinned over the front door. Tears welled up, and more tears when I got indoors, but I was home – and four-and-a-half stones lighter.' The subsequent extended leave was a time for Harold to 'pull myself together and build myself up . . . It took some gradual adjustment . . . To others you'd look bloody scared just crossing the road, and people would come over and say, "Could I help you, sir?" I suppose you could say my nerves had gone.' There was no counselling or support.

Ten weeks later, Harold was ordered to report to Horsham for 'repatriation training'. This, however, revolved almost exclusively around physical – not mental – fitness. Declared fit and having reverted to corporal, accelerated wartime promotion no longer applying, Harold Padfield joined 20 Bomb Disposal. Soon afterwards he returned to the airborne engineers, serving in the troubled Middle East and earning a 'Mention' in Palestine. It was overseas that Harold met Beryl Joy Edwards, whom he married, at Lymington Registry Office, in September 1950. The Padfields' son, David, was born in 1956, Harold continuing his distinguished army service until 12 October 1963. He then began work as Estate Foreman at Oxford University's St John's College, eventually retiring as 'Administrator of Stores and Flats' twenty-three years later. Having already returned to Arnhem on three post-war pilgrimages, in retirement Harold became actively involved with those annual events, the Arnhem Veterans' Club, the Elvington Airborne

Harold Padfield returned to Arnhem frequently and was a keen supporter of the commemorations there – pictured here below a photograph of himself after the defenders of the Schoolhouse were captured. (David Padfield)

Harold Padfield felt responsible for his men, and suffered from 'Survivor Guilt' – pictured here paying respects to his fallen comrades at the airborne marker on the Van Limburg Stirum School's former site. (David Padfield)

On 18 September 2015, Harold Padfield's ashes were interred behind the grave of Sapper Norman Butterworth at Oosterbeek. (David Padfield)

Museum, and Airborne Engineers' Reunion. Indeed, he essentially became an ambassador for Arnhem survivors – but was never at peace with his wartime experiences.

David Padfield:

Danny Neville was Dad's best friend, they were like brothers, he said. He told me that when the school was hit by the tank shell, he immediately went upstairs, finding Joe Simpson dead on the way, but nothing left of Danny. Dad was always upset about the fact that most of those killed at the schoolhouse had no known grave. As their Sergeant, he felt totally responsible for them. The guilt of the fact that they have no known graves, and especially the death of Norman Butterworth, never left him.

Aged ninety-three, Harold Padfield published *Twelve Mules and a Pegasus: Memoirs of an Arnhem Veteran*, an account of his life, mainly for family and friends. In conclusion, he wrote:

Since finishing my memoirs, I have been diagnosed as having cancer of the oesophagus, which is inoperable, and the consultant has given me twelve months. So, I have another battle to fight. I have now brought forward what has been on my mind for a long time, and that is to have my ashes interred in the cemetery at Arnhem, behind Norman Butterworth's headstone. I have permission granted from the Commonwealth War Graves Commission, and by his daughter and son-in-law, Pat and Les Crabtree, who over recent years I've kept in touch with. The War Graves Commission has sent me a letter allowing my son to take the necessary action when the time comes. This will be a fitting end to an incident that should never have happened.

Harold Padfield passed away on 13 December 2014. At his funeral in Oxford in January 2015, Harold's coffin was draped in the flag of 9 Squadron, RE, and he was carried on his last journey by six serving sergeants from his old unit (now 23 Airborne Engineer Regiment, RE). On 18 September 2015, David buried his father's ashes, as this fine man wished, behind the headstone of Sapper Norman Butterworth at the Arnhem-Oosterbeek War Cemetery. As David said, 'Dad felt that it was the right thing to do'.

Let us hope that Harold Padfield, and his friends who died so young, whether in named graves or not, have all found peace at last.

Chapter 17

Squadron Leader John Phillip Gilliard DFC, 190 Squadron, RAF

Operation MARKET-GARDEN was – and remains – the greatest airborne landing ever undertaken. The insertion of the 1st British Airborne Division and 1st Independent Polish Parachute Brigade Group by glider and parachute some eight miles from Arnhem, and transportation of the American airborne divisions involved, was an aerial feat of unprecedented proportions. Aircraft were provided by a combined fleet of the US Army Air Force (IX US Troop Carrier Command), RAF (38 Group), and RCAF (46 Group), which flew across some 200 miles of sea and enemy-held territory to deliver cargos of men and materiel sixty miles behind enemy lines – facing all the dangers such an intrepid undertaking involved.

During the three main lifts, the RAF 38 Group alone delivered 4,500 men, 544 vehicles, and the necessary anti-tank and artillery pieces. Furthermore, the airborne troops required re-supply from the air – which the Germans anticipated – meaning a further huge effort was required to sustain the surrounded and outnumbered sky soldiers. Flying low and slow to drop panniers and containers in the face of an enemy prepared and fully alerted was arguably suicidal – beyond brave. Today, newsreel footage survives, widely available via the online video channel YouTube, recorded by Sergeants Dennis Smith, Gordon Walker and Mike Lewis of the Film & Photography Unit, showing RAF aircraft being destroyed by German flak during these sorties. This sobering and tragic viewing, however, provides an immortal testament to the bravery of the aircrews and RASC air despatchers involved – amongst them 24-year old Squadron Leader John Phillip Gilliard DFC.

John was born in Paris on 18 April 1920, the second child of Lionel and May Gilliard, his elder sister, Joan, having arrived two years previously. Lionel had served in the Royal Flying Corps during the First World War, when he suffered the ill-effects of mustard-gas poisoning, which, it is believed, contributed to his premature demise in 1935. Initially, John studied at Moulton Grammar School, later attending St Paul's in Hampstead. Technically-minded, aged fourteen, John left school and began a four-year engineering apprenticeship at S. Smith & Sons. John, however, yearned to fly. This was an exciting time in aviation – and the young Gilliard wanted to be part of it. The era had seen the transition from biplanes to the fast new monoplanes, epitomised by R.J. Mitchell's iconic Spitfire, which the RAF gratefully received in 1938. On 4 April 1938,

Pilot Officer John Gilliard during pre-war flying training on Tiger Moths. (John & Vivien Gilliard)

Pilot Officer Gilliard with a Gloster Gladiator biplane fighter. (John & Vivien Gilliard)

in fact, seventeen-year-old John Gilliard volunteered for flying duties with the RAF, on that day reporting to the Civil Flying School at White Waltham for *ab initio* training.

After successfully passing the initial flying course and winning his 'wings', on 24 June 1938, John was awarded a Short Service Commission, becoming Pilot Officer 40819 JP Gilliard. Then, having completed his advanced flying training at service flying training schools in England, Pilot Officer Gilliard was sent to Egypt, there to join 216 Squadron, flying Vickers Vimy, Victoria and Valentia aircraft on transport duties around the Middle East. John was serving overseas with 216 Squadron when war broke out on that fateful Sunday of 3 September 1939. A year later, he was promoted to flying officer. By then, the Squadron was still operating the outdated Valentia in addition to the Bristol

JOHN PHILIP GILLIARD

Bombay, and, more importantly, the Vickers Wellington, Lockheed Hudson and Douglas Dakota. The unit predominantly remained engaged in transportation, although in June 1940, lone aircraft of 216 Squadron did bomb the German airfields at El Adem and Tobruk.

On 25 August 1941, Flying Officer Gilliard – who was promoted to flight lieutenant a week later – was posted from 216 to join 38 Squadron at Fayid, Egypt. His new squadron was equipped with the twin-engined Vickers Wellington bomber, and engaged on night attacks against Italian ports along the North African coast, disrupting the supply of Axis troops in the Western Desert. When Germany invaded Greece in April 1941, 38 Squadron began raiding enemy targets on the Greek islands and Yugoslavia. Joining 201 Group, 38 Squadron was then engaged on anti-shipping sorties and night torpedo attacks against enemy shipping in the Mediterranean. Under cover of darkness, radar-equipped Wellingtons known as 'Snoopingtons' would pinpoint enemy convoys and illuminate the Axis ships with flares – directing the torpedo-armed Wellingtons, called 'Torpingtons', onto the target. This was dangerous work: torpedoes need to be released very low, which at night, lacking the night vision aids of today, was often extremely difficult to judge; sometimes pilots erred and flew into the sea. Suffice it to say that by this time, Acting Squadron Leader Gilliard was a very experienced pilot – whose efforts were recognised with a well-earned DFC on 15 May 1942:

> . . . this officer has carried out many sorties both day and night. Whilst operating from Malta, Squadron Leader Gilliard has participated in attacks on shipping and other targets. On one occasion he attacked a large motor vessel in Tripoli harbour in the face of intense opposition and set it on fire. This officer has always pressed home his attacks, to the utmost limit. As flight commander he has displayed fine leadership and set a praiseworthy example.

John's time with 38 Squadron, however, soon was over: by September 1942, Squadron Leader Gilliard DFC was back in 'Blighty' and posted to the Telecommunications Flying Unit (TFU) at Defford in Worcestershire on 8 October 1942. This was a most secret unit indeed, conducting experimental flights for the 'boffins' of the Telecommunications Research Establishment (TRE) based at nearby Malvern. It was here that airborne interception radar, countermeasures and target-locating electronic devices were developed – and, coincidentally, where the German radar captured at Bruneval by (the then) Major John Frost was evaluated by the 'Backroom Boys'. Defford, in fact, swarmed with aircraft of all kinds, many bristling with various strange antennae. According to Squadron Leader Gilliard's Service Record, he flew with both the TFU's 'Offensive Section' and 'Coastal Flight'. Defford historian Dr Dennis Williams explains:

> The TFU at Defford initially comprised Offensive and Defensive Sections. The Defensive Section was divided into 'A', 'B' and 'C' Flights, and the Offensive

Section (OS) into 'A' and 'B' Flights. The Naval Section at Defford became 'C' Flight, OS, in March 1943. I presume that, as a Squadron Leader, John Gilliard was a flight commander at Defford, but cannot confirm this.

There was also the Air Defence and Coastal Flight, which provided 'target' facilities for Air Defence Research & Development Establishment based at Pale Manor, Malvern, and the Coast Artillery Experimental Establishment, which had a detachment at Earl's Croome Court. Both of these units carried out radar-directed gunnery research and development for the army and jointly used a trials field at Earl's Croome.

Although not in the Defford Operations Record Book, Derek Collier-Webb's book on flight testing accidents records that Squadron Leader Gilliard had an accident with Walrus L2201 on 10 March 1943, when the aircraft became bogged down while taxying and damaged during recovery from the mud. This aircraft was used for 1.5m Anti-Surface Vessel [radar] trials. However, Gilliard also flew other types. Squadron Leader Frank Griffiths was OC 'B' Flight, Offensive Section, and, after a tour on a Halifax squadron and evading capture in France, returned to Defford for a further tour as Wing Commander Flying. His pilot's flying log book records a number of flights with Squadron Leader Gilliard in such types as the Blenheim, Stirling, Envoy and Walrus.

At Defford, there was, amongst the ground staff, a contingent of the Women's Royal Naval Service (WRNS), billeted in the so-called 'Wrennery'. Amongst them was Leading 'Wren' Cecilie Hall – who met Squadron Leader John Gilliard when the pilot was tasked with providing the young Wren with an air experience flight and briefing on the testing of radar in a Fairey Swordfish biplane. Feeling airsick during what was her first flight, via the Gosport communication tube, Cecilie implored her pilot to 'fly more steadily'! Nonetheless, a romance blossomed. In November 1943, the couple were married by Cecelie's uncle, Frank Gillingham, at his church, St Michael's, in Chester Square, London. Thereafter, the couple returned to Worcestershire in John's Morris 8 two-seater car, and honeymooned at the famous Lygon Arms, in the picturesque village of Broadway, in the Cotswolds.

Flying radar trials in the Western Trials Airspace, away from marauding German fighters, may well have been an unsung role – but it was undoubtedly essential to the country's survival. TFU at Defford, in rural Worcestershire, could perhaps be considered a 'cushy' posting, but it was not without danger: there were a number of fatal flying accidents suffered by Defford aircrew during the war years. The shooting war, however, reached out once more for John Gilliard on 9 February 1944, when he was posted to command 'A' Flight of the recently re-formed 190 Squadron at 'Leicester East'. This was an airborne support unit, flying supply drop missions to Special Operations Executive (SOE) agents in enemy occupied Europe. This was, of course, the run-up to D-Day, in which SOE played a key part disrupting German communications and

JOHN PHILIP GILLIARD

Squadron Leader John Gilliard DFC on the occasion of his wedding to Cecelie Hall in November 1943. (John & Vivien Gilliard)

transport, mobilising and organising the resistance. Indeed, SOE, located in London's Baker Street, was ordered by Churchill himself to 'set Europe ablaze'. 'Maintenance and re-supply by air', therefore, became a key element of that objective.

John now found himself flying the huge four-engined Short Stirling Mk IV heavy bomber. Having entered service in 1941, the type had, however, been replaced by newer designs, including the Handley-Page Halifax and Avro Lancaster as a front-line bomber, and relegated to secondary duties such as re-supply. The Stirling operated with a crew of seven: two pilots, first and second, the former being the aircraft's captain; a navigator/bombardier; a front gunner/wireless operator; a flight engineer and two further air gunners (mid-upper and rear). Re-supply involved the dropping of containers and panniers by parachute, requiring, therefore, more hands – a task allocated to the Air Despatch Group, RASC. These soldiers – 'Air Despatchers' – were trained in dropping supplies from RAF aircraft, in the case of the Stirling increasing the crew during re-supply sorties to nine.

On 25 March 1944, 190 Squadron officially moved to RAF Fairford in Gloucestershire, but was actually actively operating from Tarrant Rushton, in Dorset, re-supplying SOE and the French resistance. Although in theory the Stirling required a first and second pilot, frequently there was only one pilot; on the night of 29/30 April 1944, for example, Squadron Leader Gilliard alone piloted Stirling '2253' between 2253 hrs and 0521 hrs, as one of three aircraft dropping containers to SOE operatives in France. Only Flight Sergeant McMillan, however, received a radio signal from SOE on the ground, so both Squadron Leader Gilliard and Pilot Officer Farren frustratingly returned with their loads. For some reason, John did not fly at all in May. His next flight, however, would be on a somewhat auspicious occasion: D-Day.

Squadron Leader John Gilliard DFC. (John & Vivien Gilliard)

Between 2315 hrs and 0300 hrs on the night of 5/6 June 1944, Squadron Leader Gilliard flew Stirling LK939 amongst twenty-three aircraft on Operation TONGA, dropping 426 paratroopers into Normandy to capture the bridges at Ranville, near Caen. Apart from light flak, there was no opposition, and all but one aircraft successfully dropped their parachutists. This was what everyone had been waiting for – the liberation of enemy-occupied France. Over the coming weeks, the young squadron leader flew on a number of operations: dropping supplies to SOE on 18 June 1944; likewise of 27 June, when his Stirling was hit by light and medium flak but returned safely; another similar sortie followed on the night of 20/21 July, and again ten days later. On 8/9 August 1944, thirteen 190 Squadron aircraft took off between 2230 hrs and 2355 hrs, bound for France: ten Stirlings carried 210 containers and 24 panniers destined for the Resistance; three aircraft carried high-explosive bombs for an unspecified 'Special bombing mission'. Two of the three Stirlings involved, including that of Squadron Leader Gilliard, bombed the target successfully. He then flew another container dropping sortie on the night of 10/11 August.

On 18 August 1944, however, Cecilie Gilliard gave birth, in Penzance, Cornwall, to the couple's son, also John; Squadron Leader Gilliard flew straight down to Cornwall to share the happy occasion and meet his new son. The war, however, waited for no man, and on 24 August, the new father was once more over enemy occupied France, re-supplying SOE.

On 17 September 1944, the 190 Squadron diarist recorded the following entry at Fairford:

Operation MARKET. 25 aircraft took off at approximately 1015 hrs for the Arnhem area of Holland. 6 of the aircraft acted as Pathfinders and carried 97 troops. The remaining 19 aircraft were towing gliders which contained 130 troops, 17 jeeps, 7 light and 1 heavy motorcycle, 17 trailers, 7 guns and 1 bicycle. All successfully carried out their sorties with the exception of O/O Middleton, who had to return to base as his glider cast off at South Cerney. Certain amount of flak encountered, F/L Anderson had his tail holed – and S/L Gibb received damage to his tail-plane. Enemy flak positions were well beaten up by our own fighters.

The six paratroop-dropping Stirlings were inserting HQ Company and No. 3 Platoon of the 21st Independent Parachute Company. Six more Stirlings, from 620 Squadron, conveyed the 1st and 2nd Platoons. The remaining 190 Squadron aircraft towed the gliders of HQ No. 1 Wing and 24 Flight of 'G' Squadron, Glider Pilot Regiment. Squadron Leader Gilliard flew Stirling LJ939 as sole pilot with a crew of six, between 1015 hrs and 1445 hrs. Flying Officer Reg Lawton flew as John's navigator, on this trip to drop Pathfinders:

> The day was cloudless and we had no difficulty in finding our DZ, and the men jumped successfully at 2 pm, opposition being very slight. We had to circle them at 500 feet while we tried to release some parachute supplies which had 'hung up" in the bomb bays, and while doing so we could see the Dutch civilians waving and starting to cycle towards the paratroops. The job of these paratroops was to set up their wireless homing equipment to guide in the main force which was following us in about half an hour. On the way back, we flew over this force of tugs and gliders, supported by fighters who were shooting up the few ack-ack batteries which opened up. The main force was made up of Halifaxes, Stirlings and Dakotas, each with a glider, making a continuous stream, 280 miles long.

That LJ939 was carrying Pathfinders meant that it was one of, if not the, first aircraft over the Arnhem area on this first day of battle – on which surprise had been achieved. As Reg Lawton later wrote to Mrs Gilliard, 'it was an easy trip'.

The Allied air forces in England, however, had insufficient transport aircraft to lift the airborne troops deployed in Operation MARKET-GARDEN in one go. Consequently, transportation of General Urquhart's Division was split over two days, with the Poles delivered in still more lifts, delayed due to bad weather. This meant that on the first day, when surprise was achieved, General Urquhart had less than half of his total force available to take Arnhem Bridge. The other issue was that after the first lift, the Germans were alerted and pouring reinforcements into the Arnhem area. On the first day, German fighters and flak based at nearby Deelen airfield were a concern, but in the event was not an issue. Flak positions in and around Arnhem were suppressed by

ARNHEM 1944

Allied fighter-bombers, but the Germans possessed a myriad of mobile flak weapons – guns mounted on tank or half-track chassis – meaning that flak concentrations could be moved. Indeed, the SS *Hohenstaufen* and *Frundsberg* divisions already in the Arnhem area had various such vehicles at their disposal. Moreover, after the first lift, the 4th Flak Division deployed Flak-Regiment 46, comprising, coincidentally, seven batteries totalling forty-six guns, to the Arnhem area. Commanded by *Oberstleutnant* von Svoboda, who took command of all flak guns in the Arnhem vicinity, a ring of steel soon circled the landing grounds, and subsequently the Oosterbeek perimeter. More flak units arrived in Arnhem over the coming days, joining *Kampfgruppe* von Svoboda, ultimately numbering some seventy-nine guns.

Squadron Leader Gilliard did not fly on the second lift, on 18 September 1944, a glider-towing commitment from which all 190 Squadron's aircraft returned safely. As Reg Lawton later told Cecilie Gilliard, 'the crews had drawn lots for who was going to fly, and we drew a blank'. Already, though, it was clear that XXX Corps would be unable to relieve the airborne troops at Arnhem as swiftly as had been hoped. Lightly armed and equipped airborne troops, in the absence of rapid relief, require re-supply from the air; having correctly anticipated that further lifts would follow, the Germans likewise expected such an effort – it was just a question of when. With an increasing amount of mobile flak units in the area, the re-supply effort would receive a violent reception.

The Short Stirling carried 2.64 tons of supplies (the Dakota 1.97 tons), these being stored in metal containers dropped from the bomb-bay or wicker panniers pushed out of the fuselage by Air Despatchers of the RASC. The RASC also transported the pre-packed containers and panniers from supply dumps to the airfields. There, parachutes were fitted and the all-important supplies loaded aboard waiting aircraft. Dropping these loads dictated flying at around 1,000 feet, slow and steady, to ensure accurate delivery onto pre-selected drop zones just north-west of Oosterbeek. The aircraft involved were, therefore, proverbial 'sitting ducks', easy pickings for the eagerly awaiting German flak gunners. The first re-supply drop was organised for Tuesday, 19 September 1944, involving 101 Stirlings and 63 Dakotas.

Fairford's contribution to this first, crucial, re-supply mission was provided by 190 and 620 Squadrons, which fielded sixteen and seventeen Stirlings respectively. 253 Airborne Divisional Composite Company provided the air required despatchers. In total, the re-supply effort involved 101 Stirlings, 63 Dakotas, and 454 air despatchers. Take off was delayed by poor visibility over England, but at 1300 hrs, 190 Squadron's Stirlings began roaring down Fairford's runway – bound for Arnhem, Holland. Although visibility was actually better on the northern route, the southern was decided upon so as to avoid using the same route three consecutive times. The southern route involved over-flying the landmarks of Manston-Ostend-Ghent, before turning and flying up the 'airborne corridor'. Squadron Leader Gilliard again flew Stirling Mk IV LJ939. On this trip, Squadron Leader F.N. Royle-Bantoft flew as second pilot; the remainder of John's crew were Flying Officer Reg Lawton (navigator); Flight Sergeant C.T. Byrne (flight

Stirlings dropping supplies at Arnhem.

engineer); Flying Officer C.H. Lane (wireless operator); Flying Officer R.G. Cullen (bomb aimer); and Flying Officer Norman McEwen (rear gunner). The two air despatchers aboard, both from 253 (Airborne) Divisional Composite Company, RASC, were Drivers Denis Breading and Frederick Taylor. Owing to a communications failure, however, 127 Spitfire and Mustang fighters, detailed to escort the re-supply fleet, were unaware of the delayed take-off; arriving at the rendezvous to find no waiting transport aircraft, the fighters assumed that the mission had been aborted and returned to base. It was an inauspicious start.

Flying Officer Lawton:

We were supposed to fly in formation, led by the Wing Commander, but before we left England the weather had deteriorated so much that the formation became split up and we proceeded individually. This is a nuisance for the navigator as he has to start work suddenly with no basis to work from, and as it happens we flew right over Ostend, above 10/10ths cloud. However, we were not fired on. Over Holland the weather cleared completely and we were able to map read to our target, but the opposition became considerable, and we were hit several times. We were at 1500 feet, and there was neither cloud cover nor fighter escort.

As the aerial armada droned overhead, it must have been obvious to the Germans that this was either another Arnhem-bound drop or a re-supply mission. By the time the leading aircraft droned into sight, the enemy flak gunners were ready and waiting. No. flak suppression of the Oosterbeek and Arnhem area had taken place, owing to poor weather (which had not prevented *Luftwaffe* fighters from strafing British troops at Arnhem) and communication issues. This aerial stream was heading for LZ 'V', a clearing no more than half a mile square, just to the north-west of Oosterbeek (close to where the Airborne Cemetery is now located). Without radio communications, it had been impossible for the airborne troops to inform England that LZ 'V' was in enemy hands – and aircrews had been instructed to ignore signals from the ground inconsistent with the known LZ, in case these were enticements by enemy troops to drop in the wrong place. The events of the next few minutes are beyond a tragedy.

By now, the 4th Parachute Brigade's forlorn attempt to reinforce Colonel Frost at Arnhem Bridge had failed. Turned back to Oosterbeek, there the defensive perimeter had been formed, enabling General Urquhart to both preserve his remaining force and maintain a foothold on the northern bank, in the hope that 2nd Army could throw bridges across and still cross the Rhine. Surrounding the perimeter was an ever-increasing German ring of steel, and to the enemy flak gunners the huge formation ponderously approaching was a gift.

The first aircraft to arrive over Oosterbeek were Dakotas – four of which were immediately shot down. The fourth machine, of 271 Squadron based at Down Ampney, was flown by Flight Lieutenant David Lord DFC; Glider pilot Lieutenant Ron Johnson, fighting at the 'White House' alongside the King's Own Scottish Borderers, saw what happened:

> I was at Down Ampney with David 'Lummy' Lord, whom I knew in the Officers' Mess as a quiet, unassuming, really nice chap. That day, planes were coming in, low and slow, on re-supply. The noise was dreadful, flak guns banging away. One of the Dakotas was on fire, but went round again to drop more. We could see the panniers being thrown out until the aircraft disappeared below our horizon. The supplies, however, were dropped in the wrong area, because of how the battle had gone. When this Dakota crashed, the whole battlefield went momentarily quiet, everyone, British and German, had seen what had happened. I said to my troops, 'Well, if they can do this for us up there,

we've got to put our backs into this battle'. It was the bravest thing I've ever seen, and afterwards we found out only one man escaped from 'Lummy's' aircraft. Subsequently, my CO, Peter Jackson, was one of the two officers who recommended 'Lummy' for the VC.

Flight Lieutenant David Lord VC's grave at Oosterbeek (4.B.5). (Author)

Flight Lieutenant Lord was killed in the crash. His supreme act of courage was considered a 'signal act of valour' worthy of the VC, which was gazetted posthumously in November 1945.

Following the ill-fated lead Dakotas came the Stirlings, whose turn it now was to descend to 1,000 feet and brave the maelstrom of shot and shell ahead. Squadron Leader Gilliard, however, declared the flak to be 'not a patch on Benghazi', although to Flying Officer Lawton it was 'intense', their pilot taking violent evasive action as we let our supplies go . . . I thought we were coming through all right, but suddenly the Skipper, Squadron Leader Gilliard, said over the intercom 'Prepare to abandon aircraft'. I stood up, took off my headphones, got my parachute and clipped it on . . . and turned to go down the steps when I bumped into our passenger [Squadron Leader Royle-Bantoft from 38 Group HQ], who was apparently going to the rear. I turned him round and pointed to the Bomb-Aimer's compartment, and then followed him down the steps, past the Skipper, who was still at the controls. The aircraft then swung steeply upward and I thought the Skipper was pulling her up to give us time to jump, but found out later that the aircraft was out of control. I reached past the passenger at the bottom of the steps to help the Bomb Aimer, Flying Officer Cullen, to pull open the escape hatch as he seemed to be having difficulty. When it was open, Squadron Leader Royle-Bantoft went out, and I sat on the edge and rolled out forwards without any delay. All this, from the first order, took only a matter of seconds.

According to the 190 Squadron diary, 'whilst over the DZ' LJ939 had been 'hit by two shells which severed the controls'. Later, Squadron Leader Royle-Bantoft confirmed to Flying Officer Lawton that 'the control column was useless in John's hands which, of course, was the reason we were told to bale out, and so it seems to me that the shell that hit us severed the wires in the rear of the plane which controlled the rudder etc'. Literally seconds after five parachutes blossomed from the doomed aircraft, the Stirling crashed in woodland north of the Bilderberg Hotel, south-west of the Sportpark Biderberg in the north-western area of Oosterbeek. The gallant 24-year-old Squadron Leader John Gilliard DFC, a married man and father for one month and a day, was at the controls. Killed with their Skipper were the Bomb Aimer, Flying Officer Norman McEwan (37), and both air despatchers, Drivers Denis Breading (21) and Frederick Taylor (21). All four were initially buried at the crash site (and later interred at the Arnhem-Oosterbeek War Cemetery).

The survivors of LJ939 now faced further dangers amidst a ferocious land battle. Ultimately, Squadron Leader Royle-Bantoft, Flying Officers Lawton and Cullen would survive the battle and be safely evacuated across the Rhine. Flight Sergeant Byrne, however, had broken his leg upon landing, and was captured; Pilot Officer Lane was also captured, but both came through the war.

In total, nine Stirlings and four Dakotas fell to the deadly flak. In human terms, fifty-two men were killed or fatally wounded; thirty-nine were captured; three evaded and six more landed safely by parachute within the British perimeter. Few supplies reached the airborne troops.

Like all wartime wives, Mrs Cecilie Gilliard doubtless dreaded the postman's knock – which came at her Cornish home, Mulberry House, on 20 September 1944. The priority telegram regretted to inform the new mother that her husband, 'Squadron Leader JP Gilliard is missing as a result of air operations on 19 September 1944'. Grief-stricken,

JOHN PHILIP GILLIARD

Cecilie made immediate preparations for travel to stay with her parents near Chingford in Essex. Two weeks later, correspondence arrived from Fairford's station commander, enclosing a letter found in John's personal possessions, with a request that in the event of him being reported 'missing', it be forwarded to his wife. The letter, dated 5 June 1944, read:

> My darling Cecilie
> I find it very difficult to write this letter because I know I am going to see you soon. If I am a bit late I'm sure I'll be alright on the other side, but if the worst happens, which I know it won't, I shall always be with you, my darling, and I do pray you will learn to forget, as Jonny David doesn't want to have a sad Mum. I can't write any more because my imagination runs away with me.
>
> I love you more than anything on earth.
> With every bit of my love.
> John P.
> PS. Darling, it goes without saying that all my worldly possessions are yours. Give my love to all and thanks for everything.

The family was, like so many, in suspense. John was still 'missing' – which indicated hope that he was still alive. On 30 September 1944, the Air Ministry (Casualty Branch) wrote to Cecelie, with news that three of her husband's crew had returned safely from the Arnhem debacle. Of John or the other three, however, 'no news . . . has yet been received'. The letter reassured that 'This does not necessarily mean that your husband is killed or wounded, and if he is a prisoner of war he should be able to communicate with you in due course. Meanwhile enquiries are being made through the International Red Cross Committee, and as soon as any definite news is received, you will be informed.'

On 30 November 1944, Flying Officer Lawton wrote to Cecilie Gilliard, describing what had happened, so far as he knew and could ascertain. Whilst on the ground within the British perimeter, Reg had spoken

> to many of the soldiers about the fate of our plane and they all told the same story. I could identify the plane to them by telling them it was the one which went into a very steep climb after being hit and they all recognised the one. They said they saw four men jump by parachute and that the plane fell, but no one saw it hit the ground for the simple reason that these men were dug in in thickish woodland and their view was very restricted. They were almost certain that there was no fire, for they did not see any smoke. It was impossible, of course, for me to find the wreck for it was now in, or behind, German lines . . . While I was floating down I did not see the plane. I was watching the ground all the time. We were at a thousand feet when we were hit (at 3.50 pm) which is a low height for parachute jumping, but I am sure that there was time for John to get

Debris from Squadron Leader Gilliard's Stirling still litters the Bilderberg woods today. (Luuk Buist)

out after me. Perhaps he stayed to try and crash-land, but it is no use my speculating, you see I know so little that it was not until the next day that I found out why we had baled out.

The days of anguish and uncertainty were interminable. In May 1945, after the liberation of Arnhem, those agonising days were abruptly ended – but with the worst possible outcome. It was with 'deep regret', that the Under Secretary of State for Air wrote 'to inform you that your husband, Sqn Ldr John P Gilliard DFC, 40818, is now reported to have lost his life as the result of air operations on 19 September 1944. The Air Council express their profound sympathy, his mother is being informed.'

The waiting was over. Cecilie Gilliard was officially a widow, her baby son, John David, fatherless. Cecilie never re-married. John D. Gilliard: 'When I was a child, I didn't know any different. It wasn't until adulthood did I regret not having a Father with whom I could discuss things with (my career etc), and I regretted not having brothers and sisters . . . maybe this is why I have always wanted to get in touch with my immediate cousins.'

John David Gilliard has visited his father's grave at Oosterbeek, together with his wife Vivien, and were shown the crash site of Stirling LJ939 by Robert Voskuil. Pieces of the wreck still lay scattered underfoot, a reminder in those now peaceful woods of the violence and tragedy of yesteryear. So deeply moved was Vivien, in fact, that she was inspired to write her own first novel, based upon the story of John and Cecilie Gilliard, entitled *Flight Home* (see Bibliography). As Vivien says, the book, drawing heavily upon intimate letters exchanged by the couple during wartime, 'give the reader a deeper insight into the lives of their two families, through which the "blast of war" echoed down two generations'. So too does that chilling 'blast' resonate throughout this book.

The beautiful memorial window to the RAF effort at Down Ampney church. (Author)

The Air Despatch Memorial adjacent to the Airborne Cemetery. (Author)

In cold statistical terms, the RAF squadrons of 38 Group, and RCAF units of 46, flew a total of 1,339 sorties during the Battle of Arnhem; 612 of these were re-supply flights. Three hundred and sixty-eight aircrew and passengers were killed, and 79 air despatchers. Twenty-seven American aircrew also lost their lives, a total, therefore, of 474 men lost – 40 per cent of the figure lost by the British and Polish airborne troops.

Per Ardua ad Astra.

Squadron Leader Gilliard DFC's headstone at Oosterbeek (4.B.1). (Author)

Chapter 18

Lance-Corporal Czeslaw Gajewnik, Signals Company, 1st Parachute Battalion, 1st Polish Independent Parachute Brigade

Sandwiched between East Prussia to the west, and Russia to the east, perhaps inevitably the history of Poland – a nation state dating back to the tenth century AD – is far from a happy one. During the Early Modern period, a cultural renaissance and close association with neighbouring Lithuania led to the prosperous Polish-Lithuanian Commonwealth – the independent existence of which concluded, violently, in 1795, after a series of invasions by the Prussians, Russians and the Austro-Hungarian Empire. Indeed, no independent Polish state existed again until 1918, after the three occupying powers had been defeated in the First World War. This Second Polish Republic, however, only existed until 1 September 1939, when Nazi Germany invaded, following a fabricated 'border incident'. Two days later, of course, Britain and France declared war on Nazi Germany, Hitler having ignored demands to withdraw his troops. On 17 September, the Soviet Union occupied eastern Poland. By 6 October, it was all over: Poland, the first to fight, was also the first to fall.

Although defeated and their country occupied by two totalitarian foreign powers, the Poles remained defiant, their spirit unbroken. Airmen and soldiers escaped their homeland by various and devious means, many joining the French military and fighting back until France fell in June 1940. From there, these nomadic warriors made their way to England – the last bastion of both hope and freedom. The Poles, and Czechs, were much-needed at that dark time, when Britain too faced the threat of invasion. In the air, trained Polish and Czech fighter pilots provided essential replacements to RAF fighter squadrons, and ultimately Polish and Czech-speaking squadrons made an invaluable contribution to the epic Battle of Britain's successful outcome. Indeed, the courage of and ferocity with which these young pilots fought set the scene for free Poles to fight in every campaign, theatre and major battle on land, sea and in the air – until Nazi Germany was eventually defeated in 1945.

Foremost amongst Polish heroes who emerged during the Second World War, is the name of Stanislaw Sosabowski, who had soldiered since 1913. By 1 September 1939, Colonel Sosabowski was commanding the 21st Infantry Regiment. During the siege of Warsaw, the 21st held its ground, even counter-attacking and virtually annihilating the

German 23 *Infanterie* Regiment. Ultimately the position was hopeless, the proud Sosabowski suffering the ignominy of surrender and capture. Soon afterwards, however, he escaped, joining the resistance in Warsaw under a false name, before being summoned to France by the Polish government in exile, there to report on the situation in Poland. Made infantry commander of the Polish 4th Infantry Division, Colonel Sosabowski left France, with 6,000 men, on 19 June 1940, to continue the fight from Britain's shores.

The Polish General Staff in London assigned Colonel Sosabowski to the 4th Rifle Brigade, which numbered around the same as a British infantry battalion, which was sent to Scotland. There, Sosabowski was allocated a section of the Fife coastline to defend, setting up his headquarters at Levin. The threat of invasion, however, was seen off by the 'Few' during the summer and autumn of 1940 – whilst the free Poles constantly worried about their families in Poland, of who, of course, they had no news. The inactivity of Home Defence, however, was not what these men, desperate to set their homeland and people free, had in mind. As Sosabowski himself wrote: 'There we were sitting safely in Scotland, while troops of other nations fought the Nazis overseas. In Poland, men of the Home Army were actively opposing the Germans . . . It was the ambition of all us exiles to get back and fight for the freedom of our country. We felt guilty being in Scotland.' The answer to this predicament came when London requested twenty Polish officers to complete a parachute course at Ringway, which they did, in February 1941. Sosabowski, quite simply, made up his mind to form a Polish Parachute Brigade – which he did without even consulting senior officers. Naturally, Sosabowski, this iron-hard man of action, the defender of Warsaw, aged fifty, became a parachutist himself. On 23 September 1941, General Sikorski, leader of the Poles in exiles, agreed the existence of 1st Polish Independent Parachute Brigade – the aim of which was clear: the liberation of Poland. Sosabowski, however, may have achieved a miracle, but this uncompromising man had few political allies – for which he ultimately paid a high price.

The intention was that Sosabowski's paratroopers would be trained for and deployed to support a national uprising against the occupying forces in Poland, for which reason Sosabowski fiercely resisted any attempt for his formation to be brought under British control and lose its independent status. After much political wrangling, and given the perhaps implausible objective of parachuting into Poland, it was agreed in June 1944 that Sosabowski be promoted to major general and his brigade absorbed into the 1st British Airborne Division – to participate in one Allied operation following the Normandy invasion, after which it would be at liberty to return to Poland. The brigade now moved from Scotland to the 1st British Airborne divisional area around the Peterborough and Stamford areas of the East Midlands. Along with their new British comrades, the Poles would now suffer the exasperation of repeatedly cancelled operations owing to the fluid military situation on the Continent.

On 25 July 1944, General Sosabowski, now commander of free Polish forces following General Sikorski's death in a flying accident, received a signal from General Bor, Commander-in-Chief of the Polish Home Army, indicating that an uprising was

The 1st Polish Independent Parachute Brigade marching through Markinch, Scotland, before Arnhem. (Mary Robertson)

about to start in Warsaw, in which 'The arrival of the Parachute Brigade will be of important military and political value'. The 'Warsaw Rising' began on 1 August 1944, but, as General Sosabowski painfully remembered, '. . . the call we had all been living for came. We did not answer it. It was not surprising that the whole Brigade felt very strongly over the political actions which prevented us from carrying out our pledge . . . Can you imagine our bitterness and our inner defeat?' The Rising would end in failure on 2 October 1944, with the virtual destruction of Warsaw. By that time, General Sosabowski would have parachuted into Holland with his men – many of whom would be dead. The story of General Sosabowski's 1st Independent Parachute Brigade, therefore, mirrors that of Poland itself: an unhappy one.

Amongst General Sosabowski's men was Lance-Corporal Czeslaw Gajewnik, of the 'Kompanie Lacznosci', or Signals Company, commanded by Captain Josef Burzawa, of the Polish 1st Parachute Battalion. Born on 11 August 1918, to Jan and Karolina Gajewnik in Przypisoka, Lublin, Czeslaw had a brother and two sisters. When the Soviet Union invaded Poland, however, the whole family, along with hundreds of thousands of other civilians, was deported to Siberia. Somehow – it is not known how – the young Czeslaw escaped and, doubtless after many adventures and much adversity, by 1 April 1942, was serving with 1st Polish Independent Parachute Brigade. Today, he is remembered fondly by Mary 'Bunty' Robertson, who was then seventeen:

I met Czelaw at the Markinch Town Hall, where there was dancing every night of the week. He was a marvellous dancer! I liked him. All of the Polish soldiers were great dancers, but their English wasn't very good, making communication difficult. He was a signalman, a radio operator proficient in Morse Code, and stationed with his Company in the town. They stayed in huts at the golf club and were there about six months. The friends they made in Markinch became their next of kin, really, because they had no idea or news of their own families in Poland. Because of the language barrier, however, it was impossible to discover anything about their lives in Poland. They were well accepted by the local people. The Poles used to sing as they marched from their camp to the canteen, and the people loved this. The officers, in fact, were billeted in houses in the town, so there was a close relationship and bond between us. When the Polish Parachute Brigade left Markinch, that was the last I saw of him.

Lance-Corporal Czeslaw Gajewnik, an airborne signaller. (Alice van Bekkum)

According to the 1st Airborne Division's 'Report on Operation MARKET', '1st Parachute Brigade Group, in the third lift, were to land south of the river, immediately opposite Arnhem, cross the river by the main bridge and occupy a position on the eastern outskirts of Arnhem . . . It was thus intended to form a firm bridgehead around Arnhem . . . All landings were to take place in daylight'. This third lift was scheduled to take place on Tuesday, 19 September 1944. The brigade's transport and anti-tank guns, however, were to land on the north bank, near Wolfheze, spread over the Monday and Tuesday.

Mary 'Bunty' Robertson danced with Lance-Corporal Czeslaw Gajewnik in Markinch, and never forgot him. (Mary Robertson)

On 12 September 1944, the Polish Brigade's commander and staff attended an 'Air Force conference', at which the allocation of powered aircraft and gliders were decided. The Poles were to be lifted by 114 aircraft and 45 Horsas – insufficient to transport the entire Brigade, and hence why the Poles' light artillery were to be left behind and the anti-tank battery just two men for each gun. All transport and heavy equipment, in fact, 'had to be reduced to the necessary minimum (in comparison to respective British units)'. It was an unhappy start. Previously, with certain of the other cancelled operations, General Sosabowski had considered the plans for his Brigade unrealistic, and had robustly voiced his objections. Regarding the proposals for Operation MARKET-GARDEN, on 13

September 1944, he 'had so many doubts about the Arnhem operation'. Had the Polish general been blessed with the ability to view the future, his anxiety would have been greater still. The plan, of course, assumed that the bridges at Arnhem would be safely in Allied hands by the Poles' arrival, spread over several days and separated by the Rhine, and that German resistance would be minimal. The plan also assumed favourable weather conditions. On 14 September, General Sosabowski expressed concern to General Urquhart that the proposed bridgehead was ten miles round, meaning that his defence would be thinly spread. The British commander's response was that as there would be 'no heavy German resistance', it was an affordable risk. The Pole returned to his headquarters at Stamford 'with a heavy heart, much worried over Urquhart's optimism'. The general was also appalled that reports from the Dutch underground regarding German tanks in the Arnhem area had been ignored, which he considered 'arrogant optimism completely unjustified'. Nonetheless, General Sosabowski also remembered with pride how 'the tremendous spirit of the Brigade rose as the day of action grew nearer'. Dropping into Holland may not have been the battle the Polish paratroopers would have chosen to fight, given current events in Warsaw – but it was still an opportunity, after five long years, to fight the Germans, who had inflicted so much pain and suffering on their homeland.

In the event, as we have seen, the plan went badly wrong, for many reasons, prominent amongst them the furious and rapid German reaction to the airborne landings. Use of the Driel ferry at Westerbouwing had been overlooked, the Oosterbeek railway and Arnhem pontoon bridges had been destroyed by the Germans, and only 2nd Parachute Battalion, with supporting troops had reached Arnhem Bridge – failing to seize both ends but grimly holding on to the north side. The remainder of the Division had been unable to penetrate the German blocking line to reinforce Lieutenant Colonel Frost at the Bridge, forcing General Urquhart to form a thumb-shaped defensive perimeter 700 yards wide, the base of which was on the Rhine's north bank at lower Oosterbeek, and a mile long, in an attempt to preserve what was left of his force and maintain a bridgehead for 2nd Army – XXX Corps of which had been badly held up on the south bank, preventing relief. Indeed, the Polish glider lift arrived at Wolfheze amidst a battle, as 4th Parachute Brigade, unable to penetrate the 'Wall of Steel' and reach Arnhem, withdrew, under fire, through the woods and across the LZ. Then, the Polish parachute lifts were cancelled on both Tuesday and Wednesday owing to bad weather over England. Because the actual situation now bore little semblance to the original plan, on the night of Wednesday 20 September 1944, General Urquhart selected a new drop zone for the Poles, near Driel, on the Rhine's south bank, opposite the Westerbouwing high ground. Although only one mile from what was now the Oosterbeek perimeter – the Poles still had to cross the Rhine to reach it, and not, as originally planned, via Arnhem Bridge. Instead, the British General intended that by the Poles' arrival, the British would command the Driel ferry, which could then be used to transport General Sosabowski's Brigade across the river – where they would assemble in the woods of the Hemelse Berg as both essential and most welcome reinforcements. At 0430 hrs on Thursday 21 September 1944, General Sosabowski received a signal from General Urquhart confirming that the ferry was in British hands. The die was cast.

Between 1400 hrs and 1430 hrs on 21 September 1944, the Polish Brigade's parachute lift took off from Spanhoe and Saltby airfields. General Sosabowski flew from Saltby in a Dakota, Chalk 100, of either the American 32 or 50 Squadron of IX Troop Carrier Command. That aircraft carried elements of the General's Brigade HQ and Signals Company. Lance-Corporal Gajewnik flew to Holland in the General's aircraft, dropping with the fabled national hero on DZ 'K', immediately to the south and south-east of the village of Driel. Owing to the still far from perfect weather and other reasons, many of the seventy-two aircraft were forced to turn back. Consequently, only 1,003 of the intended 1,568 Polish paratroopers reached DZ 'K' – where they were met by heavy German flak and opposition. By the end of this first day following their arrival, five Poles would be dead and thirty-six more wounded. Whilst leaving the DZ, the General happened across the dead body of one of his men; he wondered how many more would die, and 'whether their sacrifice would be worthwhile?'

At the brigade rendezvous, General Sosabowski found that Captain Burzawa's Signals Company had lost no time in setting up a transmitter and establishing from outstations their strength and state of readiness. Polish mortars laid down smoke, obscuring the DZ and impeding the enemy. Captain Burzawa had been able to contact all units except 1st Parachute Battalion, but received no response from General Urquhart across the river (for reasons the reader will be aware of). Had radio contact been established, General Sosabowski would have learned that earlier that day, 'B' Company of 1st Border had been pushed off the Westerbouwing, which was firmly in German hands (see Sergeant Tom Watson chapter), the ferry sunk. In the absence of radio communications, the Poles reconnoitred, from the south bank, the area of the ferry – confirming to their general at 2100 hrs that the Germans held the far bank and the ferry's fate. This, of course, changed everything: instead of immediately crossing over the Rhine into and reinforcing the British perimeter, the Poles were now isolated on the south bank and, like the British across the river, surrounded by strong enemy forces. Moreover, General Sosabowski, now forced to adopt a defensive posture whilst an improvised plan and means of still crossing the river was decided, had no anti-tank support owing to his guns having been delivered by glider to the north bank two days previously. Meanwhile, the Polish Brigade was under sustained machine-gun and mortar fire. The whole story, on both banks of the Rhine, was now rapidly becoming a dreadful tragedy.

At 2230 hrs, according to the Polish Brigade's War Diary, Captain Ludwik Zwolanski, the Brigade's Liaison Officer with the 1st British Airborne Division, arrived at General Sosabowski's command post with a 'sitrep'. Zwolanski had been unable to raise his Brigade via radio, so had swum the fast-flowing Rhine. The news Zwolanski brought was not necessarily the best: the Polish Brigade still had to cross the river, but had no means to do so. British troops were apparently to 'counter-attack' to 'clear a sector of the northern bank and will send over boats and rafts to enable the Brigade Group to cross the river'. Lacking appropriate equipment or training, this was a forlorn hope indeed. The British attempt to re-take the Westerbouwing failed, and the construction of rafts from jeep trailers – a somewhat desperate expedient – proved unsatisfactory. By 0100 hrs the RE contingent on the north bank had completed just one such raft. By 0200 hrs, the Polish Brigade Group had reached the proposed crossing area opposite Oosterbeek church. An hour later, neither boats nor rafts had arrived, and the Polish paratroopers' efforts to locate vessels locally produced a nil return. The Brigade returned the mile to Driel, adopting defensive positions at 0530 hrs on 22 September, but vowing to make 'all possible further efforts' to cross the Rhine.

At 0845 hrs that day, an incredible thing happened: although the scheduled drop of the remainder of General Sosabowski's brigade failed to materialise, three Daimler Dingo scout cars of the Household Cavalry arrived in Driel. This was the first link-up of XXX Corps with the 1st Airborne Division, tenuous though it was. On the evening of 20 September, in fact, the Guards Armoured Division and American Parachute Infantry Regiment had taken the bridges at Nijmegen – just eight miles or so away. The problem was, however, that just as German armour had prevented the British reinforcing their beleaguered garrison at Arnhem Bridge, the area between Arnhem and Nijmegen was swarming with enemy forces, which effectively and conclusively barred the way. Indeed, since the battle at Arnhem Bridge had been lost on 20/21 September, the enemy was able to cross the Rhine with ease and commit more troops to the battle with XXX Corps. General Horrocks, however, had not yet given up, and 'was desperately trying to force a way through to the north bank of the Neder Rhijn to join up with the embattled parachute troops. Courtesy of the Household Cavalry, General Sosabowski was at least to speak personally with both General Horrocks and General Browning. General Horrocks explained that he was pushing forward to Driel, with a squadron of 4th/7th Royal Dragoon Guards Sherman tanks, and the 5th Duke of Cornwall's Light Infantry. These elements of XXX Corps arrived in Driel at 2000 hrs on 22 September. Contact with British airborne troops in Oosterbeek also came that night, when Lieutenant Colonels MacKenzie and Myers swam the Rhine, having been ordered by General Urquhart to liaise with Sosabowski before pressing on to personally impress upon Horrocks and Browning the urgency of the situation. That was something the Polish General, although under increasing pressure from German armour, understood full-well: the Poles would cross the Rhine that night.

Darkness once more found the Poles opposite Oosterbeek church, preparing to cross the river in six two-man boats and an RAF dinghy, supplied by the 1st Airborne's REs. The boats were bound together and a pulley system was organised, enabling the ferrying of fifteen men at a time. It was hoped to transport 200 men across the river by daybreak. The river, however, was too fast and the cables broke. Thereafter, Polish sappers, untrained for the job, rowed the tiny boats across, meaning that each boat could only convey one paratrooper at a time. Inevitably, the noise attracted the enemy's attention, night turning into day by parachute flares – followed instantly by heavy machine-gun fire and mortaring, firing on both the boats and Poles on the south bank. By 0400 hrs, when General Sosabowski abandoned the attempt, 15 per cent casualties had been suffered and only fifty-two Poles had safely set foot on the north bank. Those men were led up to Stationsweg, in Oosterbeek, taken over the defence of houses there from a platoon of the 21st Independent Parachute Company.

The following day, General Sosabowski sent his Chief of Staff, Major Malaszkiewicz, to the 130 Infantry Brigade HQ at Valburg, there to beg for boats. Twelve boats, and British crews were promised – but at midnight on 24 September, only the boats arrived. Again, untrained Polish engineers had to crew the boats. This time, the crossing was supported by a barrage from XXX Corps. By 0505 hrs it was daylight and the effort concluded: 153 Polish officers and men were successfully ferried across the river, a number not including the casualties suffered during the crossing and disembarking. On the north bank, Captain Zwolanski met the new arrivals, guiding them into the woods of the Hemelse Berg estate, across the Benedendorpsweg. A short distance north into the woods are a series of pools, alongside one of which the Polish Signals Company dug in. These men had arrived in the 'Cauldron' at a high price – but were welcome reinforcements, for sure.

Entrance to the Hemelse Berg estate, across the Benedendorpsweg, in the woods of which the Polish signallers were deployed. (Author)

At 1000 hrs, General Horrocks himself arrived in Driel, for, the Polish War Diary records, a personal 'appreciation of situation and preliminary decisions concerning further crossings night of 24/25'. It was consequently decided that the further crossing would be made under command of 43rd (Wessex) Division, 'which has boats and DUKWs'. The 4th Dorset Regiment was to cross at the Driel ferry site, whilst the remainder of the Polish Brigade Group did so opposite Oosterbeek church. Sosabowski was furious. His command had been subordinated to a young Brigadier Walton, of 130 Brigade; in an emotional, angry outburst the Polish commander made his feelings known: that the crossing was on insufficient strength to influence the outcome of the Oosterbeek perimeter battle, and would only spend the lives of his men, and the Dorsets, for nothing. Horrocks firmly made clear that his orders stood, and that if Sosabowski felt unable to comply, he would be replaced. Afterwards, the seething General was entertained to lunch in Nijmegen by his Corps commander, General Browning, who had failed to support the Pole at the fractious conference. Sosabowski was appalled to see no boats in Nijmegen – and told Browning exactly what he thought of British commanders who failed to bring up boats on an operation involving crossing water obstacles.

At 1930 hrs, the remainder of the Polish Brigade, having been dropped near Grave, arrived in Driel. The proposed crossing, however, was 'delayed because of lack of boats', leading to cancellation of the proposed crossing of the Polish 2nd Parachute Battalion and Brigade HQ personnel. 1st Parachute Battalion, though, and the Dorsets, were to go ahead. This was not a successful operation. Due to the lack of boats, none of General Sosabowski's Poles crossed the river. 315 Dorsets landed on the north bank in disjointed groups, which never managed to form up as a cohesive unit. The Dorset commander, Lieutenant Colonel Tilley, having achieved the north bank high ground, had to reluctantly accept that his position, in view of the quite literally overwhelming numbers of Germans his Battalion had landed amongst, was hopeless – and surrendered. Thirteen Dorsets died and 200 were captured. The outcome was entirely as General Sosabowski predicted. It was that day, with no prospect of relief and short of all supplies, his devoted medical staff under immeasurable pressure, General Urquhart made the decision to evacuate the battered and exhausted remnants of his division across the Rhine. It was a sad end to the British and Polish commitment to this bold and daring enterprise.

The question needs answering regarding why relief did not arrive as intended. The problem was that 2nd Army had to advance sixty miles along a single-track road to reach Arnhem, an impossible task, as things turned out. Running through orchards facilitating ambush, the four-feet high causeway bisected marshy meadows unsuitable for armoured vehicles. The road was under constant fire, and frequently severed for hours. Moreover, the narrow front's spearhead was constantly under attack. The two American airborne divisions, however, successfully completed their allotted tasks, namely the seizure of Grave's Maas bridge and Nijmegen's great span across the Waal, and, being closer to 2nd Army's start line, were relieved after bitter fighting. The fact was that the German reaction at Arnhem and fighting along 'Hell's Highway' was unanticipated – providing a salutary lesson regarding the abilities of the German soldier. Arguably General Urquhart's division had landed too far from the Arnhem Bridge

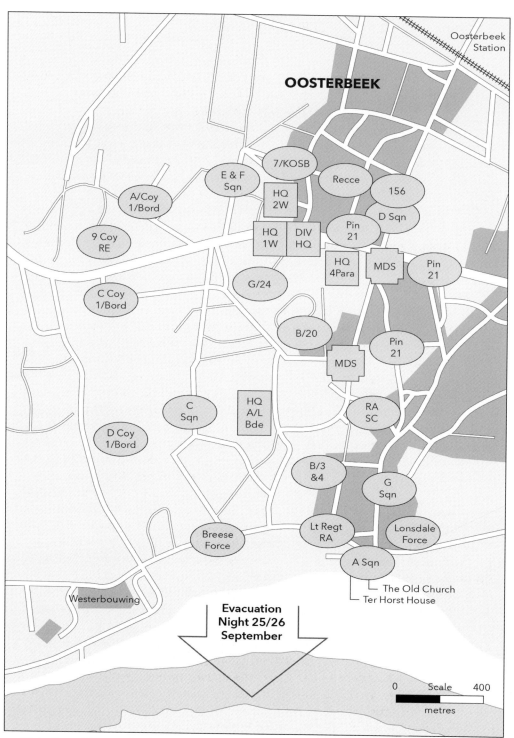

Unit dispositions in the Oosterbeek area (for colour version see plate section).

objective, and was unable to punch as a cohesive whole, being dropped over several days, owing to a lack of foresight and bad weather. All of these factors, and more, made Arnhem, to quote General Browning, 'A bridge too far'. At Arnhem Bridge and within Oosterbeek's *Hexenkessel*, however, the 'Red Devils' and their grey-bereted Polish comrades, had held out many days longer than required, generating a legend of courage and endurance beyond praise. But now, it was all over: the final nail in the coffin of Operation MARKET-GARDEN was when, on 24 September 1944, the Germans severed the road south of Nijmegen for forty-eight hours.

General Urquhart, however, knew full-well that his division was in danger of envelopment and annihilation. As a young officer, General Urquhart had studied the Allied evacuation from Gallipoli during the First World War, and it was with that equally sad undertaking in mind that his plan to save what was left of his Division was made. Whilst the perimeter reduced like a collapsing bag, the wounded staying behind manning weapons in order to deceive the enemy, the artillery of XXX Corps and machine-guns of 43rd (Wessex) Division would provide support. The medical staff were to remain at their posts, at the various Medical Dressing Stations. The evacuation took place on the night of 25/26 September 1944 – a foul one, during which rain poured incessantly. Faces were blackened, weapons and equipment rigged so as not to rattle, and strips of fabric were tied around boots, muffling the noise. Tapes were laid through the woods leading south to the Rhine, near the old church, Glider Pilots acting as guides. Sappers from 260 (Wessex) Field Company paddled their boats to and fro, whilst engineers of 23rd Canadian Field Company enjoyed the benefits of their Stormboats' outboard motors. The Germans suspected that another attempt was being made to reinforce the perimeter, so targeted the south bank and approaches. Nonetheless, some boats were hit, and others capsized owing to overloading, the swift current sweeping their occupants away. Others decided to swim for it anyway. As daylight dawned, so too did the Germans' realisation of what was actually happening – leading to heavy fire of all kinds raining down on the river and crossing. Eventually a halt had to be called: some 2,400 men had been safely ferried across the Rhine.

On 28 September 1944, the *Daily Mail*'s front and back pages graphically reported on the Arnhem battle – providing the folks back home with news of the disaster. A paratrooper from London described the Oosterbeek perimeter as 'a monster engine that spat flame and smoke and liquid death for eight nights and nine days', describing how he and his comrades had been 'seared out of the trenches by flame-throwers' before the houses in which they consequently found refuge became 'flaming charnel houses'. The *Daily Express* had a reporter, Alan Wood, embedded in 1st Airborne Division, who survived the hell of Arnhem and whose account of the evacuation made the *Mail*'s front page:

This is the end. The most tragic and glorious battle of the war is over, and the survivors of this British airborne force can sleep soundly for the first time in eight days and nights . . . We were told the password, 'John Bull'. If we became separated, each man was to make his way by compass due south until he reached the river. Our major is an old hand. He led the way, and linked our party together by getting everyone to hold the tail of the parachutist's smock of the man in front, so our column had an absurd resemblance to some children's game. It was half-light with the glow of fires from burning houses around, when we set out. We were lucky: we went through a reputed enemy pocket without hearing a shot except for a stray sniper's bullet. Another group met a machine-gun with a fixed line of fire across their path. Another had to silence a bunch of Germans with a burst of Sten fire and hand grenades. Another had to pause while a German finished his evening stroll across their pathway. But we all got through without the enemy realising that we were doing anything more than normal night patrolling. The worst part was waiting two hours by the riverside till our turn came for assault boats to ferry us across. The Germans, if not definitely suspicious were inquisitive, and kept on sending up flares and it was vital to lie flat and motionless. In our boat queue, we lay flat and shivering on a soaking field with cold rain drizzling down. Occasionally machine-guns spattered out and bullets tweaked through the grass. We were lucky again: our actual crossing was quiet. But soon after it seemed that the Germans had guessed what was going on, because they mortared and shelled heavily along the shallow riverbanks. One soldier in the next field was hit and called out for help. Men whose turn had come for a place in the boats had come after hours of waiting insisted on staying under fire a little longer so that the wounded could go first. Any wounded left behind, of course, became automatically prisoners of war: so many sick and limping left their beds to take a chance with the escape parties making their way to the river. And so this epic stand of the British airborne soldiers ended as it had been fought – with honour, high courage, with selfless sacrifice. What of the spirits of these men as they trudged back through the wet night to the billets where they are now sunk in sodden sleep? You can best judge it by the name they chose for last night's break-out. It had the same objective as they always have had, and they still mean to get in there. They called it 'Operation BERLIN'.

That dangerously flare-lit night, 160 Poles were amongst those safely ferried across the Rhine. Sadly, Lance-Corporal Gajewnik was not amongst them.

During the afternoon of 14 November 1944, two eleven-year old Dutch schoolboys, Adrie van den Berg, son of the Tienhoven-Jaarsfeld ferry skipper, and Hans van Straten, son of the Tienhoven church verger, were in a rowing boat near the small village of Tienhoven, near Ameide, on the river Lek (which linked the lower Rhine to the Nieuwe Mass and ultimately the North Sea). The two young friends were rowing in the area of the De Koekoek salmon farm, Hans later recalled:

CZESLAW GAJEWNIK

During this period all kinds of things were floating down the river. The day before, we found several sacks of flour, which had somehow fallen into the water from a horse-drawn vehicle. Inside, the flour was dry, so in those days of food shortage, this could be used to make something edible. We used to bring ashore things we found that were useful. It was high tide that afternoon and we saw what we thought was another flour sack floating amongst the rubbish on the far side of the river. We rowed over to it and discovered that it was actually a body; another was floating nearby. Both were in an advanced state of decomposition. We tied ropes around their trunks and rowed to the bank. Both bodies were naked but wore their identity discs. They were laid out on the bank, the Koekoekswaard, after which others took over. As we lived in German occupied territory, the German authorities had to be notified. During the same period, the body of a German soldier was found near the ferry-boat's jetty, still wearing uniform, with helmet, and grenades pushed into his belt.

Unsurprisingly, Adrianus recalled that 'I could not eat anything the day after we found the bodies'. The remains were initially placed in lead-lined coffins and taken to the Dutch Reformed Church at Tienhoven. On 16 November 1944, the two bodies were buried together with those of three German soldiers also found in the Lek, at Gorinchem General Cemetery. One of the bodies found by the boys was, sadly, Lance-Corporal Gajewnik; the other was a Canadian sapper, Harold 'Maggy' Magnusson.

Canadian Sapper, Harold 'Maggy' Magnusson, who body was found in the Rhine alongside the remains of Lance-Corporal Czeslaw Gajewnik. (Alice van Bekkum)

The date of both men's death is given as 26 September 1944. Magnusson, who was of Swedish origin, was amongst the Canadian engineers assisting in the evacuation of the 1st British Airborne Division: his was the first Stormboat across the Rhine – seen by a Major Tucker to have been destroyed by a mortar bomb. A friend of Lance-Corporal Gajewnik's in the Signals Company, however, Bolek Ostrowski, who survived the hell of Oosterbeek, remembered that Lieutenant Jarvilc told him that his friend held onto the side of an overcrowded boat – but was swept away by the strong current. We also know that Lance-Corporal Gajewnik was awarded the *Virtuti Militari* for his gallantry at Arnhem, although exactly what for is unknown. Whatever the facts may be, Czelaw Gajewnik would never see his homeland again – or his teenage Scottish sweetheart, Mary – who only discovered what had happened to her old friend in 2006, when contacted by Alice van Bekkum, a Dutch lady fascinated by Magnusson's lone war grave at Gorinchem and who had become interested in Gajewnik on account of the two men's bodies having been found together. After the war, Lance-Corporal Gajewnik was moved to the Arnhem-

Oosterbeek War Cemetery, where he now lies at peace with his airborne brothers.

By the reckoning at noon on 27 September 1944, according to the official account of British airborne operations, it was estimated that the 1st British Airborne Division, including glider pilots, had been reduced from 10,095 to 2,490; the balance of 7,605 officers and men were either known to have been killed or otherwise reported missing, wounded and/or prisoners of war. Figures, however, vary from source-to-source. Martin Middlebrook cites the figure of 11,920 men having participated in the Arnhem operation, comprising the 1st British Airborne Division, 1st Independent Polish Parachute Brigade, and various supporting troops. 1,485 were killed, according to Middlebrook, 3,910 being safely evacuated across the Rhine or Poles who withdrew from Driel to Nijmegen. It is no surprise that the most fatalities were suffered by the ill-fated 4th Parachute Brigade: 294, compared to 209 of 1st Parachute Brigade. For some survivors, in hiding on the north bank of the Rhine, their ordeal was not yet over, and these men would suffer yet more privations before safely crossing the Rhine in a number of operations; others, like Lance-Sergeant Harold Padfield, would escape from captivity. The 1st Polish Brigade had lost ninety-seven men killed in action, eighteen of whom remain unaccounted for to this day.

Sapper Magnusson's grave at Gorinchem. (Alice van Bekkum)

In his subsequent report on the battle, General Urquhart wrote that 'The operation was not one hundred per cent successful and did not end quite as we intended. The losses were heavy but all ranks appreciate that the risks involved were reasonable. There is no doubt that all involved would willingly undertake another operation under similar conditions in future'. The general concluded, quite simply, that 'We have no regrets'. Field Marshal Montgomery's view was that:

> A great tribute is due to 1st Airborne Division for the magnificent stand at Arnhem; its action against overwhelming odds held off enemy reinforcements from Nijmegen and vitally contributed to the capture of the bridge there. Such reinforcements as did reach Nijmegen were forced to use a long detour to the East and a ferry crossing, and there is no doubt that the delays thus imposed were instrumental in enabling us to secure the Nijmegen bridges intact. The Battle of Arnhem was ninety per cent successful. We were left in possession of crossings over four major water obstacles including the Maas and the Waal, and

Memorial to the evacuation across the Rhine at Driel. (Author)

> . . . the Wall bridgehead proved a vital factor in the subsequent development of operations, culminating in crossing the Rhine and advancing to the Baltic. Full success at Arnhem was denied us for two reasons: first, the weather prevented the build-up of our airborne forces in the battle area; second, the enemy managed to effect a surprisingly rapid concentration of forces to oppose us. In face of this resistance the British Group of Armies in the north was not strong enough to retrieve the situation created by intensifying the speed of operations on the ground. We could not widen the corridor sufficiently quickly to reinforce Arnhem by road.

General Sosabowski, however, blamed his British superior General Browning for the British failure at Arnhem. Instead of agreeing to evacuate General Urquhart's division, the outspoken Pole believed that Browning, 'Chief of British Airborne . . . did not use all his powers to encourage and persuade Horrocks, Dempsey and Montgomery to have a final go. We were so near victory at the time . . . It only needed one final effort by the units south of the river, and I am sure they would have streamed across to the relief of 1st Airborne.' It was, perhaps, a little more complicated than that, but the General certainly had a point. To the eternal shame of those high commanders involved, however, accusations were levelled at the Polish Brigade having been unwilling to fight at Arnhem. On 17 October 1944, Montgomery wrote to the Chief of the Imperial General Staff (CIGS) to the effect that he did not want this Brigade under his command. The following month, in a lengthy epistle to the Deputy CIGS, General Browning charged Sosabowski with being 'difficult to work with' and having failed at the level of command involved to appreciate 'the urgent nature of the operation . . . argumentative and loth to play his full part . . .'. Consequently, on 9 December 1944, General Sosabowski was relieved of his command. Any sensible scrutiny of the events involved, however, fail to substantiate allegations that the Poles performed poorly or were in any way to blame for the ultimate failure at Arnhem. On the contrary, those high commanders who made a scapegoat out of General Sosobowski and his brigade were the very officers actually responsible for the operation's outcome – and should themselves have been called to account. The ultimate fate, therefore, of General Sosabowski and his Brigade – which never fought again, much less in Poland, leaves a bitter after-taste to this epic tale of derring-do.

Polish memorial in Driel. (Author)

Polish graves at Oosterbeek. (Author)

After the battle, victorious German forces poured across Arnhem Bridge, stabilising the German front. Although the Allies continued localised mopping up operations and cleared certain ports, Germany itself remained intact, Hitler's forces consolidated behind the Siegfried Line and River Maas. As Sir Maurice Dean commented, 'From the high opportunities open in the summer of 1944, this was a steep and grave descent.' Indeed, this eleventh hour success emboldened Hitler to launch, on 16 December 1945, his *Wacht Am Rhine* ('Watch on the Rhine') offensive, through the Ardennes, intended to reach Antwerp, denying the Allies use of that port, and split the Allied forces in two. The offensive achieved total surprise, spreading alarm and panic. By the time order – and the line – had been restored and this last-ditch gamble defeated on 25 January 1945, the so-called 'Battle of the Bulge' had claimed 89,000 American casualties – over 8,000 of them killed in action. This was Hitler's last offensive, after which, their forces severely mauled, the Germans retreated behind the Siegfried Line, awaiting the Allied onslaught. Ultimately, the Rhine was successfully crossed, the washing hung out at last on the Siegfried Line, and Germany crushed in the vice-like grip of the Western Allies advancing from the west, the Russians a vengeful horde from the east. On 8 May 1945,

ARNHEM 1944

Germany surrendered, Hitler having committed suicide in his Berlin bunker on 30 April. The Battle of Arnhem's outcome, however, resonated into the post-war world and 'Cold War', between the western democracies and the Soviet bloc: had Montgomery's bold plan succeeded, it is interesting to ponder events had the western Allies reached Berlin first. Indeed, it is likely that the post-war map of Europe could have been quite different.

Whilst in simple terms, therefore, Operation MARKET-GARDEN was 'all about bridges', the outcome cast a long shadow indeed: the war did not end in 1944, and a great opportunity was lost, with consequences for Europe's post-war political and geographic map. Whilst the grand strategy and planning may have been wanting, one particular wireless transmission, the last from Lieutenant Colonel John Frost's men at Arnhem Bridge, best pays tribute to the all of the Allied soldiers who fought at Arnhem during that fateful autumn of 1944. This succinct signal perfectly captures the tenacity and defiance of these extraordinary airborne soldiers – who recorded a new benchmark for courage and endurance: 'Out of ammunition. God save the King.'

Lance-Corporal Czeslaw Gajewnik's headstone at Oosterbeek. (33.A.1). (Author)

Chapter 19

Gefallen: German Casualties at Arnhem

Just how many German soldiers, sailors and airmen were *Gefallen* – killed in action – or *Vermisst* – missing – as a result of Operation MARKET-GARDEN is impossible to say with any certainty. Moreover, it must be remembered that whilst this book focusses on the 1st British Airborne Division and 1st Independent Polish Parachute Brigade's effort at Arnhem, the overall operation involved fighting over many miles of 'Hell's Highway', and, for the Germans, against the British 2nd Army and American 101st and 82nd Airborne Divisions. Figures and records are at best incomplete, and difficult, therefore, to determine how many German casualties were suffered at Arnhem and Oosterbeek. Cornelius Ryan, however, believed these to number some 3,300, based upon *Generalfeldmarschall* Model's personal estimation, including 1,300 *Gefallen*. After interviewing surviving German commanders regarding their losses suffered fighting the 'breakout at Neerpelt, then along the corridor in battles at Nijmegen, Grave, Veghel, Best and Eindhoven', Ryan 'conservatively' estimated that Army Group 'B' lost 7,500–10,000 men of which perhaps a quarter were killed'. In his excellent book *It Never Snows in September*, Robert Kershaw has attempted an analysis, based upon known information and educated guesswork, concluding that enemy casualties at Arnhem-Oosterbeek between 17–26 September 1944, could have been as many as 5,175. Certainly, according to Kershaw, ten German formations suffered between 50 per cent and a staggering 92 per cent casualties – indicating that throughout this savage battle, in spite of the upper hand with heavy weapons and numbers, the German victory was won at significant cost.

Given the composite and *ad hoc* nature of the German forces committed to battle in and around Arnhem, just as it is difficult to accurately cite enemy casualty figures, it is equally difficult to quantify just how many German soldiers fought in this battle. Dutch historian Hans Timmermann suggests 18,000 – 20,000 men. It is frequently quoted, of course, that the British planners and high commanders ignored information from the Dutch underground regarding the presence of 9-SS *Hohenstaufen* and 10-SS *Frundsberg* Panzer Divisions in the Arnhem area, the inference being that these formations were at full strength with hundreds of tanks. That, however, is not so: both divisions had been substantially battered during the Normandy campaign, and, after the *Rückmarsch* east across France, Belgium and into Holland, were resting and re-fitting. Indeed, *Hohenstaufen* was actually in the process of handing over what few armoured fighting vehicles it had left to *Frundsberg*, before returning to Germany. Kershaw tells us that in reality both of these SS divisions were only at 20-30 per cent strength – 2,500 – 3,000 men – and 'possessed virtually no tanks'. Also in the area, however, was SS-*Panzergrenadier-Ausbildings-und Ersatz-Bataillon* 16, commanded by SS-*Sturmbannführer* Sepp Krafft, whose training unit's swift and positive reaction to the initial landings was decisive. All of these *Waffen*-SS units, even if not fully equipped, were dangerous adversaries, led by battle-hardened NCOs and officers who had fought in Russia, Normandy and elsewhere. All of these men, including Krafft's trainees, were highly

Captain Geert Jonker of the Royal Netherlands Army's Recovery & Identification Unit with Dilip Sarkar and the remains of a German soldier found near Arnhem, at the Soesterberg laboratory in 2015. (Karen Sarkar)

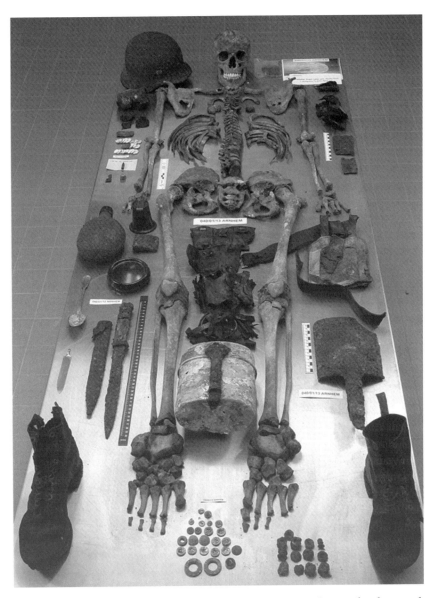

The remains of an SS panzergrenadier *found near Arnhem – 'We know what he was, but not who he was', says Geert Jonker. (Geert Jonker)*

motivated. These were far, therefore, from the rear echelon or sub-standard troops that the 1st British Airborne Division had been briefed to expect. The fact is, that this *Waffen-*SS cadre provided a backbone of steel to the composite German force which fought at Arnhem – many units of which were, contrary to the myth, inexperienced and unsuitable *Luftwaffe* and Kriegsmarine units pressed into the infantry role. For that reason, and given that the officers of most of those units had little or no experience of leading infantry in the field, high German losses are unsurprising. That fact does, though, make the German achievement remarkable. That said, the Germans still view the Battle of Arnhem and Oosterbeek as of infinitely less importance to the battle being fought around Nijmegen – which, after all, is where 2nd Army's inability to reach Arnhem was decided.

Like the British and Polish fatalities, German dead were first buried close to or where they fell, in field graves scattered all over the battlefield. The Germans also set up temporary cemeteries at various locations, and some units, contrary to policy, returned their dead to the Fatherland. This is another reason why arriving at an accurate figure concerning fatalities is so difficult. Moreover, the Germans removed their wounded from the battlefield by every means of transportation available, medical facilities moving up to be close to fighting troops. For example, initial aid posts were located at the Wolfheze Hotel and Loeren Doedel Hotel, whilst facilities better equipped to deal with serious wounds and provide ongoing care were located well behind the lines. Of course, many men died at and were buried close to those places too – in addition to the locations taken over and used by the British as field hospitals, notably the Schoonoord and Tafelberg hotels in Oosterbeek. No.-one has done more than Hans Timmermann to research the German dead, who is convinced that the majority of German field graves concerned *Kampfgruppe* von Tettau, which included airmen of the *Luftwaffe Ersatz-und-Ausbildings*-Regiment Hermann Göring, and sailors of 10 and 14 *Schiffstammabteilung* and Marine *Schützen Bataillon* 250 – many of whom remained in their field graves after the area was liberated in April 1945. After the war, these were largely exhumed and interred at the vast German War Cemetery at Ysselsteyn – where a staggering 32,000 German soldiers killed in this theatre of operations are buried. According to Hans Timmermann, at least 1,725 graves there are of Germans killed fighting in the Arnhem and Oosterbeek areas – the identities of 445 of them *unbekanst* (unknown). Like the Allied casualties, therefore, many were never identified – and undoubtedly some remain buried in long forgotten field graves in and around Oosterbeek.

Hans Timmermann, together with his brother, Dick, and friends including respected Dutch historian and author David van Buggenum, has been metal detecting on the Arnhem battlefield since 1980. In 1981, Hans and Dick found identity discs at the former German *Ehrenfriedhof Zypendaal* cemetery – launching their journey to research, recover and identify those of both sides still unaccounted for. In 1985, Dick discovered the remains of Private William Allen of 10th Parachute Battalion on Ginkel Heath, who was subsequently interred at the Arnhem-Oosterbeek War Cemetery. Perhaps appropriately, the first German soldier the Timmermann brothers found was on 3 September 1988, on a dike near Wilp. This transpired to be a 37-year-old *panzergrenadier* killed in April 1945, who was later buried at Ysselsteyn. On 18 January 1993, Hans and David, together with Robert Markus, were searching at the owner's request in the garden of the house on Van Lennepweg used as 'C' Company, 1st Border's HQ. There they found the remains of two more British soldiers, Privates Ernest Ager and Douglas Lowery, both of whom were consequently interred at Oosterbeek later that year. These discoveries led to the

GEFALLEN: GERMAN CASUALTIES AT ARNHEM

Timmermann brothers and David becoming authorised by Renkum Council to search for field graves in the Arnhem area, working in close cooperation with the Royal Netherlands Army Identification & Recovery Unit, and police. Today, although Hans has now taken a back seat, David continues this physical search with Martin Reijnen.

Desktop research with archival sources can also lead to evidence being found identifying German casualties buried as unknown – as Hans proved in 2000, with the case of *Bootsman* Alfred Steckhan, killed on the Valkenburglaan, Oosterbeek, in September 1944. Buried as *unbekanst* at Ysselteyn, information discovered in the Renkum Archive and the Deutsche Dienstelle in Berlin confirmed that Steckhan was the unidentified casualty buried in block BM, row 12, grave 283, leading to his grave being named accordingly. Likewise, in 2005, again using archival sources, Hans confirmed that the unidentified casualty buried in block M, row 7, grave 169, was SS-*Unterscharführer* Ewald Carstensen of the *Hohenstaufen* division, who had died on 20 September 1944, of wounds sustained in Arnhem. Further identifications followed. In 2008, whilst searching the Westerbouwing for missing 1st Border Lance-Corporal Eric Melling, David van Buggenum and friends discovered the remains of a German soldier. The police and Recovery & Identification Unit were immediately alerted and on site. Ultimately, the remains were confirmed to be *Oberbootsmannsmaat der Reserve* Johann Peter Grabowski, of 3.*Kompanie*, 10.*Schiffsstammabteilung*, killed, aged thirty-one, on 25 September 1944 – whose remains were subsequently interred at Ysselsteyn.

The organisation responsible for German war graves is the *Volksbund Deutsche Kriegsgräberfürsorge* (VDK) – which has a difficult job. This is because German memory of the Second World War is inextricably connected with that of National Socialism. Any German Second World War commemoration is automatically faced with the issue of to what extent or even whether this can be detached from responsibility for aggressive expansionism, a racial war and ultimately the Holocaust. Consequently, as Gerd Knischewski argued, '. . . the memory of the Second World War in general and commemoration of the dead in particular have been, and still are, far from being consensual and unifying in Germany'. The problem is that German soldiers – especially those of the SS – could be both victims of war and perpetrators of crimes against humanity. The VDK, therefore, organises Germany's national day of remembrance – *Volkstrauertag* – along the lines of a humanitarian, not patriotic, day of mourning for all the dead of both world wars and, since the early 1960s, the victims of tyranny. Indeed, the VDK's mantra is 'Working for peace. Reconciliation over graves'. Nonetheless, the VDK has drawn fire from some, critical of what they see as a shaping of German war memory around an emphasis on German victimhood, avoiding responsibility, guilt and historical explanations. Indeed, in Bill Niven's *Germans as Victims*, Andrew Beattie maintains that memory of German suffering is important to a unified German national identity today, and a 'counterweight to memory of German guilt'. Accordingly, the VDK's presentation is that the principals of reconciliation and forgiveness should be applied to all fallen German soldiers, regardless of their individual crimes. Consistent

In 2008, whilst searching for 'missing' 1st Border field graves at Westerbouwing, David van Buggenum and friends found the remains of a German soldier. (David van Buggenum)

A Kriegsmarine tunic button indicated that this casualty belonged to a German naval unit, and his wedding ring that he was a married man. (David van Buggenum)

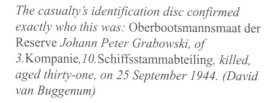

The casualty's identification disc confirmed exactly who this was: Oberbootsmannsmaat der Reserve *Johann Peter Grabowski, of 3.Kompanie,10.Schiffsstammabteiling, killed, aged thirty-one, on 25 September 1944. (David van Buggenum)*

with this stance, on 26 May 2010, at Ysselsteyn, the VDK awarded Hans Timmermann the *Peacepark* medal for his efforts to recover and identify German war dead in Holland. This work, of course, has no political basis whatsoever but is a purely humanitarian gesture – the recognition was well-deserved.

The complex issue regarding Second World War memory and commemorations in Germany generates a clear distance between today's generations and their country's Nazi past. Indeed, during the course of research for this book, it became clear that the families of German casualties were uncomfortable with putting the spotlight on their ancestors killed fighting in 'Hitler's war', for fear that this may be misinterpreted as having Nazi sympathies today. For that reason, it was (reluctantly) decided not to apply the same methodology to presenting the story of German casualties as has been possible with those of the 1st British Airborne Division and 1st Independent Polish Parachute Brigade. This is a pity, because history is deserved of a balanced account, the view from the other side, therefore, being essential. For that reason, however, the pioneering work of Robert Kershaw to present the German view, backed up in more recent times by certain specialist publications in English focussing on German units at Arnhem, are of great importance to our overall understanding of the violent past. In time, however, this may change, and the need to present the stories of German casualties will be seen for what it is: a historic, not political, enterprise. At the time of writing, the Airborne Museum at Oosterbeek is planning, for the first time, a major exhibition presenting the German perspective of Operation MARKET-GARDEN – which would have been unthinkable only recently, given the understandable antipathy of the wartime Dutch generation. The distance in time from the traumatic events concerned has made this possible, enabling, perhaps, a fresh perspective, so who knows what the future holds?

It is often written that the *Waffen*-SS units committed to battle at Arnhem fought with unexpected honour and chivalry. It is worth examining why this was, and, indeed, why adherence to the Geneva Convention – intended to ensure that warfare is conducted as humanely as possible – is considered surprising.

The so-called *Shutztaffel* – literally 'protection squad' – was formed to provide security at Nazi Party meetings. From 1925, onwards, the 'SS' was controlled by Heinrich Himmler, growing from a small, obscure, paramilitary organisation to an all-powerful behemoth responsible for security, genocide and terror throughout the Third Reich. There were two heads to this beast: the *Allgemeine*-SS and the *Waffen*-SS, the former being enforcers of Nazi laws and racial policy, the latter armed combat units. All swore an oath of allegiance to Hitler personally – not Germany. The SS formations which fought at Arnhem, principally the 9-SS *Hohenstaufen* and 10-SS *Frundsberg* divisions of II SS *Panzer Korps*, were elements of the *Waffen*-SS. At the post war Nuremberg war trials, however, the SS was collectively declared a criminal organisation by the Allied court. Ever-since, the validity of this judgement has been hotly debated, former members of the *Waffen*-SS claiming that they were simply soldiers like any others, with no part in mass murder. This is not the place to further that debate, except

Peter Grabowski was eventually laid to rest, with other 'missing' German soldiers recovered in the Netherlands, at the German War Cemetery at Ysselsteyn. (David van Buggenum)

to say that weighty evidence exists to counter any such hollow argument. Nonetheless – and this is the point – no allegations of war crimes are known to have been aimed at either *Hohenstaufen* or *Frundsberg*. In 1940, though, the SS *Totenkopf* regiment had murdered Royal Norfolk Regiment prisoners on the road to Dunkirk at Le Paradis, the 1-SS *Liebstandarte* Adolf Hitler, the *Führer*'s personal bodyguard formation, following suit shortly afterwards by massacring Royal Warwickshire Regiment prisoners near Wormhout. In Normandy, the 12-SS *Hitler Jugend* Division fought without quarter, its teenage soldiers responsible for numerous atrocities against Canadian troops in particular; in June 1944, 2-SS *Das Reich* had committed the infamous outrage against French civilians at Oradour-sur-Glane on its way to Normandy. The *Waffen*-SS, therefore, had a deserved reputation for murder and mayhem on and off the battlefield. Moreover, both SS divisions at Arnhem had previously fought on the savage *Ostfront*, where unspeakable acts of barbarity, by both sides, were commonplace. Why, then, did the 9th and 10th SS fight a comparatively decent battle at Arnhem? The answer is not necessarily easy to find.

GEFALLEN: GERMAN CASUALTIES AT ARNHEM

It could be argued that by 17 September 1944, notwithstanding the fact that the Germans had halted and were prepared to defend their homeland, all but the most blinkered Nazi fanatic realised that the war was lost. It was a question of trying to preserve Germany and buy time in the hope that either a diplomatic solution and a negotiated peace could be found, or Germany's ill-fortune reversed by Hitler's new secret weapons. Moreover, the furious storm fast approaching from the east had to be resisted for as long as possible, to protect Germany's civilians, and women in particular, from the retribution undoubtedly to follow for German crimes against humanity in the Soviet Union. The longer Germany could fight, the more chance there was, some hoped, of the western Allies and Soviets quarrelling and Germany being required as an ally of the Western democracies in a new war against Stalin. In any event, surrender, if it came to that, was preferable to the Western Allies, so some have opined that the prospect of impending judgement in the victors' court was an influencing factor on SS conduct at Arnhem. A few months later, certain *Waffen*-SS units, however, committed further crimes, against American prisoners and Belgian civilians, and that was even closer to the war's end. That, explanation, therefore, is far too simplistic. We need to delve deeper.

The *Hohenstaufen* and *Frundsberg* were formed in France in March 1943, as part of *Reichsführer* Himmler's plan to expand the *Waffen*-SS further still. These, however, were increasingly desperate times, in the wake of the German army's crippling defeat at Stalingrad, on the Volga, where 730,000 men were killed, wounded or captured. Whereas the once proud *Waffen*-SS had accepted only the most physically fit and 'racially pure' volunteers, after so many casualties such fine Aryan cannon-fodder was difficult to find. Indeed, the call for volunteers to man Himmler's new divisions met with an unenthusiastic response. Consequently, for the first time, the SS had to rely upon conscription – recruits not of the same quality or motivation as the fanatical Nazi volunteers who had conquered so much territory between 1939 and 1941. In fact, between 70–80 per cent of *Hohenstaufen* and *Frundsberg*'s strength were conscripts from the *Reichsarbeitdienst* (State Labour Force) and *Volksdeutsche* – ethnic Germans – from Hungary. The composition of these units, therefore, was somewhat different to the *Waffen*-SS units of earlier in the war – although the new divisions' officers and men were experienced combatants and from no less a formation than the *Leibstandarte*. The 9th and 10th SS were first sent to the Ukraine, fighting around Tarnopol, in April 1944. There, *Hohenstaufen* alone suffered 1,011 casualties before being withdrawn to join Army Group North's reserve. After D-Day, both divisions – now collectively the II SS *Panzer Korps* – were deployed to Caen. Again, horrendous losses were suffered and hence why Bittrich's *Korps* was re-fitting and held in reserve at Arnhem in September 1944.

It should also be remembered that throughout this time, Germany was being subjected to the Allied strategic bombing campaign, aimed squarely at liquidating Germany's ability and will to fight. Many German soldiers who fought at Arnhem, no doubt, had lost, or would lose, their families in this relentless, round-the-clock, aerial Armageddon. Indeed, when the 1st British Airborne Division descended on the heaths around Renkum and Wolfheze on 17 September 1944, II SS *Panzer Korps* was preparing to withdraw to Germany; one SS officer wrote that 'The soldiers were thinking about their families, as everything had virtually been packed for the move to Siegen. The mood was resigned to "Here we go again!" They were inevitably disappointed at first, but the officers and NCOs were able to overcome this and get the soldiers quickly into action.' The fact arguably is, therefore, that although largely conscripts, these were still well-trained and excellently commanded troops – but lacking that steely and cruel fanaticism of the *Waffen*-SS in previous years and campaigns. There is probably no one reason to explain the exemplary battle fought by the SS at Arnhem – but that, I think, goes a long way to assisting our understanding of these enemy soldiers who achieved, when all is said and done, Germany's last great victory of the war.

Of all the German casualties at Arnhem, the highest-ranking, of course, was Major-General Friedrich Kussin, the *Stadtkommandant*, whose staff car haplessly blundered into 3rd Parachute Battalion advancing into Oosterbeek on 17 September 1944. The most famous German fatality, however, has to be SS-*Hauptsturmführer* Viktor-Eberhard Gräbner, commander of SS-*Panzer-Aufklärangs-Abteilung* 9, who led that unit's ill-fated attack on Arnhem Bridge on 18 September 1944. As explained previously in this book, Gräbner passed over Arnhem Bridge on 17 September 1944 – the very day on which he had received the coveted *Ritterkreuz* for his bravery and efforts in Normandy – spending the night in Elst, on the south bank of the Rhine, equidistant between Nijmegen and Arnhem. SS-*Hauptsturmführer* Wilfried Schwarz, a *Hohenstaufen* staff officer, recalled that early on 18 September, Gräbner was passed orders via radio to re-cross Arnhem bridge, neutralise the British force clinging onto the northern end, and establish a defensive perimeter to the west. In the film *A Bridge Too Far*, a strutting, arrogant and typical steel-helmeted Nazi, Gräbner is seen standing upright in his open-top half-track and thundering across Arnhem Bridge at the head of his armoured column – when all hell suddenly broke loose from the British lines, decimating his vehicles and men. Gräbner, however, born in Leipzig on 24 May 1914, was an experienced reconnaissance specialist, having previously also fought in Russia, where he added the German Cross in Gold to his existing Iron Crosses 1st and 2nd Class in May 1942. The portrayal of him as reckless and over-confident in the famous film, therefore, is doubtless somewhat exaggerated. Nonetheless, it has made Gräbner and this particular action famous. In truth, though, rather than arrogantly assuming an easy victory, more likely, I would suggest, Gräbner probably lacked intelligence concerning the British strength – and was surprised by the total ferocity of the British reaction.

SS-*Unterscharführer* Mauga was in one of Gräbner's half-tracks: 'Suddenly all hell broke loose. There were explosions all around my vehicle, and all at once I was in the middle of chaos and confusion. A few wanted to carry on, others wanted to go back. Gräbner was in a captured British armoured car. Where he got it from we had no idea. Later, we took the car into Arnhem, but the commander was nowhere to be found; we

310

were unable to recover his body.' The British vehicle was a Humber Mk IV, a four-wheeled armoured car used for reconnaissance. Gräbner leading in this British vehicle, Marcel Zwarts suggests, is what may have at first confused the British, who allowed several vehicles, in their surprise, to pass through into Arnhem unscathed; Frost's men, after all, Zwarts argued, expected 'Allied units, not German' from the south. Zwarts emphasises that Gräbner 'was probably standing up with the top half of his body exposed above the gun turret hatch so as to have a better view. This was unwise but fairly common with armoured car commanders.' This, then, goes some way to explaining the portrayal of Gräbner in the film, and, indeed, the nature of his death in action that day: his obituary notice stated that he had been shot in the chest. It is, however, strange that his remains were not found and identified, meaning it likely that the highly decorated SS-*Hauptsturmführer* Viktor-Eberhard Gräbner is amongst the many German soldiers buried as *unbekanst* at Ysselsteyn.

What, though, do we know of Viktor-Eberhard Gräbner beyond his exploits at Arnhem? Very little. However, some years ago, an American enthusiast by chance met Gräbner's nephew, adding a twist to the story. Apparently, there Viktor had a brother, also in the SS, although nothing more is known. He also had a sister who married an American serviceman after the war and emigrated to the United States. The nephew, therefore, was very much an American, with little interest in his SS uncles, although did play, apparently, with Viktor's SS honour dagger as a child. Unfortunately, no response was received from him during the course of my research for this book – meaning that, very likely, unless the family decides to emerge onto our radar, we will never advance our knowledge of Viktor-Eberhard Gräbner the man.

Clearly, there needs to be a longer passage of time and period of healing before research into and the relating of German casualty stories will be possible.

The vast German cemetery at Ysselsteyn. (Author)

Chapter 20

Flowers in the Wind

During the battle in and around Arnhem, ferocious fighting had taken place in Dutch homes, above the occupants who sheltered in their deep cellars. Ans van Wilk-Hobé remembered those dreadful days of death, destruction, and disappointment:

> In 1944, I was ten years old. My father was the caretaker at Oosterbeek Police Station, and our family lived in that building. During the fighting, we stayed in the cellar there, and other policemen, whose homes had no cellars, brought their families to ours. We were stuck there for about ten days, and then the Germans came and told us to leave the area. There was a kind of armistice for a day, enabling we civilians to pack up a few belongings and move out. We walked about thirty kilometres to a village called Harskamp, and stayed there for nine months.

Arnhem and Oosterbeek were devastated by the battle, and were fought over again in April 1945; this is Arnhem – or what little left of it. (Gelders Archief)

FLOWERS IN THE WIND

Ans van Wilk-Hobé. (Ans van Wilk-Hobé)

Wim van Zanten, aged ten, having nearly starved during the 'Hunger Winter', with the grave of Corporal Joe Simpson. (Wim van Zanten)

Wim 'Willy' van Zanten:

> In the cellar, you could still hear everything. If you heard the artillery in the Betuwe firing, everyone was quiet: a 'whoosh' meant that the shell had passed overhead, but hearing a bang, not a whistle, we took cover, because that meant we might be hit. Many houses were destroyed. The Germans eventually came and ordered us out. Until then, we didn't even know that the British had gone. There was now less shooting and it was quieter. On 26 September 1944, the Germans forced us to leave Oosterbeek. We struggled with our carts and a delivery bicycle borrowed from Mr Köhler, a poulterer, over the mess in Weverstraat, the Utrechtseweg, the Schelmseweg, and along the railway to Mariëndaal. When we were near the avenue of trees running from the Utrechtseweg into the park of Mariëndaal, we had to shelter under the archway

because some British planes flew over and the German flak batteries on the avenue Middellaan started shooting, hit a plane which crashed. I remember the Germans congratulating each other, shaking hands. We then walked further on, and at the corner of the Schelmseweg and Apeldoornseweg was a football pitch, which was a German army camp. There, some rather old Austrian soldiers, with tears in their eyes, distributed bread to civilians. I will never forget that. We next came to Groenendaal, where a German column had been shot-up by British fighters. There were many civilians on the roads at that time, amongst them my friend, Martin Derksen, who was seriously wounded – he later died in the 'Juliana' hospital in Apeldoorn, aged sixteen or seventeen. We ended up in Het Loo, a suburb of Apeldoorn, where we stayed with Freek Gerritsen and family in their house on the Nieuwelandweg.

Luuk 'Lukie' Buist was eight years old on 17 September 1944, living at 'De Parre', Benedendorpsweg 169, with his 39-year-old father, Luitsen, a sailmaker, his mother, 'Bep', two sisters, Truusje, aged seven and four-year old Hennie, and the family dog, 'Teddie'. The family's story is a tragic one, emphasising the vulnerability of civilians trying to survive on a violent battlefield. On that fateful Sunday, Luuk remembers,

> A lot of noise in the air, people coming out of church and hurrying home through the lower part of Oosterbeek. I can tell from the adults' behaviour that something important is happening. Then comes information that parachutists and gliders have landed near Wolfheze. That the 'Jerries" do not like it is clearly visible: they leave with everything they can run away with. They use cars, carts and especially bicycles. Even a neighbour's son's bicycle is taken but, being too small, is discarded after 100 meters. The adults are talking excitedly and are waiting for things to come. The sky is full of Allied aircraft. When shots are fired nearby, we run for shelter in our house.
>
> Then, there are cheers of joy in the distance. Here are the Allied soldiers, young and fit paratroopers. Slowly they follow the road, looking around carefully, alert. Some small green vehicles pass and one drives into the Polderweg, in the direction of the brickworks and the railway bridge. A little later we hear a violent bang and see the bridge being blown. The firing increases, so we shelter in our little cellar. There is also the whistling of shells and mortar bombs, with some explosions getting closer.
>
> Parachutes are dropped again, I can see them close by. They are like large flowers in different colours with a basket or big tube attached. Some land in the trees or on the rooves. In those baskets and tubes are the supplies badly needed by the soldiers: food, ammunition, fuel and medicine. By now we are more or less living in our little cellar. Gunfire and explosions are now incessant, so we go to the air raid shelter which our neighbour had dug in their back yard.

Hennie and Luuk Buist with their mother, 'Bep'. (Luuk Buist)

Luitsen Buist, also known as Luuk – tragically killed trying to protect his family during the Battle of Oosterbeek. (Luuk Buist)

Luuk with both his sisters, Hennie and Truusje. (Luuk Buist)

ARNHEM 1944

On Wednesday, 20 September 1944, my father comes home. He has heard that there are German tanks heading in our direction. We have to leave immediately. My mother takes the packed cart and my dad takes his bike, also packed, and on top my youngest sister Hennie. I am told to hold the hand of my other sister, Truusje. Our dog Teddie is running along with us.

There we go, amongst other refugees, through the war violence along the Benedendorpsweg towards the Hemelse Berg estate. At the entrance the cart breaks down, one of the wheels folds. 'Just leave the cart', my Dad says, and on we go onto the terrain of the Hemelse Berg. More bad luck when the heel of my mother's shoe breaks off. Moving on, past the big house where people seek shelter in the cellars. My father says, 'Don't stop, we need to go into the woods as far as we can'. We arrive at the Van der Gronden family's small, crowded, farm on the edge of the Oorsprong woods. Here we spend the night. My mother gets some big gloves from Dad that she can draw on her feet. We all lie down in the hay and try to get some sleep.

The next morning, Thursday 21 September, we are wakened by heavy mortar and gunfire. We all flee from the farm into the cover of a small valley in the woods behind. Soon afterwards the farm is set ablaze. The noise is terrible. We are close to each other behind a thick tree. We children close to the tree, and then Mum, and Dad is using his body as a shield to protect us – but he gets injured by shrapnel. When the shelling stops, Mum makes Dad as comfortable as possible, with his back leaning against the tree we were using for cover. Suddenly a group of Germans storm into our valley. They are sending us away. My father, mortally wounded, told my mother to take the children to a safer place and leave him behind. There we go, mother with Hennie, and I have a firm grip on Truusje's hand. During another mortar barrage we lose sight of our mother and Hennie in this 'Witches Cauldron'". Everywhere you hear gunshots and explosions. The air is filled with acrid smoke.

We follow other people heading in the direction of Hemelse Berg, where we find shelter with many others. Again, it was not safe, though, because after the owner, Mr. Belaerts van Blokland, announced that a Red Cross flag had been raised, the house was hit and soon ablaze. Next we moved to the coach house and waited for things to get a little quieter. Over the course of the day, people take us through the woods and across Bato'swijk to a house along Bato'sweg. Food is prepared, endive stew, which is the first hot meal we have since leaving home. Meanwhile, someone went to see if my mother returned to our home. He comes back with my father's banjo. He asks me if I recognize it, which I confirm. That banjo has been with us for a very long time.

We did not stay long and moved through Nieuwland to the Grintweg, where we stay in another cellar. Here it is a bit quieter. From time to time a loud bang and further away some small arms fire. In the evening, Germans suddenly come in and want to know who we are and if there are any English soldiers among us. Immediately, we were told that a regular check would be made and if no response, a grenade would be thrown into the cellar. A schedule is then set where all the adults have a turn to stay awake. The next morning there is a discussion about what has to happen to Truusje and me. The owners of the house ask us if we have any relatives in the area. 'Yes', I reply, 'on the Backerstraat'. With a group, we then went on our way. But at Backerstraat everyone had gone. I explained that we also have relatives at Schaarsbergen. We cross the bridge over the railway line at Dreijenseweg. Along both sides of the road lie several dead soldiers. At the top of the road we are stopped by German soldiers. We get permission pass through the woods, in the direction of Amsterdamseweg. When we arrive at the forest warden's house, I notice there are several blankets in the pond around the house.

Finally, Truusje and I arrive in Schaarsbergen. There is a lot of consternation as to where our parents and Hennie are. The house is already very crowded with refugees. Our companions say 'Goodbye' and move on. All I can tell people is that my father was injured and that my mother might have decided to stay with him and Hennie. Where we are is very quiet, but in the distance we can hear the battle still raging in Oosterbeek.

The days went on and we children adapted, playing with the other children. One day there is the sharing of clothes, as what we wear is all we have. We went to see if we could get some extra clothes. There is a distribution point in a large villa. We get some clothes and I ask the lady if she has some shoes for my Mum, size 36. I told her my mother's shoes were broken during the flight. She gave me some black slippers. Meanwhile, Uncle Rinus, my mother's brother-in-law, has been searching for information about my parents and sister Hennie. Cycling as far as Hilversum, because it was too late to return he went to his brother's, who lives there. There he could not believe his eyes: my mother and sister were there! After wandering from one to another place they had reached safety there. The relief and joy of my mother when she heard my sister and I are also safe is beyond words. My mother has no information, however, regarding our father's fate.

The next day, Uncle Rinus returns to Schaarsbergen with the good news that my mother and sister are safe and in good health. Now plans are made to get us to Hilversum. On 26 October, we travel with Uncle Rinus and his daughter, Dina, on bikes to Hilversum. I'm with Uncle Rinus on his bike, and Truusje with Dina. It's a long journey on old bikes with massive tyres. Mother has never been happier as when she has us in her arms again.

It is very peaceful on 27 October, my ninth birthday. I could not have had a more beautiful gift, being reunited with my mum and little sister. Here too, the days pass, and Uncle Dirk and Aunt Marie make every effort to make everything as good as is possible. Naturally, I have to go to school again. There I get books and writing materials – and have to do homework! What is homework?! My thoughts are elsewhere! Meanwhile, in Amersfoort, the shortage of food is noticeable. Uncle Dirk knows how to organise bits of food, but it's getting scarce. Fuel is also a problem, and as a boy you are sent out to 'sprout' wood. 'Sprouting' consists of collecting logs from trees illegally sawn and chopped up.

We received a message from the Red Cross that we can move to Groningen where we have family. Early in the morning we reported to the gathering point. With our few possessions, we get a place in the full bus. In the back are suitcases and a few young boys under blankets. They are sick (diphtheria). Later, I hear that they are subversives. The Jerries are very afraid of contagious diseases. The bus is equipped with a gas generator and does not run smoothly. At Zwolle or Deventer we had to cross the river Ijssel. We all had to leave the bus and across the bridge on foot. Only the sick are allowed to stay in the bus. On we go to the north. It's already late afternoon when my mother takes a piece of bread out of the bag and divides it. It's our lunch. It's getting dark and we are not yet in Groningen. It's about 8 o'clock when we arrive at a church. Now we need to be brought to the Hortencialaan where our family lives. Due to the curfew, however, we are no longer allowed to travel, but receive wonderful help from a big policeman in uniform who takes care of us. Hennie, my youngest sister, is exhausted from the bus journey and is being carried by the policeman. My Aunt raises big eyes when she sees the policeman with Hennie on his arm, and my Mum, with Truusje and I behind them. Quickly she lets us in. The policeman sniffs and says, 'From the smell of the kitchen, I can tell you arrived at a good home!' My Aunt is roasting meat, which smells delicious. We say 'Goodbye' to the friendly policeman. Inside it is warm and there is bread, jam and more food on the table. We could eat as much as we wanted! It feels like a feast after all those weeks of a slice of bread with no butter. It is very late when we get to bed, Mum still up talking with my uncle and aunt.

In Groningen, life just goes on. I go back to school. Following the lessons in the Gronings dialect is not easy. Initially, there is no sign of the war. There are many Jerries, but no fighting. My youngest sister Hennie gets seriously ill and needs extra food. My mother walks many miles to get a few eggs at a farm. But here too, the peace does not last for a long time, the Canadians arrive and the city is bombarded. The centre of the town is in flames. Shells also land in our area of the town and we quickly try to find shelter. My uncle and aunt are laughing at us a bit, but if there is an explosion close to us, they join us in our shelter. When our liberators enter the city, the Jerries flee to Delfzijl. Some officers in an open car are also trying to get away, but they are unlucky: the bridge is open and can't be lowered. The only way is over the lock gates. What a party, we are liberated!

FLOWERS IN THE WIND

Soon, the first Canadians walk through our street, cautiously on both sides of the road. Later, German prisoners were marched through our street and the citizens were shouting at them. A number of boys have found a German car and cruise triumphantly through the street. A German home is looted, clothes, pots and pans, everything loose is dragged away. Meanwhile, the Canadians have transformed the end of the street into a camp. Every now and then I see Truusje who is staying with cousin Rie due to lack of space in our house. Life goes on – but we have heard nothing about my father's fate. We need to go to Oosterbeek. My mother, Uncle Wubbo and I make the long trip to Arnhem. The city looks desolate, everything is destroyed. A military lorry serving as a bus takes us to Oosterbeek. We stay with my grandparents where we get the devastating news that my father died of his injuries; he was found where we had left him. Every time I pass this spot, which is often, I see those horrible images from the past. My father was buried at the Oosterbeek Cemetery on 6 July 1945.

We also visit our house at the Benedendorpsweg. 'De Parre' has been hit by several grenades and is a ruin. Inside, books are all over the floor and all our furniture is broken. It's terrible. The streets are full of debris and the Benedendorpsweg is screened on the south side with some sort of wicker mats, a German barricade. All doors were taken from the houses by the Germans and were used to strengthen their defences. After a few days we travel north again. It's a journey with many obstacles. From Arnhem by train to Utrecht. Then we are told there are no trains to the north as the railway bridge at Zwolle is being repaired. My uncle finds us a place to sleep and next day we continue our travel to Groningen. There we get back to everyday life. At school, I try to follow the lessons as best I can.

Meanwhile, my mother is working hard for our return to Oosterbeek. It's a difficult job to find housing, but eventually it's possible to get a few rooms in my birthplace on the Weverstraat, number 124. After the summer of 1945, we moved back to Oosterbeek. On return we have nothing but the clothes we wore and the few things picked up during our evacuation. We literally are in need of everything, clothes, furniture, and the everyday things required to live. Through the Damage Survey Office and the Red Cross, mother was able to get a few things to make a new start.

For boys of my age, life in a devastated village is a paradise. We searched for all kind of things in the destroyed houses – but danger is everywhere: unexploded ammunition and other war debris lies everywhere. There are several accidents involving young and old killed or severely injured. In September, I go to school again at Wilhelminastraat. My old school in the Weverstraat has been destroyed. Also, I commemorate the 'Battle of Arnhem' for the first time. From school, we children walk with flowers to the Airborne Cemetery and stand by the crosses. This makes a big impression on me too because my father is one of the civilian victims.

In 1945, the Buists returned to Oosterbeek, finding their house, 'Parre' on Bendendorpsweg badly damaged. (Luuk Buist)

The Buist family's story really emphasises the human suffering of the stoic Dutch people. During the Battle of Arnhem, Dutch records indicate that at least 453 Dutch civilians lost their lives. Evicted from their battered, looted, homes by the Germans, after the battle the Dutch faced a famine. A German blockade prevented distribution of farm produce, and many low-lying areas were flooded as a defensive precaution. Some 4.5 million people were affected, many surviving only because of emergency soup kitchens. Dutch historian Loe de Jong estimated that at least 22,000 deaths occurred during the 'Hunger Winter'. Another Dutch

In 1945, Luuk became one of the first 'Flower Children'. He is seen here at the grave and with the widow of Driver Gilbert Gwilliam (18.B.19), killed near the Driel ferry on 21 September 1944. (Luuk Buist)

historian, Leen van Bekkum, adds that 'Due to the failure of Operation MARKET-GARDEN, the supply routes from the Limburg coal mines in the western Netherlands were blocked. Because no coal could be delivered, many factories fell silent and homes could not be heated. The Germans punished the Dutch by not permitting food from other parts of the country to be brought in.' The crisis was in part alleviated through the Allied air forces airlifting food in, the Germans agreeing not to fire upon these flights of mercy, Operations MANNA and CHOWHOUND, but the situation was only fully resolved through the complete liberation of the Netherlands in April and May 1945. Wim van Zanten was still alive by then, but, as he said 'Only just. I nearly starved to death'.

After the liberation of Arnhem by Canadian forces in April 1945, one of the first British officers to visit the area was Major Ernest Watkins, RA, a War Staff Writer; his description of Arnhem and Oosterbeek at that time, before the Dutch returned, is evocative:

> It was 11 o'clock in the morning of a fine day in April. The sky was clear and the sun was brilliant . . . (the road) ran straight into Arnhem, down a broad boulevard lined by blocks of excellent flats. Structurally most of them were intact, but they had been shelled, machine-gunned and fought through, and the debris still lay in the street.
>
> After the withdrawal of the men of 1st British Airborne Division last September, the Germans, resentful of the welcome the inhabitants had given them, cleared the whole town of every person living in it. Then they divided it into four zones and proceeded to systematically loot each in turn. The loot they sent to four bomb-damaged towns in Germany, with a message that it was a free-will offering from the Dutch to their less fortunate neighbours. After that, the town remained empty. I do not like the German sense of humour.
>
> I drove out to Wolfheze and then back again into Oosterbeek, in a jeep. The country was like the higher lands in Surrey, the same woods of fir and patches of open sandy ground, the same country cottages, some thatched, that looked so attractive. Some had been burnt out. A great many had been shattered by shell-fire. Occasionally alongside the road there was an empty container or a wrecked jeep with the airborne flash still on its wing. They said the woods were still full of other souvenirs.
>
> Oosterbeek was much worse. The Germans had built fire positions along the whole length of the lower road, just above the flat fields alongside the river, and had thrown together road blocks of furniture and felled trees across the roads leading away from the river. They had buried the dead. Otherwise, they had left the place untouched.
>
> Hartenstein, the big hotel that had been Airborne Div HQ, was still there, wrecked, but the grass had grown over the shell and mortar holes in the gardens and on the tennis court. Oosterbeek Church still stood, roofless and scarred, and

in the churchyard, just outside the porch, was a 17-pdr ATk gun, still pointing east [Author's note: see Chapter 12]. Alongside it a wrecked artillery tractor lay half on its side.

A few hundred yards to the east a burnt-out Mk IV tank blocked most of the road [Author's note: this was probably the StuG III knocked-out by Sergeant Jack Baskeyfield VC, still *in situ* in 1945, a kilometre or so east of the Old Church]. Beside it a parachute was still draped around the wrecked gable end of a small cottage, its red silk now very faded. The whole suburb had remained as it had been left. Except, of course, for the graves. There was one on the corner just opposite the church. An airborne helmet hung from the wooden cross, with a big rent in the steel above the left eye.

The place is not quite as it was left. Then the leaves were turning brown and the gardens of the houses looked very neat and Dutch. Now they are overgrown and new leaves are on the trees and another year's growth is hiding the traces left last autumn. The place has a defiant, bedraggled air. Nature had got out of hand and knew it. Somehow, the uncut lawns, so very small and suburban, looked worse than the wrecked houses.

When we reached the centre of the town again I left the car. This was where, seven months before, the 350 or so men of the Airborne Division who did get into Arnhem had held the northern approaches to the road bridge over the Rijn for four days.

It was very quiet. The main supply route did not pass near it, and there was no other traffic. The bridge itself was wrecked, the span over the river neatly cut by the charges and dropped into the stream. There was the embankment that carried the road south to Nijmegen up to the level of the bridge. There were the ornamental gardens, with a lake in the centre, at the foot of the embankment. There were the carriageways, on either side of the gardens, and the two met at the foot of the embankment. After the fighting in September the Germans had built two palisades of wood and sand across the roads and blown a crater in between them. The stretch of roadway up to the bridge had been left as it was, unused and unusable. On it still stood the remains of more than twenty trucks that the airborne men shot-up that first morning. They lay at all angles across the road and verges, a light rusty brown, their wheels gone, the chassis members resting on the tarmac and edged with little ridges of sand and dust blown up against them by wind over the winter months. With all the woodwork burnt away, the wrecks looked small and unimpressive.

I walked up the embankment towards the river. On the left, the east side, were the ruins of the school which some fifty engineers had held for four days until the fires started in various corners and the building had spread to their store of explosives and the roof blew off. It was an empty shell, the outside curiously unmarked. On the right, to the West, were the houses that had been Brigade HQ and the other strongpoints of the main body at the bridge. They too had burnt out. Some had completely collapsed.

It was very silent in the hot sunshine and the clear light seemed to take away all emotion, as though the sunshine was an antiseptic for that too. But not quite all. There was the contrast between what had died, and what was growing . . . All that man had made had been destroyed. And Nature mocked him with an artifice of which the satire was too pointed, for the trees were undamaged and in full leaf, the grass along the embankment was thick and rank. The candles on the chestnut trees were in bloom and already their petals were falling like a fine, intermittent snow. And these were the flowers.

I climbed over a pile of rubble, formerly a house, to the gardens behind. One end of the garden, the nearest to the house, was buried by fallen brickwork, the other erupted by a recent bomb crater, a smooth, perfect, circle in the sandy soil. There were perhaps five yards of undisturbed ground in between. In the centre of this five yards was a flower bed, unaffected by seven months of neglect. It was a mass of yellow and red tulips in full bloom. They moved gently in the little wind, apart from and indifferent to the wreckage that lay around them.

I should not like to stay in Arnhem now. It is too empty of people and the ghosts have it all their own way.

To others, however, that desolate landscape was home, ghosts and all. Ans van Wijk-Hobé remembers returning to Oosterbeek: 'My father had to return as soon as possible, because the policemen needed to start work again. My father was very happy to do his old job again, but the police station's roof was very badly damaged – the holes in it had to be covered by a tent. Although everywhere was badly damaged, as a child I was very happy to be back home.'

After the liberation and German surrender, Europe was in chaos. Countless people were on the road, heading for home – if that still existed – and searching for their families – often without even knowing whether their relatives were alive or dead. Much of the continent was in ruins, ravaged by five years of war, cities decimated by bombing and shelling. Everywhere lay the detritus of war, from rusting tanks to bayonets – and innumerable graves of friend, foe and civilians that now had to be gathered up from field graves and interred at formal cemeteries. The precise death toll of 1939–45 will never be known, but between 35–40 million people are believed to have perished in Europe, out of a total number of 60 million deaths. For the immediate post-war world, both the reconstruction of shattered countries and dealing with the dead, was a colossal task.

For centuries, the dead of battle had been buried anonymously in mass graves, generic memorials commemorating the collective dead. In 1862, during the American Civil War, however, the Union Army's Adjutant General decreed that plots would be created within battlefields for military cemeteries comprising individual graves, headboards identifying, 'where practicable' the identities of those interred. This represented a major shift in the treatment and commemoration of war dead, other nations adopting the new practice. Europe's first head-on collision, of course, with the aftermath of industrial warfare came during and in the wake of the First World War, eighteen million casualties representing mass death on an unprecedented scale owing to the efficiency and destructive power of modern weapons. Death in battle came to be seen as sacred, a selfless sacrifice for the cause and nation. Consequently, the people demanded that their loved ones were laid to rest in communal military cemeteries in individual, named, graves.

The Imperial (now Commonwealth) War Graves Commission was founded by Royal Charter in 1917, vast military cemeteries subsequently created, with their equality of death, all men, regardless of rank or status, being treated the same. The nature of twentieth-century warfare, though, dictated that millions of casualties were never found or identified, the latter buried as 'Known unto God'. Another issue, for the British, was that the war had been fought on foreign shores, and so the graves of loved ones were not immediately accessible to grieving relatives. For this reason, every parish erected a memorial to its dead sons, their names inscribed thereon to provide a local focus. Likewise, the missing were commemorated by name on memorials dedicated to those with no known grave, at home and abroad. Indeed, all nations involved paid homage to the missing through dedication of an unknown soldier's tomb. As the French General Weygand said, these places provided a focal point where 'all those mothers who had never found their sons could pray'. Such places of pilgrimage and rituals of collective mourning became the accepted means of commemorating and honouring the 'fallen' – and it was in this way that Britain dealt with both its grief and lost sons in the chaotic aftermath of the Second World War.

In the wake of the liberation in 1945, as the Dutch survivors of the 'Hunger Winter' returned to their homes, or what, if anything, was left of them, the immense task of reconstruction began. Concurrently, 2nd Army Graves Registration Units moved into the Arnhem and Oosterbeek area, to clear the dead from the field and collect them in a military cemetery. The Dutch government offered a site on 'perpetual loan' to Britain for this purpose, located within the woods just north of the railway line at upper Oosterbeek, east of the Dreijenseweg. This became known as the Arnhem-Oosterbeek War Cemetery, designed by P.D. Hepworth and completed in February 1946. To that hallowed place, known locally as the 'Airborne Cemetery', many of the British casualties from September 1944, known and unknown, were brought and interred. Others were buried in the smaller cemeteries around the area. Some casualties, washed away by the Rhine whilst trying to cross the river, ended up many miles from where they died. In 1945, seventy-three Poles were exhumed from their field graves at Driel and brought to Oosterbeek, joining six of their countrymen already there. Today, 1,774 burials can be found at the 'Airborne Cemetery – 244 of them unidentified. At Groesbeek, ten kilometres east of Nijmegen, is the memorial to the missing of this theatre of operations, which records the names of 1,032 British and Commonwealth soldiers with no known grave.

The manner of the 1st British Airborne Division's exit from Oosterbeek that sodden night of 25/26 September 1944 was somewhat different to its proud and triumphant arrival by glider and parachute nine days previously. In that time, the city of Arnhem and environs, and the lovely, up-market, village of Oosterbeek had been virtually laid waste. Not evacuated before the battle, Dutch civilians, sheltering in their cellars, had endured the privations and terror of battle along with the 'airbornes' who had so bravely come to liberate them. When General Urquhart returned to the battlefield in 1945, he did so quietly, expecting to face resentment from the Dutch for his Division's failure to liberate them, and for visiting unprecedented death and destruction upon them. Nothing, however, could have been further from the minds of the still grateful Dutch. By the time of the British commander's return, Jan ter Horst – husband of Kate, the revered 'Angel of Arnhem' – was deputy mayor of Oosterbeek, at that time residing at the Bilderberg Hotel, and greeted the General warmly – much to the latter's surprise. Sophie Lambrechtsen-ter Horst: 'My father sent the Hotel's driver, Mr Gademan, to fetch a crate of Dutch jenever (gin). Having a drink at the Hartenstein, the General and my father then planned the first commemoration, as it has been ever since.So began a unique bond and friendship between the civilian population and the veterans of that bitter battle fought in the autumn of 1944. As Glider Pilot Regiment survivor Ron Johnson says, 'All we brought them was suffering'. Jan Crum, a five-year old during the battle, explains: 'The point is, they tried to liberate us. They came to help. Many died. We cannot forget that. Not ever. We will always owe a debt that can never be repaid.'

In September 1945, the first annual service of remembrance took place at the Arnhem-Oosterbeek War Cemetery. The order of service records that:

> We have gathered here to remember before God the men who died last September at Oosterbeek and Arnhem. In this battle British soldiers and Dutch civilians shared the same dangers. This cemetery will remain as an imperishable link between the citizens of Oosterbeek and the 1st Airborne Division. It will set a seal on the friendship of the peoples of Holland and Britain, and thus, please God, contribute to the brotherhood of mankind.

Wim van Zanten:

> At that first service, Oosterbeek's Padre Dÿker had the idea of asking local schoolchildren to lay flowers on the graves. I was one of those children, and I 'adopted' the grave of Corporal Joe Simpson. This led to many years of deep friendship between Joe's family and mine. The bond between us is unique.

ARNHEM 1944

Ans van Wijk-Hobé:

I was one of the 'Flower Children' who laid flowers on the graves at that first service. Later, I met a couple who had lost their son, and had come with their daughter-in-law and grandson to visit the grave of their son, husband and father. I took care of that grave and it was very emotional to meet those people. In 1957, I married a boy from Arnhem, and we were involved with the annual commemorations as a host family for Arnhem veterans. Our first family came from Tiverton in Devon. Sadly, the veteran concerned was later killed in a motorbike accident, so his son and family were thereafter our guests. We remain in contact today. Our second family came from Lincoln, and again we became very close friends. I still have contact with their daughter and have visited them in England several times.

Wil Rijken with the grave of Trooper William Edmond. (Wil Rijken)

FLOWERS IN THE WIND

Corry Tijssen-Rijken:

> The battle was horrendous, the noise, the dreadful suffering, but we remain eternally grateful that the British and Poles tried to liberate us. Afterwards the Germans were awful, making us leave Oosterbeek, and we knew hunger – I never throw food away, even now. The battle, however, was defining; it made me who I am. Now I read about it all the time, because back then all you saw and heard was what was immediately around you, which when sheltering in a cellar isn't a lot. So now, aged eighty-five, I want to know more. I was also amongst the first Flower Children in 1945, and still have lasting friendships with the families of those whose graves I looked after.

Every year since 1945, in fact, the 'Flower Children' have placed their flowers on the graves every annual service of remembrance. Near the entrance to the Arnhem-Oosterbeek cemetery is the 'Flowers in the Wind' plaque erected by the Arnhem Veterans Club 1944, dedicated to 'the children of this region who grace this cemetery ever year paying homage to the men who gave their lives for Liberation'. The nearby Hartenstein Hotel, once General Urquhart's Divisional HQ, now houses the Airborne Museum; across the road, on the green, is the Airborne Memorial; close-by is another tribute to the 'Flower Children': a bronze statue of an airborne soldier and a flower girl. Clearly, this unique tribute by Dutch children has touched the lives of countless people.

Since that first service in 1945, annual pilgrimages have taken place, and still do. Veterans, their families, enthusiasts and local people descend upon Arnhem, Oosterbeek and Driel every September for a full programme of commemorations over a number of days. This includes ceremonies at the many memorials across the battlefield, the dropping of parachutists over Ginkel Heath, communal walks and tours of the area by expert guides – but the focal point, the culmination of all these activities, is always the cemetery service. There, the Flower Children continue this deeply moving gesture, to the appreciation and rapturous applause by all. As Corry said, 'It is very important that the unique relationship between the British and Dutch people continues – and that the battle and sacrifices of those involved are never forgotten'.

Trooper Edmond's headstone at Oosterbeek today (16.B.9). From Musselburgh in Scotland, efforts to trace his family during the research for this book proved fruitless, because, it seems, he was an only child and the family now extinct. (Author)

An aerial photograph taken in 1945, after Arnhem's liberation by the Canadians, mainly showing the area east of Arnhem Bridge. After the airborne battle, the bridge was targeted by Allied bombers and destroyed, hence the devastation. The pontoon bridge was erected by the liberators as a temporary expedient, the buildings around the northern end being some of those stubbornly defended by Lieutenant-Colonel Frost's men in September 1944. (Keith Brooker)

The western side of the destroyed road bridge in 1945, showing the destruction wrought around Arnhem Bridge by Allied bombers. The zig-zag lines of German trench networks, constructed after the airborne battle, can clearly be seen. (Keith Brooker)

Significantly, in 2006, Sophie Lambrechtsen-ter Horst, like her parents a pronounced humanitarian, founded the annual 'Bridge to the Future' Conference (www.bttf.nl), focussing upon love, peace and reconciliation arising from violence, death, devastation and despair. That, concurrently with the annual pilgrimage, has surely to be the Battle of Arnhem's lasting legacy.

Epilogue:
Walking with Ghosts

Fascinated by the story of Arnhem since childhood, it was inevitable that one day I would go there and walk with the ghosts Major Watkins decided in 1945 'had it all their own way'. Having now done so, I can categorically state that in my experience nowhere has brought me closer to the events of 1939–45; nowhere is the violent and emotive past so palpable. The battle-scarred houses and trees, the proliferation of memorials and battlefield markers all combine to make the battles fought long ago at Arnhem and Oosterbeek omnipresent. Our visits there during the research for this book are a kaleidoscope too of happy and moving memories.

Following a flying visit whilst working near Utrecht in 2013, my wife, Karen, and I were able to visit the Arnhem area at greater length in August 2015, with our friends John and Jan Fidoe. It was on that occasion that the warmth and friendship of the Dutch people became immediately apparent. Kitty Brongers, a volunteer at the Airborne

Dilip and Karen Sarkar at the Airborne Museum 'Hartenstein'. The research for this book involved many visits to the Arnhem area, and was a special journey in more ways than one. (John Fidoe)

Museum who provides guided tours of the Airborne Cemetery, kindly gave us – four strangers – a guided tour of the main sites. It was almost overwhelming, in fact, to stand on the landing zones, visit the Airborne Museum at the former Hartenstein Hotel, see the St Elisabeth Hospital and surrounding area, the 'White House', the spot where Major-General Kussin met his death on the Utrechtseweg; walk in the woods around Oosterbeek and along the lower road – through the railway culvert near which the Gronert twins lost their lives, the Ter Horst house and Old Church, the Westerbouwing; to stand on John Frost Brug – and the site of the former Van Limburg Stirum School – was all beyond inspirational. The list of landmarks, in fact, all within a surprisingly small area, is virtually endless. Then, as described in the introduction to this book, began a very special relationship with that unique place, the Airborne Cemetery. Luuk Buist too ferried us about, taking us to Groesbeek to see the memorial there to the missing. Inspiration was also found at nearby Nijmegen's 'Grenadier Bridge', that great span across the mighty Waal. This, however, was a reconnaissance, a look at the battle through a wide lens before sharpening focus and getting down to serious, specific, research.

By the time of our next visit, in May 2016, the project had a clear direction. A number of families had been traced, some through media appeals, most through the great work of genealogist Michelle Baverstock. By that time, I was also in regular contact with Captain Geert Jonker, Commanding Officer of the Royal Netherlands Army Recovery & Identification Unit, based at Soesterberg. A visit to the laboratory to meet Geert, and discuss various issues and projects revolving around the missing, was an unforgettable experience. There, the sad remains of various human beings were laid out, with their equipment and personal accoutrements, on mortuary tables. Geert explained that:

> I have been involved with this important work since 1989, and did my first dig two years later – the recovery of Private Frederick Harrington, of Onibury in Shropshire, who was killed fighting with the King's Shropshire Light Infantry. Our Unit was established in January 1945 under the Dutch Free Forces of the Interior, when half of Holland was still occupied, and became part of the Ministry for War in August 1945. Today, we work on around forty cases annually and are responsible for the recovery and identification of missing Dutch civilian and military personnel, and both Allied and German personnel – this is still something that that the Dutch government considers both a duty of care and a debt of honour.

The physical recovery of human remains, however, is only the start of a long process for Geert and his small but dedicated unit:

> What we have to do is combine military history with forensic archaeology and physical anthropology. Identification is frequently very difficult, and can take anything from just three days to over a decade. Oxygen and strontium isotope analysis of tooth enamel can confirm where in the world an individual came

One who is no longer missing is Corporal George Froude of 1st Border, whose field grave was discovered on Van Lennepweg, Oosterbeek. Here the author examines Corporal Froude's Sten Mk V at Soesterberg in 2017. (Karen Sarkar)

The missing are remembered by name on panels in two buildings at the Groesbeek Canadian War Cemetery. (Marcel Boven)

Memorials and markers to the battle are abundant: Airborne Memorial on the green opposite the Hartenstein. (Author)

from, and DNA, essentially genetic fingerprinting, can confirm beyond doubt the link to a known living relative. Dental records, however, are crucial evidence, but we still need luck because many were destroyed and not preserved with army service records. Successfully identifying a casualty's remains, providing families with closure at a military funeral, however, is the ultimate reward, making all the time and effort involved completely worthwhile.

Geert estimates that two-thirds of cases concern German casualties. Some 140 British airborne soldiers, however, remain missing from the Battle of Arnhem. Thanks to the Royal Netherlands Army Recovery & Identification Unit, that number has reduced and

Tribute to the 'Flower Children' at the Airborne Cemetery. (Author)

Tribute to the 'Flower Children' and annual 'airborne march' in front of the Airborne Memorial at Oosterbeek. (Author)

Memorial outside the Old Church in lower Oosterbeek. (Author)

Memorial from the people of Gelderland – which perfectly captures Dutch feeling – at the Airborne Museum. (Author)

will hopefully continue to do so. In 2004, for example, the CWGC cited the figure of 1,759 burials at Oosterbeek, 253 unidentified; in 2017, whilst the number of burials have increased to 1,774, the quantity of 'unknowns' has decreased to 244. The total figure of burials is greater because more human remains have been uncovered on the battlefield – and, after often painstaking work, identified, providing families with long-awaited closure. The decreasing number of unidentified graves is also due to desktop and archival research confirming the identities of certain of those hitherto known only to God. These successes then permit the erection of named headstones. Never a year goes by, or so it seems, that an airborne soldier recently discovered is laid to rest at Oosterbeek with full military honours, or a headstone rededication ceremony takes place. In the majority of cases, however and as indicated by some of the stories in this book, the evidence is either inconclusive, ambiguous or non-existent. The collaboration of Geert's Unit and historians, as the years advance, should still, nonetheless, achieve more identifications through thorough investigation. That first visit to Soesterberg, standing amongst the dead of battle, was a deeply moving experience. Identifying the missing is a subject with which I have personally been involved for many years, a subject I feel passionately about, and I cannot commend Geert and team highly enough.

EPILOGUE

The highlight of that trip, though, was undoubtedly dinner at the Old Vicarage with Sophie Lambrechtsen-Ter Horst – daughter of Kate and Jan ter Horst. After the battle, when evicted by the Germans, Kate had collected up her children, gathered a few meagre belongings, and walked away from her devastated home. As she did so, Sophie remembered that her mother 'put a blanket over our heads so that we didn't see the bodies outside awaiting burial, or graves in our garden. Our father was still hiding in Wolfheze, but caught up with us after burying the dead in our garden, helped by Father Bruggemann, who happened to be passing'. Sophie's parents, were undoubtedly exceptional and remarkable people, philanthropists and forward-thinking humanitarians whose ethos was to generate positivity, for the greater good, out of the inconceivable past. Immediately after the war, they restored their home, above the front door of which is a carving of a phoenix rising from the ashes. In the garden a sculpture of Pegasus and Bellerophon falling to earth – reflected in a small pool, the image is reversed, symbolising hope and, indeed, the resurrection. In practical terms, the resurrection was the reconstruction of Oosterbeek, an undertaking, typically, Kate and Jan became driving forces behind.

Something so sad about the number of unidentified burials at the Airborne Cemetery . . . (Karen Sarkar)

In 2012, the remains of Driver John Kennell were found on Ginkel Hiede; he was interred at the Airborne Cemetery in 2015. (Geert Jonker)

ARNHEM 1944

To have some idea of the agony and suffering that went on within the Old Vicarage, and know of the burials in the garden, was sobering indeed. 'How can you still live here after everything that's happened?', was an obvious question to ask. Sophie, who was five years old in 1944, and sheltering with her siblings in the cellar, replied 'It is because of the love in the house. The friendships made that have lasted a lifetime, the bond between our peoples arising from these dreadful things. People never stop coming here, wanting to learn about what happened. I feel it vitally important to tell them, so that these things are not forgotten.'. Sophie, however, is no stranger to personal tragedy: in 1947, her eldest brother, 'Peik', was playing on the adjacent polder with his friend and neighbour, Henk Winterink, when they stepped on unexploded ordnance and were killed; in February 1992, Kate and Jan were hit by a car outside their home on Benedendorpsweg: Kate suffered fatal injuries and died on 21 February 1992, aged eighty-five (although it was feared that Jan would never walk again, happily he did – and died on 30 July 2003, aged ninety-eight).

Driver Kennell's headstone. (Kitty Brongers)

There is an aura about Sophie, an indefinable serenity, clearly inherited, I daresay, from Kate – whose mantle and positive, philanthropic, approach to life Sophie has naturally adopted. At the time of our visit, Sophie's daughter had just married a German, regarding which, Sophie says, her parents would have been 'delighted'. There is no question that in this house there is, indeed, much love and a focus upon healing and reconciliation. Like many others, the Battle of Arnhem has been a defining factor in Sophie's life – who sees the John Frost Brug as not a bridge too far, but 'A Bridge to the Future'. Spending time with Sophie in this hallowed place, was, it must be said, an almost spiritual experience.

On an earlier trip, Karen was most taken with the exhibition at the fabulous Airborne Museum on the suffering of Dutch civilians. Included therein was reference to the selfless sacrifice of Private Albert Willingham, who threw himself on a grenade to save Mrs Voskuil and her son, Henri. That day we also met Robert Voskuil, the Museum archivist and a mine of information concerning the great battle. Back home, Albert's family were soon traced, Kim, Brian and Rosie enthusiastically helping piece together the story of Albert's short life. It was deeply moving, therefore, to stand outside 2 Annastraat, off the Utrechtseweg in Oosterbeek, where this incident occurred. Pretty

EPILOGUE

Sophie Lambrechtsen-ter Horst with Dilip Sarkar at her historic home in May 2016. A committed philanthropist, Sophie sees Arnhem today as the 'bridge to the future', and is heavily involved with international youth projects. (Karen Sarkar)

The incredible sculpture Kate and Jan ter Horst commissioned in their garden, showing the winged horse Pegasus and rider, Bellerophon, falling to earth – reversed in the water's reflection, representing the resurrection. (Author)

much unchanged, the property has an aged appearance – a veritable one-time house of horror. To those aware of the history, there are many other buildings with similarly tragic pasts.

On a subsequent trip, we were engaged by the warmth and friendship of Jan Crum, a retired languages teacher (and a five-year-old Renkum resident in 1944). Years ago, Jan had formed a deep connection with the Airborne Cemetery and kindly sent me a copy of his excellent book, *Oosterbeek: Forever England*, exploring epitaphs on the headstones. Over several trips, in fact, Jan was our guide, showing us outlying locations and taking us to visit the grave of Private Patrick Taylor at Jonkerbos, Nijmegen. Jan also kindly drove us to the enormous German military cemetery at Ysselsteyn, fifty

Kitty Brongers, a tireless volunteer at the Airborne Museum and cemetery tour guide, with British battlefield enthusiast John Fidoe at the Airborne Cemetery. (Author)

The author's wife and companion, Karen Sarkar also made a deep connection with the Airborne Cemetery – seen here with the Gronerts' graves on a wet and windy day in August 2015. (Author)

kilometres south of Nijmegen. With 32,000 graves, the scale is vast – but owing to the sloping geography of the site, at ground-level it is impossible to observe all the graves simultaneously. Walking to the horizon, the graves just go on . . . and on. If ever there is a reminder of the consequences of voting a madman and his murderous henchmen into power, Ysselsteyn is it. Under the pines on a swelteringly hot day in June 2017, Jan and I sat and had some deep conversations about Germany's past and how this is perceived today by younger generations. The vast cemetery was also the place to reflect upon the consequence of a misguided nation democratically electing a madman to power – who was hell-bent upon waging a racial, total, war, ultimately destroying Germany. Indeed, many of those German soldiers who fought gallantly at and survived Arnhem doubtless perished before Germany finally surrendered, unconditionally, on 8 May 1945: German military losses were as high in the war's last ten months as they were between

EPILOGUE

3 September 1939 and July 1944. According to Professor Sir Ian Kershaw in his superb study *The End: Germany 1944-45*, of the 18.2 million men to serve in the German armed forces throughout the war, 5.3 million lost their lives; 2.6 million of these, 49 per cent, were killed in those terrible last ten months (1.5 million of them on the *Ostfront*). German civilians also paid the price: 400,000 were killed and 800,000 injured by Allied bombing, which destroyed 1.8 million homes and displaced five million people. The total death toll of the Second World War will never be known but is estimated at a staggering 60 million. As Jan and I walked through the endless rows of stark crosses that memorable summer's day, we were both agreed that in war there are no real victors, just tragedy and suffering, regardless of nationality or politics.

In September 2016, in Arnhem we met Gordon Anderson, the brother of Private Gilbert Anderson, and his daughter Tanja, both totally dedicated to identifying Gilbert's last resting place – and still very much bereaved. We have become good friends, and walking from our hotel up the Utrechtstraat towards Bovenover, the Museum, St Elisabeth Hospital, and returning to Arnhem via the Onderlangs, the lower road, with Tanja was another time of many deep conversations. Somewhere on the Onderlangs,

A service of Remembrance at the RAF memorial in the Airborne Museum's grounds, September 2016. (Author)

The author with Dutch author Jan Cruum, a four-year-old living in Renkum in 1944, on a moving visit to Ysselsteyn in 2017. (Karen Sarkar)

Gilbert had met his death in the terrible fighting on 19 September 1944, so it was a moving journey for us to re-trace with Tanja her missing uncle's footsteps.

That September, we attended the annual service of remembrance at the Airborne Cemetery. Having not previously attended but having heard much about the event, it was still difficult to know what to expect. This, of course, is the culmination of many acts of commemoration in Arnhem, Oosterbeek and Driel, which take place every single year. People go on that annual pilgrimage for different reasons: for some, although increasingly fewer in number, it is to pay respects to fallen comrades and maintain the all-important bond of friendship with the Dutch; for others it is to remember fallen comrades; some visitors are military history enthusiasts and re-enactors who have an annual occasion to socialise with like-minded people in an atmospheric place; currently serving British, Polish and Dutch servicemen are also heavily involved, joined by Americans on the mass parachute drop on Ginkel the day before each annual cemetery service. The Dutch, of course, come to pay homage to those who tried to set them free from German occupation – losing their young lives in the process. In a way, the period of events leading up to the cemetery service has somewhat of a

Not a manipulated image, the light eerily picking out the grave of an 'unknown'. (Karen Sarkar)

EPILOGUE

pervading carnival atmosphere, with military vehicle parades and the British take-over of the famous Schoonoord and other hostelries. Thousands of people descended on the Airborne Cemetery that Sunday, 18 September 2016. It was immediately clear that whatever carnival atmosphere pervaded in advance, this was a sincere and reverential act of remembrance. Hundreds of Dutch schoolchildren and students arrived by the coachload – waving their flowers in the wind before solemnly placing them on each grave. This was really something to see and experience. Afterwards, it was fascinating to meet our friends Wim van Zanten and Ans van Wijk-Hobé by the grave of Corporal Joe Simpson, and talk about their experiences, having lived through the battle and been amongst the first 'Flower Children'. Suffice it to say that for anyone even remotely interested in the Battle of Arnhem or study of remembrance, attending this unique service is pre-requisite.

The lack of closure reverberates down generations: Tanja Anderson at the grave which may be that of her 'missing' uncle, Private Gilbert Anderson (see Chapter 8). (Karen Sarkar)

The woods around Oosterbeek are peaceful now, but for some, even those unborn at the time, the scars remain deep and real. One afternoon, we being driven along Van Borsselenweg by Luuk Buist – Glider Pilot Regiment expert of experts – who stopped just north of the farm used as the 'D' Company, 1st Border HQ. We walked along a well-used track through the woods, a small valley carved by a stream (the Eastern Brook, by which Oosterbeek got its name) hurrying south to the nearby Rhine. 'In that field up there', Luuk explained, 'was the farm my grandfather took his family to shelter at until forced to evacuate when it caught fire. My grandparents brought their children, including my father, here, to shelter in this wood'. Our friend then told us the story of his grandfather's tragic death trying to protect his family (see Chapter 20). It was beyond moving. 'This is why', Luuk said, 'I got so interested in the battle as a boy, and have studied it is ever since. It is personal.' I totally get that. In fact, it would be hard to have a more personal local connection – making us appreciate how much the battle resonates today.

Another Dutchman born long after but equally fascinated by the events of 1944, is David van Buggenum – the highly respected author of the excellent and much sought-after book, *'B' Company Arrived* (see Bibliography). In addition to our historical interests in the Battle of Arnhem, David and I share a passion, with Captain Geert Jonker, for recovering and identifying the missing, and for battlefield archaeology. David and I

The 'Flower Children' at the Airborne Cemetery service in September 2016. (Author)

The author with Ans van Wijk-Hobé and Wim van Zanten at the grave of Corporal Joe Simpson in September 2016. (Karen Sarkar)

EPILOGUE

Dutch historian and archaeologist David van Buggenum presenting a delighted Dilip Sarkar with a British canteen recovered near the Old Church at lower Oosterbeek. (Karen Sarkar)

very much connected, and I was honoured when my friend presented me with a British canteen found some years ago near the Old Church at Oosterbeek – whether it belonged to a casualty or was discarded on Operation BERLIN we will never know – but the last person to secure the cork stopper was undoubtedly the unknown original owner.

David, together with Martin Reijnen, is officially authorised to search for field graves in the Renkum district. In August 2017, Karen and I had the privilege of joining David and Martin on an excavation at Westerbouwing, and there had the pleasure of also meeting Hans Timmermann. Watching an exploration of the former 'B' Company, 1st Border positions with metal detectors was incredibly exciting: but dangerous, given the potential presence of unexploded ordnance and hence why unauthorised searches are banned. Almost immediately finds appeared: an unfired 9mm Sten gun round; a fired Sten round; a German Kar 98 cartridge case, and, best of all, an exploded French rifle-calibre round from one of the Char B-1 *Flammpanzers* destroyed there. Inevitably a mountain of shrapnel was soon accumulated, mainly from the heavy artillery of 2nd

ARNHEM 1944

Army firing from Nijmegen on the Westerbouwing after 'B' Company was forcibly ejected from that high-ground by the Germans (see Sergeant Tom Watson chapter). The digging went down to a depth of 1.5 metres, in several locations. These excavations took place in former trenches and fox holes, into which, after the battle, the debris of war was thrown and buried. Very interestingly, the remains of several particular German ammunition baskets were found. The weave had long rotted away, but the metal framework and holders for shells and fuses remained. These parts belonged to ammunition containers for the 7.5cm *Leichtes Infanteriegeschutz* 18 – a light infantry howitzer designed and manufactured by Rheinmetall. There is no record of a German unit so equipped at Arnhem, so this was a very interesting discovery indeed. This weapon was also used by German airborne troops because it could be broken down and transported into four 140kg loads. It is likely, therefore, that this battery of guns belonged to the *Luftwaffe Ersatz-und-Ausbildings-Regiment* Hermann Göring, which seized Westerbouwing from 1st Border, and then fired from there onto the Oosterbeek perimeter. It is discoveries like this which make 'conflict archaeology' so important – the ground itself can be an archive, and delving into it, like when researching with dusty, long forgotten documents as source can yield exciting new information. That day, our search for field graves – the purpose of the exercise – was fruitless, as such searches more often than not are – but it was incredibly interesting and a great day spent with like-minded friends.

As the sun went down over the Rhine that afternoon, we walked away from the woods and bid the ghosts farewell. Along the journey that researching and writing this

During this excavation, no field graves were discovered, but artefacts were found proving the presence of this light infantry howitzer.

The metal remains of ammunition baskets for the 7.5cm Leichtes Infanteriegeschutz *18. (Author)*

book represents, we have been privileged to make many friends, in both the Netherlands and back home, to reach out and touch the traumatic past in a very up-close and personal way. That war is a tragedy is well evidenced by the stories in this book – but the remarkable thing about this battle is the positivity and friendships arising from it, even so long after the event. Moreover, Binyon's lines, 'At the going down of the sun, we will remember them' are oft quoted; there is no danger whatsoever of the sun ever setting on the dead of Arnhem, such is the interest and strength of feeling involved with the ongoing commemoration of these sacrifices. Indeed, part of us now, like many others, remains in Arnhem-Oosterbeek – and we look forward to returning many times in future to see our friends, pay homage to the fallen and walk with ghosts.

Today, birdsong, not the 'Morning Hate', reverberates across the Airborne Cemetery and the woods of Oosterbeek – where, perhaps, we walk with ghosts. (Karen Sarkar)

Acknowledgements

The research and production process of any book always represents a personal journey, and new friends made along the way. Indeed, this book has only been made possible due to the cooperation, collaboration and kindness of numerous friends all over the world, some old, some new, many of whom spared no effort in their kind assistance.

This book could not have been produced without the essential contribution of the relatives of the casualties concerned. Genealogist Michelle Baverstock, in fact, deserves a special mention for so efficiently tracing many of these families on my behalf.

I would like to thank the relatives of the fallen: Annie Amos, the late Rob 'Tim' Taylor and David Townsend; Gordon and Tanja Anderson; Pamela Francis-Bondy; Lesley Boosey and Colleen Dowler; Brian Brazier, Christine Campbell, Rachel Wyatt and Vanessa Kirkbride; Janice and Ben Chapman; Margaret and Eunice Collett; Alec Colvin-Smith and Nell Saunders; Pat and Les Crabtree; the late Margaret Davies; Susan and Ian Bonser, Trudi Hale and Glen Harper; Brian Gerrett and Mrs E Gerrett; Bernard Gronert and Debbie Hosking; Anne Wilton and Martin Gueran; Don and Owen Holloway, Peggy Holloway-Pearce; Dave, Sally and Diane Hayward; Kim and the late Brian Hymers, Rosy Tee and the now late Laurie Beekes; Angie Jenkin; Nadine Jesko; Ted and Shirley McSkimmings; Tracey Lodwig; Kevin Neville, David and Nora Noonan; John and Vivien Gilliard; Wanda Orysczak; Parnell Seabrook; John and Bernard Tate; Irene Thomson and Denise Watson; Andy Wilkins; the late Diana Wright; Paul Wright, Betty and Lynda Ross; Mary 'Bunty' Robertson also deserves a mention in this category.

Historian, enthusiast, and original 'Flower Children' friends in the Netherlands (in no particular order): Sophie Lambrechtsen-ter Horst for the moving foreword, love and friendship; Captain Captain Geert Jonker; David van Buggenum (who also proof-read the manuscript, making many helpful observations); Sophie Lambrechtsen-ter Horst; Kitty & Fred Brongers; Dr Robert Voskuil; Jan Crum; Tim Streefkerk; Luuk & Astrid (and Maron!) Buist; Marcel Boven; Sarah Heijse; Paul Hendricks; Ans van Wijk-Hobé; Corry Tijssen-Rijken; Will Rijken; Wim van Zanten; Chris van Roekel; Alice & Leen van Bekkum; Arno Baltussen; Hans Timmermann; Geert Maassen; Roland Boekhorst; Martin Reijnen & Eugenè Wijnhoud.

Worldwide: Lieutenant General Sir John Lorimer KCB DSO MBE, Colonel Commandant The Parachute Regiment; Captain Tom Clark, ADC to Lieutenant General Lorimer; Glider Pilot Regiment veteran Ron Johnson; Dave Baverstock; David Padfield; Roy 'Lofty' Tolhurst; Neil Holmes; Adrian Saunders; John & Jan Fidoe; Andy Long; Gordon Blakeman; Patrycja Bury; Niall Cherry; John Howes; Nigel Simpson; David Pasley; Allan Price; Bill Gaynor; Geoffrey Abreu; Simon Cooper; Graham Cooke; Glenn

ACKNOWLEDGEMENTS

and Catherine Gelder; Uwe Pinnau; Darrell Graham; Paul Pariso; Mike Vockins; Duncan Holley; Mike Shuttleworth; Dr Dennis Williams; Keith Brooker; David Bull; my son, James Sarkar.

I would also like to acknowledge assistance provided by The Airborne Museum, Oosterbeek; Commonwealth War Graves Commission; The Gelders Archief; Gerry McArdle & staff at the Ministry of Defence Army Personnel Centre; The Keeper & Staff of The National Archives; The Dorsetshire Regimental Museum; BBC Radio Hereford & Worcester, BBC Radio Solent; *The Forest Review*; *The Bromsgrove Messenger*; Bromsgrove School.

Martin Mace and team at Frontline Books were a pleasure to work with and have my sincere thanks for making this book a reality.

Finally, I must, of course, thank my wife, Karen, for her essential support, company on trips to Arnhem, her photographs – and proof-reading skills!

Bibliography

Unsurprisingly, the Battle of Arnhem has an enormous bibliography; the following are documents and publications that I found particularly helpful.

A number of official War Diaries were consulted, which are preserved at The National Archive, Kew:

- 1st British Airborne Division HQ — WO171/392 & 395
- HQ RA — WO171/396
- 1st Parachute Brigade HQ — WO171/592
- 1st Parachute Battalion — WO171/1236
- 2nd Parachute Battalion — WO171/1237
- 3rd Parachute Battalion — WO171/1238
- 1st Airlanding Anti-Tank Battery — WO171/957
- 1st Parachute Squadron RE — WO171/1509
- 4th Parachute Brigade HQ — WO171/594
- 10th Parachute Battalion — WO171/1243
- 11th Parachute Battalion — WO171/1244
- 156th Parachute Battalion — WO171/1247
- 1st Airlanding Brigade HQ — WO171/589 & 590
- 1st Battalion The Border Regiment — WO166/15077
- 2nd Battalion The South Staffordshire Regiment — WO171/1375
- 7th (Galloway) Battalion King's Own Scottish Borderers — WO171/1323
- 1st Airborne Reconnaissance Squadron — WO171/406
- 21st Independent Parachute Squadron — WO171/1248
- No. 1 Wing Glider Pilot Regiment — WO361/638
- No. 2 Wing Glider Pilot Regiment — WO361/505
- 4th Battalion, The Dorsetshire Regiment — WO171/1286
- 190 Squadron RAF, Operations Record Book — AIR27/1154

Very helpfully, all of the above war diaries, and that of the 1st Independent Polish Parachute Brigade Group are available online via The Pegasus Archive (see below).

In addition to my own personal correspondence and interview of Glider Pilot Regiment veteran Ron Johnson, the following publications were all very helpful, some essential, not least in helping reconstruct the socio-economic background:

BIBLIOGRAPHY

Anker, M., *The Lost Company: 'C' Company 2nd Parachute Battalion in Oosterbeek & Arnhem, September 1944*, Maca Publishing, Duiven, 2017.

Anon, *By Air to Battle: The Official Account of the British Airborne Divisions*, HMSO, London, 1945.

Beatie, A.H., 'The Victims of Totalitarianism & the Centrality of Nazi Genocide: Continuity & Change in German Commemorative Politics' in Niven, B. (ed.), *Germans as Victims: Remembering the Past in Contemporary Germany*, Palgrave MacMillan, Basingstoke, 2006.

Branson, N., & Heinemann, M., *Britain in the Nineteen Thirties*, Weidenfeld & Nicolson, London, 1971.

Buggenum, D. van, *'B' Company Arrived: The Story of 'B' Company of the 2nd Parachute Battalion at Arnhem, September 1944*, Sigmond Publishing, Renkum, 2003.

Buggenum, D. van, *'B' Company Arrived The Men: Supplement to the book "'B' Company Arrived" Arnhem, September 1944*, self-published, Arnhem, 2016.

Cherry, N., *Red Berets & Red Crosses: The Story of the Medical Services in the 1st Airborne Division in World War II*, Sigmond Publishing, Renkum, 1998.

Cheery, N., *With Nothing Bigger Than A Bren Gun: The Story of the Defence of the Schoolhouse at the Arnhem Road Bridge September 1944*, Brendon Publishing, Warton, 2014.

Cholewczynski, G.F., *Poles Apart: The Polish Airborne at the Battle of Arnhem*, Greenhill Books, London, 1993.

Clapson, M., *The Routledge Companion to the Britain in the Twentieth Century*, Routledge, London, 2009.

Clark, L., *Arnhem: Jumping the Rhine 1944 & 1945, the Greatest Airborne Battle in History*, Headline Publishing Group, London, 2008.

Cooper, A.W., *Air Battle for Arnhem*, Pen & Sword, Barnsley, 2012.

Crum, J., *Oosterbeek: Forever England*, Kontrast, Oosterbeek, 2004.

Dean, Sir M., *The Royal Air Force & Two World Wars*, Cassell, London, 1979.

Eastwood, S., Gray, C., & Green, A., *When Dragons Flew: An Illustrated History of The 1st Battalion The Border Regiment 1939-45* (second revised edition), Regimental Museum in association with SLP, Kettering, 2009.

Evans, R.J., *The Third Reich at War: How the Nazis Led Germany From Conquest to Disaster*, Penguin Books, London, 2008.

Fairley, J., *Remember Arnhem*, Peaton Press, Bearsden, 1978.

Frost, Major-General J., *A Drop Too Many*, Cassell, London, 1980.

Frost, Major-General J., *Nearly There: The Memoirs of John Frost of Arnhem Bridge*, Leo Cooper, London, 1991.

Fullick, R., *Shan Hackett: The Pursuit of Excellence*, Leo Cooper, London, 2003.

Gallagher, M., *With Recce at Arnhem: The Recollections of Trooper Des Evans, a 1st Airborne Division Veteran*, Pen & Sword, Barnsley, 2015.

Gerritsen, B., & Revell., S., *Retake Arnhem Bridge: An Illustrated History of Kampfgruppe Knaust, September-October 1944*, RN Sigmond Publishing, Renkum, 2014.

Gijbels, P., & Truesdale, D., *Leading the Way to Arnhem: An Illustrated History of the 21st Independent Parachute Company 1942-1946*, RN Sigmond Publishing, Renkum, 2008.

Gilbert, M., *The Second World War: A Complete History*, Phoenix, London, 2009.

Gilliard, V., *Last Flight Home*, Aspect Design, Malvern, 2014.

Glenn, H., & Spezzano, R., *Kampfraum Arnheim: A Photo Study of the German Soldier Fighting In & Around Arnhem September 1944*, RZM, Stanford, CT, USA, 2013.

Goldman, W., *William Goldman's Story of A Bridge Too Far*, Hodder & Stoughton Ltd, London, 1977.

Graves, R., & Hodge, A., *The Long Weekend: A Social History of Britain 1918-1939*, Hutchinson & Co (Publishers) Ltd, London, 1985.

Greenacre, Major JW, 'Assessing the Reasons for Failure of 1st British Airborne Division Signal Communications during Operation MARKET-GARDEN', *Defence Studies*, 4:3, 2004, pp. 283–308.

Greg, P., *A Social and Economic History of Britain 1760-1980*, Harrap Ltd, London, 1982.

Hackett, General Sir J., *I was a Stranger*, Chatto & Winduss, London, 1978.

Harclerode, P., *Para! Fifty Years of the Parachute Regiment*, BCA, London, 1992.

Hey, J., *Roll of Honour: Battle of Arnhem, September 1944*, Society of Friends of the Airborne Museum, Oosterbeek, 5th revised edition 2011.

Hill, Colonel E.R., & Rosse, Captain the Earl of, *The Story of The Guards Armoured Division 1941-1945*, Geoffrey Bles, London, 1956.

Hilton, R., *Freddie Gough's Specials at Arnhem: An Illustrated History of the 1st Airborne Reconnaissance Squadron from Official Records & Personal Accounts of Members of the Squadron*, RN Sigmond Publishing, Renkum, 2017.

Hoekstra, A., *All Men Are Brothers: The Polish Roll of Honour Battle of Arnhem 1944*, Market Garden Foundation, Arnhem, 2015.

Hook, P., *Hohenstaufen 9th SS Panzer Division*, Ian Allen Ltd, Hersham, 2006.

Holt, Major & Mrs, *Battlefield Guide to Operation MARKET-GARDEN*, Pen & Sword, Barnsley, 2012.

Horst-Arriëns, K.A. ter, *Cloud Over Arnhem: Oosterbeek-September 1944*, Kontrast, Oosterbeek, 2009.

Howe, J.C., *Point Blank Open Sights*, Hough Publishing, Reigate, 1999.

Junier, A., & Smulders, B., with Korsfloot, J., *By Land, Sea & Air: An Illustrated History of The 2nd Battalion The South Staffordshire Regiment 1940-1945*, RN Sigmond Publishing, Renkum, 2003.

Kershaw, R., *A Street in Arnhem, The Agony of Occupation & Liberation*, Ian Allen Ltd, Addlestone, 2014.

BIBLIOGRAPHY

Kershaw, Sir I., *The End: Germany 1944-45*, Penguin, London, 2012.

Kershaw, R, *It Never Snows in September: The German View of MARKET-GARDEN and the Battle of Arnhem, September 1944*, The Crowood Press, Marlborough, 1990.

Knischewski, G, 'The Role of the *Volksbund Deutsche Kriegsgräberfürsorge* in Commemorating the Second World War' in Andrews, M., Bagot Jewitt, C., & Hunt, N (eds), *Lest We Forget: Remembrance & Commemoration*, History Press, Stroud, 2011.

Longworth, P., *The Unending Vigil: The History of the Commonwealth War Graves Commission*, Pen & Sword, Barnsley, 2010.

Longson, J., & Taylor, C., *An Arnhem Odyssey*, Leo Cooper, London, 1991.

Lowe, K., *Savage Continent: Europe in the Aftermath of World War II*, Penguin, London, 2013.

Maanen, A. van, *Tafelberg Field Hospital: Diary, Oosterbeek 17-25 September 1944*, Kontrast, Oosterbeek, 2015.

MacKenzie, Brigadier C.B., *It Was Like This! A Short Factual Account of the Battle of Arnhem & Oosterbeek*, Airborne Committee, Oosterbeek, 1964.

Margry, K., *Operation MARKET-GARDEN: Then & Now, Volumes I & II*, After the Battle, London, 2002.

Michaelis, R., *The 10th SS-Panzer-Division "Frundsberg"*, Schiffer Publishing Ltd, Altgen, PA, USA, 2008.

Middlebrook, M., *Arnhem 1944: The Airborne Battle*, Penguin, London, 1995.

Montgomery, Field-Marshal the Viscount B., *Normandy to the Baltic*, Hutchinson, London, 1947.

Mowat, C.L., *Britain Between the Wars, 1918-40*, Taylor & Francis Books Ltd, London, 1968.

Niven, B., *Facing the Nazi Past: United Germany and the Legacy of the Third Reich*, Routledge, London, 2002.

O'Reilly, J., *156 Parachute Battalion: From Delhi to Arnhem, Includes Operations PEGASUS I & II*, Thoroton Publishing Ltd, Thoroton, 2009.

Padfield, H., *Twelve Mules and a Pegasus: Memoirs of an Arnhem Veteran*, Graffiti Press, Oxford, 2013.

Pallud, J.P., *Ruckmarsch! The German Retreat from Normandy*, After the Battle, London, 2006.

Peatling, R., *Without Tradition: 2 PARA 1941-1945*, Pen & Sword, Barnsley, 2004.

Peters, M., & Cherry, N., with Howes, J., & Francis, G., *Desert Rise – Arnhem Descent: The 10th Parachute Battalion in the Second World War*, Brendon Publishing, Warton, 2016.

Peters, M., & Buist, L., *Glider Pilots at Arnhem*, Pen & Sword, Barnsley, 2014.

Piekalkiewicz, J., *Arnhem 1944*, Ian Allen Ltd, Shepperton, 1977.

Pijpers, G., & Truesdale, D., *Arnhem Their Final Battle: The 11th Parachute Battalion, 1943-45*, RN Sigmond Publishing, Renkum, 2012.

Pontilillo, J., *Murderous Elite: The Waffen-SS and its Complete Record of War Crimes*, Leandoer & Ekholm Publishing, Stockholm, 2009.

Pope, R., *War & Society in Britain 1899-1948*, Longman, London, 1991.

Powell, G., *The Devil's Birthday: The Bridges to Arnhem 1944*, Leo Cooper, London, 1993.

Powell, G., *Men at Arnhem*, Leo Cooper, London, 1998.

Pugh, M., *We Danced All Night: A Social History of Britain Between the Wars*, Bodley Head, London, 2008.

Revell, S., with Cherry, N., & Gerritsen, B., *Arnhem A Few Vital Hours: SS-Panzergrenadier-Ausbildings-und Ersatz-Bataillon 16 at the Battle of Arnhem, September 1944*, RN Sigmond Publishing, Renkum, 2013.

Revell, S., *A Piece of Coloured Ribbon: An Insight into German Award Winners at the Battle of Arnhem*, Historia House, Aus, 2015.

Richards, A., *Braziers: Builders of Bromsgrove, 1850-1990*, B&M Ltd, Bromsgrove, 1996.

Roekel, C. van, *The Torn Horizon: The Airborne Chaplains at Arnhem*, Jan & Wendela ter Horst & Chris van Roekel, Oosterbeek, 2000.

Ryan, C., *A Bridge Too Far*, Hamish Hamilton, London, 1974.

Sarkar, D., *Spitfire Ace of Aces: The Wartime Story of Johnnie Johnson*, Amberley Publishing, Stroud, 2011.

Saunders, T., *Nijmegen: US 82nd Airborne & Guards Armoured Division*, Pen & Sword, Barnsley, 2001.

Sigmond, R.N., *Off at Last: An Illustrated History of the 7th (Galloway) Battalion The King's Own Scottish Borderers 1939-1945*, self-published, Renkum, 1997.

Sims, J., *Arnhem Spearhead: A Private Soldier's Story*, Imperial War Museum, London, 1978.

Sliz, J., *Engineers at the Bridge*, self-published, Toronto, 2010.

Sosabowski, Major General S., *Freely I Served: The Memoir of the Commander 1st Polish Independent Parachute Brigade 1941-1944*, Pen & Sword, Barnsley, 2013.

Smith, C., *History of the Glider Pilot Regiment*, Leo Cooper, London, 1992.

Stargardt, N., *The German War: A Nation Under Arms 1939-45*, Vintage, London, 2015.

Steer, F., *Arnhem: The Bridge*, Pen & Sword, Barnsley, 2013.

Steer, F., *Arnhem: The Landing Grounds & Oosterbeek*, Pen & Sword, Barnsley, 2002.

Weeks, J., *Assault from the Sky: The History of Airborne Warfare*, David & Charles Publishers plc, London 1988.

Truesdale, D., *Steel Wall at Arnhem: The Destruction of 4 Parachute Brigade, 19 September 1944*, Helion & Company Ltd, Solihull, 2016.

Truesdale, D., Conelissen, M., & Gerritsen, B., *Arnhem Bridge Target Mike One: An Illustrated History of the 1st Airlanding Light Regiment RA 1942-1945 North Africa-Italy-Arnhem-Norway*, RN Sigmond Publishing, Renkum, 2015.

Urquhart, Major-General R., *Arnhem*, Cassell, London, 1958.

BIBLIOGRAPHY

Vockins, M., *Chig: Sky Pilot to the Glider Pilots of Arnhem*, Helion & Company, Solihull, 2017.
Waddy, Colonel J., *A Tour of the Arnhem Battlefields*, Leo Cooper, Barnsley, 1999.
Warner, P., *Horrocks: The General Who Led From the Front*, Hamish Hamilton, London, 1984.
Warrack, G., *Travel by Dark*, Fontana, London, 1976.
Watkins, Major E., *Arnhem: 1 Airborne Division*, first published by the Army Bureau of Current Affairs 1944–45, compilation by Books Ulster, 2016.
Wilkinson, P., *The Gunners at Arnhem*, Spurwing Publishing, Northampton, 2002.
Woollacott, R., *Winged Gunners*, Quote Publishers Ltd, Harare, Zimbabwe, 1994.
Zwarts, M., *German Armoured Units at Arnhem, September 1944*, Concord Publications, Hong Kong, 2001.

The Friends of the Airborne Museum, Oosterbeek, publish a quarterly newsletter full of information. The following 'Ministory' provided unique references:

Berends, Peter, 'They Also Called Themselves "*Freikorpskämpfer*"', Ministory 60, October 1998.
Cherry, Niall, 'The SS 9th *Hohenstaufen* Panzer Division at Arnhem, and Colonel Boeree', Ministory 111, March 2012.
Jensen, Helmut, 'The 14th *Schiffsstamm-Abteiling* During the Battle of Arnhem', Ministory 62, May 1999.
Kok, Ruurd, 'Archaeology of the Battle of Arnhem: The Significance of Excavated Finds as an Historical Source', Ministory 89, June 2006.
Maan, Ingrid, & Timmermann, Hans, 'German Eye-Witnesses', Ministory 103, February 2010.
Maassen, Geert (based on information supplied by Hans Timmermann), 'Thirty Years Searching & Researching: Investigation into Missing & Unknown Soldiers in the Arnhem Area', Ministory 110, December 2011.
Roekel, Chris van, '*Sturmgeschütz*-Brigade 280', Ministory 70, May 2001.
Timmerman, Hans, 'German Field Graves in Oosterbeek', Ministory 84, December 2004.
Velden, Hans van der, '35 Years Searching the Former Battlefields at Arnhem', Ministory 98, September 2008.
Zwarts, Marcel, 'SS-*Panzer-Aufklärungs-Abteilung* 9 and the Arnhem Road Bridge', Ministory 78, June 2003.

Web Resources
Details are where casualties are buried can be found via the Commonwealth War Graves Commission casualty search facility: https://www.cwgc.org/find-war-dead.aspx
   Details of burials at specific cemeteries can be found here: https://www.cwgc.org/find/find-cemeteries-and-memorials

Anyone interested in supporting the work of the Airborne Museum is encouraged to join the Friends at: http://www.friendsairbornemuseum.com. The Airborne Museum is also on Facebook.

The Arnhem Fellowship remains the primary umbrella organisation furthering research into the Battle of Arnhem: http://www.arnhem1944 fellowship.org/

A huge amount of information concerning British airborne forces can be found on these two excellent web sites: http://www.pegasusarchive.org & https://paradata.org.uk/

Much information regarding the German defence of Arnhem can be found at http://www.defendingarnhem.com/

Inevitably, there are numerous Arnhem-related interest pages on Facebook.

Bridge to the Future Conference: www.bttf.nl

Films

A Bridge Too Far, directed by Richard Attenborough (United Artists, 1977).
Theirs is the Glory: Men of Arnhem, directed by Brian Desmond Hurst (Carlton Film Distributions, 1946).

Documentaries

Last Words: The Battle for Arnhem Bridge (Simply Media, 2015).
Britain at War, Disc 4, *Arnhem* (Simply Home Entertainment, 2009).

Other Books by Dilip Sarkar (in order of publication)

Spitfire Squadron: No. 19 Squadron at War, 1939-41
The Invisible Thread: A Spitfire's Tale
Through Peril to the Stars: RAF Fighter Pilots Who Failed to Return, 1939-45
Angriff Westland: Three Battle of Britain Air Raids Through the Looking Glass
A Few of the Many: Air War 1939-45, A Kaleidoscope of Memories
Bader's Tangmere Spitfires: The Untold Story, 1941
Bader's Duxford Fighters: The Big Wing Controversy
Missing in Action: Resting in Peace?
Guards VC: Blitzkrieg 1940
Battle of Britain: The Photographic Kaleidoscope, Volume I
Battle of Britain: The Photographic Kaleidoscope, Volume II
Battle of Britain: The Photographic Kaleidoscope, Volume III
Battle of Britain: The Photographic Kaleidoscope, Volume IV
Fighter Pilot: The Photographic Kaleidoscope
Group Captain Sir Douglas Bader: An Inspiration in Photographs
Johnnie Johnson: Spitfire Top Gun, Part I
Johnnie Johnson: Spitfire Top Gun, Part II
Battle of Britain: Last Look Back
Spitfire! Courage & Sacrifice
Spitfire Voices: Heroes Remember
The Battle of Powick Bridge: Ambush a Fore-thought
Duxford 1940: A Battle of Britain Base at War
The Few: The Battle of Britain in the Words of the Pilots
Spitfire Manual 1940
The Last of the Few: Eighteen Battle of Britain Pilots Tell Their Extraordinary Stories
Hearts of Oak: The Human Tragedy of HMS Royal Oak
Spitfire Voices: Life as a Spitfire Pilot in the Words of the Veterans
How the Spitfire Won the Battle of Britain
Spitfire Ace of Aces: The True Wartime Story of Johnnie Johnson
The Sinking of HMS Royal Oak
Douglas Bader
Fighter Ace: The Extraordinary Life of Douglas Bader, Battle of Britain Hero
Spitfire: The Photographic Biography
Hurricane Manual 1940
River Pike
The Final Few: The Last Surviving Pilots of the Battle of Britain Tell Their Stories

Index

A
Ager, Private Ernest 304
Allen, Corporal Bob 48
Allen, Private William 304
Allsop, Captain 81
Anderson, Flight Lieutenant 273
Anderson, Gordon 98, 102-4, 109-10, 339
Anderson, Private Gilbert 97-103, 105-11, 230, 339
Armstrong, Major Tom 207, 211-12, 214
Arnold, Major 234, 257
Ash, Lieutenant 58

B
Bamsey, Griffith & Louisa 49, 61
Bamsey, Lance Corporal 44, 48-49, 51, 59, 61
Bamsey, Private Charles 59, 61
Bamsey, Private William 45, 47, 49-51, 53, 56, 59, 61
Bannatyne, Captain 226
Barker, Lieutenant Alan 91, 94-95
Barlow, the late Arthur 71-73, 76-79, 85-86, 88
Barlow, Colonel Hilaro 88
Barneki, Feldwebel 257
Barnes, Sergeant Jack 201
Barnett, Gunner 191
Barr, Private 170
Barry, Lieutenant Peter 39
Barton, Platoon Sergeant George 231
Baskeyfield, Lance Sergeant Jack 171, 178, 322

Bass, Private 239
Bates, F. 108
Baxter, Lieutenant 58
Beardsley, Flight Lieutenant Bob xviii
Bennett, Private Henry 44, 46
Berthon, General Thomas 226
Best, Private 97, 102-5, 108, 110-11
Bittrich, General Willi xxiv, 23, 207, 211, 309
Bondy, Driver Robert 1, 5, 7-8, 10-13
Bonome, Staff Sergeant 235-38
Boosey, Lance Corporal Jack Ronald 62-66, 68
Bor, General 284
Bower, Sergeant 194, 235
Bradley, General xix
Brawn, Fred 81
Brazier, Captain Edward Sydney John 163
Brazier, Dr David 145
Brazier, Jonathan 142
Brazier, Lieutenant Peter 141-45, 147-49, 153, 156-60, 162-64
Brazier, Philip 143-44
Brazier, Roger 142, 163
Breading, Driver Denis 275, 278
Breese, Major Charles 214
Bretherton, Sapper Johnny 258, 261
Briscoe, Lieutenant 156, 158, 162
Browning, General xxvii, 18, 148, 289-91, 293, 297-98
Bruggemann, Father 335
Bucknall, Lieutenant Peter 76-77
Buist, Luitsen 314-15
Burbridge, Lance Bombardier 235

INDEX

Burzawa, Captain Josef 285, 288
Bush, Flight Lieutenant Mike 141
Bush, Major Alan 173
Butterworth, Sapper 243-47, 249-50, 256, 262-63, 265-66
Byrne, Flight Sergeant 274, 278

C

Cain, Major Robert 94, 171-73, 175
Campbell, Colin 177
Cane, Lieutenant Peter 37, 40
Carr, Sapper Steve 258
Carstensen, SS-Unterscharführer Ewald 305
Casey, Lieutenant T. 235
Cassidy, Private 217, 219, 221, 223, 225, 227-33
Chamberlain, Neville 16
Chapman, Staff Sergeant Freddie 180
Chatterton, Colonel 147-49
Chennell, Private Sidney 59
Chignell, Captain Reverend 89, 151, 156-58, 165
Christie, Sergeant 80-81
Churchill, Winston 18, 21, 140, 147-48, 243, 271
Clay, Corporal 10
Cleminson, Lieutenant 45-46, 51, 53-54, 56, 58, 87-88
Cochran, Major Alexander 217-21, 223, 225-29, 231-33
Coke, Major 220, 225-26
Collett, Private Percy 87, 89-91, 94-96
Collier, Lieutenant-Quartermaster Tom 81
Colvin-Smith, Alec 227
Cooke, Trooper 81
Cope, Corporal 239
Coulthard, Captain 226
Crawley, Doug 29
Crighton, Lieutenant 226

Croot, Major 168-69, 194, 202
Crosson, John 230-31
Cullen, Flying Officer 275, 278
Cunningham, Sapper 239
Czelaw, Lance Corporal Gajewnik 285-87, 289, 291, 293, 295

D

Dauncey, Lieutenant Mike 169
Davis, Sergeant 158-60, 162-63
Dawson, Major 128
Dennison, Major 58, 65
Derksen, Martin 314
des Voeux, Lieutenant Colonel Richard 113
Dietrich, Sepp xxiv
Dinwiddie, Major 226
Dobie, Lieutenant Colonel 62-66, 99-100
Dover, Major Victor 39
Dryden, Lance Bombardier Lionel 54

E

Edmond, Trooper 326-27
Edward, George 186
Edwards, Private Jack 40, 42
Eisenhower, General xxi-xxii

F

Fairley, John 71, 80
Farren, Pilot Officer 272
Fellows, J.G. 108
Fitch, Lieutenant Colonel 44-45, 57-58, 66, 87-88, 94
Fitchett, Sergeant 238
Flavell, Lieutenant Jim 31, 33
Fleming, S. 247
Fletcher, George 72
Flower, Sergeant 168
Foulkes, Lieutenant 79
Frost, Lieutenant Colonel John 12, 14,

20-21, 24, 26-29, 31, 33, 37, 39, 53, 66-67, 79, 87, 89, 92-93, 112-14, 117, 123, 127, 156, 169, 197, 235, 244, 249, 269, 276, 287, 300, 311, 328
Froude, Corporal George 331
Fullriede, Oberst Fritz 211, 214

G

Gajewnik, Lance-Corporal Czeslaw 283, 285-86, 288, 294-95, 300
Gater, Stan 108
Gentle, Sergeant 238
Gilliard, Squadron Leader John Phillip 267-74, 277-82
Gillie, T 247
Goodman, Lieutenant Thomas 201
Goodrich, Corporal Horace 29
Göring, Hermann 18, 211, 304, 344
Gort, General The Viscount 5, 189, 245
Gough, Freddie 29, 37, 62-63, 74, 76-78, 240
Gould, Staff Sergeant 140-41, 145, 149, 151, 153, 155, 157-60, 162-65
Gourlay, Captain 219
Gräbner, Hauptsturmfuhrer 26, 28, 39, 54, 92, 255, 310-11
Grabowski, Johann Peter 305-6, 308
Graham, Sergeant 225-26
Grant, Staff Sergeant Reg 153
Grantham, Corporal 239
Gray, Sapper David 'Tommy' 255
Grayburn, Lieutenant Jack/John 31, 33
Greenacre, Major John W. 218
Greer, Charlie 261
Griffiths, Squadron Leader Frank 270
Gronert, Bernard 42-43
Gronert, Claude 34, 36-37, 39-43, 46, 64, 250, 330, 338
Gronert, Thomas 36-37, 39-43, 46, 64, 250, 330, 338
Gueran, Sapper Sidney 243, 247, 249, 251-55, 257, 259, 261, 263
Gueran, Stanley 66, 192, 252-54
Guildford, Lord 248
Gwilliam, Driver Gilbert 320

H

Hacker, Sergeant Henry 40
Hackett, Brigadier xxvii, 88, 97, 112-14, 117-18, 122, 124-25, 127-30, 168, 219-20
Hannah, Lieutenant 226, 231-32
Harding, Lance Corporal 197
Hardman, Sergeant 238
Hare, Gunner Ronald 191, 194-95
Harmel, Heinz 257
Harrington, Private Frederick 330
Harzer, SS-Obersturmbannführer Walter 28, 92, 211
Haslam, Bombardier 235
Hasler, Dicky Minns 77
Hasler, Reg 77
Hauser, SS-Obergruppenführer xix, xxiv
Hay, Captain 79-80
Hazelwood, Twiggy 261
Helle, SS-Sturmbannführer Paul 118, 212
Hendy, Lance-Corporal Arthur 258
Herford, Lieutenant Colonel Martin 241
Hibbert, Sergeant Maurice 152-54
Hickmott, Gunner Ernest 179
Hicks, Brigadier R.H.W. 87-89, 91, 97, 99, 112-13, 117, 122, 148, 158
Higgins, Sergeant Geoff 235-40
Hill, Major 219
Himmler, Heinrich 307, 309
Hindley, Lieutenant 255-58
Hitler, Adolf xxiv, 16-17, 19, 23, 140, 150, 188-91, 283, 299-300, 307-9
Holloway, Staff Sergeant Eric 'Tom'

INDEX

166-69, 171, 173, 175, 177, 179, 181, 183, 185
Hopwood, Private Frederick 44-45, 47, 49, 51, 53-55, 59, 61
Horrocks, General
Howe, Lieutenant John C. 234
Hughes, Private 207
Hughes, Sergeant P.H. 235
Hughes, Sergeant Tom 235
Hummel, Hauptmann Hans 257
Hunter, Corporal 211-13
Hunter, Lieutenant 226
Hurst, W. 247

I

Imber, Squadron Leader Bob 193

J

Jackson, Major 149, 157
Jackson, Peter 277
James, William 246
Jarvilc, Lieutenant 295
Jenkin, Private Harry 97, 99, 101, 103-5, 107-11
Jensen, Helmut 207
Johnson, Air Vice Marshal 'Johnnie' xviii, 89
Johnson, Lieutenant 141, 152, 158, 162, 182, 200, 221-23, 224, 276, 325
Jones, Lieutenant Glynn 162
Jonker, Captain 103, 105, 107-8, 215, 239, 241, 261, 302-3, 330, 334-35, 341
Jukes, Signalman Bill 28

K

Kaufman, Lieutenant 226
Kennell, Driver John 335-36
Kesselring, Feldmarschall Albert 264
Knaack, Leutnant 257
Kohnken, SS-Hauptsturmführer Hans-Heinrich 51, 53
Krafft, SS-Sturmbannführer Josef 'Sepp' 24, 37-38, 46-48, 51, 53-54, 58, 63-64, 77, 87, 118, 123, 125, 127-28, 302
Kussin, Major-General Friedrich 47-48, 51-53, 59, 81, 87, 154, 310, 330
Küster, Unteroffizier 47, 59

L

Laker, Ted 264
Lane, Pilot Officer 275, 278
Larkin, Gunner 238-39, 242
Lathbury, Brigadier 26, 37, 45, 53, 57-58, 62, 66, 69, 76, 87-88
Lawton, Flying Officer 273-75, 277-79
Lea, Lieutenant Colonel George 97, 99, 113
Leaver, Staff Sergeant 168-69, 171, 175, 177
Leiteritz, Günter 53
Leslie, David 217
Lewis, Lieutenant 57, 186, 195, 261-62, 267
Lippert, Hans Michel 156
Loder-Symonds, Lieutenant Colonel Robert 180
Lonsdale, Major Dickie 169
Lord, Flight Lieutenant 276-77
Lorimer, Lieutenant General 137
Loudon, Lieutenant Colonel 137
Lowery, Douglas 304

M

MacGregor, Lance-Sergeant 77
Mackay, Captain 251, 254, 258, 260-61
MacKenzie, Lieutenant Colonel 88, 226, 289
Madeley, Reg 54
Magnusson, Sapper 295-96
Malaszkiewicz, Major 290
Malley, Joe 251, 258

Maltby, Lieutenant 206
Marr, Billy 262
Masterson, Sergeant 238
Matthews, Private 44-47, 49, 51, 53-54, 56, 59-61, 98-99, 101-3, 105-11
Mauga, SS-Unterscharführer 310
May, Oberleutnant Alfred 156
McArthy, Trooper 81
McCardie, Lieutenant Colonel 88-91, 94, 99
McCarthy, Trooper 80
McCullock, Bombardier 191, 195, 197
McDowell, Corporal Jim 208
McEwen, Flying Officer Norman 275, 278
McGladdery, Alfred 214
McGowan, Father 100, 102-5, 107-8
McGregor, Sergeant 77
McMillan, Flight Sergeant 272
McMurbury, Lieutenant Colonel 249
McSkimmings, Trooper Ray 69, 73, 70-86
McWhirter, Private 232
Meagher, Lance-Sergeant 235
Meikle, Flight Sergeant Colin 182, 184-85
Meikle, Flight Sergeant David 181-85
Meikle, Lieutenant Ian 166, 169, 171-77, 179-85
Meikle, Ormiston 181, 184
Meikle family 177, 179, 181, 184-85
Melling, Lance Corporal Eric 305
Meredith, Ray 163
Meredith, Ted (pilot) 163
Mervyn, Sergeant 152
Millard, Corporal Jack 264
Minchin, Flying Officer Tony 14
Model, Generalfeldmarschall xix, xxiv, 23, 58, 224, 301
Montgomery, General xix-xxii, xxiv, 185, 296-98, 300
Munford, Major Denis 28, 194
Murray, Lieutenant Colonel Iain 58, 168

N

Neary, Sergeant 235-36, 238-40
Neville, Lance-Corporal Daniel 243-47, 249, 251, 258, 260-61, 263, 266

O

Ottaway, Captain 114, 117

P

Padfield, Bertha Daisy 246
Padfield, Harold 243, 246-51, 253-59, 261, 263-66, 296
Palmer, Corporal 80-81
Pare, Reverend Arnold 58
Pare, Reverend George 151, 158
Parkes, Private 108-9
Patton, General xix
Payton-Reid, Lieutenant Colonel 218-20, 223, 225, 233
Pearson, Lieutenant Colonel Alastair 20
Pearson, Lieutenant Hubert 80-81
Peatling, Bob 20
Perrin-Brown, Major Chris 64
Peters, Private Johnnie 206, 216
Peterson, Private Herbert 106
Philip, Jonathan 142
Pierce, Jimmy 77
Pijpers, Gerrit 107
Place, Lieutenant Colonel John 149, 154, 206-7
Pluemer Jr, Captain Herbert 115
Potter, Sergeant 154
Poulson, Stanley Thomas 241
Powell, Major Geoffrey 113-14, 117, 128, 130
Pridmore, Lance Corporal Wilf 170

INDEX

Priest, Captain Maurice 168

Q
Queripel, Captain Lionel 125

R
Ransmayer, Leutnant Hans 29
Richardson, Gunner Albert Cornwall 238-39, 242
Rigby-Jones, Major 263-64
Robson, Gunner George 54
Robson, Sergeant Cyril 28
Rommel, General 120, 179, 211
Roseberry, Lord 228
Royle-Bantoft, Squadron Leader 274, 278
Rubenstein, Sergeant 239

S
Salmon, Trooper James 81
Schramm, Oberst 214
Schwarz, SS-Hauptsturmführer Wilfried 310
Scott-Malden, Pilot Officer David 190
Scrivens, Corporal 115
Sharples, Lieutenant 226
Sharrock, James/Jim Johnson 186-87, 189, 191-95, 199-203
Shaw, Lieutenant 195
Shipley, Sergeant Bob 175, 180
Sikorski, General 284
Simpson, Corporal Joe 243-46, 249, 251, 258-60, 266, 313, 325, 341-42
Simpson, Lieutenant 249, 251, 258, 261
Simpson, Sapper W.L.G. 244
Simpson, Sergeant Robert 201
Smith, Geoff 151
Smith, Private Don 40
Smith, Sergeant Dennis 267

Smyth, Lieutenant Colonel 113, 118, 122-25, 128, 131-34, 137
Sosabowski, General xxi-xxii, xxvii, 125, 283-91, 297-98
Southall, Samuel 45
Spindler, Obersturmbannführer Ludwig 124
Stalin xx, 309
Steckhan, Alfred 305
Steer, the late Frank 208
Stevens, Private Thomas 115
Student, Oberst Kurt 18, 22, 140
Sutton, Major Arthur 187
Swanston, CSM 226

T
Tait, Drum Major 220
Tate, Bernard 15, 35
Tate, John 15, 19
Tate, Joseph Bayliss 14
Tate, Major Francis Raymond 14, 16-21, 23, 26, 28-29, 31, 33-35
Tatham-Warter, Major 24, 29, 31
Taylor, Captain Willie, 23 88
Taylor, Flying Officer Peter xix
Taylor, Frederick 275, 278
Taylor, Maxwell D. 264
Taylor, Private Patrick 112-17, 119, 121, 123, 125, 127, 129, 131, 133, 135, 137, 139, 337
Thomas, Sergeant George 186-91, 193-99, 202-3, 205
Thomas, Taffy 77
Thompson, Arty 65
Thompson, Colonel 169
Tijssen-Rijken, Corry 10, 13, 132, 327
Tilley, Lieutenant Colonel 291
Timmermann, Hans 307
Tucker, Major 295
Twynham, Sir Henry 227

U

Urquhart, General xxvii, 12, 26, 29, 53-54, 57-58, 61, 64, 66-67, 76, 78, 87-88, 97, 113, 117, 124, 127, 130, 151, 209-10, 218-19, 236-37, 273, 276, 287-89, 291, 293, 296-97, 325, 327

V

van Wijk-Hobé, Ans 132, 312-13, 323, 326, 341-42
van Zanten, Wim 1, 4, 10, 14, 260, 313, 321, 325, 341-42
Vernon, Captain Dennis 244
Vlasto, Lieutenant Robin 39-40
Vockins, Reverend Mike 151
von Kluge, Feldmarschall xix, xxiv
von Runstedt, Feldmarschall Gerd xxiv
von Svoboda, Oberstleutnant 274
Voskuil, Robert 132, 134-35, 137, 139, 161, 174, 178, 281, 336

W

Waddy, Colonel John 12, 57
Waddy, Major Peter 45-46, 57
Wade, Sergeant 153
Wadsworth, Lieutenant John 82
Walker, Captain 180-82
Walker, Sergeant Gordon 267
Wallis, Major David 26, 29
Walton, Brigadier 291
Wareing, Lieutenant Colonel Andrew 137
Waring, Staff Sergeant Stanley 199, 201
Warr, Major 122, 130-35, 137
Warwick, Gunner Thomas Stanley 234-35, 237-42
Watkins, Major Ernest 321, 329
Watson, Corporal 232
Watson, Sergeant Tom 204-7, 211-16, 288, 344
Wavell, Archibald 17
Weaver, Staff Sergeant 249
Weigand, SS-Hauptscharführer 77-78
Weiner, Sergeant 129
Weygand, General 324
Wilkinson, Peter 195
Wilkinson, Sapper 'Ginger' 26
Willeke, Gefreiter Josef 48, 51, 59
William, David 177
William, Thomas 199
Williams, Jim 200
Willingham, Albert 112-13, 115, 117-25, 127, 129-39, 336
Willingham, George 118-19
Wilson, Lance Corporal 'Ginger' 212
Winder, Sergeant Fred 81
Winterink, Henk 336
Woollacott, Lieutenant 182
Wossowski, Oberleutnant Artur 211-12, 214
Wright, Major Philip 108
Wright, Staff Sergeant Leonard 201-2
Wrightman, Gunner Stan 197

Y

Younger, J.C. 108

Z

Zwolanski, Captain 288, 290